Rhineland

Rhineland

THE BATTLE TO END THE WAR

W. DENIS WHITAKER
DSO & BAR
& SHELAGH WHITAKER

St. Martin's Press
New York

Photographs are used by permission of Imperial War Museum (IWM, Public Archives of Canada (PA), U.S. National Archives (NA), United States Army Military History Institute (USAMHI), Carlisle, Pennsylvania, Bundesarchiv-Militaer, Freiburg, West Germany (BAM), Wilfrid Laurier University (WLU), Waterloo, Ontario.

Library of Congress Cataloging-in-Publication Data

Whitaker, Denis.
    Rhineland : the battle to end the war / Denis Whitaker and Shelagh
  Whitaker.
        p.   cm.
    ISBN 0-312-03419-9
    1. World War, 1939–1945—Campaigns—Germany (West)—Rhineland.
  2. World War, 1939–1945—Personal narratives, American.
  3. Rhineland (Germany)—History. I. Whitaker, Shelagh. II. Title.
  D757.9.R49W47 1989
  940.54'21—dc20   89-35333
                                                      CIP

First published in Canada by Stoddart Publishing Co. Limited.

First U.S. Edition

10 9 8 7 6 5 4 3 2 1

This book is dedicated to the young men of four nations who were given a job to do. Some won, some lost — but they all did their utmost.

Contents

Preface

From its inception to its final draft, *Rhineland* absorbed four years of our lives — four very pleasurable years. My wife, Shelagh, and I gathered material for the book during two lengthy periods in the United Kingdom and Europe, and had two protracted visits to the United States. The trusty Volkswagen that spun us around Europe in 1983 while we researched our first book, *Tug of War*, again became our floating office, complete with computer, printer, and files, as we travelled from town to town searching out and interviewing men who had fought in the Rhineland Campaign.

Our pursuit of British veterans was made easier by their tendency to stay put. We tracked down Seaforth Highlanders in Inverness, Gordons in Aberdeen, Black Watch in the Kingdom of Fife, Welch Fusiliers in Wrexham, and Monmouthshires in Abergavenny. The Somersets and Wiltshires are still — many of them — Wessex men. The Guards' headquarters is still on Birdcage Walk, a short stroll from Buckingham Palace.

In Holland we met the Burgemeester of Groesbeek, Mr Van Hil, who took us to see the Canadian cemetery so carefully tended by the Dutch. In the next village, Bredeweg, a Roman Catholic priest, Father Thuring, has painstakingly given the dignity of a name to scores of solidiers whose bodies were lost in the mudded ruts of the Reichswald. In the Rhineland itself, we were warmly hosted by the Buergermeister of Cleve, Mr Brock, and a number of citizens of the area.

Several Canadian foundations were generous in awarding us the grants — the lifeblood — that made this research possible. We are indebted to the Social Sciences and Humanities Research Council of Canada, the Canada Council, the Ontario Heritage Foundation, and the Ontario Arts Council for their invaluable support — and to the historians in Canada who recommended us for these grants.

The book could not have been written without the cooperation and help of all of the military historians, archivists, and regimental and association secretaries identified in our list of sources in the appendix. To single out just a few: Dr Alec Douglas and Brereton Greenhous of the Department of National Defence; Rod Suddaby of the Imperial War Museum; Lt-Col Martin Andresen of the U.S. Army Military History Institute in Carlisle, Pennsylvania; Richard Boylan of the National Archives in Washington; and Oberst Kindler of the West German Bundesarchiv-Militaer in Freiburg im Breisgau. In addition, our colleagues in military and civilian circles in the United States, Great Britain, Canada, and West Germany — including Col James "Trapper" Drum of Washington, Maj-Gen Heinz Guderian of Bonn, Erwin Jaeger of Hamburg and Oakville, and our good friends in the British Light Infantry, Maj-Gen Peter Bush, Maj-Gen Barry Lane, and Lt-Col Alastair Brown — opened many doors for us.

All these people provided us with the facts of the battle — the skeleton, as it were. As well, we acknowledge the help of Jack Stoddart, Bill Hanna, and Donald G. Bastian, of Stoddart Publishing, our cartographer, Linda Risacher Copp, and her husband, Terry Copp, who generously loaned us photographs and maps from his book, *Maple Leaf Route: Victory*.

It was the interviews, however, that became the heart and breath of *Rhineland*. We are deeply indebted to the veterans who took the time to dig out old records and let their minds go back to those raw days of February and March 1945 in the Rhineland.

Finally and especially, our own daughter Martie Hooker was all things to our book. As well as providing her skills as a consultant in military history, and as the painstaking editor for the manuscript's evolution, she gave unstinting encouragement and inspiration to its authors for four long years.

Prologue

THE AUTUMN OF 1944 was the wettest and coldest of the century in central Europe.

To 120,000 American soldiers of Lieutenant-General Omar N. Bradley's 12th U.S. Army Group, the dark mass of the Huertgen Forest was wetter and colder than any other battleground. Its 200 square miles of sharp slopes, deep gorges, and fast-moving streams — in times of peace a playground in the Eifel Massif near Aachen — had been transformed by the autumn rains into a morass of mud.

From mid-September through the early winter chill of December, American troops of Lieutenant-General Courtney H. Hodges's First U.S. Army fought four full-scale engagements in the Huertgen Forest. Hodges's objective was to reach that last German defence bastion: the Rhine River. Before this could be achieved, the American troops had to breach the Germans' Siegfried Line defences and then establish a bridgehead across the Roer River, some 25 miles west of the Rhine.

Ill conceived and ill commanded, the battle to reach the Roer — still remembered with bitterness by American troops as the Battle of the Huertgen Forest — was a grim affair that resolved little and cost much. It was a battle that never should have been.

Many of the dead and even some of the wounded were abandoned where they fell, left to rot through the long months of fall and early winter. In 12 weeks of fighting, the playground became instead a burial ground, an obscene resting place for thousands of American and German troops.

Hodges and his boss, Bradley, recklessly expended division after

---

See Map 2 (Appendix B).

1

division of troops in the Huertgen Forest, ignoring the safer alternate routes that would outflank it. Ignoring, too, the fact that even if they conquered the lethal woods, even if they reached the banks of the Roer, the enemy still held the trump card to stop them from forcing a crossing: the Roer dams.

The river was overshadowed by the concrete bulk of the 180-foot-high Schwammenauel Dam, one of seven such dams that had been constructed over the years to control the flow of the Roer and its tributaries. As long as the German engineers held the floodgates of these dams, the danger remained that they could inundate the river, making it impassable to assaulting troops. Worse, if any battalions reached the far side of the river, they could be cut off and annihilated. Bradley's 12th Army Group planners were slow in appreciating this fact.

By forcing a head-on confrontation in the dense Huertgen woods, Hodges handed the determined enemy forces such an overwhelming advantage that even the Germans were puzzled. As one Wehrmacht officer observed, "The fighting in the wooded area denied the American troops the advantages offered them by their air and armoured forces."

There, the Siegfried Line's interlocking fortifications of camouflaged pillboxes, barbed wire, and trip wire were at their most formidable. Thickly sown anti-tank and anti-personnel mines carpeted the forest's narrow mudded trails. German artillery was sited on every crossroad they approached, every minefield they encountered.

Overhead, the thickly intertwined canopy of green was soon stripped to shell-splintered branches that stabbed the sky. German mortar and artillery shells exploding high among the treetops cascaded millions of lethal metal fragments, killing and maiming the helpless troops beneath. Ernest Hemingway called the Huertgen battle "Passchendaele with tree bursts."

Exposure was knocking out more soldiers than rifle fire. Greatcoats became so sodden that many men, nearing the point of exhaustion from the prolonged battle, could no longer bear the weight of them. Many, too, could no longer walk. Feet that were constantly wet became swollen and gangrenous. Cases of battle fatigue were abundant.

The toll on the men who slogged valiantly through the slippery trails of the Huertgen Forest became horrifying. In all, 33,000 Americans — one-quarter of the assaulting force — became casualties before the forest was conquered. More than 24,000 of these were killed, wounded, missing, or captured. Another 9,000 men succumbed to the misery of the forest itself, the wet and the cold, respiratory disease, exhaustion, and that old World War I bugbear, trench foot.

It was "sheer butchery," as even one of its authors, General Bradley, was later to describe it. The 120,000 men were thrust into suicidal terrain in quest of an impossible objective.

Major-General James Gavin, commanding the 82nd U.S. Airborne Division in a ground role in the conflict, was appalled by the grisly scene he encountered when he arrived later on the battleground. He saw "a shambles of wrecked vehicles and abandoned trucks . . . . All along the sides of the trail there were many, many dead bodies . . . . Their gangrenous, broken and torn bodies were rigid and grotesque."

In mid-September, the 9th U.S. Infantry Division initiated the action, fighting their way 3,000 yards into the dread forest. In four weeks, 4,500 of their number were killed, wounded, or missing — more than one man lost for every yard gained.

Then, early in November, all three regiments of Major-General Norman ("Dutch") Cota's 28th Infantry Division, wearing the distinctive red Keystone shoulder patch of the Pennsylvania National Guard, were thrust into the battle. Almost immediately, forward troops seized the village of Schmidt, which overlooked the Roer and its dams. However, senior officers of First U.S. Army, commanding from a map instead of from first-hand knowledge of the land (as Gavin criticized), failed to take into account that tanks and anti-tank weapons could not follow the lead troops. The wooded trails and steep gullies precluded any such support.

"In launching Cota," Bradley later noted, "we grossly underestimated both the terrain and the German defences. The ensuing battle was a disaster."

The next day, Generalmajor Siegfried von Waldenburg's crack 116th Panzer Division laid on a violent counter-attack from the high ground behind. Employing tanks and self-propelled guns, the Panzer troops drove back the American troops. Many ran, panic-stricken, back to their own lines. Two hundred were ignominiously captured.

A week later, the Keystone Division reeled out of Huertgen Forest. It had been one of the war's most costly attacks. Over 6,000 men were casualties, including the 200 taken prisoner. The red shoulder patch, taking on a more sinister connotation, would be ever known as the "Bloody Bucket."

Hurtled after them into the killer woods was a major force comprising six divisions from Bradley's First and Ninth Armies. An air strike of unprecedented strength was laid on to launch the attack: on November 16, 4,000 planes from the Royal Air Force and the Eighth U.S. Air Force dropped 10,000 tons of bombs on the Siegfried defences.

Even this show of power did little to quell the stubborn defenders. Their resistance was almost beyond belief. The Americans reported many instances of wounded German troops refusing to give up the fight. An entire platoon was found at its post, dead to the last man.

In the days that followed, the effect of the enemy's fierce effort was heightened by the incessant rain and cold of that raw autumn.

General J. Lawton ("Lightning Joe") Collins, GOC (General Officer Commanding) 7 U.S. Corps, saw his 1st Infantry Division struggle bravely for three weeks for a gain of six miles — and a loss of 4,000 men. There were 4,053 combat casualties in 4th Infantry Division, plus another 2,000 men stopped by disease and exhaustion. The casualty rate was equally bad for the 8th Infantry Division, the Combat Command of 5th Armored Division, and 2nd Ranger Battalion, who had also amassed 4,000 combat casualties (in addition to 1,200 from non-combat causes).

The assault limped on into December. By then, Bradley was apparently aware of the value of the Roer dams — not sufficiently to assign them as an objective, but enough to cause him "worry and discussion," as he later wrote in his memoirs, defending himself against critical American historians.

After stubbornly insisting that the dams could not be breached, the RAF finally consented to tackle the job. But despite five attempts, each with several hundred Lancasters, no significant dent was made on the concrete structures. First and Ninth U.S. Armies eventually broke out of the forest and closed on the Roer River at the end of the first week of December. Detailed plans had been drawn up for an assault across the river, but Allied commanders dared not proceed in the face of the looming threat that their bridgeheads would be cut off. The drive for the Rhine, the powerful thrust to end the war with Germany, was fizzling out on the marshy banks of the docile Roer.

When finally the Americans could force a crossing, the river was no longer docile: the flooded waters of the Roer had become as hostile as the enemy troops that defended it.

1

The Little Watchmaker

BEHIND HIS BACK, General der Infanterie Erich Straube's more irreverent contemporaries in the German Wehrmacht called the wizened corps commander the *Uhrmacher* — the Watchmaker. It was hardly a compliment.

Although 36 years in the German Imperial Army had earned Erich Straube the Knight's Cross — his country's highest award — his hesitation in committing himself to decisive action and his obsessive fretting over each petty detail had won him this unfortunate sobriquet. It was understandable in those bitter days of January 1945, in the wake of repeated German defeats since the Normandy invasion, that few of his staff could take the tiresome commander of 86 Infantry Corps with the seriousness and respect his rank demanded — especially when the focus of his tirade of the moment was the fate of a single Allied prisoner of war.

For a second time, Straube thumbed impatiently through the stack of intelligence reports on his desk. "I need more information before I can make a judgment about the enemy's intentions," he snapped peevishly at his corps intelligence officer. "I want to see that Canadian prisoner."

"He has been removed to Gestapo headquarters in Cleve for questioning, sir," the chagrined officer started to explain.

"Bring him to my headquarters immediately!" Straube interrupted. "I will personally conduct the interrogation."

Straube badly wanted that Canadian. It was the sixth January of Hitler's war. American troops had broken out of the Huertgen Forest and closed to the banks of the Roer, although they still had not gained control of the dams that controlled the waters. Berlin's

---

See Maps 1 and 2 (Appendix B).

bold gamble in counter-attacking American positions in the Ardennes in December had failed. Casualties on both sides had been heavy, but the Germans had managed to extract almost all of their equipment except that which was destroyed in battle or lost through lack of fuel.

Now the Americans were massed on the Roer; the British were holding strong positions along the Maas River near Venlo. The Canadians had formed a defensive line at Nijmegen, on the Dutch border.

It was only a matter of weeks or even days before the combined Allied force poised along the German border would make its next move. Inevitably, the enemy would advance to close the 20- to 25-mile gap to the Rhine. But where, on that long front, would the great Rhineland offensive be launched? Speculation was rife among senior staff officers of the Wehrmacht.

Historically, the Germans had always believed that the Rhine was a water barrier of formidable might that could repel any enemy invasion. Flowing northward from Switzerland to Holland, the 820-mile-long river passed through some of central Europe's most dramatic scenery.

In the upper (southern) Rhine, German fortifications along the steep, vine-covered eastern banks could more easily resist a water assault. Even if the Allies forced a bridgehead, the terrain was too forbidding to permit rapid penetration by tens of thousands of men and their armour.

It was downstream, where the lower Rhine flowed through flat green plains into the great industrial northern basin of the Ruhr, that Germany was most vulnerable to a large-scale assault. The only point on which the Wehrmacht High Command was in agreement was that this area offered the sort of terrain where the Allies could profitably make an assault over the Rhine.

If one were to heed the views of Generalfeldmarschall Gerd von Rundstedt, it would be the Americans who would launch the main attack, from their sector on the Roer. This would probably be followed in a few days by an attack by British troops across the Maas River from Venlo, midway between the American and Canadian positions.

This theory was supported by the newly appointed Commander-in-Chief of Army Group H, Generaloberst Johannes Blaskowitz. As a result, he had sited his reserves — including the force that

had held up the Americans in the Huertgen Forest, von Waldenburg's 116th Panzer Division — in readiness for attacks across either
the Maas or the Roer.

An attack across the Roer, Straube mused . . . . A ridiculous
notion! Had Blaskowitz forgotten that — despite the bitter and, in
Straube's opinion, stupid fighting by the Americans throughout
the fall in the Huertgen Forest — the Germans still controlled the
Schwammenauel Dam near Schmidt and could inundate the river
at will? Straube himself had seen the directive of General der Fallschirmtruppen Alfred Schlemm, commander of the elite First
Parachute Army, ordering his engineers to disable the discharge
valves and flood the valley to thwart such an attack.

No, in Straube's view it was much more realistic to anticipate
the main attack coming from the British sector at Venlo. It was true
that German guns were heavily entrenched along the Siegfried Line
defences facing the enemy across the Maas at this point. But once
the British forced a crossing over the river they would find the open
Rhineland plains vastly more suitable than the Reichswald for an
armoured blitzkrieg to the Rhine.

There was one other theory upon which Straube now speculated
sourly. Straube's boss, General Schlemm, argued vehemently with
his superiors that the Allied attack would be renewed late in January by the British or Canadians through what was known as the
"side door to the Ruhr" — the Canadian positions facing the Reichswald Forest near Nijmegen, 60 miles north of the American sector.

Schlemm's request for reinforcements in that sector had been
rejected by the Wehrmacht planners, who obviously also thought
the theory of an invasion in the north was ludicrous. He was told
that, despite extensive patrolling, scouts could find no evidence
of any concentration of forces there. Straube disagreed with
Schlemm, a matter of little consequence to the Para leader, who
privately considered the corps commander a *langweilig* (a bore).

The Canadian forward defence line (FDL) fronted on what
Straube considered to be a most unrewarding strip of German territory, stretching some 20 miles between the Maas and Rhine rivers.
A large part of this area was covered by a state forest — the Reichswald — a heavily wooded eight-by-five-mile tract. The forest's only
transportation links, beyond two narrow roads running south
through the wood, were rough paths, or rides, that crisscrossed
the densely planted area. Straube considered it impenetrable to

large-scale armoured assault. The remainder, the low-lying marsh-lands along the Rhine, could easily be flooded and rendered impass-able by sabotaging the dikes.

How to discover the Allied intentions? Reconnaissance by air was no longer possible; after the Ardennes battle, German reconnais-sance aircraft had been virtually wiped out by the RAF. There were scarcely any trained agents left behind Allied lines. Intensive patrol-ling and information forced from captured Allied prisoners were the only means to seek the intelligence he needed.

Straube had ordered long-distance patrols to be sent across the river through the Allied FDLs. Although they probed as deeply as 10 miles behind the lines, maintaining a watch for two or three days at a time, none of these scouts brought back information that would indicate any unusual activity. Invariably, they returned with the same story: no insignia of fresh new battalions being moved forward, no increased traffic, no evidence of a step-up of armour or artillery pieces — just the same troops of the 2nd and 3rd Cana-dian Infantry Divisions that had been headquartered in those regions all winter.

It was as Straube thought: if any attack came through the Reichs-wald, it would be a minor diversion to the main thrust at Venlo. But the Watchmaker's penchant for detail was not entirely satis-fied. Nor would it be until Straube himself had questioned the Canadian.

"Bring that prisoner to me. Now!" he repeated. "I will find the answer."

At that moment, the man Straube hoped could shed some light on his dilemma was executing a bold plan of escape. Hugging the dark shadows, he worked his way cautiously to the outskirts of Cleve, grateful that an earlier RAF raid on the city had left bomb-shattered skeletons of buildings to shelter him from the menacing search party.

For Lieutenant S.W. Nichols of Canada's Black Watch Regiment, the past four days had blurred into a confused nightmare that had begun when he led a patrol into German territory in the Reichs-wald Forest. It had been his second patrol of the night, the first having encountered strong enemy fire that killed one of their band and forced the remainder to withdraw. Nichols had returned a few hours later to recover the body, and again his patrol came under fire. It was while he was giving aid to one of his wounded men that he was captured.

That night his German captors moved the young Canadian to their platoon headquarters, an earthwork bunker in the forest. They identified themselves as paratroops known as the "Green Devils." From there he was evacuated under escort of an officer to another HQ in the southwest corner of the Reichswald. Here, Nichols was subjected to the first of three interrogations, each more unpleasant than the last. The Germans informed him that they had found the bodies of some of their soldiers shot in the head. Nichols would be held responsible for the atrocities and regarded as a common criminal, he was told angrily. He would be taken to Major-General Heinz Fiebig's 84th Infantry Division HQ and handed over to the Gestapo for questioning.

The second interrogation took place in Cleve several days later. After violent grilling by a Gestapo captain, he was escorted back to his cell with the final threat of "retaliation."

It could have been a moment of bleak despair. However, the Canadian had a plan of escape. Since his first meal, he had been hoarding part of any food given him. By feigning dysentery, he had managed during frequent trips to the latrine to make a limited reconnaissance of the prison area. Now he would make his move.

Early that same evening he was escorted to the latrine by two guards armed with rifles. Seizing an opportunity when they glanced away, he leaped over a wall. At once he came upon a hedge that proved to be thickly wired. After struggling in vain to get through it, he spun around in another direction and made off through the shattered city. The two guards fired several shots, all wild, and then gave the alarm. (For this negligence, General Fiebig was to fire his divisional intelligence officer and confine the guards to barracks.)

Now Nichols was back in the forest, desperately groping his way along the rough paths that crisscrossed the woods as he strove to elude his pursuers. He heard the howl of the guard dogs as they raced across the flatlands of the Rhine seeking the scent of their quarry. Moving swiftly, he cut even deeper into the profound blackness of the Reichswald. The sounds became fainter. Thank God — his captors were still searching in the north.

For three days, the bold Black Watch officer clung to the dense woods, thankful for the obscurity of the thickly planted trees. By day, he hid in the enemy slit-trenches that abounded in that area of the Siegfried Line, shivering almost uncontrollably in the near-freezing temperatures. Once, a column of German soldiers with their usual horse-drawn transport passed not 10 feet from his narrow trench. Peering through the branches, he could see the frosty breath of the horses.

When darkness fell he clambered stiffly up to the ice-rutted rides and resumed his nine-mile trek through the woods towards Canadian lines, carefully circling enemy outposts and noting their strengths and positions.

The little Watchmaker would have to make his decision without benefit of the cool-headed Canadian even now crossing the line into friendly territory.

There was one circumstance that would have truly dumbfounded the perplexed German, had he but known it. At the very moment when he was struggling to discern the enemy's next plan, the Allied camp was still floundering in indecision and dissension. There *was* no new plan.

In the final months of 1944, the three Army Groups under General Dwight D. Eisenhower's command — numbering some two million men — were massing on the German border along a 600-mile front that stretched from the North Sea to Switzerland.

The focus of the Supreme Allied Commander, Eisenhower, had turned to the Rhine River, the enemy's last western defence line. Eisenhower insisted that before any major operation was attempted east of the Rhine, it was essential to destroy the main enemy armies west of the river.

Sandwiched between the Allied line on the German border and the Rhine lay the Rhineland — a stretch of territory 20 to 30 miles wide that had to be penetrated before the Rhine could be reached. Two major rivers blocked entry to this strip of land: the Maas and the Roer. As well, the many rivers that coursed through the area and Hitler's Siegfried defences were effective obstacles to Allied armour and infantry.

Closing his forces simultaneously to the Rhine during the latter months of 1944 had thus far proven an elusive objective for the Supreme Commander. In southern France, General Jacob L. Devers's 6th U.S. Army Group (comprising General Jean de Lattre de Tassigny's First French Army and General Alexander M. Patch's Seventh U.S. Army) was fighting its way northeast to the Rhine through the difficult terrain of the foothills of the Vosges Mountains. The armies had become stalled by a large and troublesome German bridgehead on the west bank, known as the Colmar Pocket. Even if they did break through, no crossing so far from the industrial north was feasible.

On Devers's left or northern flank, the three armies of General Bradley's 12th Army Group — the flamboyant Lieutenant-General George S. Patton's Third Army, Hodges's First Army, and Lieutenant-General William H. Simpson's Ninth Army — were extended along the German border fronting Belgium and Luxembourg.

By an accident of geography, Bradley's Army Group faced the Saar district, whose rugged terrain made it impractical for a killing strike on Germany. Their assigned objectives were to advance on both sides of the Ardennes Forest — its steep hills and gorges all the more treacherous in winter — and close on a long stretch of the upper Rhine from Cologne south to Mannheim.

Field-Marshal Sir Bernard L. Montgomery's 21st Army Group (comprising British and Canadian troops), the most northerly of the three Army Groups, held the line that fronted the flat terrain of the Ruhr, where much of Germany's industry was located. This was a considerably more viable passage into the heart of Germany.

As fall progressed into winter, each commander proposed that the major thrust be made from his sector: Bradley advocated the Frankfurt corridor in the upper Rhine, and Montgomery argued for crossing the lower Rhine at Wesel. The Saar-versus-Ruhr debate became distorted by the more subjective side issues of Bradley versus Montgomery and the U.S. versus Britain. Each commander was passionately determined to be the one to spearhead the final drive to victory. National feelings hardened from irritation to anger and outright jealousy.

The events of the autumn months had exacerbated the situation. Following the sweep through France and Belgium in August and September of 1944, Montgomery had persuaded Eisenhower to let him attempt a ''single full-blooded thrust'' to establish a bridgehead over the Rhine at Arnhem. Although it did slice a valuable 65-mile-long corridor deep into the Netherlands, almost to the German border, the attempt failed to gain that final, vital bridge. The price was high. Operation Market-Garden cost the British, American, and Polish armies 11,850 casualties.

More subtly, it fired up smouldering American doubts concerning Montgomery's ability as a military commander. It also confirmed Eisenhower's innermost belief that the best strategy was to extend all his armies across a broad front for a massed sweep into Germany.

The Americans thought that in Montgomery they had an over-cautious ''master of tidiness,'' as his own Intelligence chief,

11

Brigadier Edgar T. (Bill) Williams, described him: a man who hesitated to commit himself to decisive action until he had all the details neatly together — in short, a sort of British "Watchmaker."

The prevailing sentiment at Supreme Headquarters Allied Expeditionary Force (SHAEF) was "If anything has to be done quickly, don't give it to Monty."

As General Bradley defined their two widely varying approaches: "When Montgomery prepared to attack, he dragged up everything he had for an all-out campaign. . . . We Americans, on the other hand, constantly nibbled away on the key positions of an enemy. . . constantly kept him knocked off balance."

It was this very "nibbling" that was outraging the British. "The Americans would never learn the principle of concentration," the field-marshal lamented to his diarist, Lieutenant-Colonel Christopher Dawnay. "They are obsessed with the idea of keeping everybody fighting all the time and consequently in Bradley's Army Group he was never able to concentrate for one full-blooded thrust. In 21st Army Group, I always tried to avoid having two armies fighting at the same time. This is something the Americans never learned."

Montgomery maintained that Bradley's persistence in dissipating the efforts of 12th Army Group by probing ineffectually "here, there and everywhere" had resulted in minimal progress with maximum casualties. By focussing on the wrong objective — the Huertgen Forest instead of the Roer dams — Bradley had caused his divisions to become immobilized on the banks of the Roer, leaving the Germans in control of the river.

Colonel Charles B. MacDonald, the official U.S. Army historian and himself a company commander in the Northwest Europe campaign, explains the lapse as "a kind of torpor that enveloped American commanders and their staffs as the exultation of the pursuit passed and the hard realities of continued bitter fighting followed."

MacDonald recently commented to the authors, "A lethargy seemed to settle over the American command. They just kept throwing in one division after another. They seemed to have the feeling, 'Surely one more will do it.' Well, one more didn't do it. They finally just ground the Germans down, but in the meantime Huertgen had become a meat-grinder for us as well."

"We were mired in a ghastly war of attrition," Bradley reflected sourly in his memoirs. "Monty promptly seized on our failures to position himself for a renewed political offensive inside the high command to have his own way."

Indeed, Montgomery was not backward in spotlighting Bradley's "strategic reverses," as he somewhat tactlessly termed them, to make his own point. The American commanders had lost both their grip on the battle and the confidence of their troops, he remonstrated to Eisenhower on November 28. The Allies, he argued, must now strike out for the Rhine in a single, powerful thrust.

Montgomery proposed that two almost simultaneous assaults be launched across the Rhineland to secure the west banks of the Rhine: Operation Veritable, a northern thrust from Nijmegen by a combined British and Canadian force of 470,000 men (under command of First Canadian Army); and Operation Grenade, an assault across the Roer River by 375,000 American troops in Ninth and First Armies 60 miles to the south. The dual forces would burst out on the Rhineland Plain in an armoured sweep that would converge at the Rhine at Wesel, cutting off the retreating Germans.

The Germans would be left with two options: stand and fight on the west bank of the Rhine, with the possibility of having their last cohesive forces eliminated; or abandon their positions in the Rhineland and retreat to form a new defensive line on the Rhine's east bank. Either way, the Allies would have secured a firm launching pad on the Rhine from which to attack eastward into the Ruhr.

In principle, Eisenhower was in full accord with Monty's strategy. His own chief of staff, General Walter Bedell Smith, concurred that the factories and blast furnaces of the Ruhr were pumping "lifeblood" into the German military system. Once the Ruhr was sealed off, he said, "the heart would cease to beat." But it was Montgomery's suggestion that he himself head up this massed force of Anglo-American divisions that rocked Allied unity.

Between them, Bradley's First and Ninth Armies held a front north of the Ardennes of some 55 miles. Montgomery urgently needed those forces for his Grenade operation. He proposed that they be consolidated under his command. But, he said, if this were not acceptable, then he would serve under Bradley's command in this assault.

Bradley set up a storm of protest against the proposal, complaining that he was being shafted by Montgomery's "megalomania," made the more dangerous, he thought, by Eisenhower's "anglophilia."

"[Montgomery's] plans were almost always designed to further his own aggrandizement," he scoffed, threatening (along with Patton) to resign if Montgomery's 21st Army Group were given the glory of finishing off the Germans.

Bradley had suspected that Montgomery might try to commandeer his most northerly American army to augment the ranks of 21st Army Group. Cannily, he had inserted his inexperienced Ninth Army between Hodges's and Montgomery's armies, thereby preserving for his own purposes the vastly more experienced First Army.

This newcomer to the group, commanded by Lieutenant-General William H. ("Simp") Simpson, was to surprise them all. The name "Simp" began as a somewhat uncomplimentary reference to the fact that the lanky, rawboned 56-year-old Texan had been a very poor student in his West Point days. In the Rhineland campaign, the nickname softened to respect and affection for the American who proved himself one of the most astute of the commanding generals in World War II.

Of all the American commanders, Simpson was most suited to serve under British command. Mild and unassuming, he was one of the few American army commanders to get along with the crusty British field-marshal. Like Montgomery, Simpson had the charisma of a born leader, and his tall, lean frame with the distinctively clean-shaven head was often seen bent in conversation with the ranks. Both men were energetic, dedicated, and skilled. But Big Simp was not burdened with the sometimes overbearing pride that was often attributed to Montgomery — and perhaps in a team of two there was room for only one such ego. As Bradley himself put it, the Ninth Army, "unlike the noisy and bumptious Third and the temperamental First," was "uncommonly normal."

Simpson also had, as Bradley recalled, "a wonderfully earthy sense of humour." One of the anecdotes that Simpson loved to tell related to an evening when he and Georgie Patton substantially reduced the level of a bottle of brandy as they rehashed their army careers under their new bosses:

Patton said, "Well, here we all are under Eisenhower and Bradley, both six years our junior. Hodges flunked out of West Point Class of ought-eight [1908] and had to enlist and now he commands First Army. I was turned back from ought-eight and it took me five years to graduate — with ought-nine — but I command Third Army. You came out second from the bottom in our class in ought-nine and you command Ninth Army. Isn't it peculiar that three old farts like us should be carrying the ball for those two sons-of-bitches?"

It was precisely this strong bond — this old boys' net shared by Bradley, his three army chiefs, and Eisenhower — that was to become a critical factor in determining the direction of the war. Lamentably, during the acrimonious debates of early winter when a battle plan was so sorely needed, their very enthusiasm to win became obstructive to the quest for peace. Each of Bradley's three commanders intensely desired to "carry the ball" to victory — an American victory — over Nazism. They did not want to sit idly by while Montgomery administered (and got the credit for) the death blow.

Eisenhower was inwardly sympathetic. As his biographer, Stephen Ambrose, observed: "In the back of Eisenhower's mind, perhaps if only in his subconscious, was the desire to give Bradley the leading role in the campaign if the opportunity presented itself."

At the Maastricht conference on December 7, Eisenhower announced his decision. The outcome was termed by Bradley "a classic Eisenhower compromise that left me distinctly unhappy":

I would retain control of Hodges' First and Patton's Third armies (both north and south of the Ardennes); . . . Hodges, Patton and Devers would continue aggressive operations against Germany.

Now Monty had been chosen to make the "main effort", and henceforth my operations would be "supporting". Monty would be given my Ninth Army. Ten U.S. divisions would be compelled to serve directly under a British commander who would make certain they never received any credit.

Still Eisenhower wavered, later informing his staff that he was referring the entire issue to a committee "to work out a plan."

Appalled at the lack of direction, Montgomery complained on December 16 to SHAEF's chief of operations, General Sir John Whitely, that unless the Supreme Commander made up his mind quickly as to what he wanted to do and issued definite orders, they were likely to "drift into an unfavourable situation, vis-a-vis the enemy."

It was a prophetic remark. That same morning, 200,000 German tank and infantry troops, spearheaded by parachutists and blanketed by heavy air cover, launched Hitler's surprise counter-offensive in the Ardennes against Bradley's dangerously thin line of 83,000 Americans. Montgomery voiced his dismay to the British Chief of the Imperial General Staff (CIGS), Field-Marshal Sir

Alan Brooke: "It looks as if we may now have to pay the price for the policy of drift and lack of proper control of the operations which have been a marked feature of the last three months."

This "drift," or torpor, of Eisenhower and his senior staff only accentuated the fundamental differences between them and Montgomery.

"[Monty] could think only as a soldier," his intelligence officer noted. "He thought he saw a chance to win on his front. He could see only that.

"Ike was a military statesman. He could see the strategic angles. He could see that you couldn't win without public opinion."

There was a difference in another dimension as well: wartime lifestyle. In Paris, the staff of SHAEF — a bureaucracy of some 100,000 officers and men — could have filled a small city. Politicians and military personnel from America were frequent visitors.

Eisenhower's tactical headquarters in Reims, with 16 master bedrooms and innumerable lounges, had been the opulent residence of Monopole, the "Champagne king" of France. Both Bradley and Hodges were headquartered in luxurious châteaux in Luxembourg and Belgium.

By the early winter of 1945, Eisenhower's main headquarters in Versailles at the Trianon Palace Hotel bustled with the constant flow of Stateside guests, often bearing gifts of American delicacies. (On one occasion, Eisenhower gleefully apportioned out to his dinner guests, one by one, a gift of 100 Malpeque oysters.)

Eisenhower's commanders had a penchant for sharp dressing and high living. There were always female companions for bridge in the evenings or weekends in the south of France. Eisenhower himself set the pace: he included his former driver, English-born Kay Summersby, as his constant companion, as his aide at top-secret meetings, and even as his hostess at high-level dinner parties. (At one point he offended British protocol by seating their prime minister at the place of honour on her right.) Whether the pair were emotionally involved was immaterial; what mattered was that many of the SHAEF commanders followed suit with equally non-military and highly distracting conduct.

By contrast, Montgomery lived a solitary and ascetic life at the front. His habitual dress was a shabby pullover and baggy corduroy trousers; his preferred Tac HQ consisted of a caravan in a field near the front, in tandem with similar vehicles and tents serving as map lorry, mess, and sleeping quarters. He ate sparingly and abstained from alcohol and tobacco.

By day, his boundless energy propelled him on tireless visits to his various command units. There was always time to stop and talk to the men. He loved the troops and they loved him. "He always let us know everything that was going on," Corporal Peter Huntley of the 53rd Welsh Division recalled. "He put us in the picture. We knew we would not be sent into battle until he had everything just right."

By evening, regardless of what VIPs might be his dinner guests, he retired firmly to his quarters. He believed that a period of quiet reflection on the events of the day was essential for a man in senior command.

Montgomery had evolved an intelligence system that provided him with fast, first-hand, detailed reports on all fronts. They were brought to him verbally (to avoid security risks) by his liaison officers (LOs), who daily risked their lives travelling hundreds of miles, even behind enemy lines. These LOs became Montgomery's "family," sharing simple comforts in an environment totally dedicated to war.

One of these officers, Lieutenant-Colonel T.S. Bigland, described the ritual in the map lorry each evening:

After the 9 o'clock news we went across to the map caravan to hear what the "boys" had to say. The boys are the ADCs and liaison officers, British, American, Canadian. [They] have been out to various fronts during the day, driving immense distances in cars or jeeps — a tough job in the winter, a wearing one in any weather. Now each in turn comes to the great map on the wall and tells the chief what he knows: "The 21st are through the wood; it's a bit sticky by the windmill; 44th will attack at 0400" and so on. Chief asks few questions . . . makes few comments. It might be somebody else's battle. But it isn't. These are his chosen men at work using his ways and so there is nothing much to say.

"When he had seen these fellows at night," Lieutenant-Colonel Trumbull Warren, Montgomery's Canadian personal assistant, recalls, "he would write out a lengthy report in longhand. He wouldn't dictate anything. We would put this into code and send it to London. So by midnight the War Office also had right up-to-date information of what was going on."

Thus it was that while Eisenhower, Bradley, and Bedell Smith were interrupted while playing bridge in Versailles to hear the first confused word of the German attack against Bradley's troops in the Ardennes, Monty's LOs were already bringing in detailed reports from American frontline units. It clearly didn't endear him to his opposite numbers or to Eisenhower or SHAEF HQ that his knowledge of *their* affairs was often greater than was their own.

Small wonder that Montgomery viewed his American counterparts' sybaritic lifestyle with lofty disdain, shrugging off their successes as he harangued and humiliated them for their failures. Small wonder that this intolerance was met with such strong feelings from Eisenhower's commanders that "what previously had been merely contempt had grown into active hatred."

It took Montgomery's ill-fated press conference on January 7 to finally blow the lid off Allied unity, causing a chain reaction that put the pending Veritable and Grenade operations into jeopardy and nearly cost Eisenhower his job.

2

One Could Go Mad

THE ANIMOSITY AMONG the Allied generals had become so intense that even Hitler had begun to relish the rivalry as a secret weapon of his own. In December, from his concrete-entombed bunker deep below the Chancellery, Adolf Hitler sent off a diatribe to his generals, prophesying his own victory through the disintegration of the Allied union:

In the whole of world history, there has never been a coalition which consisted of such heterogeneous elements with such diametrically opposed objectives. On the one side a dying world empire, that of Great Britain, and on the other a "colony," the United States, anxious to take over the inheritance.

Montgomery's statement to the media of the United States and Great Britain at the infamous January 7 press conference not only fuelled the dictator's rhetoric. In the words of his liaison officer, it "caused more bad feeling [among] the Americans than anything else in the war." It was classic Monty: as full of conceit as it was of good intentions.

The fact that Montgomery had been given temporary command of First and Ninth Armies during the Ardennes crisis had been a keen embarrassment to Hodges and Bradley. Press censorship withheld the fact from the public until the first week of January. Its inevitable disclosure, two days before the press conference, incited strong response from the American media and people; the victory in the Ardennes that they had thought was achieved by Americans had in fact come about under British command. Now — with permission from Eisenhower, Brooke, and Churchill — the field-marshal set about to redress the situation.

Ostensibly, Montgomery's motive was to reduce the mudslinging between the American and British media by describing how the "whole Allied team rallied to the call" in stopping the enemy offensive in the Ardennes. In delivery, however, Monty's condescending attitude and air of self-importance enraged the American commanders, and even appalled many of the British ones. What particularly stung was that Montgomery was taking credit for a victory that he claimed was achieved by American troops fighting alongside British ones, when in fact he had held back the British forces in reserve to the Americans as much as possible in order to preserve them for the coming Veritable operation.

"The text in a sense was innocuous; the presentation quite appalling," Brigadier Bill Williams, Montgomery's chief of Intelligence, told author Nigel Hamilton in an interview. "I was there. . . . It seemed to me, well, *disastrous*. I couldn't stop it.

"It was meant to be a tribute to the American soldier and so on — but it came across as if he . . . had rescued the Americans — 'Of course they were jolly brave,' and so on and so forth, but he used that awful phrase, 'a very interesting little battle,' or words to that effect.

"The newsmen were not fools," Williams added. "They reported the cocky air in which he gave the interview."

Never slow to seize such a heaven-made opportunity, Goebbels's propaganda people wrote a doctored version of the speech and broke in on a BBC overseas wavelength to deliver it. It was this slanted version that reached Bradley's headquarters in Luxembourg and rekindled the feud.

By mid-January, the ruckus had put an end to any hopes Montgomery might have had of taking over total command of Bradley's armies for the major thrust on the Rhine. He had completely alienated the 12th Army Group commander, who protested to his staff that Montgomery was treating the Americans like "country cousins."

If it had not been for the Americans "pulling them along," Bradley said angrily, the British would have had difficulty ever establishing the Normandy beachhead or advancing across France. It was unthinkable that Montgomery expected the Americans to step back and let him win the war — using American troops. "The British would get the glory. Monty would get the glory primarily."

This only deepened Eisenhower's dilemma. If he denied Montgomery the reinforcements he needed for his Rhineland campaign, the operation would be jeopardized. Putting 14 American divisions back under Montgomery's command for the dual operations, however, would not only further alienate Bradley; it would also outrage the American people. Yet each day's delay brought the increased risk that the usual early-spring thaws would endanger the Veritable and Grenade operations. Their success depended upon being launched over still-frozen ground to allow a full-fledged armoured breakout.

Montgomery had insisted all along that his two pincer assaults be mounted more or less together, on the 8th and 10th of February. He would not risk British and Canadian lives in a watered-down Veritable operation if Grenade were delayed or cancelled. Before Grenade could be launched, however, two essential tasks had to be achieved.

The first was a massive movement of troops to bolster the strength of Simpson's Ninth Army and place it under command of Montgomery's 21st Army Group for the operation. Eisenhower issued the order that a total of 12 divisions be moved up from Bradley's armies.

Yet he waffled on the timing of the move. Bradley was still engaged in a mopping-up offensive in the Ardennes, which he hoped might lead to a breakout to the Rhine for Hodges or Patton. Ninth Army's buildup "would depend on whether operations in the Ardennes were allowed to proceed or were closed down," Eisenhower said, giving Bradley the OK to continue "until the first week in February." Thus the units designated for the transfer were still employed.

Such a delay in reinforcing Ninth Army would forestall the launching of Grenade. It could also cancel its sister operation to the north — Veritable — as the two were interdependent.

Eisenhower reminded a protesting Montgomery that two-thirds of the forces in the Northwest Europe campaign were American (61 U.S. divisions versus 15 Anglo/Canadian). Therefore, Eisenhower said, while he supported the strategy of an assault on the Ruhr, he also intended to send Bradley's armies south of the Ruhr at Frankfurt. The people of the United States would never stand for any other arrangement.

The response totally frustrated Montgomery, who was back where he started, with Eisenhower seemingly playing both ends of the field. Monty complained to Brooke that Ike was "useless . . . quite out of his depth in dealing with such matters . . . a complete amateur compared to Rundstedt."

Nor were Ike's staff any better, Montgomery maintained. There

21

was no one at SHAEF who could give him sound military advice. Consequently, Eisenhower simply collected advice from everyone and then worked out a compromise to satisfy them all.

"Twelfth Army Group takes no interest in Grenade," Montgomery said plaintively to Brooke. "[They] openly said they were off to Cologne and Bonn. . . . One has to preserve a sense of humour these days, otherwise one would go mad."

The situation shifted somewhat during the final week of January. First, the British chiefs of staff, disturbed by the Supreme Commander's vacillation, requested a high-level strategy review. The subsequent Combined Chiefs of Staff meeting in Malta (prior to the Yalta conference) resulted in "the most violent disagreements and disputes of the entire war," during which even the possibility of demanding Eisenhower's resignation was raised. It was only resolved by the verbal assurance of Bedell Smith that "Montgomery's Army Group would have top priority and would cross the lower Rhine as soon as possible and without waiting until all the Rhineland had been cleared."

Then, as January came to a close, it became clear that Bradley's operation had faltered badly in the Ardennes. The operation was cancelled, freeing 12th Army Group for other duties. Eisenhower's long-delayed directive authorizing Operations Veritable and Grenade and giving Montgomery command over them was finally issued on February 1, just a little over a week before the proposed D-Days of the assaults. Simpson's Ninth Army was to be fully reinforced, as planned, and put under Montgomery's operational control for the Grenade attack.

To facilitate this, Patton was given written orders to go on the defensive so that supplies and reinforcements could be diverted north to support the Grenade operation. The directive was somewhat farcical, having been hedged by a reluctant Bradley who instead gave Patton a verbal command to stay on the "aggressive defence." ("We laughed about that," Bradley admitted later. "Actually we were keeping up the attack. . . . I suppose it did give them [Third Army] some merriment.")

"As a sop to our pride," Patton reported, "we were told that we could continue to attack until the tenth and thereafter, providing casualties and ammunition expenditure were not excessive. . . . We were all very much upset. We felt it ignoble for the American armies to finish the war on the defensive."

The second task necessary before Grenade could be launched was the capture of the Roer dams. As recently as January 17, Eisenhower's Intelligence chief, Major-General K.W.D. Strong, had warned Bradley that the enemy could flood the dams.

Incredibly, even as Eisenhower was giving the go-ahead for Veritable and Grenade, there was still no plan in the works to seize this long-term obstacle. Bradley received his orders to concentrate his resources on the dams only when his southern operation was finally cancelled. It wasn't until February 4 — just four days prior to the Veritable launch and six before Grenade was scheduled — that Bradley relayed the order to Hodges to seize the dams.

The next evening, at Hodges's HQ in Spa, Bradley reviewed the assault plans. On the 7th and 8th, his diarist, Major Chester Hansen, noted, "Brad stays in office working on plans for capture of Roer dams. . . . He continues to appear relaxed, jokes easily."

Meanwhile, on February 5, Montgomery arrived in high spirits at a conference in Namur, where Eisenhower had ordered Bradley to set up his new headquarters ("to be closer to Montgomery"). Montgomery seemed strangely unaware of Bradley's hostility towards him, or of the resentment the staff of 12th Army Group harboured because he had stopped their offensive and made off with their divisions.

"Even Kay Summersby objected to being seated at the table with Montgomery," Hansen noted, "assuring us that she would, undoubtedly, become embroiled in a controversy if she did."

Captain William C. Sylvan, Hodges's personal assistant, noted waspishly that his boss had made a private bet that, "true to form," Montgomery would find an excuse to foist the brunt of the coming operations onto the Americans: "The General bet . . . that Monty would work it somehow that the Ninth Army would attack first."

The "dying world empire" and the "colony" had reached an all-time peak in animosity and were causing serious damage to the progress of the war. The mismanagement of failing to secure the dams, and the repeated delays and indecision had stalled the Veritable-Grenade attack until thaws and floods robbed it of much of its potency.

The operation that had been mired in controversy throughout the fall and early winter now faced the prospect of being mired in mud. Instead of launching three-quarters of a million fighting men across the Rhineland's frozen terrain, it would propel them into a quagmire. The success of the battle plan would now depend not on weapons and armour, but on the sheer guts of every one of those men.

While the Allied strategists, having finally settled on a plan, believed that they were placing Hitler in an untenable position, the dictator in fact acknowledged no such quandary.

His most competent commanders were astute enough to recognize how desperate the German plight had become. Hitler, however, refused to allow his commanders to yield a single yard to the enemy.

Generalfeldmarschall Gerd von Rundstedt, a shrewd and professional strategist who by Hitler's whim had been twice fired and rehired as commander-in-chief of the western army, appealed to his chief to abandon his policy of "clinging to every foot of German soil." Instead he urged withdrawal to prepare the defence of the eastern banks of the Rhine. General der Panzertruppen Hasso von Manteuffel reported bitterly that by refusing to withdraw to the Rhine, Hitler was sacrificing what was left of a courageous and loyal fighting force.

Ignoring their advice, Hitler issued an uncompromising directive. His commanding generals must report directly to him every decision to carry out an operational movement, every attack, and every plan for disengaging, withdrawing, or surrendering their forces. Hitler reserved the right of veto over the heads of even his most senior commanders and threatened "draconian punishment" to anyone who disobeyed.

"The pressure from behind," Rundstedt lamented, "was always far worse than the pressure in front. As Commander-in-Chief West my only authority was to change the guard in front of my gate."

The Nazi dictator's obstinate refusal to heed his subordinates' advice was based in part on his belief in his West Wall (as the Germans called the Siegfried Line) — the fortified barrier that stretched all the way along the western borders of Germany from Holland south to Switzerland.

In 1936 a world inattentive to the first rumblings of imminent war had watched idly as Nazi troops defied the Treaty of Versailles by marching into the demilitarized Rhineland. Two years later, under the skilled direction of Dr. Fritz Todt, half a million labourers were employed in creating the Siegfried defences. Using one-third of the country's annual production of cement, Todt constructed more than 3,000 concrete pillboxes, bunkers, and observation posts, strung two or three lines deep.

The pillboxes, with walls and roofs up to eight feet thick, were compact subterranean fortresses of steel-reinforced concrete with a warren of small rooms for troop quarters, ammunition storage, and mutually supporting gun casements. Some were camouflaged as houses or barns. Chains of "dragon's teeth," ungainly concrete anti-tank obstacles embedded in rows in the ground, formed a further defence. Steel beams anchored in concrete protruded along roads, prohibiting vehicular advance.

At the outbreak of war in 1939 the line was extended north, though in diminishing strength, as far as Cleve in the lower Rhineland. No further work was done on the Siegfried defences until the autumn of 1944, when the Allied advance towards Germany inspired frantic efforts to improve the line. Although the fortifications were in some aspects outmoded, they still provided a formidable defence. Moreover, the Siegfried Line had soared as a symbol in the minds of the German people. Hitler's propaganda had created an unshakeable belief that the wall was impregnable.

Above all else, Hitler believed his own propaganda. He knew his Germans. He demanded their loyalty; he touched their hearts with fear. Hitler reminded them of their strategic strengths: a dedicated Wehrmacht, the much-vaunted Siegfried Line defences, the German superiority of weapons. He terrified them with accounts of the destruction of their homeland if they should be overrun by the Allies.

He warned the people that an Allied conqueror would subjugate them; enemy troops would pillage and desecrate their homeland. He cited the Morgenthau Plan — a proposal made in 1944 by the U.S. Secretary of the Treasury, Henry Morgenthau — which would reduce Germany to a pastoral land. Even if this plan were not adopted, meetings were being held at Yalta in January 1945 by Roosevelt, Churchill, and Stalin that would slice up Germany like so many pieces of pie to be handed over to the victors.

Hitler appealed to his people's nationalistic pride with expansive boasts of his new miracle weapons. With the technological brilliance for which they have historically been renowned, the Germans had already devised a jet airplane, a remote-controlled flying bomb, a rocket plane even faster than a jet, a rocket missile that homed in on an enemy plane by tracking the heat rays from its motors, and a torpedo that reacted to sound. Development of a ground-to-air missile had been completed.

Although he would not release details of these inventions — some had not reached the production stage — Hitler could and did flaunt the destructive use of several of them to *das Volk*, the German populace.

The V-2 rockets continued in full production with the use of slave labour in subterranean plants under the Harz Mountains, safe from Allied bombs. They would not cease in their silent flights of destruction on London and Antwerp. The new Me-262 (Messerschmidt) jet fighter-bomber — the first of its kind and 125 miles per hour faster than any existing plane — was released in January 1945, with a production rate of 210 craft each month.

One by one, Hitler mocked his adversaries, playing one ally against the other. The American soldier has no will to fight, he assured his people. German weapons will inflict such heavy casualties on them that the people of the United States will demand a negotiated peace. The British Empire is doomed, he declared, and their colonial subjects, the Canadians, will pull out of the war when they realize it. "Against the coolly scheming Stalin, Churchill hasn't got a ghost of a chance," he assured them.

His propaganda machines pumped out their vitriolic description of the Allied commanders: Roosevelt, the "fire-side chatterer with a poor knowledge of geography"; Churchill, the "drunkard."

"Stalin, Churchill, Roosevelt, and their abettors bring poverty and death," he exhorted. "Retain your loyalty to the Fuehrer! Adolf Hitler is the guarantor of our future."

His two most powerful propaganda weapons had been outright gifts from his enemies: the dissension among the Allied commanders and the issue of unconditional surrender.

The demand for Germany's "unconditional surrender" had been adopted primarily to appease the Russians. The phrase was coined by Roosevelt and first aired with Churchill over lunch before the press conference at which it was announced, just prior to the 1943 Casablanca conference.

Roosevelt's son Elliott, who was present, reported: "Churchill, while he slowly munched a mouthful of food, thought, frowned, thought, finally grinned and at length announced, 'Perfect, and I can just see how Goebbels and the rest of 'em 'll squeal.' "

Instead of "squealing," skilled propaganda chief Joseph Goebbels capitalized on the Casablanca Formula, calling it "world-historical tomfoolery of the first order."

"I should never have been able to think up so rousing a slogan," Goebbels gloated. "If our Western enemies tell us: we won't deal with you, our only aim is to destroy you . . . how can any German, whether he likes it or not, do anything but fight on with all his strength?

"Nothing better could happen to us than to have the English . . . openly proclaim their intention to destroy Germany completely, that is, not only the Nazi regime, but the entire German people."

A young American infantryman of the 104th Division, John S. Wade, Jr., saw the results of this policy from the front line and wrote to his family:

These people back home that publicly announce their opinions on what to do with Germany after the war make me mad. Especially when it is an opinion that does not give the Germans any choice but slavery. Why in the hell they can't shut up until we have beaten the Germans, I don't know. Maybe they think the war is over already. It just makes the Jerries fight longer, and believe me there is still quite a lot of fighting in them . . . . All the post-war talk is only convincing them that they might as well keep shooting because if they give up, they'll be as good as dead anyway.

There is strong evidence, borne out by the testimony of many Allied and German commanders, that this no-compromise approach merely stiffened the German will to fight and prolonged the war. Hitler managed to convince even the most reasoned and influential anti-Nazis that because of the Allied insistence upon unconditional surrender, there could be no alternative to stubborn resistance, no thought of a negotiated peace.

Hitler commanded a well-trained, superbly disciplined, and obedient army that had already proven its defensive skills by staving off the Allied powerhouse from invading Germany for five months. Logistically, the German army had been defeated at least as early as July 1944, after the overwhelming success of the Allied invasion of Normandy. It was defeated again when the Ardennes counter-offensive failed in January 1945. Yet, fuelled by desperation, this beaten army continued to fight and win battles.

The cost of this prolongation was staggering. American casualties in the fighting in Northwest Europe from January 1945 until the end of the war in May amounted to 222,360 dead and wounded. Add to this figure more than 17,000 British and Canadian casualties in the Rhineland campaign alone, in addition to the French and Polish and the huge numbers of Russian casualties — and a substantial proportion of the estimated four million German military and civilian casualties from the war — and this innocent-sounding phrase ''unconditional surrender'' reveals how truly expensive it was.

The chief of staff of the 116th Panzer Division in Schlemm's First Parachute Army during the Huertgen and Rhineland campaigns, Major-General (then Lieutenant-Colonel) Heinz-Guenther Guderian, recently described to the authors the frustration of many in the Wehrmacht who were given no choice but to fight on: ''There was no other solution.''

Guderian's father, Heinz, the famed Panzer leader who was Chief of the General Staff in 1945, was advocating to Hitler that he negotiate peace with the west.

His son recognized the futility of the advice. ''There was no possibility of making an honourable peace,'' he recounts. ''There was only unconditional surrender. We would have been completely destroyed.

''The German army did not fight for the Nazis; we fought for our Fatherland.''

3

The Tide's In

Top Secret. Personal and Eyes Only for CIGS from Field-Marshal Montgomery, 6 Feb 45:
I visited the Veritable area today. The ground is very wet and roads and tracks are breaking up and these factors are likely to make progress somewhat slow after the operation is launched.

THEY CALLED IT "Edinburgh Castle," an innocent-seeming barracks in the Dutch town of Grave, now expropriated as the Canadian Reconnaissance Report Centre. The heavy traffic of men of the 51st Highland and the 15th Scottish, two divisions of Lieutenant-General Brian Horrocks's 30 Corps, could account for the Scottish brogues that echoed in its halls — and the distinctly un-Flemish name with which it was christened.

When Field-Marshal Montgomery finally won approval on February 1 for his mammoth dual assault to the Rhine — Operations Veritable and Grenade — preparations had to be hastily finalized for the February 8 and 10 D-Days.

The job of launching Veritable was given to General H.D.G. (Harry) Crerar, Commander-in-Chief First Canadian Army. No Canadian had ever commanded so large a force: its "ration strength" exceeded 470,000 men. Veritable — the northern arm of the pincer attack — would advance from Nijmegen directly through the Reichswald Forest and beyond it across undulating farmland and wooded countryside, clearing the area between the Maas and the Rhine.

In early winter the paths and narrow roads would have been frozen hard. Armoured vehicles could have swept through the

---

See Maps 3 and 4 (Appendix B).

forest and broken out in a 20-mile dash for the river at Wesel before the enemy had an opportunity to raise a defence.

That was the theory. In February, however, meteorology reports indicated the strong possibility of an early-spring thaw — an occurrence that would reduce communication lines to a morass of mud and jeopardize Veritable's success.

Crerar's American counterpart, Lieutenant-General Bill Simpson (also under command of Montgomery), would head up Operation Grenade, the southern arm of the pincer movement, 60 miles to the south. The 300,000 men of Simpson's Ninth Army would be augmented by an additional 75,000 from Hodges's First U.S. Army. Simpson's plan was to launch Grenade across the Roer River two days after Veritable had commenced and join up with First Canadian Army at the Rhine to cut off the enemy. But whereas in early winter the Roer would have been a placid stream, the February thaws could wreak their havoc there as well.

It was a good plan, one that might have gained the Allies a firm position on the west bank of the Rhine within 48 hours, had it been launched on schedule under winter conditions. However, policy disputes among the Allied commanders and the Ardennes battle had delayed it until the second week of February. Now Montgomery could only gamble that the hard ground would hold — and that the thaw would hold off — just a little longer.

His *real* gamble, as it transpired, depended more on men than on meteorology: could this huge operation be salvaged, despite its flaws?

No wonder the little Watchmaker had not deduced his enemy's plans. With his passion for examining every facet of an operation, Straube could never have overlooked the basic fact that a campaign designed for one season is not necessarily adaptable to another. He would not shrug off the meteorological warnings of the usual February thaws.

Nor would he have devised a plan whose very success depended on the uncertain assumption that the Roer dams could be captured by the Americans in the next few days when the Germans had defended them successfully for five months. He knew that as long as German forces had firm control of the dams, they could stop the Americans at will by flooding the river. He certainly would not have ignored this critical fact.

Crerar's operation would be in three phases, each expanding on the previous one as the front gradually enlarged.

He gave Horrocks the responsibility of launching the first phase of the attack — Operation Veritable. After breaking out of the Nijmegen bottleneck, 30 Corps was to smash the enemy's Siegfried Line defences and clear the Reichswald and its environs. It was intended to be a blitz against an enemy stunned both by the surprise of the attack and by a massive pre-invasion bombardment.

Three paved roads encircling the forest and two in its interior would thereby be freed. Although limited, these roads were essential to get the armour forward. The narrow front of attack would thus be extended to form a new V-shaped wedge some 20 miles long, incorporating Cleve on the east, the small farming hamlets of Hekkens and Asperden below the Reichswald, and, in the west, the Siegfried Line fortifications around Gennep on the Maas.

When Horrocks had completed the opening phase, an additional force — Lieutenant-General Guy Simonds's 2 Canadian Corps — would be brought in on his left to strengthen the front for the second phase, called Operation Blockbuster. First Canadian Army would now include seven infantry divisions, three armoured divisions, three independent armoured brigades, and a Commando brigade. The enlarged force was to breach the second enemy line of defence east and southeast of the Reichswald. It would then seize the towns of Weeze, Goch, Udem, and Calcar, freeing additional roads to keep the armour on the move.

Finally, in the third stage of the operation that would wrap up the Veritable-Grenade pincer attack, Crerar envisioned a massive armoured sweep to clear the Hochwald Forest, joining forces with the Ninth U.S. Army's assault to close on the Rhine at Wesel.

The three phases would employ 500 tanks and another 500 specially adapted tracked vehicles, brought up to support the attack. Over a thousand guns would lend their devastating power. The operation would also involve the Second Tactical Air Force, with a potential of 1,000 fighters or fighter-bombers, 100 mediums, and 90 night-fighters. Bomber Command would attack targets in the enemy's battle area with up to 1,000 heavy bombers, and the Eighth U.S. Army Air Force medium and heavy bombers would also be engaged. The RAF's 84 Group were alerted to provide close infantry support with their spunky Typhoon rocket-firing planes.

"If everything breaks in our favour — weather, ground, air support, enemy dispositions, and reactions — I would not be surprised if armour of 30 Corps reached the Geldern-Xanten-Wesel line in a few days," Crerar remarked to his commanders at an Orders Group on February 4. "On the other hand," he warned them, "if conditions are against us, I see three 'set-piece' operations [deliberate attacks with artillery support], one for each phase, and the battle may well last three weeks.

"I am quite certain," he added, "that the close tactical relation of Grenade and Veritable will be of the utmost mutual assistance to Bill Simpson and myself." Crerar had no inkling that he would be out on a limb without that assistance for 15 critical days.

Few commanders were as qualified to handle an operation of such complexity — and precariousness — as 57-year-old Harry Crerar.

"He is no flaming personality . . . no Montgomery," broadcaster Matthew Halton commented. "But he has proved . . . that he would have cool judgment and cold nerves in the hard hours when great decisions are in the scales."

The logistics of Operation Veritable demanded just such a man at the helm. "Keeping the offensive going was a fine piece of work," commented Major-General (then Lieutenant-Colonel) Roger Rowley, CO (Commanding Officer) of the Stormont, Dundas & Glengarry Regiment. "With those masses of troops and artillery, and that long, incredibly tenuous supply line, it was a masterful piece of planning and a gigantic operation to coordinate and control."

However, Crerar had other pressures to contend with. He had the demands of the Canadian Parliament and its prime minister, to whom he was accountable first and foremost. He had also to contend with a boss — Montgomery — who couldn't have liked playing second fiddle to a "colonial" government.

General (then Brigadier) Geoffrey Walsh, at the time CRE (Commander Royal Engineers), First Canadian Army, remembers an incident at Tac HQ that typified the squeeze on Crerar:

Monty came up to our HQ and we had some of the divisional commanders in for dinner. Despite this, at 9 o'clock Harry Crerar got up from the table, excused himself and said he had to get his daily dispatches back to Prime Minister Mackenzie King.

It was pretty hard to lead an army in a difficult operation plus having to write to and hold the hands of the politicians back in Ottawa. I doubt if many generals could have done this as well as Crerar did. He was a great staff officer and a fair tactician too. He was simply more cautious because he had to report to the politicians directly.

Getting along with Montgomery was not easy in the face of the latter's thinly cloaked disdain for the Canadian commander. Montgomery had only accepted Crerar as Commander-in-Chief in the first place as a lesser evil than General Andrew McNaughton, whose resignation he had helped to engineer.

"Monty's opinion of General Crerar was, I would say, rather strained," considers Lieutenant-Colonel Trumbull Warren, Montgomery's personal assistant. "I think the reason behind this is that Montgomery had commanded everything in the infantry from a platoon to an army group.

"Crerar served in the First World War as an artillery battery commander. Then he went on staff and never commanded anything else until he was given command of 1 Canadian Corps in England.

"When the corps was sent to Italy, Montgomery suggested that Crerar take over the 1st Division himself (with a drop in rank) to gain some experience. Crerar wouldn't do this, and that didn't help the tension any."

Montgomery's own dominant personality created even more problems for Crerar, who was by nature a reserved man, loath to seek publicity.

"I think he suffered a bit from having Montgomery as his boss," Horrocks suggests. "Not in the tactical sense but because Montgomery was such a personality it was difficult for his army commanders to show any personality of their own."

Crerar would suffer further from being handed this massive project — Veritable — that was already beginning to fall to pieces. It would demand all of his skill, and a lot of luck besides, to pull it off.

If the authors of the battle plan had faltered in underestimating thaw and enemy flooding, they shone brilliantly in devising an ingenious deception plan to mask their intentions. The element of surprise was critical to the operation's success. Throughout the frantic weeks of Veritable's buildup the planning staff managed to disguise both the force and the direction of the coming attack.

A stockpile of supplies that Horrocks himself termed "awesome" was stealthily moved up to the battle zone. The Allied strategists also succeeded in filtering key 30 Corps officers across Canadian lines, up to the front for a good look, and out again without arousing the slightest suspicion that 30 Corps was even in the Canadian sector.

6   This masterpiece of tight security escaped the most penetrating of General Straube's probes. The "usual" Canadian traffic, comprising the "usual" 2nd and 3rd Canadian Infantry Division troops that Straube's patrols had been observing all winter, continued to move about freely. What the German scouts failed to note were the carefully coordinated jeeploads of Scottish, Welsh, and English officers reporting to Edinburgh Castle to reconnoitre the battle area.

Here the men were outfitted in the darker khaki Canadian uniform (which the British admired as more stylish than their own) and apportioned strictly regulated passes. They were then driven in Canadian vehicles to Canadian OPs (observation posts) on the front line.

Sentries were posted to check their passes at intervals and to ensure that the area was cleared before the next lot of "Canadians" came through. By this means, every brigade, battalion, and company commander had a thorough look at the battlefield without arousing suspicion.

There was more. No 30 Corps officers or their vehicles were permitted north of the Maas without insignia blanked out. Special canvas blinds were devised that pulled down to mask regimental markings.

A company commander with the 5th Queen's Own Cameron Highlanders of Scotland spotted a soldier wearing a tartan patch and thought it was one of his men. "I nearly had him by the throat when I discovered that by pure chance we had assembled in the lines of the Cameron Highlanders of Canada. The Canadians were allowed to wear their regimental patches but we of the Highland Division had to take them all off!"

Strict blackout regulations were enforced. By day, all gatherings of men, even for meal parades, were forbidden unless under cover.

A camouflage pool of specialist officers were attached to each Royal Canadian Artillery HQ. They devised a comprehensive scheme to hide the enormous concentration of weapons, vehicles, and ammunition brought forward each night. These were concealed close to their final positions, covered with nets, tarpaulins, and brushwood in farmyards, barns, hedges, and haystacks.

As some observation was deemed inevitable, a cover story was concocted. Its objective was to convince the enemy that, because of political pressure by the Dutch, the resumed offensive would be in a northerly direction to liberate Holland, rather than an eastern push into Germany.

Full-sized, inflatable rubber dummies of tanks and artillery pieces were positioned along the imaginary battle line where they might attract the attention of enemy patrols. Bogus reconnaissances were carried out in the northwest sector and bogus billets arranged. One Scottish officer got the feeling that things were getting a little out of hand when his sham reconnaissance of the Maas elicited an insistent invitation from the unwitting Canadians that he climb a nearby tower for a good look around.

As enemy mortars were falling at regular intervals on this tempting target, the Scot declined the offer. "I'm afraid I left the impression of being somewhat cowardly," he recalls wryly, "but it really wasn't worth getting my head shot off when we were only acting out a charade."

On the American front, preparations for Operation Grenade's launch on February 10 were also in full swing. A total of 303,243 men from 10 divisions of Ninth Army, augmented by 75,000 men from four divisions of First Army, were being assembled at the front.

It had been a tremendous feat to move up and assimilate this mass of manpower on such short notice — a feat that Montgomery himself described admiringly as an example of the "truly extraordinary mobility of American units when regrouping."

Tens of thousands of troops had toiled their way forward along rutted roads clogged with traffic to reach the Roer's front. To some units it was unfamiliar territory. To others, it was like coming home. Men found themselves back in the same cellars they had abandoned when they had been rushed out to stem the German winter offensive in the Ardennes.

Men of the 35th Infantry Division were startled to be greeted by a cordial message from the enemy, posted on lampposts in the towns:

Welcome Men of the 35th Division:
Considering the fact that you are newcomers, we would like to do everything to make you feel at home. . . . You have tried to veil your arrival here by doing such things as removing your divisional insignia. Nevertheless, a little bird told us all about it.

Simpson's three corps used the time to assimilate and train the five extra divisions that were being reluctantly shifted from Bradley's armies. Lead assault troops were moved north to practise river crossings on the Maas.

Those not immediately involved were sequestered from enemy view in the relative comfort of rear echelon.

"Little things made life better," the 29th Division history noted. "The Coca-Cola ration began to appear, amounting to one bottle per man per week. But it was an unbelievable luxury, to be sipped slowly and raved over." There was warm food and hot water for showers. The supply sergeant had piles of dry socks. Homesick troops were cheered by the arrival of mail and packages from home.

One highlight was a personal visit by Katharine Cornell and Brian Aherne, who staged a production of "The Barretts of Wimpole Street" for the troops.

As D-Day for Operation Veritable drew nearer, the seven-by-eight-mile Canadian front became increasingly crammed. Ninety thousand men of six divisions and their equipment were transported in total blackout from their staging areas to the forward assembly lines near Nijmegen. To carry all this required 35,000 vehicles, using 1,300,000 gallons of fuel. More than a thousand guns and over half a million rounds of ammunition (weighing 11,000 tons) were brought up to ammo dumps, along with 200,000 tons of stores — all funnelled across two sorely bottlenecked bridges that crossed the Maas at Mook and Grave.

Many of the troops were quartered in dugouts; others, with strict orders to remain hidden, slept on the floors of schoolhouses, factories, and assembly halls. The surrounding fields began filling up with camouflaged tanks, field guns, and anti-aircraft guns.

The Canadians became accustomed to playing host to some highly placed officers — gunners, engineers, signallers, and the like — in their makeshift rooftop or even treetop observation posts. Crerar was a frequent visitor, as were Horrocks and, on occasion, Montgomery. But perhaps the most unusual of all were the only two representatives from their branch of the service to visit a frontline OP: two young women from the Canadian Women's Army Corps (CWAC).

Obliging scouts from the South Saskatchewan Regiment outfitted the intrepid females in greatcoats and steel hats and escorted them to an OP — a monastery on the banks of the Maas. They were in luck. Not 150 yards away, German troops could be seen going about their routine duties.

Major Bill Gaade of 4th Royal Welch Fusiliers recalls his battalion OP: "There was a very high building about 2,000 yards from the edge of the Reichswald where we took all our officers and section commanders to have a look. This way we could actually point to specific features and explain exactly where their positions would be. It was the first time I'd ever been able to do a complete reconnaissance of the ground before a battle.''

As far back as November, the CRE, Geoffrey Walsh, had been anticipating and preparing for the special problems that could arise for the engineers. Even before First Canadian Army had left England, the CRE had developed the technique of crossing wide rivers — and staged what to the men must have been interminable rehearsals on the Trent and Medway rivers.

"The main job of the chief engineer was to be ready months ahead," Walsh recalls. "We found that it took a high degree of training, organization, and discipline to pull the thing off properly."

Under a strict cloak of secrecy, Walsh had a fresh rail line laid into Nijmegen to handle the vast stores of supplies. He insisted that there be two trainloads of gravel and logs available at all times for road improvement.

He even contrived to construct a large airfield just outside of Nijmegen. "I couldn't start working on it until Veritable was launched," he remembers. "At H-Hour the bulldozers began levelling the field so the Typhoons could land. We had them operational in five days, working day and night, by floodlight too."

Providing a landing strip for the Typhoons was vital. These rocket-carrying fighter-bombers, flown by the RAF and the RCAF, operated in an infantry support role. Each carried eight powerful 60-pound rockets (four under each wing) of devastating striking power, capable of destroying a 56-ton German Tiger tank. In addition, they carried small 20mm cannons and machine guns for harassment of enemy troops, gun emplacements, or vehicles.

Throughout those pre-D-Day preparations, the men worked at fever pitch. British and Canadian sappers constructed and improved some 100 miles of road. This impressive effort required 20,000 tons of stones, 20,000 logs, and 30,000 pickets. Four hundred and forty-six freight trains lifted 250,000 tons to the railheads. It was reckoned that the ammunition alone — 350 different types, stacked side by side and five feet high — would line the road for 30 miles.

Army engineers constructed five bridges across the Maas, using 1,880 tons of bridging equipment. The longest was the "Quebec Bridge," a Bailey bridge 1,280 feet long.

The forward defence lines were strengthened and camouflaged against counter-attacks.

Mine-lifting parties went out each day on their dangerous missions. The CRE of 2nd Canadian Infantry Division, Lieutenant-Colonel L.G.C. Lilley, concentrated his engineers on this task almost exclusively during the final week of preparations. ''In this period some 10,000 mines were lifted,'' he reported. ''Enemy opposition prevented the lifting of mines in the Wyler area, and these mines caused a number of casualties among our infantry during the initial phases of Veritable.''

Since 3rd Canadian Infantry Division was responsible for maintaining half of the front, its engineers worked around the clock to improve the roads in the sector where the 15th Scottish Division would be moving up. The area lay under unimpeded fire and observation range (and earshot) of the enemy a short distance away across the Rhine, and repairs had to be effected at night and in silence. The engineers found the solution: ''The difficulty was overcome by carrying rubble down onto the road in sandbags under cover of darkness, and there spreading it as quietly as possible.

With similar ingenuity the Canadian sappers — often under shellfire — devoted seven nights to laying a Bailey bridge atop an existing inadequate bridge; during the operation an officer and sapper of the 6th Field Company were killed by an enemy patrol.

Training was stepped up. While none of the troops knew the exact map reference of the attack, they could make some shrewd guesses when they were suddenly subjected to exhaustive practice in forest fighting, house-clearing, and night marches by compass readings.

The ''Funnies,'' the support vehicles that had won the hearts — and saved the lives — of so many troops in the Scheldt operation in October 1944, would return as trusted allies in this new challenge. The 79th Armoured Division, under the innovative command of Major-General Sir Percy Hobart, had devised the ingenious assortment of tracked vehicles that came to be known collectively as the Funnies. Each was designed to overcome a specific obstacle. The Flail was a special kind of tank carrying a rotating drum with chains attached that would precede the infantrymen into a minefield and detonate the mines. The Crocodile was a flame-throwing tank that was an effective — and terrifying — weapon. The AVRE (armoured vehicle Royal Engineers) could perform as a cannon. It also carried bridging material to span narrow gaps such as the anti-tank ditch, a favourite enemy defensive tactic. Finally, in this strange menagerie, there were the Buffaloes or LVTs (landing vehicle tracked). These marvellous creatures could swim in water or slither in mud, making them invaluable as amphibious troop carriers. Intensive training in these specialized vehicles was essential.

The final days of January and early February brought the kind of weather that could make a North American homesick: crisp, cold days with sunny skies and daily snowfalls adding to the high snowbanks on the sides of the narrow roads. The Queen's Own Rifles of Canada noted without enthusiasm in their history that the men had been given snow-clearing jobs.

Diversions of a more agreeable nature were also arranged. In Nijmegen, the Winter Gardens cinema was so popular that soldiers attended in drawn lots; Betty Grable was everybody's pin-up girl. A hamburger at a spot called IT's was a popular reminder of home. British troops stationed around the Tilburg area staged dances and films — or, as the Royal Scots Fusiliers history recalls, "enjoyed a quiet seat by the stove in mine host's kitchen with a bairn on each knee."

The largest battalion canteen ever, officially called Stirling Castle but known familiarly to all ranks as "Uncle Tom's Cabin," relieved the tedium for the 2nd Battalion of the Argyll & Sutherland Highlanders of Scotland.

Before the battle of bullets came the battle of propaganda. As the pre-attack momentum rose, each side probed for even the smallest scrap of intelligence that could ultimately save lives or gain yards on the battlefield.

And each side indulged in the histrionics of war, seeking to confuse and demoralize the other. In mid-January, the Germans dropped planeloads of leaflets vilifying Churchill as a warmonger and a drunkard. Still others played up Goebbels's favourite theme: while the Americans were being slaughtered by the thousands, Monty's troops were still indulging in a "Dutch holiday."

The 2nd Canadian Infantry Division fired back a defiant reply in the form of shells stuffed with anti-Nazi propaganda material. Enemy amplifiers across the Maas blasted out messages of defeat and surrender. "Arnhem Annie" broadcast seductive invitations to the men to lay down their arms — for her arms.

Every battalion posted to frontline duty was instructed to intensify its patrol activity. Each night, small groups of men were sent into no-man's-land, their white camouflage suits blending with the snow-covered ground to offer at least some slight protection against snipers' bullets. Their mission: to seek information about the enemy and, most importantly, to bring back prisoners for interrogation.

"All winter long we lived by the philosophy of General Daniel C. Spry [GOC 3rd Canadian Infantry Division]: 'Be masters of no-man's-land; make your presence felt 24 hours a day in front of your enemy,' "remembers Major-General Rowley. "We put in company raids, platoon patrols, section patrols, always trying to dominate no-man's-land. It was pretty delicate stuff. You got where you knew every blade of grass by its Christian name."

On the morning of February 4, Horrocks briefed his commanders at an Orders Group. Officers from each of the assaulting divisions — the 51st Highlanders, the 15th Scottish, the 53rd Welsh, and the 2nd and 3rd Canadian Infantry (temporarily under command of 30 Corps) — plus senior men from all the supporting arms were relayed into the packed cinema at Tilburg. Also attending were representatives from the two divisions being held in reserve until the completion of the first phase: the 43rd Wessex and the Guards Armoured.

The shrill whine of RAF fighters soaring high above the rooftops offered the only interruption as the intent officers discovered their mission. The Intelligence Section had prepared 500,000 current air reconnaissance photographs and 800,000 special maps. (Paper abandoned by the retreating Wehrmacht was put to use for some of these maps. On the back of one set, the men were astonished to see a complete diagram of the proposed invasion of England in 1940.)

As usual, the popular English corps commander drew a warm response. Horrocks was deeply committed to his men. Dressed in the plain brown corduroy trousers and battlefield jacket that reflected his own lack of pretension, he could frequently be seen mingling with the troops at the front line. The men felt that wherever they were sent in battle, "Jorrocks," as he was nicknamed, would not be far behind, his tall, lithe figure moving from group to group with a friendly and humorous word.

Horrocks was known as "the general who led from the front." His style of command was "intensely active," his biographer stated. "He was not a general who could sit in a rear headquarters, studying reports and maps . . . he had to be up there, up with the leaders. He was also intensely ambitious, not in the personal sense, but in the bulldog determination that his Corps be the fastest and best of the British Army."

Many of the "Jocks" (as the Scottish troops were universally called) had served under Horrocks and Montgomery in North

Africa. There was a deep-rooted bond among the men with "sand in their shoes" who had shared the horrors and the ultimate victory of the Desert War.

It is rare indeed for a pair of Englishmen to have earned such fierce loyalty from Scotsmen. "Sassenachs" (as the Scots gruffly called their neighbours to the south) and Jocks frequently exercised the debate. "There were endless brawls in pubs after North Africa because some wretched Englishman would make a derogatory remark and promptly get beaten up by a Jock," one Black Watch officer smilingly recalls.

Unhappily, Horrocks was beginning to show the strain of six months' gruelling combat in the Northwest Europe campaign. Although he strove to hide the fact — particularly from his commanding officer, General Crerar — he had never fully recovered from wounds incurred less than two years before when he had served as Montgomery's corps commander in the North African campaign. Strafed by a German fighter plane, Horrocks was seriously wounded in the lungs, intestine, spine, and leg. Even after 14 months' recuperation, his physician had warned him against ever taking on active field command again.

At Montgomery's urging, however, he agreed soon afterwards to take command of 30 Corps — "the Corps of the Black Boar." He led its advance across the Seine and on into Belgium in its historic armoured dash in September 1944, stopping only as it neared the Rhine at Arnhem. In those five months of fighting, Horrocks had never really been fit. He was prone to horrific attacks of high fever and illness, which he sought to camouflage by taking medication and eating and drinking sparsely.

As recently as December 27, 1944, Monty had signalled Brooke, the Chief of the Imperial General Staff:

I am sending Horrocks home on leave tomorrow. During the past 10 days he has been nervy and difficult with his staff and has attempted to act foolishly with his Corps. He is definitely in need of a rest and I want him to have 3 to 4 weeks quietly in the U.K. He is a valuable officer and I want him back.

Horrocks's ill health was to become an increasingly difficult burden in the coming days as he struggled to keep his grip firmly on the battle ahead. He later admitted: "During part of this long-drawn-out battle I was feeling very unwell . . . though I managed to conceal it from everybody other than my ADCs and senior members of my staff. The outward and visible sign was that I became extremely irritable and bad-tempered, yet Crerar bore with me very patiently.''

Nevertheless, Horrocks radiated his usual confidence as he conducted the Orders Group. Using a map the size of the cinema screen, he outlined concisely the tasks ahead.

"He had us all there, down to company commanders. What a memorable occasion — and what a marvellous target that cinema would have been if the planes overhead had been hostile!'' remembers Colonel Brian A. (Bill) Fargus, then a captain and adjutant of the 8th Battalion Royal Scots.

"We'd never fought for him before. In two hours he convinced us that he'd got it all worked out, that we'd all get to Berlin.''

"It was very dramatic,'' adds Major-General Bruce Matthews, GOC 2nd Canadian Infantry Division. "He never used a note. My God, it was good: you'd leave his conferences full of steam.''

The officers left not only with a great deal of confidence, but certainly with a full comprehension of the unique aspects of the initial stages of the operation. The narrowness of the start line — six miles — and the paucity of paved roads leading from it — two — limited the number of divisions that could be committed in the initial assault to a single corps — Horrocks's.

The Northwest European war's largest battle would take place on the war's smallest battlefield.

That same day, the North Shore Regiment of Canada turned out for a hockey practice in Nijmegen and found pools of melted ice. For the next three days it rained, a relentless, driving downpour that transformed the accumulation of snow into slush and mud.

Two days later, on D-minus-Two, the 90,000 men of the initial Veritable force moved up from the Tilburg area into their forward billets in Nijmegen. The rain and floods coincided with the mammoth exodus. A special Traffic Office employing 1,600 men maintained rigid controls along the roads.

The entire move was made under strict blackout conditions, in trucks creeping along the tops of narrow dikes that sloped off steeply into the flood waters. The 6th Battalion Royal Scots Fusiliers noted in their war diary: "The night was black as pitch, and it was an agonizing strain to peer continuously through the wind-screen at a vague blur . . . of the vehicle in front, and so avoid collision at every check or stop.'' The speed was 10 miles per hour; it took from 4 p.m. until daylight the next day to cover 37 miles.

Then on February 7, D-minus-One, the men of 1st Canadian Scottish Regiment climbed out of their bunks and gazed with wonder at the surrounding fields. "The tide's in!" they exclaimed. As a precautionary measure, the Germans had detonated holes in the Rhine's winter dikes, allowing the already rain-soaked marshlands to fill up. Where yesterday most of the routes leading to the enemy's forward defended localities were still approachable over dry land, now a foot of water covered the entire area.

Two hours later the flood level had reached 30 inches and was rising at the rate of one foot per hour. A liquid barrier as formidable as any made of concrete or steel had been created. Along the polderlands bordering the Rhine, nothing could be seen but water, punctuated here and there by the red-tiled roofs of farmhouses or the top branches of a clump of trees.

Crerar's hard crust of frost that would make rapid movement of men and armour possible had disintegrated. Before his very eyes, the roads were slowly sinking. Half of his battlefield now lay under five feet of water. The rest had been transformed by the thaw into a morass of mud.

At his command post, Horrocks listened in silence as the reports of the disaster filtered in. In 24 hours, he thought, 90,000 men would be funnelled into an arena of war that had murky water for battlefields and mudded ruts for roads. They would need ammunition and food, and transportation back for their wounded. How could he keep them supplied through this God-forsaken mire?

The responsibility for this massive first phase of Operation Veritable rested on the shoulders of this great — and ailing — general.

The lines were drawn; Brian Horrocks prayed it might be the final battle of this long, long war.

4

Cratering Is to Be Accepted

Top Secret. Personal and Eyes Only for CIGS from Field-Marshal Montgomery, 8 Feb 45:
Operation Veritable was launched this morning according
to plan. The movement problem involved in getting formations and units in position for this very large scale attack
has been a remarkable achievement in view of the very
bad state of all the roads . . . . Today's operation has been
98% successful and we now hold Wyler, Kranenburg,
Frasselt, Grafwegen and have secured a good footing in
the Reichswald Forest.

AFTERWARDS, AND FOR THE rest of his life, Brian Horrocks would
have continuing nightmares about the bombing of Cleve. The
scenes that so bedevilled his sleep were of a blackened sky exploding in flashes of light as 900 heavy bombers dropped their loads
of high explosives.

It was February 7, the night before the launching of Operation
Veritable — the night to "soften up" the enemy. Two hundred
and eighty-five Lancasters, led by 10 Mosquito Pathfinders,
dropped 1,384 tons of high explosives on Cleve alone that night.
The city of Cleve was the gateway to the Rhineland, and the key
communications and rail centre through which the Germans could
funnel reinforcements. But other nearby towns were targeted for
the raid as well: Goch, the hub from which Veritable's massive
force would pivot, was smashed, killing 30 local people and 150
forced labourers from Holland, Italy, and Russia who had been
brought in to dig local defences. Known enemy strongpoints in
the enemy's Rhineland defences — Weeze, Udem, Geldern, and
Calcar — were also flattened.

See Maps 3 and 4 (Appendix B).

But it was the bombing of Cleve that would haunt Horrocks. The events that led to his decision to unleash the RAF on the Rhineland targets began the morning that General Harry Crerar, overall commander of the Veritable operation, came to Horrocks's 30 Corps headquarters.

"Crerar said, 'Do you want Cleve taken out?' " Horrocks recalled. "By 'taken out' he meant, of course, 'totally destroyed.' This is the sort of problem with which a General in war is constantly faced and from which there is no escape. I knew that Cleve was a lovely old historic Rhineland town. Anne of Cleves, Henry VIII's fourth wife, came from there. No doubt, a lot of civilians, plus women and children, were still living there. Their fate depended on how I answered Crerar's question, and I simply hated the thought of Cleve being 'taken out.' "

Horrocks believed there were tactical advantages to the bombing. The success of Veritable depended on his troops' breaking out through the Reichswald bottleneck, anchored at one end at Cleve, and onto the German plain with their armour before the enemy could bring up reserves to stop them. It was a race.

His men had the initial advantages of surprise and logistical superiority. Should they lose their advantage to a swiftly retrenched enemy, the operation would be seriously jeopardized. Horrocks had seen this very phenomenon at Antwerp and Arnhem; he could not countenance it again.

A bombing raid would not only knock out General Fiebig's division headquarters in Cleve; it would also destroy the roads and rail lines needed by the Germans to bring in fresh troops. Horrocks reasoned that if the enemy were delayed in reinforcing their line, the blitz to the Rhine would be achieved in a matter of days. Many British and Canadian lives would be saved.

Horrocks said yes. "It was the most terrible decision I had ever had to take in my life," he remembered. "I felt almost physically sick when . . . I saw the bombers flying overhead on their deadly mission."

Ironically, the decision so backfired that the raid actually helped the Germans' defences while disrupting his own attack. It was to play a paramount role in transforming what was intended to be a lightning strike into a 31-day slogging match, costing many more lives than Horrocks dreamed.

For this, Horrocks blames the RAF. "I had specifically asked for 'incendiaries' to be used," he was later to protest, "but through some error 1,384 tons of high explosive had been dropped, and the huge craters in Cleve not only held up the German reserves but our own troops as well.''

But Bomber Command cannot be saddled with the responsibility for the "error" committed that night, nor for Horrocks's nightmares. At a conference held in "A" Mess, Main HQ, First Canadian Army, at 1630 hours on December 17, 1944, the air policy concerning Veritable had been determined. Officers attending included General Crerar, his chief of staff, Brigadier Churchill Mann, his general staff officer, Lieutenant-Colonel Walter Reynolds — as well as Horrocks himself. Their conclusions were formally recorded:

— The main routes into the battle area are to be denied to the enemy by the complete destruction of Cleve, Goch and Emmerich.
— Cratering is to be accepted.

Even more damning was a top-secret document circulated to the chiefs of staff on February 5 that referred to the expected "ruins" of Cleve.

By midnight of February 7 there was not much left that Anne of Cleves would have recognized in the town of her birth, little that Wagner would find to inspire again a work such as *Lohengrin*. Emerging from the Lancaster raid was a city of cellars, its historic spires toppled, its monuments smashed. It was a "staggering sight," BBC Radio recounted. "Cleve is blazing . . . lit like London on its brightest day.''

It was not so much on Cleve's historic buildings that Horrocks focussed his frustration and anguish. Nor were the casualties to German civilians a significant factor. Most had already been evacuated to a tented refugee centre at Bedburg, three miles southeast. What he regretted bitterly was the same phenomenon that was to strike Major-General (then Major) John Graham, commanding D Company, 2nd Battalion Argyll & Sutherland Highlanders, when he entered Cleve two days after the raid.

Appalled by the chaos and confusion that had overtaken the city, Graham observed that the bombing was actually helping the enemy. By destroying the buildings, it had created an almost impenetrable barrier of rubble. This offered the enemy better emplacements for their defences than if they had been in normal houses. By cratering the roads, the way was blocked for Allied vehicles more effectively than any anti-tank ditches the Germans could contrive.

But regrets belonged to the future. The result of the massive bombing on the night of February 7-8 was a city more completely devastated than any other city of its size in Germany at any other time in the war. And a determined reserve of German infantry was dug in behind that wall of rubble, alerted now to the British attack and fully prepared to delay its advance.

In nearby Bedburg, a German mother, Lotte Seiler, and her young daughter, Edith, were among the 28,000 evacuated civilians who endured the "night of horrors." She wrote to her Marine husband, Fritz: "At 2200 hours I was awakened by the shooting. For fully 20 minutes bombs were coming down all around us. The air blast effect was so intense it prevented me from reaching Edith's room."

At dawn, while the fires of Cleve still blazed brightly, 1,334 guns thundered the opening salvo of Operation Veritable. It was one of the most massive artillery bombardments ever staged in Northwest Europe: greater than anything in Normandy, more formidable than the historic bombardment at El Alamein.

The fire was to continue unceasingly for over 24 hours in support of the assault. Its functions were several: to saturate German defences, to destroy known strongpoints, to provide immediate supporting fire for those on attack, and to so demoralize the enemy that he would no longer have the will to fight.

On this grey morning the enemy felt the entire weight of the combined field artillery guns of the British and Canadian armies: the 25-pounders of seven divisions, augmented by the medium and heavy guns of five AGRAs (Army Group Royal Artillery), the 3.7-inch ack-ack guns of two anti-aircraft brigades, and the devastating power of 1st Canadian Rocket Battery.

"We had so damn many guns, we didn't have enough real estate to put them down on," recalls Brigadier Stanley Todd, who commanded 2 Canadian Corps Artillery. "We had to put two batteries in every position. The crews at the guns were so close they could give hand signal acknowledgments instead of the usual radio signals to the GPO [gun position officer] — and that's the only time that happened in Northwest Europe."

Forward troops who had forgotten their cotton-wool were deafened for many hours to come. Gunners turned their heads, mouths askew, to minimize damage to eardrums.

"The guns were almost turning red," recalls Major-General Roger Rowley, whose battalion formed part of the 3rd Canadian Infantry Division's left-flank attack across the flooded plains. "They were

47

just fired right out. The gunners had to have spare guns behind the batteries which could be put in.''

Incredibly, 21st Army Group recorded that over half a million rounds were fired without a single report of a round falling short. These were, as Todd recalls, the unavoidable "battle risks" in amassing so great a concentration of batteries. If a single gun was worn or its calibration was faulty it would fire short, endangering the very infantrymen it was striving to assist. And if this occurred in one of the hundreds of guns firing in a barrage, it would be impossible to identify the malfunctioning artillery piece. There were then two courses of action: the barrage could be cancelled, but this would deprive the advancing troops of support, and heavy casualties could result. Or the officer commanding the infantry could reroute his men around the shortfall of shot.

The greater the number of guns, the greater the odds that some would malfunction. An artillery officer had to accept this fact; while his guns would save many lives, they could also cause casualties to his own men.

The coordination required to amass, supply, and program this unprecedented assembly of artillery pieces was unique. "We had to have a thousand rounds of ammunition dumped at each gun position for the artillery bombardments," Major R.K. MacKenzie, second-in-command of 14th Field Regiment, Royal Canadian Artillery, said. "This was the biggest inventory of ammunition we'd ever experienced. Getting it in place made for a lot of confusion."

Unique, too, were the unorthodox tactics with which the guns were employed. From 0500 hours until 0945 on the morning of the assault, over six tons of shells were targeted on every one of the known enemy strongpoints, headquarters, or communication centres. The list was long; 2nd and 3rd Canadian Infantry Divisions had been holding the area since November and had had ample time to pinpoint the German defences.

Midway through the bombardment, the guns fell briefly silent and a smokescreen was fired across the whole front. This was a tactic to trick the enemy into returning the fire and thus revealing his battery positions to sound-ranging and flash-spotting troops waiting to take bearings.

The "pepperpot" fire plan, first introduced at Veritable, added impressive weight to the bombardment. Its role was to deny all movement to the enemy in the forward area by a constant sweep of fire across the front.

For Major H.Z. ("Zooch") Palmer, commanding 30th Canadian

Anti-Aircraft Battery, the pepperpot gave him the strange experience of shooting his 40mm Bofors ack-ack gun in a ground role:

> Almost every weapon available of various sorts and sizes was employed: medium machine guns, Bofors, medium mortars, 3.7 ack-ack guns and whatever else we could lay our hands on. We concentrated all our fire on a single target for an agreed period — say, five minutes or so — and then simultaneously moved our line of fire to the next target, and then the next. The guns were positioned side by side, 10 or 15 yards apart, which was an unusual thing for an anti-aircraft battery to do. We fired over open sites. It was all a hell of a lot of noise — I hadn't heard anything like that since the Caen breakout.

Also adding its considerable power to the deafening cannonade was 1st Canadian Rocket Battery. This new form of rocket warfare, the brainchild of a one-eyed British guardsman and an over-age Canadian artillery officer, first came into operation during the Battle of the Scheldt in November 1944.

It comprised a collection of what looked like long metal pipes mounted on a truck. Each of these cylinders fired a canister carrying ten pounds of high explosives. When ten such vehicles were concentrated together, with all their rockets firing simultaneously, the collective weight of fire — called a "mattress" — landing on a small target would create a terrifying and destructive force. Over 10,000 three-inch rockets were allocated for the land mattress.

Infantrymen waiting out the opening bombardment from the safety of their billets and FUPs (forming up places) found that the noise and tension of pre-battle hours created curious little inconsistencies. Joe Illingworth, war correspondent with the *Yorkshire Post*, wrote: "Before the attack, a medical officer in the 53rd Welsh Division pottered irritably round his billet, oiling the doors with castor oil because their squeaks denied him sleep. An hour or two later the house was rocking under the fire of 1,400 guns."

Shortly before dawn, General Alfred Schlemm, commander of the German First Parachute Army, was awakened at his headquarters in Xanten by the ominous rumbling of artillery in the direction of the Reichswald Forest. Ascending one of the twin towers of the Romanesque St. Victor's Cathedral, he watched with awe as the sky came alight in flashes of vermilion and gold.

"I smell the big offensive," Schlemm signalled General Blaskowitz, Commander Army Group H. Reports streamed in, detailing the damage caused by the RAF raid. Schlemm was distressed to hear that his artillery commander, General Windig, had been killed in the raid that morning at Terborg, near Emmerich. Evidently, the Allied bombers had been trying to knock out the main telephone exchange. He was relieved to hear it was still operational.

Schlemm's tactical skill had marked him as one of the Wehrmacht's outstanding general officers. He alone had surmised correctly that the Allied attack would be launched through the Reichswald. But he had been unable to convince his commander-in-chief, General Blaskowitz, who had persisted in massing his reserves farther south. The obdurate Blaskowitz kept the armoured reserve of Army Group H (15th Panzer Grenadier Division and von Waldenburg's 116th Panzer Division) sited in the Roer sector opposite the American lines and his infantry reserve at Venlo opposite the British.

Schlemm feared that — should his theory prove correct — the Allied steamroller would overrun his defences before he could shift these divisions north. Ignoring Blaskowitz's views, he had ordered his battle-smart 6th and 7th Parachute Divisions moved up immediately from the south to plug the holes in the 84th Division line before the Allied troops could break through. These troops were just now arriving but their employment had not yet been approved by the German High Command.

Despite the strength of the opening salvos of the barrage, Blaskowitz refused to acknowlege that it was more than diversionary to the main attack, which he still expected at Venlo or the Roer. German Intelligence was not yet aware of the presence of British troops on the Canadian line.

For the moment, the German defence was under the command of a man who hardly inspired Schlemm's confidence: Straube the Watchmaker. General Straube's sole guardian of the Reichswald was Major-General Heinz Fiebig, whose 84th Infantry Division headquarters was in the city of Cleve. The division, recently re-formed and retrained after being virtually wiped out in Normandy, comprised some 8,000 to 10,000 men. In addition, he had several units of men grouped together because of specific health problems: a "Magen" (stomach) battalion, comprising troops suffering from digestive ailments, and an "Ohren" (ear) battalion of troops with hearing difficulties. Straube preferred the former, protesting that the Ohren battalions could not even hear a barrage.

Equally dismaying were his Volkssturm units. These consisted of men of the district between the ages of 16 and 60, capable of bearing arms for local defence. They were conscripted following Hitler's levée en masse of October 18, 1944, when every able-bodied German man was expected to rise to the defence of the Fatherland. Untrained, often without uniforms and armed only with short-range anti-tank and infantry weapons, these units were expected to provide the last-ditch defence of the homeland.

These forces were strung in three thin defensive lines across the forest. Even Fiebig had little optimism that they would hold against a concentrated attack.

The first line was weakly held and would probably crumble almost immediately under any onslaught. The second line was anchored to the West Wall. ("A farce," Straube remarked caustically. "It wasn't a wall; it was an idea.") Just two days before the attack, this line had been reinforced by the 2nd Parachute Regiment, three strong battalions of newly equipped and newly trained men. These constituted the strongest fighting unit in the Reichswald, and Fiebig had inserted them into a vital part of the front in the southwest corner of his sector — directly, as it evolved, in the path of the 51st Highlanders.

The third line extended along the eastern border of the forest at Cleve. As a further precaution, Fiebig had blocked the probable point of any main effort of the enemy along the Nijmegen-Cleve road as well as parts of the Reichswald Forest, flooding the northern sector. The day before, Fiebig had further ordered that the rear positions along the road be bolstered.

Adhering to Hitler's mandate that commanders report every operational decision to him, Schlemm rushed a top-secret situation report to Berlin, where an emergency meeting had been called to discuss the attack.

At dawn on the same morning, 20 miles northwest of Schlemm's HQ, General Horrocks climbed wearily to his observation post, a wooden platform high up in the trees. It was a miserable day.

Horrocks peered through the branches, shrouded by low-hanging cloud — the harbinger of more rain, he thought dismally. Gone was his air support. Gone was the frozen ground that would allow a swift breakthrough by his tanks.

In the distance, the still-burning city of Cleve glowed crimson. Haphazard yellow streaks cut through the smoke and cordite fumes that swept across the area as the pyrotechnics of the bombardment exploded over the battlefield. The gaunt trunks and torn limbs of trees, the shattered farm buildings, and the slain animals were evidence enough of the deadly efficiency of the artillery.

The area teemed with vehicles: Kangaroos (tanks with the turrets cut off to transport troops), tanks, Flails, and flame-throwing Crocodiles. Not a single man was on foot. The air was filled with the noise of engines. Tracked vehicles carrying the troops across the tight little six-mile start line pitched and heaved as they wallowed through the mud. Tanks ploughed into the woods, crashing and roaring like angry elephants.

Horrocks glanced at his watch; the second hand swept to H-Hour — 1030 hours. The barrage thickened, offering a moving umbrella of protective fire that advanced forward apace with the troops who clung to it: 100 yards every four minutes.

The Veritable line-up has been likened to a string of soccer forwards: two Scottish divisions (15th Scottish and 51st Highlanders); one Welsh (the 53rd); and two Canadian infantry divisions (2nd and 3rd). "It was some team!" exclaimed one sports-mad Jock.

A prime player, the 15th Scottish, starred as centre forward. This division had been assigned the key objective of capturing Cleve, seven miles due east.

On their left, the 5th Canadian Infantry Brigade (2nd Canadian Infantry Division) moved up with the important task of clearing German strongpoints from the towns of Wyler and Den Heuvel to open the main Nijmegen-Kranenburg-Cleve road. With their supply route thus opened and their rear positions protected, the Jocks could then rush Cleve and overrun its defences.

The Welsh division — in the inside right position — was swallowed up by the formidable bulk of the Reichswald. The troops would follow the narrow forest rides, cutting the anti-tank ditch and Siegfried fortifications as they forged into the very heart of the forest. An essential priority was to secure the two roads that bisected the Reichswald and converged below it at the village of Hekkens. Only a matter of eight miles, Horrocks realized — but a dangerous and punishing mission. The thaw and heavy rains in the dense woods would make those roads almost impassable.

Finally, in right-wing position, the 51st Highlanders plunged into the western edge of the Reichswald. It was the Highlanders' job to clear the enemy from the sector between the western edge of the Reichswald and the Maas, where the Siegfried fortifications were strongest.

Later in the day, as the Scottish and Welsh divisions fanned out through the Reichswald and towards Cleve, the 3rd Canadian Infantry Division would round out the Anglo-Canadian attack at the extreme left of the battle front. They had the unenviable assignment of launching an amphibious assault under direct observation of the enemy across the now-flooded flatlands bordering the Rhine.

In the sidelines, the 43rd Wessex and the impressive weight of the Guards Armoured Division were poised to join the line when the front opened up.

At first, everything went according to plan. Apart from one or two contested areas, the leading elements in the attack found resistance relatively light. "The enemy had been over-awed by the bombardment," Captain Peter Dryland observed.

"Our worst enemies that day were mines and mud," Horrocks noted. Within an hour, almost all the tanks and armoured vehicles bogged down. Some sank in mud caused by the flooding and rain. A number hit mines, others were roadblocked by trees felled by enemy demolition or halted by craters created by their own bombing and artillery bombardment.

Two battalions of 5th Canadian Infantry Brigade — the Calgary Highlanders and the Régiment de Maisonneuve — crossed the start line under the Veritable barrage. Initially, the Canadians also found that the gunners had effectively silenced the Germans. A Maisonneuve officer reaching his objective at Den Heuvel reported a count of 46 enemy dead in a small area, "without examining slit-trenches." Those that had survived were stunned.

Coming in with his platoon to the attack, Lieutenant Guy de Merlis tossed a 36 grenade into a small cellar and was surprised to see German troops emerging unscathed. "They had been lying along the sides of the walls and although the ceiling was blown out, they weren't injured. They were pretty well shell-shocked by then, though."

With Den Heuvel captured, it remained for the Calgary Highlanders (Lieutenant-Colonel Ross Ellis in command) to attack the main objective — the town of Wyler astride the Cleve highway. Speed was of prime importance; the 15th Scottish were depending on the road being freed from enemy interference by 1600 hours.

From the beginning, the attack met with bad luck when lead troops struck a field of schu-mines. These were German-designed anti-personnel mines that would explode when stepped on, causing severe damage to the legs or genitals of the victims. Not being made of steel, they could not be detected by conventional sweep equipment.

The field was laid out with diabolical precision. Several rows of the mines lay quite openly on the ground, but in trying to avoid them the troops detonated others that had been interspersed and hidden below the surface. Twenty-four men were killed or wounded. A party of 18 Germans, captured as they moved up to counter-attack, were forced to go back through the minefield carrying out the wounded. While they were performing this task, two of the enemy were blown up.

Casualties from mines and snipers and stiff opposition at Wyler disrupted the momentum of the attack. Nevertheless, at 1830 hours — two and a half hours behind schedule — the Calgarians finally sealed the town from the rear, trapping 322 Germans who became some of the first POWs of Operation Veritable.

The toll, however, was heavy for the Highlanders. Sixty-seven men were casualties, including 15 killed. ''[They]were too thin on the ground to do the job effectively and there were numerous enemy in the vicinity,'' was the explanation of their brigade commander, Brigadier W.J. Megill.

By contrast, the Régiment de Maisonneuve lost only two killed and 20 wounded. It had been a short engagement, but surprisingly sharp. The 2nd Canadian Infantry Division was now withdrawn, pinched out of battle.

Charged with the responsibility of protecting the main assault from enemy harassment on its exposed left flank bordering the Rhine, the commander of 3rd Canadian Infantry Division, Major-General Dan Spry, found his only recourse was to take to the waters.

Indeed, when Spry expounded the principle that his officers ''keep one foot on the ground,'' he was forgetting the reputation his three brigades had earned as masters of amphibious warfare: first on the Normandy beaches, then across the flooded polders to the Scheldt River in Holland, and now over the Rhine's overflowing banks. The sobriquet ''Water Rats'' had stuck to the waterbound division.

In the coming days, getting a foot — a dry foot — on the ground — dry ground — was to become an unattainable luxury for many of the Water Rats. ''The so-called dry was just plain mud,'' Spry recalls.

Two of Spry's brigades, the 7th and 8th, crossed the start line at nightfall, eight hours after H-Hour. Because the darkness and water would undoubtedly add untold problems to the attack, three sophisticated aids to modern warfare were laid on: Buffaloes to swim the troops to battle, "artificial moonlight" to show them the way, and a transplanted London fog to mask their movements.

Artificial moonlight was produced by searchlights. The purpose was to provide visibility that would allow infantry and armour to fight more effectively at night. It worked particularly well when conditions were such that the beams of light could be bounced off low-hanging clouds.

"It was like walking out onto a pitch-black stage with a spotlight on you," Spry commented. "Some of the men hated it, and they probably did get shot at more in the first few minutes because of it."

One hundred and fourteen of the amphibious troop-carrying Buffaloes that had played so prominent a role in freeing the Scheldt Estuary in the autumn were again employed, with troops from the 79th British Armoured Division again serving as their skilled drivers. DUKWs (two-and-a-half-ton, six-wheel American trucks, converted to amphibious use with a propeller) were also used for transporting troops.

As the units were under continuous enemy observation and fire from the high ridges and tall factory chimneys on the far bank of the Rhine, the war's longest smokescreen was created. First Canadian Army Smoke Control HQ, under Major J.T. ("Tempy") Hugill, Royal Canadian Artillery, had assembled 1,350 all ranks for the task, comprising four British smoke companies and chemical warfare and meteorological specialists from Canada and Britain. The latter were of utmost importance as the effectiveness of the smoke was dependent on the speed and direction of the wind. "Whenever the winds changed, gaps would open up and the Germans would start firing through them," Hugill recalls.

Originally intended as a four-day exercise, the screen was so successful that its use was continued for six weeks and extended some 25 miles along the Rhine. In that period, 3,500 tons of smoke stores, including 400,000 gallons of fog oil, were used. Besides concealing the movement of troops from enemy observation posts little more than a mile away, the screen enabled sappers to proceed with road maintenance and mine-clearing, free from direct enemy fire.

Despite this back-up, 8th Brigade soon discovered the insoluble complication posed by a night attack across water: the essential elements of support that were normally transported by carriers — anti-tank guns and flame-throwers, for example — had to be left behind.

"It was straight infantry fighting out on the polders, and it was terrible," Captain Blake Oulton, a company commander with the North Shore Regiment, remembers. "The great lack was in getting any kind of vehicles forward. There was some support from artillery but even that posed problems as they had to fire across our front instead of from behind us."

On the 7th Brigade flank, 1st Canadian Scottish Regiment encountered serious difficulties when it ran into "Little Tobruk," an enemy strongpoint at Niel. Named for its concrete fortifications, Little Tobruk was to claim Veritable's first victim from the ranks of commanding officers — the first of a tragic and unparalleled number of senior commanders to be killed or seriously wounded in the fierce fighting of the Rhineland campaign.

"There were pockets, isolated to some extent by water, which were well defended by the Germans," Major William Matthews, second-in-command, explained. "Wallowing along in those Buffaloes, you never knew as you approached these little 'islands' whether they were defended or not. Everything had to be dealt with on the spot, usually as a platoon-plus effort. And of course communications were bloody awful. We were fair spread out over a couple of miles and it was pretty hard to maintain contact.

"That's where poor old Des Crofton came a cropper. He couldn't establish communication with his companies out in front."

Lieutenant-Colonel Crofton, the CO (Commanding Officer) of the Canadian Scottish, had been caught in a dilemma. The 7th Brigade commander, Brigadier Jock Spragge, was pressing him for a report on the exact location of his companies. Crofton was unable to get through on the wireless. Rationally, he knew his place was at Battalion HQ. His inclination, however (for which he had been admonished in the past) was to go forward and find his men. The insistent brigadier decided the issue; Crofton and his group clambered aboard Buffaloes and headed for the forward position of his two missing companies, which he believed to be near the village of Niel.

Unknown to him, both companies had had problems maintaining their direction in the lurching craft and had not yet reached their objectives. Map references had proven almost useless in the darkened and waterlogged floodlands, and the metal vehicles sent compass needles wheeling.

Crofton approached two buildings that loomed silently out of the water in the half-light of dawn. His Buffalo slipped between them. Suddenly there was an explosion. He had stumbled on a stronghold held firmly by the enemy. The craft was hit by a rocket from a German Panzerfaust (a hand-held rocket-firing anti-tank weapon). Four men were instantly killed and another six were wounded.

Crofton's arm was badly smashed. Accompanied by his intelligence officer, he managed to crawl to a nearby barn where the two wounded men lay helplessly for almost 12 hours before anyone reached them.

While the battle raged towards Cleve, the "noble mariners" of 9th Canadian Infantry Brigade were up to their waists in February's icy waters. Their job was to break through the Siegfried Line defences — now partially submerged — on Veritable's left flank.

Afloat in Buffaloes, the Stormont, Dundas & Glengarry Highlanders (SD&G), the North Nova Scotia Highlanders (NNSH), and the Highland Light Infantry (HLI) silenced German outposts in one "island" village after another. They were immeasurably grateful for Smoke Control's effective screen as they sailed almost under the noses of enemy OPs.

The flooding that had caused so many serious problems for 7th and 8th Brigades had if anything worsened. When the Germans pierced the winter dikes on February 7, engineers from 16th Field Company, Royal Canadian Engineers, consulted with Dutch experts as to how to correct the flooding. On their recommendation, the Canadians breached the main dike at Nijmegen to allow the flood water an escape hatch into the Waal River.

"An initial gap of 100 feet was blown and this was increased within 36 hours to 900 feet," reported Lieutenant-Colonel F.A. McTavish, CRE 3rd Canadian Infantry Division. "Shortly afterwards, the enemy further complicated the problem by blowing the lock gates of the Spoy Canal and making a 165-foot breach in the dike."

Witnessing the explosion, General Spry could not resist a sly gibe at his friend:

I had an OP up on the high ground looking down on the attack and I happen to have been looking in that direction when the Germans blew the dike, and this very thick chunk of stuff — about 300 yards of a 20-foot-thick dike — went up in the air. I called on my telephone to the Chief Engineer 3rd Division, Alec McTavish. 'Did you see what I saw?' I asked him. 'Well, try sticking your finger in that!'

The SD&G were assigned the task of advancing on 9th Brigade's right flank to secure the final 3rd Division objective of the village of Rindern, just one mile northwest of Cleve. With this stronghold lost, the enemy would no longer have a safe exit across the flooded flatlands from Cleve to the Rhine.

They had their first hint of what lay ahead when German armour-piercing shells, directed from Rindern, blasted off a portion of the roof of the house that the CO, Lieutenant-Colonel Rowley, had just set up as his headquarters and personal OP to organize the attack.

At twilight, lacking supporting arms and with two of its companies still delayed by the floods, the battalion advanced to Rindern. It appeared to be an innocent German village, obviously abandoned in haste — ''sauerkraut still on the tables, coal embers still in the hearth.'' The Glens soon discovered that Rindern was bristling with fortifications. They had stumbled on a strongly reinforced village on the Siegfried Line, with houses of reinforced concrete and gun emplacements lining the basement windows.

''We got in there all right,'' Rowley recounts, ''but they were waiting for us, German parachutists. It was my first experience with that sort of hand-to-hand fighting and there was a good deal of it, people rolling grenades through casement windows and that sort of thing. But the boys did very well. We took a lot of prisoners and held them in a sort of a barnyard.

''Then we got counter-attacked. These parachutists came along a canal from Cleve. We had one company commander there — Gordy Clarke — who handled that counter-attack marvellously but it was quite dicey.''

The next day, Rowley had a bizarre experience in this most bizarre of villages. ''I glanced at the wall, and there was a picture of a young German officer and next to it, a photograph of our pre-war Canadian Olympic hockey team. The goalie was Major Don Daley, the DAQMG (deputy assistant quartermaster general) of our brigade, who was a great hockey player. I got Daley to come and look at this picture, and he said, 'I know that German guy, sure, he was a good player.' ''

Later that morning, General Spry raised his binoculars (of German manufacture, yielded without enthusiasm by a prisoner of war) and focussed out across the polders. ''We were on our objectives, but the enemy got a lot of our people en route. The Germans on that front were do-or-die boys. They stuck to their weapons and kept firing until the last moment and then threw down their arms, hands up, and that was it.

"But now we were under water. I could see Canadian soldiers sitting on rooftops of farmhouses and barns or standing in water holding their weapons over their heads."

The flood level had risen to five feet in some places, and the Nijmegen-Cleve road was disappearing. Great navigational care had to be taken to avoid hedges, fenceposts, and other obstructions that were now under water.

The critical issue was getting ammunition and food up to the water-beleaguered troops. Each man carried a 24-hour ration kit and a tin of self-heating soup. This provided life-saving nourishment to troops in cold, wet slit-trenches. The tin had a tube filled with a flammable substance running up its centre and a seal on its top. To activate it, the seal was pulled off and the fuel heated the soup. Cocoa was sometimes issued in this ingenious form as well.

"Resupply and the evacuation of casualties became terrible problems," Spry recalls. "The roads were falling apart as we were using them. They were only Class 9 country lanes and not built for five-ton trucks and 40-ton tanks. We were just grinding them to mush. The engineers worked day and night dumping rubble and logs to fill in enough holes to make them passable."

Sappers of 3rd Division built four ferries to handle traffic along the flooded areas. Then, in an incredible feat of engineering, a two-mile stretch of a one-way Class 9 road was widened into a two-way road in a non-stop three-day marathon by all the division's engineers, under command of 18th Field Company, Royal Canadian Engineers. Nine tipper lorries and 50 Royal Canadian Army Service Corps lorries hauled rubble (stored at a church in Wyler) and gravel.

The Water Rats completed their final objective on the floodlands and reverted inland to their infantry role. The "left wing" had completed its tasks of blocking the enemy; the way was now clear for the rest of the team to surge forward.

5

Four Generals Outraged

Top Secret. Personal and Eyes Only for CIGS from Field-Marshal Montgomery, 8 Feb 45:
The main difficulty has been mud and mines and not so much the enemy who were greatly taken by artillery fire. We have captured today about 1000 prisoners. Our casualties have been light in all divisions engaged. Operations are being continued tonight with "movement light" and we hope by daylight tomorrow morning to have secured the Materborn high ground immediately west of Cleve and a high ridge running southwest through the forest.

MINEFIELDS, MUD, AND disintegrating communications posed a triple threat to the advancing Jocks as the 15th Scottish team burst forth across the start line on February 8 in its drive for Cleve.

The narrowness of the front dictated the tactics: two brigades, the 46th and 227th, would spearhead the attack as far as the Siegfried Line and a third, the 44th, would then advance through them to actually breach the fortification. The infantry were supported by tanks of the Grenadier, Coldstream, and Scots Guards of 6th Guards Tank Brigade — and by a generous tot of rum issued at the start line.

Almost immediately, they ran into minefields. The first was a legacy from the debacle of Arnhem five months before — an American minefield still littered with parachutes and skeletons of gliders. A gap was found and taped so that the riflemen could safely traverse it.

Beyond this, the enemy had sown thick beds of schu-mines blocking the approach. Many of the Flails, which could have beaten a

See Map 4 (Appendix B).

60

path for them through the minefields, had fallen far behind, bogged in the churned-up mud. The 10th Battalion Highland Light Infantry incurred a number of casualties, and eight stretcher-bearers were themselves wounded trying to reach the casualties lying in the fields.

The 2nd Battalion Argyll & Sutherland Highlanders also scrambled desperately to find a way through the minefields as they strove to keep up with the barrage. "It seemed likely the success of the operation would be in jeopardy," recorded the Scots Guards war diary. "Unless something could be done quickly the barrage would be lost for good."

Timing was essential in this operation. If a battalion could not keep apace with the barrage, moving forward under its protective umbrella each time it lifted, the entire momentum of the assault would be lost. If the troops were held up by the heavy going or by the mines, or if they panicked and went to ground in the chaos of screaming shells falling around them, the barrage would move on but the men would not. The attack could falter and severe casualties would certainly result. Yet if they advanced into the minefield before the lethal mines in their paths were cleared, they would suffer even worse casualties.

One such crisis with the Argylls was averted by cool thinking on the part of a Scots Guards lieutenant, who led his troop through a tiny gap he had spotted. The tanks preceded the riflemen, exploding the schu-mines as they went, and the infantry and the remainder of the squadron were able to follow through in the tracks with the loss of only two tanks.

Maintaining communications with the lead companies was becoming increasingly difficult. The two-way radios, designed as the primary means of communication between a battalion's headquarters and its companies, were often a source of frustration to the infantry. In close quarters, on the flat, and without obstruction they worked adequately. However, the range was very limited and any physical obstacles, natural or man-made, rendered them partially or completely unserviceable (US) or disabled (DIS). Further, any jarring action could result in a confusing alteration of frequency.

The CO of 9th Battalion Cameronians, which — along with 2nd Battalion Glasgow Highlanders — led the 46th Brigade assault, found that his radio was malfunctioning. "My communication with the forward companies now failed owing to the 18-set going 'dis,' "

Lieutenant-Colonel Edward Remington-Hobbs noted. "Therefore it was necessary to move forward on foot and keep personal contact with them."

As the Jocks neared the Siegfried Line, the awesome effects of the artillery became evident.

"The whole countryside had been devastated by the colossal barrage," reported Major K.J. Irvine, adjutant of the 2nd Battalion Gordons. A young Highland Light Infantry lieutenant leading a patrol stumbled on a grotesque example of this destruction. "The night of the attack," Lieutenant Robert Jackson reported, "my platoon was sent out to establish communications with the other companies and we came to a graveyard. All the gravestones and caskets had been blown up."

The fire had, however, temporarily stunned the Germans. Only a few pockets of resistance remained. Here, the enemy had not had the opportunity to put his defensive tactics to work: trees prepared for demolition as roadblocks had not been detonated, artillery pieces were unmanned.

"We found many guns about," Irvine noted, "but they had been deserted by their crews who had taken refuge in huge concrete underground bunkers. They were so 'bomb happy' that they were incapable of any real fighting."

Not so subdued was the German shellfire. Irvine owes his life to a bar of soap — one that slipped under the table at field headquarters that night. As he dived to retrieve it, an enemy shell made a direct hit, killing 11 Gordons and wounding nine.

One Argyll company managed to lean so closely into the barrage that when it lifted, the men were literally on top of their objective. In 10 minutes the company took 80 prisoners without firing a single shot. They also captured intact and unfired an 88mm gun, beautifully sited, ammunition neatly stacked beside it, leather covers still on breech and muzzle. Still, as a veteran NCO, Sergeant Alex Kidd, reflected, "If the Germans *had* been manning those guns, things would have been pretty hot for us."

By now, both brigades were on their first objectives. But the real enemy of the day was declaring itself: the deteriorating roads — and in their wake, chaos for the attacking force. Schlemm's flood tactics coupled with the relentless rain had taken their toll on an axis road that even before the invasion was poor. The tanks, carriers, and lorries that carried troops and supplies forward had chewed up what was left. In low-lying areas, the ditches, damaged by gunfire, were actually draining water into the area.

By afternoon there was only one road — 46th Brigade's axis — to carry the transport of two brigades, and it was a narrow dirt track with deep ditches on either side. Added to its load would be the transport of five field artillery regiments, which had to advance in order to provide covering fire for the troops moving forward. And there was still 44th Brigade to follow.

"It was to be a nightmare night," the 15th Scottish history records, "throughout which every officer and man in the 46th Brigade was to be at work without a let-up on traffic control and vehicle recovery in an effort to produce some sort of order out of chaos."

The division commander, Major-General C.M. Barber, had sternly issued a blanket order that any vehicle found blocking the axis would be immediately bulldozed into the ditch. It was Barber's own jeep that became one of the first victims of the edict.

The next morning, D-plus-One, the Scottish division sent in its third brigade, the 44th, with orders that its three battalions smash through the Siegfried defences. The spirited CO of 6th Battalion King's Own Scottish Borderers (KOSB), Brigadier (then Lieutenant-Colonel) Charles Richardson, recalls an anxious night as they struggled through mud and rain just to reach the assembly area.

"H-Hour was postponed again and again because of the traffic congestion ahead. It wasn't until early morning that my battalion at last managed to reach the start line."

The main route had by now collapsed completely, leaving the whole force, including 6th KOSB infantry, to proceed on a single muddy track. As dawn was breaking, the exhausted men reached the Siegfried Line.

The Siegfried defences in this sector included minefields and an immense anti-tank ditch. A chain of concrete gun emplacements gave the enemy fire support. The Funnies of 79th Armoured Division were tailor-made to meet the challenge: the Flails to clear the minefields, and the AVREs to lay bridges across the anti-tank ditch. An armoured breaching force of 4th Battalion Grenadier Guards, supported by 6th KOSB and two squadrons of the Funnies, was given the job of punching a hole through the line so that the infantry and armour could drive through.

By luck, Major Pike of the Grenadier Guards found a stretch of anti-tank ditch unmanned by enemy defenders and manoeuvred the force across a hastily bridged gap. Within an hour, Richardson's men had poured through the hole aboard their Kangaroos.

"As the battalion went over the Siegfried Line," the CO recalled with a smile, "an irrepressible gentleman, Sergeant-Major John Walls, MC, who had enlisted in the regiment 23 years before, carefully stopped and ceremoniously hung up his token line of washing." The song "We're going to hang up the washing on the Siegfried Line" was hummed by many a Jock that day.

With weary satisfaction, 6th KOSB set about consolidating on their objective. Then fresh orders came in for Richardson. "I really wasn't particularly pleased to be contacted by my brigadier and told that the Royal Scots Fusiliers simply could not get through to continue the second phase of the advance. So would I please just go on and capture two very dominant features that overlooked Cleve."

There was no use arguing, so Richardson piled his men back in their Kangaroos, made a rapid plan, and executed a canny left hook onto the first of two hills that barred the way to Cleve. "The attack was wildly successful," he recounted, "and we managed to capture 240 Germans and about 12 officers, including one or two quite senior ones."

Despite the bold efforts of the Scots, however, their seven-hour delay in crossing the start line and the unavoidable problems they had since encountered had put them a dangerous 11 hours behind schedule. The risk was grave that counter-attacking Germans would reach the final objective — the Materborn hill just one mile from Cleve — before the Scots could seize it. Richardson was summoned yet again to his radio set.

"We had been in our Kangaroos for about 15 hours by then," Richardson explained. "But the brigadier came on the blower again saying we had to push on to take Materborn. We rushed ahead and took it — by a margin of a half an hour or so — just in time to beat off the German counter-attack."

The POW "bag" revealed insignia for the first time from the 6th and 7th Parachute Divisions, Schlemm's hastily drawn-up reinforcements that had been rushed to the front to secure this strategic strongpoint. After a sharp action on the slopes in the gathering dusk, 6th KOSB consolidated their position on the feature.

"We felt we'd really put in a good day's work," Richardson noted. "A little later, our wonderful quartermaster, J.W.A. Smith, came up with the only rations that anyone got that day because of the flooding."

Inadvertently, this brilliant and hard-won victory — for which both Richardson and Major Pike were awarded the DSO (Distinguished Service Order) — was to be one of the main catalysts that provoked Horrocks into making the most serious mistake of his career.

The impressive achievements of the 15th Scottish Division during the first 36 hours of Operation Veritable were to persuade Horrocks that, despite the manifold problems that were unfolding — rain, floods, and stiffening opposition — the operation was a success. The glow of optimism had not yet been dimmed by reality. In a climate of overconfidence, Veritable was about to be sabotaged by one of its own architects.

Top Secret. Personal and Eyes Only for CIGS from Field-Marshal Montgomery, 9 Feb 45:
Progress in the Veritable operation has been good today. We now hold the following line from north to south. Millingen on the Rhine — Keeken — Donsbrueggen — Materborn — Hekkens then west to Middelaar on the Maas. You will see from this that we hold the key high ground in the Reichswald forest and control the roads running to it and from the Materborn feature we look down into Cleve. Tonight 43rd Div from reserve are moving up to Kranenburg and Cleve to move on Goch from the north and I hope to have secured Goch by tomorrow. The prisoners taken in Veritable now total 3,000 and our own casualties to date are about 500.

Back at his command post, General Horrocks and his staff had spent a watchful day and night. With 39 infantry battalions committed, in addition to armoured, artillery, and sapper units, it required all of the veteran campaigner's tactical skill and experience to read and evaluate the vital signs of the operation's progress from the myriad reports that were filtering back from the front line.

Above all, Horrocks feared losing the impetus of the battle. "Too often in the war I had witnessed a pause in the battle when one division was ordered to pass through another, which allowed the enemy time to recover. I was determined that our attack should flow on."

Encouraged that the campaign was going well, Horrocks had put the 43rd Wessex Infantry Division on one hour's notice to join the attack the instant that Cleve was captured. Now, as D-plus-One drew to a close, his optimism seemed justified. Each of the original divisions had reached its objectives. Sixty thousand Allied troops had planted their claim on German territory, and 3,000 prisoners had been taken. The enemy had seemingly run out of fight.

The Welsh and the 51st Highlanders had penetrated the dank gloom of the state forest; the 15th Scottish had breached the dreaded Siegfried Line, gaining the essential commanding position over-looking Cleve; the Canadians had secured the exposed left flank of the attack and opened up the paved Nijmegen-Cleve road (now unfortunately under two feet of water at its eastern end).

The artillery had overcome untold problems to fulfill its role mag-nificently, although some unique employment of guns resulted. So wet were the gun areas that one troop of the 14th Field Regi-ment of the Royal Canadian Artillery had to set up for action right in the middle of the main road, halting all traffic whenever the guns fired.

On the other hand, most of the major roads were near collapse. The vehicles and armour had snarled and bogged in the mud, and the situation was becoming ever worse from floods and ceaseless, belting sleet and rain. Here, too, getting ammunition and warm food up to the bone-cold men at the front and getting casualties back out were major problems.

Air support had petered out with the inclement weather. The Germans were detonating the Rhine dikes. Worse, Horrocks had just been informed that the Roer River dams had been sabotaged, making the American Grenade attack unlikely.

A fresh sense of urgency was added with the news that the crack German 7th Parachute Division had joined ranks with Fiebig's 84th Division just in time to establish defences in some sectors. The Scots' seven-hour delay had permitted German reinforcements to begin filtering into the line. Horrocks saw the race for Cleve becom-ing all the more imperative.

Then, in the dying hours of February 9, came the electric news that the 8th Battalion Royal Scots and 2nd Battalion Gordons had succeeded in following 6th KOSB onto adjacent objectives. The 44th Brigade had secured the Materborn feature, he was told, and was even now moving into Cleve.

Horrocks reacted swiftly to news of the city's pending capture. "This was the information for which I had been eagerly waiting," he remembered. "Speed in capturing Cleve before the German reserves got established there was essential. So I unleashed my first reserve, the 43rd Wessex Division, which was to pass through the 15th Scottish, to burst into the plain beyond and advance towards Goch."

Horrocks thereupon instructed the Scots to proceed in the capture of Cleve; he ordered 43rd Wessex to pass through them at the city's outskirts and press on south a further eight miles to Goch.

These orders had three immediate results. Horrocks inextricably entangled the two divisions. He created a traffic jam "of huge and bewildering proportions," as one of his brigade commanders described it. And he placed no fewer than three major-generals — one Scottish, one English, and one German — in a state of outrage and shock.

The first of these was Major-General C.M. Barber, commander of the 15th Scottish Division. "Tiny" Barber, six feet, six inches of towering rage, was startled and furious to find the Wessex division headed for *his* objective on *his* road. For Horrocks's information had been incorrect: Barber's Jocks were still a mile short of Cleve, and the renewed assault was not scheduled until some hours hence. In fact, the enemy still firmly held the town and its periphery and were rapidly reinforcing their position there.

The second general officer affected was the commander of the 43rd Wessex Division, Major-General G.I. Thomas. Considerably more diminutive than Barber in stature, but not in anger, Thomas sat in a leaky reconnaissance car, glowering in impotent fury at the drenching downpour — stuck in the mud.

The problems Horrocks had caused by ordering the 43rd into battle were exacerbated by Thomas's own unfortunate decision to attempt to shift his reconnaissance regiment from the rear of his line to the front. His three-mile-long column of vehicles and the troops of three brigades had snarled to a stop on the single-lane, mudded road.

The lead battalion of his 129th Brigade, having pushed forward to explore a route, had not been heard from in some hours. And all the while, a giant Scot was thundering at him to get off the road. Get off? Where?

Thomas finally agreed to pull his remaining troops and vehicles to the side of the road for two hours, to allow Barber to move his 227th Brigade through them and into Cleve on its assigned mission. At the appointed hour, however, the Wessex found there was simply nowhere to go. Secondary roads were impassable. Mud and craters made the sole axis too narrow to allow the tanks and vehicles of one brigade to pass through another.

Meanwhile, Lieutenant-Colonel John Corbyn, CO of the errant battalion, 4th Wiltshires, was holding an impromptu midnight Orders Group in a shattered roadside cottage. Cleve, Corbyn informed his astonished officers, was still held by the enemy, although defences were thought to be disorganized. When he had alerted "higher authority" to this fact, he was ordered to "bash on" through Cleve to the original objective, Goch. Corbyn himself led the column by a secondary road branching southeast into Cleve.

It was to be a nightmare journey for the men of 4th Battalion Wiltshires. As wheeled vehicles would never have negotiated the road, the riflemen rode "quick lift," 13 men hanging onto the outside of each tank and tracked vehicle. Icy rain and sleet lashed against the troops. Many were very young soliders, in action for the first time in circumstances that would have tested the hardiest veteran. They had been warned that they would be riding through enemy lines where no road reconnaissance had been made and where the German positions were not known. Their vulnerability provoked "an awful feeling of nakedness as we sat perched on top of tanks driving down this single road."

At the sharp end, clinging to an ungainly, slithering tank, Captain Derek Ford of 7th Somersets describes the unnerving experience. "I hadn't realized how few handholds there were on these tanks, especially if your hands were full and you were wearing all your kit. With so many of us hanging on, it was extremely hard to keep a position. Then of course you had to watch for the exhaust. It was red-hot, and if you put your hand on that, you were really in trouble."

Throughout the stop-and-start journey, the men dared not dismount and stretch cramped limbs for fear that the tanks would start up again before they could clamber aboard. Overhanging trees and telephone wires swept off a few unfortunates. To make matters worse, the Luftwaffe began spasmodic bombing. Groping through the confusion of twisting, narrow, darkened lanes, the battalion entered Cleve and crossed the town towards its southeastern exit without meeting any German opposition.

"At first light [on February 10]," the 4th Wiltshire war diary recorded, "the whole battalion was strung out along one road and the streets on either side had not been cleared. 75 POW were taken . . . consisting mainly of people who were surprised sleeping in the cellars, and runners and ration parties . . . who did not realize that we were there."

The battalion could hardly have been in a more dangerous position. Having "missed its turning" (as the Scottish peevishly supposed), the Wiltshire battalion had taken over the proposed objective of the Jocks. The Wessex had no orders to attack Cleve, but it would be impossible to get out of town without extensive road clearance. They were surrounded by enemy who were just coming to life. They had no option but to consolidate and fight it out.

In Cleve, the Westcountrymen of 129th Brigade saw the effects of Horrocks's "cratering is acceptable" decision. "There were bomb craters and fallen trees everywhere, bomb craters packed so tight that the debris from one was piled against the rim of the next in a pathetic heap of rubble, roofs and radiators. There was not an undamaged house anywhere, piles of smashed furniture, clothing, children's books and toys, old photographs and bottled fruit, were spilled in hopeless confusion from sagging crazy skeletons of houses."

"We swarmed into the town, thinking it had been cleared, but instead we had wandered slap-bang into the middle of a German position," remembers Major Victor Beckhurst, company commander in the 4th Battalion Somerset Light Infantry (SLI), which followed the 4th and 5th Wiltshires into town. "We just got to a crossroads around the centre of the town. Then the firing started from all sides.

"We had to formulate a plan; it was nearly impossible. Finally, all we could do was to mop up enemy pockets as best we could."

General Thomas's surprise in finding the town still strongly occupied by the enemy was matched only by that of the third general to be astonished by Horrocks's move: the striking and usually debonair German 84th Infantry Division commander, Major-General Heinz Fiebig.

All day, Fiebig had been expecting to hear that the main Allied attack had been launched farther south, as Blaskowitz had insisted. He thought that this was merely a "diversionary" attack launched only by the Canadians, which would concentrate on the Materborn Heights behind Cleve where he had dispatched his reinforcements as they came in.

Now here were these "bewildered and belligerent" Westcountrymen, some 1,800 of them, appearing in his midst from behind his lines, engaged in a free-for-all, Western-style shooting match around his very headquarters. Fiebig was startled to identify British formations and he realized belatedly that they, as well as the Canadians, were engaged in the operation. This *was* the main attack. He, Fiebig, stood in its vortex.

February 10 was to be a long and nerve-racking day for German and Wessex alike, a day of small, desperate dogfights, of bizarre encounters rather than major engagements. A sergeant of 4th Battalion Wiltshires saw a group of Germans walking towards him. Thinking they were POWs, he jerked his thumb to the rear and said, "Go on, fuck off!" A German officer drew his pistol and said in excellent English, "*You* fuck off!"

Communications were chaotic. Three company commanders and the battalion carrier officer of 5th Battalion Wiltshires were returning from an Orders Group when a shell exploded in their midst, killing two company commanders and severely wounding the remaining two. As there were no witnesses, the acting CO of the battalion, Major Hyde, did not know for some hours that he had lost his key officers and that his orders had not been delivered.

By now, the enemy had had time to profit from the confusion and delay. Fiebig noted that the "lull in the attack" gave him time to "patch up the gaps" and bring 7th Parachute Division into battle. As these fresh reinforcements arrived in Cleve, the veteran commander formed them into a counter-attack force.

The Wessex Brigade's tactical headquarters was counter-attacked and a senior staff officer was killed. Regimental Sergeant-Major J.G. Smith desperately rallied what manpower was available around the headquarters — signallers, cooks, and drivers — and fought off the attack so effectively that 29 dead Germans were counted in the back garden. Another German counter-attack at dawn the next day was subdued at the cost of 180 enemy parachute troops being taken prisoner.

Sergeant Leslie Knight of the 4th Wiltshires' anti-tank platoon saw a German medical officer firing his revolver. Taking him prisoner, Knight and his men discovered that his ambulance was full of ammunition.

Later, the men of Knight's company were told they were moving out. "We had got our six-pounder guns hooked up to the tractors, facing west. Then we were counter-attacked from the east by a force of two tanks, a Panther and a Tiger, and about 10 infantry." Finally, they were able to drive off the attackers.

The narrow front had become *too* narrow. Allies were colliding with other Allies. Still encountering pockets of resistance in the hills around Cleve, 8th Battalion Royal Scots reported caustically that they had incurred no casualties, "except from the fire of 43 Division artillery."

Major Tony Parsons of 4th Battalion Wiltshires reported that on one occasion "a Canadian unit was flaming a wood from the north at the same time as one of our companies was due to beat it [attack] from the south!"

While the Wessex were isolated and fighting it out alone on the 10th, the roads leading to Cleve had become almost unnavigable and troop movement was impossible. The mud had worsened, the craters were silt-filled lakes. All routes were frozen to normal administrative traffic.

On Sunday, February 11, the 8th Royal Scots came into Cleve to relieve the exhausted Wessex troops. They saw an incredible sight, as Bill Fargus recalls: "There were Canadians and Borderers milling about . . . two brigadiers were arguing in the middle of the road and a sniper at the far end was firing at us all. Absolute chaos!"

The casualties were fewer, the 43rd Wessex believe, than if their 129th Brigade's "daring attack" had not so precipitously preempted the Scots' assigned task of capturing Cleve. And they were surely fewer than would have been the case if the Germans had had more time to dig in behind that "barrier of rubble" while waiting for the Scottish attack the next day.

"It is certain that a deliberate attack with artillery support [a "set-piece" attack] would have been slower and more costly," the 4th Wiltshires history asserts. The Scots, unimpressed, counter caustically that the unexpected presence of the Wessex "queered the pitch" considerably for the 15th Scottish Division.

Clearly, whether the 43rd Wessex stumbled on Cleve by accident or arrived by bold intent, their unauthorized attack did prevent the Germans from becoming entrenched in the ruins of Cleve to mount a prolonged defence. Although the bizarre combination of circumstances had set back Veritable by two days, the Wessex error had inadvertently salvaged the operation — and Horrocks's reputation.

Little else can be said in defence of Horrocks's flurry of over-optimism that committed two divisions into battle on a road that could not even bear the weight of one. It was, in the words of one senior Wessex brigade commander, "an error in judgment" — but one that should, he thought, be viewed charitably. "The spirit which animated this dramatic decision is beyond criticism," Brigadier Hubert Essame, commander of the 214th Brigade, 43rd Wessex Division, wrote. "The need to debouch into the open country south of Cleve . . . was urgent and justified the obvious risks.

"However, his decision was to produce in the next forty-eight hours a situation unrivalled in its exasperating complexity throughout the campaign."

Essame forgets that there were actually *two* errors in judgment. One — ordering the Wessex Division into battle prematurely — could be attributed to impulsiveness, although it is an incongruous label for such an astute and experienced corps commander. The other — the cratering of Cleve, an act that made the town and its approaching roads a nightmare for the attackers and a haven for the defenders — is harder to understand. From early December, when a calm, decision-making mood prevailed, right up until February 5, the plan to flatten Cleve had been approved by Horrocks.

Yet Essame, whose own division suffered the most severely from this error, bitterly blames the RAF for the "oafish stupidity" of Bomber Command, even though the decision actually was made by his own corps commander.

An explanation that could account for these two crucial errors — two in a brilliant wartime career — might be found within the physical makeup of Brian Horrocks. He was under the enormous strain that only the command of close to 200,000 men in perilous times could impose. The most significant factor to influence his command was probably his health.

These two faulty decisions were made by a man who by his own admission was unwell — and whose senior commander, Montgomery, *knew* him to be unwell. Yet the field-marshal had urged-him back into the battle, knowing that he might not be fit for the rigours of serving as corps commander.

Tragically, the errors caused the very situation that Horrocks had dreaded all along: 48 hours of chaos, and a standstill to the Rhineland offensive.

"I moved 43rd Division up too quickly," Horrocks later conceded. "I should have fought 15th Division right out — should have captured Cleve with them before I put the 43rd through. [But] it might have been another Passchendaele and I had a horror of that.

"This turned out to be one of the worst mistakes I made in the war," Horrocks acknowledged regretfully. "I very nearly snarled up everything."

The inescapable fact is that the fighting men of three nations were to pay a severe penalty for this lapse.

Sixty miles to the south, Lieutenant-General William Simpson had heard the opening salvos of Operation Veritable on February 8 with dismay. The countdown, he knew too well, was on. In two days' time, Operation Grenade — the Ninth U.S. Army's prong of the dual assault — was to be launched across the Roer River. But the Roer was still dominated by the Germans, who held firmly to the dams. Unless Hodges's First Army could move quickly to seize the dams in the next two days, Grenade was off.

On February 5, Hodges's 78th Infantry Division had renewed the thrust to clear the final two miles from the eastern outskirts of Schmidt to the Schwammenauel Dam. The attempt faltered. The enemy had hung on in fierce, house-to-house fighting as the Americans inched their way ahead.

Livid at the lack of gains (which he attributed to "poor management"), Hodges directed the battle-sharp 9th Infantry Division to take command of a fresh two-divisional attack. Forty artillery battalions, comprising 780 guns, added their weight to the assault.

Yet daybreak on February 9 saw a determined enemy still holding out. Ninth Army's command post was in final preparation for Grenade's pending offensive on the Roer when a message was transmitted at 1657 hours. The assault, Simpson told his regimental commanders, would be delayed "at least 24 hours."

Exactly one hour later, just as midwinter darkness closed on the embattled troops at Schmidt, a single battalion of the 78th broke through the line. Accompanied by specially trained engineers, the raiders made a dash for the Schwammenauel Dam. By midnight the engineers were racing across the top of the dam, ducking heavy enemy fire as they rushed the entrance to the inspection tunnel that ran through its interior to the vital machinery. They stopped short. The Germans had demolished the entrance.

Desperately, the men slid down the treacherous 200-foot face of the dam to the lower entry of the tunnel. The engineers tore through the tunnel to the power room, fully expecting further explosions to engulf them in a torrent of water and smashed concrete.

They were too late. General Schlemm's demolition orders had already been executed. But instead of releasing a rush of water, Schlemm had cannily instructed his engineers to disable the discharge valves in such a way that the water would escape in a steady, continuous flow. This would maintain flood conditions for a much longer period than would a major torrent.

Hodges's aide-de-camp noted in his diary of February 9: "We have the dam tonight — or at least one-half of it. The damage was no surprise . . . damaged or undamaged, that was the objective."

If Horrocks's misjudgment gave three generals cause for alarm and outrage, Hodges's "mismanagement" of the Roer dams campaign would add a fourth general — William Simpson — to the list of disgruntled commanders.

First Army's prolonged neglect in seizing the dams was only eclipsed by this casual admission that Hodges never really expected success anyway. He was not in the least surprised to find the dams sabotaged. SHAEF Intelligence had produced a captured German map on January 17 delineating the proposed areas of flooding, and SHAEF had issued repeated warnings of this likelihood. (Even Kay Summersby, Eisenhower's personal assistant, noted: "E. always [thought] this would happen.")

Hodges must surely have realized that such an event would cripple Simpson's Operation Grenade and jeopardize Veritable, yet he delayed launching the final assault until five days prior to the proposed attack.

On February 10, 375,000 Americans stood poised for attack on a 17-mile front along the river. Simpson watched helplessly as the Roer spilled over its banks. The swollen waters were forcing them back as effectively as could enemy shellfire.

Simpson faced a crisis decision: if he launched Grenade now, before the extent of the flood could be determined by his engineers, he risked having his forward divisions isolated by the rising water, cut off from supplies, and massacred by ambushing Germans.

If he cancelled the operation, enemy forces massed across from the American front could be safely diverted to stop First Canadian Army's attack on Cleve and the Reichswald. This would seriously threaten the entire operation.

The fierce German defence of the dams and their shrewd demolition tactics had immobilized the Americans. These factors had also created an unexpectedly powerful enemy opposition for the British and Canadians, who were at that moment themselves beset with problems of flooding and cratered roads.

Montgomery's double-pronged armoured breakout was now faltering on both fronts. He had underestimated both the weather and the enemy. Now it would be up to the commanders and men at the sharp end to adapt the "paper" operation into battlefield reality. Veritable had been reduced to a single, slogging infantry combat against a strong German force fighting for its Fatherland.

The 56-year-old Texan turned away from the inexorable water and gave his command. Until the waters subsided, Grenade was off.

6

The Magic Armies

Top Secret. Personal and Eyes Only for CIGS from Field-Marshal Montgomery, 9 Feb 45:
As regards Grenade, the Roer is in spate and not even patrols are able to get across in boats and I have therefore postponed the launching of the operation 24 hours. I shall visit 9th Army tomorrow afternoon and give a decision then as to whether to launch Grenade on 11 Feb.

10 Feb 45:
I have had to postpone Grenade for a further 3 days as the Germans have blown the dams and the Roer River is quite impassable.

THE STATUE OF BISMARCK dominated the town square of Dueren. Originally, it had faced west towards the American enemy, just a grenade's-throw away across the Roer River. Bismarck's stern and threatening expression appeared to be directed at the 104th U.S. Division.

The statue was all that was left standing in the town square. The modern and prosperous city of 40,000 people had been transformed into one gigantic rubble heap by Allied bombs and shells. Ironically, the concussion of shells and bombs had rotated the statue to face the east. Its wrath now appeared to be directed at Berlin and at Hitler.

When the Allies' battle plan for Operation Grenade was formulated in November, the Roer was a tranquil 25-yard-wide stream — no great obstacle for a massed river assault. In February, the combination of the spring thaws and sabotage of the dams had transformed it into a treacherous and seemingly insurmountable

---

See Maps 4 and 5 (Appendix B).

barrier. Again, the "paper" plan had to be scrapped. Again, front-line commanders had to adapt it to reality.

Over the length of the 17-mile front, the Roer's temperament was now multifaceted. At Dueren, Grenade's southernmost point of attack, the narrow ribbon had become a seething torrent. Here the waters tumbled down the craggy Eifel hills before plunging sharply between 15-foot banks into the riverbed.

Just five miles downstream, at Juelich, the midpoint of General Simpson's proposed assault crossing sector, the terrain began to soften and the river flowed a more sedate course northwards. For three months, the 29th U.S. Infantry Division had been staring across the Roer's banks at Juelich, detesting it for its stubborn refusal to crumble. Once the granary of the Holy Roman Empire, Juelich had been ravaged by successive armies through the ages. Aerial strikes by the USAF and constant artillery poundings were now gradually reducing the city to a skeleton of half-walls and shattered roofs. Yet the 13th-century Witches' Tower and the 16th-century Citadel, with its massive 144-foot-thick walls, obstinately stood.

Still farther downstream, at Linnich, the Roer could be forded in several places at mean levels. Here the water had risen 11 feet and had overflowed its marshy banks to form lakes over a mile wide.

In the war room at Siersdorf Castle, a large wall chart showed the hourly changes in the waterline. Engineers drove stakes into the riverbanks to measure the rising water. During the night of February 9-10 the river rose two feet. The current ("watched and recorded like a patient's temperature") was running dangerously fast, over 10 miles per hour.

Eighteen thousand German troops were positioned opposite the Americans along the Roer on February 8. These included two Panzer divisions and one Panzer Grenadier division. The launch of Veritable on that day changed the situation. First Canadian Army Intelligence spelled out what it hoped would be the German quandary: "The enemy's major problem is whether he can divert reserves designed to protect himself against an attack across the Roer to our expanding threat. If he does, he leaves a road to the Ruhr open. If he does *not*, he leaves a road to the Ruhr open."

But with their flooding tactics, the Germans had solved this quandary. Reserves were hastily sideslipped north to the First Canadian Army front at Cleve and the Reichswald, with the commanders safe in the knowledge that a token force could contain Simpson's immobile forces. Ninth U.S. Army was powerless to attack.

In his daily communications with 21st Army Group HQ, Simpson followed the tortured fighting of 30 Corps. Obviously, Bradley's error in not seizing the Roer dams was giving the Germans the opportunity to exercise their uncanny ability to retrench. Against a reinforced enemy line, the Veritable thrust had been reduced to a mile-by-mile slogging match.

If the postponement of Operation Grenade on February 10 was creating serious difficulties on the First Canadian front, it was at least giving Simpson badly needed time to better prepare for the assault. His engineers calculated a delay of at least six days. He threw himself into intense planning.

In all, 303,243 men from 10 American divisions were assembled to funnel across the treacherous Roer on a front only a little more than 17 miles wide. In addition, 75,000 men of First U.S. Army would cross on the southern periphery at Dueren to protect Grenade's right flank.

A river assault by night of such a magnitude was unprecedented — and risky. Confusion was inevitable. Panic could sabotage the effort.

Simpson was staking the success of the operation on sheer power. Two supporting arms — the engineers and the artillery — were crucial to the success of the assault. The weight of artillery was massive. With over 2,000 guns, its bombardment would be greater even than Veritable's opening salvo on February 8. There would be an artillery piece for every 10 yards of front. A shuttle system was designed to keep the ammunition moving forward with the troops. Tanks and self-propelled guns were moved up to thicken the fire.

To heighten the surprise element, the artillery commanders devised two fire plans: a plan of deception and a plan of support. Shelling would commence three successive nights prior to D-Day: the first two would be feints to lead the enemy into thinking the attack was on, and the third would be the real thing.

Operating in direct infantry support, the engineers bore heavy responsibilities. It was their job to furnish engineer guides to the crossing sites and then to operate the assault boats. Across the river, they were required to clear mines and other obstacles from the enemy banks and roads, lay white tape to guide the troops, and evacuate casualties. They had also the critical challenge of constructing the bridges: footbridges for the infantry, treadway, pontoon, and Bailey bridges for vehicles and heavier supporting arms.

Also in direct support of Ninth Army was 29 Tactical Air Command, with five groups of fighter-bombers (375 planes) and a tactical reconnaissance group. Another supporting arm — the armour — would take on vital importance after the crossing. A total of 1,394 tanks, mainly Shermans, would be employed to achieve the hoped-for armoured breakout.

The logistics of organizing such a large force of men, with their vehicles, armour, and weapons, demanded round-the-clock planning and dedicated effort.

Simpson also took advantage of the holdup to move vast tons of supplies forward in readiness for the campaign. In a single five-day period, the Ordnance Corps organized 6,000 railcars to haul in over 40,000 long tons of supplies to the front. The cellars and backyards of every house and barn were crammed with material. Three million gallons of fuel were held in reserve, along with 46,000 tons of ammunition. In case anything should go wrong and the frontline troops across the river were cut off, 500 C-47s were already loaded with emergency supplies and prepared to make an air drop.

The signal corps laid many miles of telephone line to establish lateral communication on the west bank, in readiness for an immediate hookup when the assault troops jumped the river. Medics set up well-stocked regimental aid posts. A detailed traffic control program was evolved; a single stalled vehicle on a bridge could sabotage the momentum of the attack.

All this activity would be cloaked in a shroud of smoke produced by the Chemical Smoke Generator Units. The 30th Division alone assembled 50 pots to produce a 32-hour screen 2,000 yards across, three to four miles long, and 2,200 feet high.

The stretch of river between Linnich and Dueren was originally chosen because it had the narrowest crossing sites. But the February floods had transformed them. Now the Grenade battle plan was considerably adjusted to allow for the adverse conditions.

The six divisions making the initial assault would face six sets of problems in six differing conditions of terrain and current. Three American corps — 13 and 19 from Ninth Army and 7 Corps from First Army — would make the initial assault, each with two infantry divisions forward. A fourth corps, 16, would cross in the north a few days later.

General Alvan C. Gillem's 13 Corps (84th and 102nd Infantry Divisions) was assigned the most northerly assault position through the flat terrain of Linnich. So narrow was the only feasible crossing in the 84th Division sector that the "Railsplitters" were forced to plan the assault on a 500-yard, one-battalion front. On their right, however, 102nd Infantry Division faced a crossing site where the Roer had overflowed its marshy banks to form a broad lake.

Just five miles upstream in the 19 Corps sector, the terrain dictated two quite different approaches. The 29th and 30th divisions would share a three-mile front at Juelich.

At the town itself, where the river was channelled between two high banks, Major-General Charles Gerhardt, 29th Division's commander, came up with a startling plan to force the crossing. His patrols had discovered submerged coils of barbed wire that would make a normal amphibious assault difficult. Gerhardt decided instead to try an unorthodox and highly dangerous tactic. He ordered his combat engineers to erect a bridge under the very noses of the defenders, gambling that the high banks on the enemy side (at the site of a destroyed highway bridge) would shelter them from German fire.

To their right, the 30th Infantry Division was assigned a crossing place whose only advantage — it was deemed by the division itself to be a totally illogical selection otherwise — was to surprise the enemy. The river was swollen to a width of 400 feet of strongly moving water. As the floods started to recede, the engineers realized with dismay that the banks would be too soft and spongy to sustain heavy vehicles. Assault boats would be essential to move the first wave of troops across until bridges could be erected.

Finally, 19 Corps's exposed right flank would be protected by two divisions of First Army: the 104th Division (the "Timberwolves") and the 8th Infantry Division would force a crossing at Dueren. There, steep banks channelled the floodwaters into treacherous currents of more than 10 miles per hour.

Six divisions — six crossings — six potential cataclysms. Simpson had worked brilliantly at pulling together this instant army, at jelling the loyalties and honing the skills of its 375,000 men, at amassing its unparalleled artillery and armoured support and providing the fuel, the ammunition, and all the other logistical supplies to get it going and keep it going.

Once over the river and its elevated east bank, Simpson hoped that it would be "downhill all the way" in an armoured breakout to the Rhine — a mere 25 miles east.

This was Bill Simpson's magic army. His only hope was that it would be powerful enough to defeat the turbulent water and the enemy beyond. For now, all he could do was study the waterline charts — and wait.

Top Secret. Personal and Eyes Only for CIGS from Field-Marshal Montgomery, 12 Feb 1945:
Counter-attacks were put in today by 15th Pz Division and
by 116th Panzer Division but all these have been seen off.

Cleve fell on February 12, two days after the Germans had immobilized the Americans on the banks of the Roer. Berlin was finally
convinced that the attack from the Canadian sector was not a diversionary feint, but the main Allied thrust it had been expecting. This
direct threat to barge transport of coal and other essential goods
from the Ruhr to the North Sea ports presented a severe crisis to
the German High Command. The enemy was now just 20 miles
from strategic targets on the Rhine.

On February 13 von Rundstedt issued a fiery propaganda message to the troops at the front, warning them that the loss of the
Ruhr would leave the "Wehrmacht without weapons, the Heimat
[homeland] without coal." He urged them to "protect the Heimat
which works for you steadfastly; protect our women and children
from foreign despotism."

Once the floodgates of the Schwammenauel Dam had been
opened, General Schlemm was satisfied that the Americans would
be unable to establish a bridgehead over the Roer. He could safely
relieve Lieutenant-General Heinrich von Luettwitz's 47th Panzer
Corps from that front and swing the powerful force north against
Horrocks's divisions near Cleve.

Schlemm also shifted General Eugen Meindl's 2 Parachute Corps
and General Walther Wadehn's 8th Parachute Division north from
their positions in front of the American front, confidently replacing them with a weak and inadequately equipped unit of low combat value. Meindl now took over the vital sector at Goch, eight miles
south of Cleve.

Prior to the Veritable invasion, Schlemm had backed his hunch
about the direction of the expected assault by ordering up 7th
Parachute Division to bolster General Heinz Fiebig's 84th Division's
defences. It was not until the battle was a day old that he was able
to confirm his suspicions with the news that four British divisions
had been identified in the order of battle. Only then did he finally
receive permission to commit 7th Parachute Division to battle.

"We were wrong," admitted Army Group to the parachute
commander.

Now two new divisions — Major-General Hermann Plocher's
potent 6th Parachute and General Bernhard Klosterkemper's 180th

Infantry — were rapidly moved in. Schlemm rushed these rein-forcements piecemeal to the front as they arrived. It was these troops that Lieutenant-Colonel Richardson's 6th Battalion King's Own Scottish Borderers had driven off Materborn hill and that the 43rd Wessex had struggled against in Cleve.

Schlemm was desperately trying to build a new front, stretch-ing from the Rhine, near Cleve, diagonally southwest across the Reichswald to Gennep on the Maas. Morale in the units was high, despite long route marches to reach the line.

When Cleve fell on the 12th, orders shot back from Berlin: estab-lish a new line. Above all, Cleve must be retaken. Although he had little optimism about its outcome, Schlemm instructed von Luettwitz to launch a counter-attack by 116th Panzer Division to recapture this key city. Tactically, Schlemm was thus setting the pace for his defence of the Rhineland. While the attack would prob-ably fail, it would buy time for his forces to organize and mount a stronger defence in the next confrontation — which might be just a mile or two back.

With the bulk of its forces left behind at Muenchen-Gladbach, the 116th Panzer Division was at little more than 50-per-cent strength. Major-General Heinz Guderian, then a lieutenant-colonel and chief of staff of the division, describes the logistical dilemma to the authors: "When we first reached the Reichswald, our divi-sional tail was still in the Eifel. We came in parts. Because of a lack of fuel, we had to leave behind our reconnaissance battalion and our engineers, who had stayed to repair our tanks. We were not all motorized owing to the shortage of vehicles."

The 15th Scottish Division, taking over the final clearance of Cleve, was alerted to the planned attack through the interception of German transmissions by Ultra (the deciphering system that en-abled the British to intercept many German high-echelon plans and orders). The German Panzer division had joined battle only that day, taking over Fiebig's sector and, because of the manpower cri-sis, absorbing what was left of his men. The counter-attack — hastily planned and with only 14 hurriedly assembled tanks — was easily repelled by the Wessex and Scottish divisions.

Von Luettwitz was no fool. A member of the old Catholic nobil-ity (although the great-grandson of a baptised Jew), his military career dated back to World War I. "The red face, fat body, peaked nose and horn-rimmed spectacles . . . disguise the real man," a British interrogation report summarized. "He might be a college professor or a successful business man rather than a German general of the Wehrmacht. But after a few minutes of conversation his true personality reveals itself. Each word becomes a command, each gesture portrays a person accustomed to having his own way. He is consumed by a bounding energy."

The fact that he had lost one son on the World War II battlefields did not deter him from total commitment. On September 2, 1939 — the day before war was declared — von Luettwitz had been seriously wounded during the German invasion of Poland. After his recovery, he fought on the Russian front. D-Day saw him commanding 2nd Panzer Division in Normandy. Despite being severely wounded again, he managed to extricate his division from the Falaise Gap.

As commander of 47 Panzer Corps during the Ardennes battle, it was he who sent an ultimatum to the American defenders in Bastogne, eliciting the now-famous response of "Nuts!" from Brigadier-General Anthony C. McAuliffe.

Now, after being driven from Cleve, von Luettwitz was determined to stall the British in their advance south to Goch. He launched an attack along the western fringes of the Reichswald near Hau and Bedburg, inserting 15th Panzer Grenadier on the left to maintain pressure on the Welsh troops in the state forest. On the right, he dispatched Major-General Siegfried von Waldenburg's 116th Panzer Division to intercept the Wessex. It would not be the first time that the sleek "Windhund" (greyhound) Division had been brought in to stem threatening Allied forces.

It was aptly named. "In the winter campaign of 1942-43 the commander [Schlemm] took a greyhound with him to the front," Guderian explains. "It became the insignia of our division."

In the months following the Allied invasion of Normandy, the division saw six months of bitter fighting in France, Aachen, Arnhem, and the Huertgen Forest. It achieved a reputation to match its insignia — sharp to identify its prey, swift to pounce on it, and staunch to defend against enemies. Schlemm might also have appreciated that the greyhound's brainpower was as keen as its speed.

In September 1944, however, the morale of the division was shaken when — as had happened to the 51st Highland and the 3rd Canadian Divisions a few weeks earlier — its commander had to be replaced. But it was not incompetence or wounding that led to Lieutenant-General Count Gerhard von Schwerin's dismissal, as it had been for the British or Canadians, but the far more devastating charge of conspiracy and treason. The circumstances were extraordinary.

Von Schwerin, a member of the old guard of the Wehrmacht, had commanded long and intense loyalty from his staff and the troops of 116th Panzer Division. These were for the most part Rhineland men. The Allied enemies penetrating their borders were encroaching on the very villages and towns of their birth.

When von Schwerin was assigned the defence of the city of Aachen on the German-Belgian border, he was convinced that the war was nearing its end and that Aachen would fall within hours to Hodges's advancing First Army. Thirty-two Holy Roman Emperors of the German nation had been crowned in this magnificent 9th-century city. Rather than see it and its populace destroyed, von Schwerin wrote a letter to the American commander pleading that Aachen and its civilian population be spared further destruction.

Hodges never received the letter. Believing that Aachen was strongly defended, he decided to bypass the city. Count von Schwerin's damaging missive fell instead into Nazi hands.

It was not the aristrocrat's first insubordination towards Hitler and his regime. Reputed to have been in support of the July 1944 conspiracy against Hitler, he was described by one noted American historian as ''a non-Nazi, almost an anti-Nazi.'' Fortunately for him, von Rundstedt intervened and his life was spared. ''He was relieved and court-martialled,'' Guderian relates, ''but he was only reprimanded. Afterwards, he became commander of a division in Italy and later he was corps commander there.''

On September 14, von Waldenburg took over the disheartened division. Its numbers had been badly mauled in the Normandy fighting. ''Our officer corps and NCO corps were decimated,'' Guderian states. Von Waldenburg, 47, was a young, energetic officer specifically chosen to succeed von Schwerin because he was ''tactful and adroit in dealing with subordinates.'' He would need all of those qualities to rally the division.

Success bolstered the morale of the formation. On September 17 it helped fend off the Market-Garden assault at Arnhem's last bridge over the Rhine. In November, it stalled the American advance in the horrors of the Huertgen campaign. In December and January, it was a strong adversary in the Battle of the Bulge in the Ardennes. Now it was to form Schlemm's key defence against the Veritable and Grenade forces.

At first light of February 14, 4th Battalion Wiltshires, wide open on both flanks, advanced south on the Cleve-Goch road. The battalion was subjected to shelling "as bad as the worst it had received in Normandy." Two hundred shells fell on Battalion HQ in a 15-minute period. The bombardment was followed by a full-scale counter-attack by von Waldenburg's 116th Panzer Division.

Both sides suffered heavy casualties as counter-attack after counter-attack was beaten off. Corporal Mobel Rexing, a young German soldier in First Parachute Army whose home was in Cleve, recalls the confused and violent fighting that day: "I knew the area, so my commander used me as a driver. He ordered me to bring up some ammunition. When I got to a certain point I was to ask an officer where the fighting was. There was very much shooting everywhere. I had to unload the lorry. The soldier with me was shot. My lorry was full of holes and the motor was damaged. At first I couldn't turn it around."

The two Wiltshire battalions lost 300 men, 200 of them from 5th Wiltshires, whose casualties included the CO and all their senior officers.

Sergeant Leslie Knight scored "a beautiful kill" on a Panther with his six-pounder. One forward platoon allowed the enemy to approach within 20 yards before opening fire. "Coolness and good fire discipline saved the day," the battalion history noted.

In a letter to historian Chester Wilmot in 1946, Major Tony Parsons described the anxiety the 4th Wiltshires had in their vulnerable position:

> In the fighting beyond Cleve the trouble . . . was that our necks were well out with two open flanks. On the German side, the mounting of a large scale counterattack by 116th Panzer Division so soon after their arrival must have been a good piece of staff work. . . . Their tanks and infantry . . . committed all the errors in field craft and tactics which we were apt to imagine are peculiar to British troops. If they had only been content to contain us and whistle something on our right flank we would never have made it.

While Parsons was critical of the enemy's fighting ability, he was not, of course, aware of the juggling act that Schlemm had conjured up to assemble this ad hoc defensive force.

The Wehrmacht — desperately vulnerable at the outset of battle — had been given a reprieve when Horrocks's initial attack lost its momentum. ''We gained time for reorganizing our forces and assembling the reserves that had been moved up,'' General Fiebig noted with relief.

In a handful of days, they had re-created an army — another magic army. They had achieved just such an instant army once before, after being chased over the Seine and then routed out of Antwerp; now another miraculous recovery was in the works.

''The Germans could have the pants knocked off them and next thing you know, they would have exercised this terrific ability to regroup — and there would be a battleworthy formation,'' Major Fred Tilston remembers.

''They seemed capable of creating coherent units out of a ragbag of people who had never seen each other before in their lives — and doing damage,'' Lieutenant-Colonel G.P. (''Timber'') Wood agrees. ''For years, even before the war, they had an amazing training system where every man functioned two up. A private could do a Feldwebel's [sergeant's] job; a Feldwebel could do a captain's. It worked. It produced a skilled army.''

''They fought brilliantly in the Rhineland,'' Major James Gammie considers. ''I think they were brought up from their very youngest days to believe that becoming a German soldier was the very finest thing they could be. They were trained to it: trained to the attitude of being military and trained to the attitude of war. Our chaps were good fighters when it came to the pinch, but they were never trained to that attitude of war.''

This magic German army continued to create havoc with all the British and Canadian units it encountered in the next weeks.

''At the start of our attack we had been faced by one division approximately,'' Horrocks noted. ''Now, nine divisions had been drawn into the battle against us.

''It became a soldier's battle fought by the regimental officers and men under the most ghastly conditions imaginable. It was a slog in which only two things mattered, training and guts.''

7

Chewing Gum Alley

Top Secret. Personal and Eyes Only for CIGS from Field-Marshal Montgomery, 11 Feb 45:
I visited the Veritable area today to study the situation and
to see the conditions for myself. The whole problem is one
of opening up road centres and developing communications. To be in a good condition for further operations to
the southeast we require the full and free use of the road
Nijmegen-Cleve-Goch-Afferden and of all roads inside this
boundary.
   The total prisoners are now about 4000 and our own
casualties about 1000.

THE VILLAGE OF Ramsbury, Wiltshire, was just two flying hours
from the Reichswald, but it seemed a million light-years from the
shell-torn havoc of Hitler's state forest.

For centuries, Ramsbury had nestled sleepily in England's green
and tranquil hills. Now six years of war had had its impact; there
was a new bustle in the air. The young men were long gone, but
many of the villagers were caught up in work on the land or in
one of the nearby wartime factories.

Along the High Street, women with market baskets moved purposefully, ration books in hand, children firmly in tow, to join the
shop queues.

An ancient oak dominated the village green and its aged pub,
the Bell Inn. The usual cluster of older men chatted under its
branches as they awaited opening hours. Over a pre-lunch pint,
the war would be refought (the enemy air raid on Newbury, just
14 miles away, was still uppermost in many thoughts) and won.

See Map 4 (Appendix B).

It won't be long now, lads . . . our boys will be back.

A young woman, Elsie Huntley, stood at the doorway of her parents' tidy stone cottage on the High Street, fair head cocked apprehensively at the sound of approaching aircraft, green eyes focussed on the line of barren trees at the crest of the hill above the town. Beyond, on the plain, was the strip where air ambulances landed their wounded from the battlefields of Northwest Europe. In her arms, her daughter Jean wriggled with an 18-month-old's exuberance, understanding not at all her mother's concern for the father whom she had scarcely seen.

As Elsie Huntley watched anxiously, the first planeloads of casualties from Operation Veritable were landed. It was her torment throughout the war that from her parents' walk she would see ambulances bringing the wounded down the hill from the airstrip, speeding towards the military hospital 13 miles away at Swinden. This "widow's watch" told her, far more accurately and speedily than the news broadcasts, when a battle had been launched and what was its scope.

"They're bringing in a terrible lot of casualties today," she said worriedly to her father. "I'm afraid that there's a big attack going in, over where Peter is."

Over where Peter was, on a dismal February morning, a chain of men braved unceasing fire as they groped through icy, mist-clad bogs to rescue the wounded lying in the battle-stricken Reichswald. Most of the injured men would be moved back to safety and medical help at the regimental aid post (RAP) a mile or two back. The desperately wounded would be rushed by plane to the airstrip in Ramsbury that was Elsie Huntley's monitor of the progress of war and the work of her husband.

Peter Victory Huntley was born to peace. His father had given him the middle name of "Victory" to commemorate his birth at end of World War I. As a lad of 20, he joined up just three weeks after World War II was declared, volunteering as a stretcher-bearer. It would, he thought with youthful optimism, get him out of the drill and discipline of being an infantryman. It would keep him safe.

After five years' continuing service and eight months of non-stop combat, Huntley had learned the irony of that decision. Somewhere along the line, the quest for personal safety had taken a low priority against the survival of the wounded. Time and again he had darted into heavy enemy fire to rescue casualties. During the

Ardennes battle, he had volunteered to stay behind enemy lines with the wounded — surrounded for two days by attacking Germans. (For this act of courage he was awarded an immediate Military Medal by Field-Marshal Montgomery.)

When Operation Veritable unleashed its violence, Lance-Corporal Huntley was again at the forefront as his band of stretcher-bearers plunged into battle. This time it was into the black murk of the Reichswald.

Nothing in the Northwest Europe campaign had prepared Huntley or any of the men of the 53rd Welsh Division for the fearful conditions and awesome challenges of the Reichswald. It was an evil place; it stank of danger. Mature trees formed pillars canopied by thickly interwoven branches, blotting out even glimpses of the sky. The barrage had stripped many of these branches, strewing them about and blocking the narrow paths or rides — now mere ruts of mud — that zigzagged through the woods.

For eight days and nights the Welsh were enveloped by the dark, dank forest, fighting a battle where all the precepts of modern warfare were convoluted, where supporting arms no longer could support, where tactics learned in battle school had little relevance to the realities of forest fighting. The Reichswald was conquered tree by tree, step by painful step, as in battles of an earlier era.

The attacker was committed to advancing along the rides, or else floundering knee-deep through the thick brush beside them. Hulking Churchill tanks followed, roaring and grinding and slithering in the muck. The defender could be just a few yards away, silent, waiting, as he crouched behind a trunk with machine gun or Panzerfaust. Each intersection offered him an ideal location for siting machine guns and 88mms. Small clearings were lethal hunting ground for snipers. The forest became one huge natural ambush.

In the first 48 hours of the Veritable attack, from February 8 to February 10, some 5,500 Welsh troops with their supporting artillery, tanks and vehicles were committed to battle over a track — not 30 feet wide — that was slowly sinking. The heavy traffic concentration on that single, narrow dirt road had rendered it a clinging morass of mud that all who trod it would remember with loathing. They called it "Chewing Gum Alley."

The division's only axis was totally impassable to wheeled vehicles and extremely difficult even for tracked vehicles — the trusty, cumbersome Churchill tank being the sole exception. Jeeps, carriers, and anti-tank guns, even the Crocodiles and Flails from the Funnies of 79th Division, bogged and were abandoned helter-skelter along the route. More than one tank was seen sinking to its turrets in mud.

The Welsh troops (and the English and Scotsmen who served in the 53rd Division) were cut off from contact with the world, swallowed up by the despised Reichswald. They came to be known as the men of the 53rd Woodland Division.

Enemy shells and small-arms fire soon claimed hundreds of casualties, many of them severely wounded and with only the most primitive first aid treatment to ease their pain and discomfort. For many, it would end with a wounded soldier's anguished cry of intense pain and unbearable fear echoing through the darkness: "Stretcher-bearer! Over here! Help me, for God's sake, help me!"

Moving loads back out of the quagmire was a terrible challenge, for this was human cargo. Normally, jeeps were used to carry stretcher patients to RAPs. Nothing was normal in the Reichswald; there was only one way to get the wounded out. For the first four days and nights, the stretcher-bearers braced aching arms and weary backs to lift each litter — one man behind, another in front — and carried the casualties one by one to safety along the hell of Chewing Gum Alley.

"At first, the trees were so dense it was literally dark," Huntley recalls. "Later, after much shelling, the woods became a skeleton. The shrapnel had stripped the branches from the trees; there were just the trunks left. Then it became light, but there was no protection from the shells exploding overhead, not even in the trenches.

"You could hear this cry going up, all along the front, a cry for help. You didn't know where to go first. You had to feel in the dark where his wound was and put on a shell dressing or tourniquet. There was no chance to do anything more, not even to administer a shot of morphine. We just had to get him out fast and get back to the next one, lying there waiting his turn."

For four days and nights the slight, 136-pound stretcher-bearer carried load after grim load out of the forest, and then ploughed back again into its darkness. "You just couldn't let yourself think about it. You couldn't dwell on the fact that you were carrying a man whose legs had just been blown off or who had some really devastating wounds from shrapnel. If you thought about it, you'd never do it."

The dead, he found, must wait upon the living. "There just wasn't time to bring them out, at that point. We concentrated on the living, on the wounded — ours and the enemy's.

"But," the Wiltshire man grins, "we did make use of German

prisoners on occasion and made them carry the stretchers. Some from the Panzer division were pretty defiant about that, but the ordinary German soldier, he'd do it without any objections.''

In its initial thrust, the 53rd Welsh Division entered the forest from the west to secure a narrow strip of high ground along the top of the forest. Welsh units near the edge of the woods on the left flank of the attack glimpsed battalions of the 15th Scottish fighting within a few hundred yards of them as both divisions forged eastwards towards Cleve and its environs.

Only when the Welsh reached the Reichswald's most easterly periphery — a distance of eight miles — would they wheel south to complete the clearing of the 40-square-mile state forest. On the right flank, also fighting within sight and earshot of the Welsh, Jocks of the 51st Highland Division were struggling to secure the lower reaches of the woods on the south and west.

Like the 15th Scottish, the lead elements of the Welsh met a ''bomb-happy'' enemy who had been subdued by the bombardment. They also met the same overwhelming problems of mud and mines. Two brigades of the division swiftly achieved their initial objectives. The 71st Brigade — 1st Battalion Highland Light Infantry, 1st Battalion Oxfordshire & Buckinghamshire Light Infantry, with 4th Battalion Royal Welch Fusiliers in the lead — penetrated the forest on D-Day, securing the high ground to the northeast.

Then 160th Brigade — 6th Royal Welch Fusiliers, 2nd Monmouthshire Regiment, and 4th Welch Regiment, with 1st East Lancashires under command — leapfrogged through them the next day to break through the Siegfried Line and push further eastwards towards Cleve. Finally, Huntley's battalion, 7th Royal Welch Fusiliers, took up 158th Brigade's attack along with 1/5th Battalion Welch Regiment.

By now, the rain had become incessant. The sullen skies had another message for the men: there would be no air support. Communication, forward or back, became impossible. Radio sets ceased to operate in such close country. Battalion commanders, unable to contact their forward companies by wireless, were compelled to move their own headquarters forward with the lead units. Brigade commanders then sought to relay messages to the battalions by runners, who themselves became mired as the mud sucked at their boots.

Sappers of the Royal Engineers worked around the clock, often under fire, clearing mines and laying timber across mudded tracks.

Signalmen toiled to lay lines — and lay them again when accurate German mortar and shellfire cut them. The Quartermaster section performed miracles hauling ammunition, food, and even the morale-boosting rum to the forward troops.

At the sharp end, men crouched in their slits, isolated by the darkness and mud. The eyes betrayed and the ears deceived. The faint stirring heard through the brush could be his buddy, or his commander, or his enemy. Decisions had to be made, and they were made — alone. Initiative and courage soared and heroic acts became commonplace at every level of command. The rulebook was thrown out.

"The majority of casualties were from shell and mortar fire," war correspondent Joe Illingworth of the *Yorkshire Post* reported. "Inevitably they lost a number of officers and platoon commanders, and in the thick of the fighting, junior officers and NCOs suddenly found themselves with increased and urgent responsibilities. There were many instances of platoons being commanded by corporals. Conversely there were instances of battalion commanders who went forward to take the places of wounded company commanders."

In the depths of the Reichswald, commanding officers — out of communication with artillery or armour — forged on without either arm. Devoid of help from the air, isolated from the guidance of senior officers on the ground, they coolly improvised every attack.

The 6th Battalion Royal Welch Fusiliers won its prestigious Siegfried Line battle honours in this fashion. About to put in the attack, the battalion CO, Lieutenant-Colonel K.G. Exham, discovered that it was impossible to get through to Brigade on any available wireless net. This meant that the battalion would have to advance without the support of the pre-arranged artillery plan. Worse, Exham was out of communication with the battalion on his right, which was to put in a simultaneous attack. Nevertheless, he boldly ordered the attack to commence. With the support of a squadron of Churchills from the 9th Battalion Royal Tank Regiment of 34th Armoured Brigade, the battalion took its objective handily.

The 1/5th Battalion Welch, Lieutenant-Colonel J.S. Morrison-Jones in command, advanced from the start line by the light of "artificial moonlight" at 0200 hours on the 9th but were delayed by severe traffic congestion just inside the forest. They finally elected to leave their supporting armour and carriers behind and push on alone. Despite enemy Spandau (light machine gun) and mortar fire, the battalion successfully captured their objective.

To Major Bill Gaade, a company commander in the 4th Royal

Welch Fusiliers, the threat of enemy counter-attack was an ongoing worry. "In very close fighting we knew we would have no support at all. The tanks were bogged. We had no anti-tank guns; the ground was so muddy and quagmired, they couldn't even be man-handled forward. Artillery would have been useless in the trees."

Nevertheless, by improvisation and dogged determination the Welsh Division achieved all its first-phase objectives by 1600 hours on February 9.

But now the battle paused. The momentum of advance was in peril. Throughout the early hours of Veritable, the weather had been the principal enemy. Chewing Gum Alley had deteriorated to the point that it was finally closed down for 24 hours to allow feverish maintenance work. The 71st Brigade persevered in its thankless task of traffic control. Essential movement to the forward areas had to encroach on the 15th Scottish axis, itself a sodden mess. Commanders thought back to Passchendaele in 1917 when troops became bogged down in mud and stayed there, mired in a battle of attrition.

By D-plus-Two, February 10, the horrors of weather had paled in comparison to the hazards of the enemy opposition. If the Germans had been momentarily quelled by the surprise of the attack and its crushing bombardment, they soon rallied. Here too, the Allied delay in breaking out had given them the chance to bring in fresh troops. They were fighting for the first time in defence of their Fatherland, of their homes, and of their families. The Rhineland was their last stand. Never before had the Welsh Division witnessed such vicious counter-attacks or endured such devastating mortar and shellfire.

Just briefly, the fate of the operation hung in the balance. The dream of a rapid "Blitzkrieg" had evaporated all across the Veritable front; the threat of stalemate grew. The 43rd Wessex, just a few miles to the east, was caught up in confusion and traffic chaos; the 51st Highlanders, to the west and south, had run into raging opposition. The American operation had that day been cancelled.

"We have today made definite progress . . . and have captured the Reichswald Forest," Montgomery fibbed to his boss Alan Brooke on February 11, apparently intent on masking the bleak outlook of his campaign.

"It was a close thing," the 53rd Division history recorded with more accuracy. "Conditions became steadily worse from day to day and, if this could have been foreseen in advance, it is likely that the operation would have been postponed. . . . The greatest credit was due to the administrative services who laboured by day and by night to provide the fighting troops with the means to continue their forward move and fight a very determined enemy.''

On the morning of February 11, D-plus-Three, the Welsh offensive resumed in a blinding snowstorm. The 160th Brigade's 2nd Monmouthshires continued their push down the eastern edge of the forest.

Because of some canny foresight by Major John Chaston, company commander of 2nd Mons, infantry had ''married up'' with the tanks of 9th Battalion Royal Tank Regiment with outstanding success. During the pre-Veritable training period near Helmond, in Holland, they developed a new method of fighting with tanks in the forest.

''We came to the conclusion that if the trees were thick enough to stop a tank, they'd be wide enough apart for a tank to drive between them; if they were too close for a tank to drive between, they'd be small enough to be squashed down by a tank,'' Chaston recalls. ''This actually proved to be so. The tanks got through with us. We also had 17-pounder self-propelled Canadian anti-tank guns, of 56th Anti-Tank Battery, Royal Canadian Artillery.

''We used the rides. We would have one company forward with a platoon on either side of the track. They moved up in single file. We kept the tanks and anti-tank guns back. When the riflemen met some opposition which held them up, they'd wiggle up to a tank or to an anti-tank gun and it would get into position and fire a few rounds. This would usually drive out the enemy. We really made quite a lot of progress leapfrogging forward like that.''

The 9th Royal Tank Regiment history records: ''The German Sector Commander, a full Colonel, was captured in the melee at first light. Convinced that the forest was completely 'tank-proof,' the officer protested that such a use of tanks was 'not fair.' ''

The 160th Brigade, with 158th on their right, reached the eastern edge of the forest and wheeled south. At the same time, the 43rd Wessex Division paralleled the pivot, turning south from Cleve along the outside perimeter of the forest.

One of the most critical objectives was to open up the main roads and relieve the supply and communication problems. The enemy's main objective was to delay this advance. Their tactics were shrewd and unnerving.

Major Jack Catley was a ''Canloan'' officer with 1/5th Battalion Welch Regiment, 158th Brigade — one of 673 Canadians who had volunteered in 1944 to fill Britain's shortfall of junior officers, often taking a reduction in rank to do so. By the nature of their job, leading patrols and commanding platoons into action, these junior officers had high casualties. Seventy-five per cent of the Canloan volunteers were wounded and 20 per cent were killed; 49 men were decorated. In the Reichswald, Catley remembers the incessant day and night patrolling that made for those statistics.

"All we could do was advance until fired upon and take out each enemy position as we found it. Then we'd have to go to ground and give covering fire for another platoon to get around our flank for the attack. If you were in the lead platoon it was pretty frightening."

The only cover they had was tree stumps. Even the Churchill tanks weren't much support: "They were too cumbersome for that kind of fighting," Catley believes. "They had no manoeuvrability.

"What the Germans were doing was withdrawing from one position and moving rapidly to a new one where they could keep us from advancing up those tracks. They would bring up their SPs [self-propelled guns], using the tracks as their line of fire, and all they had to do was stand at the far end and shoot. Then they would quickly get into a protected or defilated position by just backing out of the way. That tactic was successful in keeping us off the tracks. By the time we got there, they were gone."

It was on one of these rides that 19-year-old David Edwards, a private in 2nd Battalion Monmouthshire anti-tank platoon, had a bizarre and emotionally charged encounter with death. It was his second such unnerving experience in the Reichswald. During the advance into the forest, Edwards happened to glance into the doorway of a wooden shed on the side of the road. Startled, he saw preparation already under way for those of his unit who would perish in the coming action. "They were making crosses there, little white crosses, all lined up. It didn't help when I realized that these were being made ready for those of us who were about to be killed."

Then, after a week of vicious fighting, a week of wholesale killing, the young Welshman found himself inexplicably conducting an impromptu funeral for an enemy soldier. Edwards and a buddy had come across the dead body of a German paratrooper that was obstructing their field of fire and had rolled it into a trench:

At first it was not a "burial." Then I found myself thinking of his relatives. I took his papers from his pocket. There was a photo of his wife and baby son and a letter to her. In a way, at that moment, it became a burial and I was conscious for the first time of a feeling of futility.

I put the papers in my pocket and in the next moments became involved and forgot about them. It wasn't until four years later that the incident came to mind and I wrote the German wife in Hamburg. She replied to my letter, Frau Wilma Kuhler. She said, "Many women still live in uncertainty and are waiting in vain for their husbands to return home. As painful as it is to get the news that your husband has fallen, it is better than living in uncertainty. You are quite right, wars settle nothing."

On D-plus-Four, February 12, 36 Weasels (small, broad-tracked carriers of American design) were sent up to the forward units to carry the wounded back to the RAPs. The task of Lance-Corporal Peter Huntley and his band of stretcher-bearers was immeasurably eased.

There was little else of cheer in this bleak campaign. Captain Peter Dryland, adjutant of 7th Battalion Royal Welch Fusiliers, recorded dismally in his field diary:

Monday, 12 Feb: Another day of pushing on in this miserable forest through wet and cold. Supply problems for food etc. most difficult. Only a couple of thousand yards from edge of forest.

That same evening, Dryland's sister battalion, the 6th RWF, endured a vicious counter-attack. Newly arrived troops of von Luettwitz's 47 Panzer Corps, supported by self-propelled guns, infiltrated between the forward companies near Battalion HQ. They were finally driven back by aggressive action of infantry and tanks of 9th Royal Tank Regiment attacking on their flank.

It was to be 9th RTR's last action in the Reichswald; their strength was too depleted to continue. Of the 52 tanks that had begun the operation, only 14 remained battleworthy six days later. Many that had bogged had to be left for weeks as irrecoverable. Some had their traverses wrecked by guns hitting trees. A few had been shattered by 88mm projectiles moving with incredible speed down the track, smashing the hulks of the tanks and killing their crews.

On D-plus-Five, Dryland wrote:

Tuesday, 13 Feb: O Group at 0700 hrs. We eventually moved at 1130 hrs to clear a few more blocks of the Reichswald. The rides are now very bad, only tanks and "Weasels" are of any use, carriers get bogged. Another small battle to get our objective in SE corner of the forest.

That same day, 71st Brigade was finally released from its road maintenance tasks, and it joined the division in the attack. Patrols probed enemy positions as the brigade neared the edge of the wood.

By the 14th, the Reichswald had been cleared (though not completely mopped up), marking the end of this phase of the battle. The good news of the day was that the weather finally improved. "It was the first good flying day for some time," the division history recorded. "84 Group RAF flew 804 sorties on the 30 Corps front on this day. Typhoons accounted for 32 separate cab rank attacks."

The "Typhies," as they were affectionately known by grateful riflemen, operated as close as 250 yards ahead of the lead infantry battalions and were particularly effective in knocking out enemy threats such as 88mm gun positions. In attack, a squadron of 12 Typhoons would fly in tight formation in a circle over the target (usually identified by the field artillery firing pink smoke). Each Typhoon would peel off in order, one at a time, to commence its deadly dive. This squad attack earned the nickname of "cab rank."

The good weather added a bonus to the men who had been slogging through the Reichswald mud. "Had my boots off for the first time since the beginning of the operation. Had my first wash and shave only yesterday," Dryland noted happily on the 14th.

However, the forward battalions of the 53rd Welsh Division were to discover that fighting their way into the Reichswald — dangerous and difficult as it had been — was not the end of their problems. Fighting their way *out* of the forest would pose even greater problems as they faced a fresh and determined enemy.

8

The Highland Fling

THOMAS RENNIE WAS A MAN with a mission: to avenge the German capture of the 51st Highland Division at St. Valéry.

On June 12, 1940, Rennie, then a major, crouched helplessly by the bomb-shattered ruins of the small French fishing village of St. Valéry-en-Caux. The Nazi Blitzkrieg that had swept through Belgium, Holland, and France was descending on the division, forcing it back into the sea.

The rest of the British Expeditionary Force had already been evacuated from the beaches of Dunkirk. For eight days, the Highland Division had fought on in a futile attempt to hold back the waves of German tanks and infantry. Their numbers were decimated; all hope had vanished. They were cut off and alone. The Luftwaffe crammed the airspace as they dive-bombed and strafed the beleaguered and battle-weary Highlanders. Scottish guns fell silent, their ammunition gone. The bitter order was sent out from the 51st's commander: Surrender!

Suffering the humiliation and anguish of capture and imprisonment by a mocking enemy, the proud Scots swore that they would force the Germans back across their borders to ultimate defeat.

Rennie made a bold escape from his captors, rejoining the reconstituted 51st as commander of the 5th Battalion Black Watch and later as a brigade commander, as the division fought in the North Africa campaign at El Alamein and later in Sicily.

In 1944, Rennie was given command of the British 3rd Division, the first to land on the Normandy beaches. But his Highlanders, fighting on the same beaches, were in trouble. The long years of combat had taken their toll. Not only had casualties depleted their

See Map 4 (Appendix B).

numbers, but the keenly honed fighting spirit of the Highlanders had dulled. Their commander inspired little confidence.

On July 16, 1944, Field-Marshal Montgomery sent a message in code to Alan Brooke:

Top Secret. Personal and Eyes Only for CIGS from Field-Marshal Montgomery:
Regret to report that it is the considered opinion of Crocker, Simpson and myself that 51 Div is at present not, repeat not battleworthy. It does not fight with determina- tion and has failed in every operation it has been given to do. It cannot fight the Germans successfully. I consider the divisional commander to blame and I am removing him from command. I consider that the best man to put to 51 Div in its present state is Rennie and I have confidence he would bring it up to its former fine state.

Late in July, his arm still in a sling from wounds incurred in the Normandy battle, Thomas Rennie — now Major-General Rennie, CB, DSO, MC — was brought in to replace the hastily deposed division commander. An officer of 7th Battalion Black Watch describes the electric effect of this new command: ''The morning we knew he was coming back — he was arriving at 11 a.m. — you just *felt* the morale go up. We were back on top again. Rennie under- stood the Scots; he was an old friend coming back.''

From that moment, the 51st regained their spark. ''He was the most accessible and least pretentious of generals, of whom every officer and man could boast as a friend,'' the chronicler of the Black Watch related. ''He had an impish sense of humour, and a cheer- fulness which was proof against every crisis or disaster. . . . He had a great flair for doing things the right way, and complete con- fidence in his judgment, which was shared by all around him. His courage was far beyond the ordinary, but there was nothing flam- boyant about him. . . . There was no Jock in the Division who did not know his duffle-coated figure.''

Rennie made it his business to ensure that non-Scots — the English and Irish reinforcements, and the Canadian Canloan officers who came into the line with the Highland Division — were quickly assimilated as ''instant Jocks.'' These honorary Scotsmen soon picked up the flavour of their adopted fighting mates: the wry humour, the verve, the clannish loyalties, and — above all — the flat-out, hell-for-leather Lochinvarian courage.

Now, on February 8, 1945, Operation Veritable was bringing these feisty Highlanders closer to their day of vengeance. Just planting a boot firmly on enemy soil sent spirits soaring.

With inelegant haste and satisfied gleams in their eyes, Jocks paused at the German border to unbutton flies and anoint the hostile land. Soon they would push their enemy back to the Rhine, back to Berlin — just as they had been pushed back to the sea in France five years before.

Top Secret. Personal and Eyes Only for CIGS from Field-Marshal Montgomery, 10 Feb 45:
Today has been spent in trying to cope with the very difficult situation regarding roads and communications leading forward in the Veritable area. There are plenty of troops available but the difficulty has been to get them and their supporting weapons forward. The delays caused by these factors have given the enemy time to scratch up some units to oppose us and heavy fighting has taken place today in Cleve and Hekkens.

While the 15th Scottish and 53rd Welsh Divisions found that their main enemies in the early days of Veritable were weather, floods, and chaotic traffic, the 51st Highland ran smack into strongly organized enemy resistance. One of the division's first main objectives was Hekkens; its final one was the major town of Goch, six miles beyond — and the Germans' most heavily defended fortification.

Because of the narrow front, General Rennie decided to use only one brigade to spearhead the attack — Brigadier James Oliver's 154th (two Black Watch battalions, the 7th and 1st, and 7th Battalion Argyll & Sutherland Highlanders with 5/7th Battalion Gordon Highlanders under command). The 152nd Brigade (2nd and 5th Seaforth battalions and 5th Queen's Own Cameron Highlanders) was to pass through them and cut the important Kranenburg-Hekkens road that bisected the forest from north to south. Both brigades would emerge from the Reichswald some five miles distant at the important crossroads town of Hekkens.

The third brigade — the 153rd (5th Black Watch and two Gordon Highland battalions, the 1st and 5/7th) — was assigned the task of seizing the wooded plateau in the southwest corner of the forest, a known enemy observation post. From there they would fan westwards, back towards the forward defence line of First Canadian Army on the Maas. This move was intended to clear the enemy from the flat ground between the river and the Reichswald on the extreme right flank of Veritable's thrust. In addition, it would free up the vital Mook-Gennep and Hekkens-Gennep roads.

In their first phase, the 51st would be penetrating the Siegfried Line's strongest defences, but intelligence reports had made light of the opposition they could expect.

"One thing I learned in the Reichswald Forest was never to believe your briefing," recalls Major Donald Callander, Commander of B Company, 5th Queen's Own Cameron Highlanders. "You are told you will attack a 'stomach' battalion, all over 40. What happens overnight is that the Germans change units and send in incredible fighters. I learned always to say to my men, 'We've got the best German troops against us, but we're the best British troops in 51st Division. They're going to be tough; we've got to be tougher.' Those Reichswald men *were* tough."

The lead battalions for the 51st attack were the 1st and 7th Black Watch. The latter found out within a few minutes just how tough those Reichswald defenders were. As the 7th Battalion approached the forest, snipers suddenly opened up. Company commander Major Allan Lowe and two of his platoon commanders were the first of the Watch to fall.

Major Thomas Landale Rollo, who was responsible for the 7th's start line, remembers the eerie circumstances of Lowe's death: "Allan Lowe's company came up for the attack. I said to him — he was an old friend — 'I'll see you soon.' He said, 'You'll never see me again. I'm going to be killed.'

"Of course I replied, 'Don't talk nonsense.' But it shakes you — two nights before, he had cleared out and gone away to Brussels, unknown to anybody. When I saw him later he said it was 'the last chance I'll ever get.' It wasn't that he was depressed; he was completely in control of himself. Yet he had a feeling that that was it.

"Allan crossed the start line. He had his signaller with him carrying the wireless. It was a mad thing to do because the Boche picked up right away who the commander was. Within 200 yards a bullet went right through him."

The 5/7th Gordons incurred their first casualties from friendly guns when Major James Gammie, commanding B Company, was wounded. Gammie was experiencing that very battle risk that had deeply concerned Brigadier Stanley Todd of First Canadian Army.

"One gun began firing short and we were getting hit from behind," Gammie relates. "Our own artillery people tried to stop it but they weren't successful. There was just nothing they could do."

Despite the most dedicated effort by the artillerymen, there were to be other instances throughout the campaign where a single recalcitrant Allied gun would kill or maim their own troops. Some shortfalls would hit a tree and explode. These tree bursts — from friendly or hostile guns — were lethal. Shell splinters and shattered branches spiralled down on the helpless men below. Slit-trenches offered only partial protection.

Yet most men advancing under a barrage were quick to forgive the odd errant shell. Major-General John Graham (then a major with 7th Battalion Argylls) was himself wounded when one of his own supporting guns fired 300 yards short. "We were just so glad to have it. We'd rather it was too close than too far away."

Despite stiff opposition, the brigade reached its objectives on time. Next morning it was the turn of 152nd Brigade to leapfrog their positions forward.

Canadian Canloan officer Lieutenant Ross LeMesurier, a platoon commander with B Company of the 5th Queen's Own Cameron Highlanders, spent only 24 hours in the Reichswald and advanced only one mile. But during those hours he was locked in dramatic, two-fisted fighting that culminated in one of the most bizarre charges in the history of the entire campaign. Emerging bloody but clearly unbowed, LeMesurier was proof of the infectious nature of Highland ferocity. He was indeed one of Rennie's "instant Jocks."

The battalion had advanced only a few hundred yards into the forest when the trouble began. The lead company met heavy fire from Panzerfausts. B Company, Major Callander in command, was ordered to right-flank the enemy.

"Machine-gun fire began spraying the area and there was a terrible crack in my ear," Callander recalled. "I went down. Somebody shouted, 'The company commander's hit!'

"I got up and shouted back, 'I'm bloody well not!' and ran on. (I later discovered that a bullet had gone through my mess tin.) Three of the Jocks were badly knocked out — Spandau fire is so rapid it can almost cut you in two — and the men were pinned down, scared to get up in the heavy fire."

Callander rallied two platoons for a bayonet charge, personally leading them across a 50-yard clearing towards the enemy position.

"I jumped over a ditch and looked back. A German came out of a trench and started shooting at my men. His back was to me. I shot him with my Schmeisser; I had no choice.

"Then I called Battalion HQ and asked them to send somebody up on the left. A very brave man — Jim Melville — came up with his company and cleared them out."

Meanwhile, LeMesurier, who commanded the lead platoon in the day's events, had been wounded three times during the morning. A sniper's bullet had pierced his steel helmet, making a neat crease across his head before exiting out the back. An hour or so later, a piece of shrapnel lodged in his back. Not long after that, another fragment punctured his left arm. "Just nicks," the Canadian shrugged off to his concerned commander.

These were heady times for a 21-year-old, fresh out of college and tasting adventure. LeMesurier had on this day seen men perform such acts of courage as were rarely witnessed even once in a single lifetime. He was crackling with excitement, beyond fatigue, beyond fear, even beyond pain from his wounds.

Night fell. It was pitch black and bitterly cold, and B Company moved forward under a steady downpour. Each man had to hold onto the bayonet scabbard of the fellow in front to avoid losing his way. Ahead was the company objective, a track crossing the muddy ride on which they were advancing into the forest. Ahead, on this cross-track, a squad of Germans were laying mines.

"Panzerfausts opened fire on us and hit my wireless operator," Callander remembers. "He was very badly wounded and his moans were attracting German fire. I said to LeMesurier, 'For Christ's sake, Ross, you've got to do something!' "

At this point, LeMesurier grabbed a phosphorus grenade (normally used to create heavy smokescreens) from his pouch. "I pulled the pin," he recalls, "but as I was about to throw it, a bullet hit the grenade and caused it to explode in my face, throwing bits of flaming phosphorus on me. I had my eyeglasses on and got a big blob of phosphorus on my right lens so I couldn't see — but the glasses saved my eye. I scooped up handfuls of snow and mud to rub on my face and stop the burning."

By now the Germans were advancing towards them. LeMesurier rallied his platoon to charge. He fell to one knee to fire his Sten gun. To his horror, the gun — never a reliable weapon — jammed.

"Ross threw down the weapon, grabbed his trenching tool, and went roaring off after the Germans," Callander continued. "He was a big man, Ross, and when he ran at them screaming like a madman and waving the shovel, the enemy took off!''

"I remember hitting one of them in the back of the neck,'' LeMesurier recalls. "He crumpled; I thought he was dead. I swung at another, just a glancing blow on the shoulder, but he kept going in the dark. I was getting too far in front of my boys by then so I figured I'd better get back to my platoon.''

"I met Ross soon after,'' Callander said. "He still had a lot of mud and phosphorus on his face where he had rubbed it on. Bits of the phosphorus glowed in the dark.

"I told him he had to go back but he refused. He said, 'I'll see you through, Donald.' My two other platoon commanders had been killed. Ross and I were holding the show together. He wouldn't go back until it got light and the Seaforths came through. I put him up for an MC — it should have been a VC.''

The 2nd Battalion Seaforth Highlanders had been battling forward on a parallel line to the Camerons, meeting the same stubborn resistance. The Seaforths, accustomed to open battlefields, had had little experience in forest fighting. They soon discovered its hazards.

"The Reichswald was a mean sort of place to try and fight in,'' recalls Captain Maurice Carter, Canloan officer and company commander with 2nd Seaforths.

"We hadn't gone very far on our first night when we ran into heavy sniper fire. A lot of men were killed or wounded. We also found that our artillery shells bursting in the trees were doing almost as much damage to our own people as they did to the enemy. Then we started receiving Spandau fire: just two German Spandaus, but each with a good firing position on opposite sides of our trail. They held up our entire battalion. We tried to outflank them, tried all the tactics, but we just couldn't seem to find our way around in any strength. In the morning, when we laid on an attack, we found they'd gone.''

Those woods were mean and ugly for the enemy troops as well. On February 9, Lieutenant Hans Hueneborn, 22, a platoon commander with the German 2nd Parachute Regiment, led a reconnaissance patrol of 10 men into the Reichswald.

"I was three days in the woods,'' Hueneborn recounts. "My commander, a major, said I was to report to him in the cellar where he had his headquarters. I was just 50 metres from the house when I saw the British soldiers — there were many tanks. I shot three tanks with my Panzerfaust. I believe they were damaged. Then a grenade hit the trench where we were and I was wounded. We were in danger of being surrounded and captured. I called to my men, 'Run and duck, run and duck! Get under cover in the cellar!' and we got away. That night, I walked out of the forest and went to my parents' house in Haversum.''

On D-plus-Two, 2nd Battalion Seaforth Highlanders incurred over 100 casualties in a bitter action to clear the Kranenburg-Hekkens road, which cut through the heart of the forest. Two forward companies came under intensive mortar and shellfire from Germans dug into the rear of the road. An anti-tank gun opened up on the lead tanks with the Seaforths, temporarily immobilizing them. Still under fire, the two Highland companies fought their way across the main road and dug themselves in.

The acting CO of 2nd Seaforths, Major Ian Murray, gambled boldly and saved the situation. ''Profiting from the enemy's concentration on our two forward companies, I pushed through my two reserve companies and they reached positions flanking the two forward companies on this road. We'd have been rather a thin red line if there had been a counter-attack. It was tough going. Fortunately the Camerons came through us with flame-throwing Crocodiles.''

By now, the Jocks were experiencing that ''other enemy'' — the miserable conditions of rain, mud, and deteriorating roads that had been tormenting the 53rd Welsh and the 15th Scottish.

There was only one track that led into the forest, and it was a bad one. To make matters worse, they had to share it with the Welsh. It was, as one Jock recalls, chaos: ''Up this one route quantities of vehicles, guns and men were sweating, swearing and squabbling for priority rights. The Argylls wanted to come through on to their objective, the gunners wanted to come through and take up their positions for the morrow's shooting programme, the battalions of the Watch wanted to get up their food and greatcoats: nobody knew what the hell the Welsh wanted.''

''Very quickly the axis began to go,'' recalls Lieutenant-Colonel G.P. (''Timber'') Wood, then commander of the Pioneer Platoon of 7th Battalion Argyll & Sutherland Highlanders. ''I was bringing carriers and mortars forward. It was black and wet and the track was in a terrible mess. The road was suddenly blocked and I — a lowly lieutenant — went barrelling up, saying, 'What the hell are you doing here?' This chap boomed at me that he was Brigadier

CRA [Commander Royal Artillery] 53rd Division reconnoitring how to get his guns forward on the same track!

"At that stage the whole thing had become an administrative problem rather than a bloodbath. How do you get the guns forward? How do you get warm food up to the soldiers, how do you get the casualties out — this became an increasing problem."

Looping south and west, the final brigade of the 51st Highlanders' assault — 153rd Brigade — had the task of clearing the entire area between the Reichswald and the Canadian line along the east bank of the Maas.

Encountering ruts of mud two feet deep, 1st Battalion Gordon Highlanders also had to leave most of their transport behind. They did retain one Weasel carrying 500 tins of self-heating soup, "a notable example of good-housekeeping in the field," the Gordon history observed drily.

By the afternoon of D-plus-One, the acting CO of 1st Gordons, Major Martin Lindsay, was nearing the Mook-Gennep road a mile or two short of the Canadian FDL. Lindsay had reduced the operation to a series of ten carefully planned limited objectives, with artillery, mortars, and a troop of tanks from 107th Royal Armoured Regiment (34th Tank Brigade) coordinated to shoot the men onto each of their objectives. As they were moving due west, their supporting field regiment was sited to the north and northwest. The Gordons had the somewhat discomfiting experience of advancing towards the very fire that was protecting them.

A sharp encounter with the enemy was resolved with typical Highland verve. C Company had crossed a deep valley, thick with dugouts and deep trenches, and was approaching the small hamlet of De Hel, unaware that it was a German battalion headquarters.

"The Germans were all around us," Company Sergeant-Major George Morrice describes. "I was able to get our company piper — Piper McLaughlin — into a trench and he played the pipes. It had a great effect on the Germans. We fixed bayonets and charged and were able to round them up. We captured an enormous number of prisoners at their headquarters. I caught the CO of the battalion and disarmed him myself."

The day closed with another bayonet charge — and yet another shrill note from the bagpipes — that again saved the day for the Jocks. Lindsay had received urgent instructions to knock out a German strongpoint astride the Mook-Gennep road that was threatening the brigade advance. Taking command himself, Lindsay organized a company attack that night. As they left the start line, the lead platoon was ambushed and the platoon commander was wounded in the leg by a stick grenade (a high-explosive grenade with a wooden throwing handle). Fighting their way out, they advanced to a group of farm buildings where the enemy was entrenched. Lindsay ordered two minutes of rapid fire from every available weapon and then rushed the buildings — from the rear. The ruse was successful. Six Germans were killed in the first rush and a great many were taken prisoner.

"There was a cheer and a burst of Sten," Lindsay recalled, "and a wild surge forward, and in a moment a shout of 'Kamerad' and a column of Huns, seventy-one in number, came running out with their hands up. . . . We went forward in the moonlight, climbing over broken walls and piles of rubble interlaced with a honeycomb of trenches. I was afraid some enthusiast in the [Canadian] front might shoot at us, so I passed the word back to the two pipers with Company HQ to play the regimental march, and before long we heard the distant strain of 'Cock o' the North.' . . . [Then] we heard the pipers of the Camerons of Canada and knew we had not far to go."

But Lindsay had another hurdle to surmount before he reached safety. As three of the men in the lead platoon led the way to the Canadian line, there was a sudden explosion and the company commander 10 yards in front of Lindsay fell groaning to the ground.

"It was obviously a schu-mine," Lindsay decided. He yelled at everyone to stand exactly where they were. "We shouted at the top of our voices to the Canadians for pioneers with mine-prodders and stretcher-bearers. I looked around and realised now that we were in a narrow no-man's-land, only fifty yards wide, between the German and Canadian positions."

Lindsay waited, frozen to the spot, standing on one leg, not daring to put the other to the ground. Finally the wounded men (for one of the Canadian rescuers had by now also stepped on a mine) were carried out by stretcher-bearers. Each step of the way was carefully prodded first. Lindsay followed them to safety, planting his feet precisely in the footsteps of the Cameron ahead.

On D-plus-Two, 5th Battalion Black Watch made a dawn assault across the Niers River and entered the village of Gennep. The Germans reacted sharply and the battle raged for two days with many close, hand-to-hand fights. Major Alec Brodie, whose zany antics could be counted on as a powerful morale-booster in any Black Watch operation, was seen "walking down the street, which was whipping with bullets, carrying an umbrella, up. When asked why he was doing this, he replied that it was raining. And so it was," the battalion reported, "although nobody else had noticed it."

The capture of Gennep freed the Allied engineers to construct a 4,000-foot Bailey bridge across the Maas that would be opened on February 20 to become the axis of the 52nd Lowland Division and units of No. 46 Royal Marine Commando when they joined battle two weeks later.

The main artery of the Siegfried Line ran through the market town of Hekkens. It was strongly fortified with concrete blockhouses and elaborate defences. Enemy troops were lined up, waiting, along the anti-tank ditch with automatic weapons sited on the road leading from the forest. At 0100 hours on February 11 (D-plus-Three), 5th Seaforths laid on an attack but were pinned down for a day and a night by the heavy fire. They could neither advance nor retreat, and their only cover — a short length of road ditch — was not even deep enough for a man to stand in. At one point troops had to lie three deep to avoid being shot.

Spandaus fired tracer at stomach level. Shells burst in the trees, throwing great splinters of metal and wood at the men lying prone in the ditch. Some of the forward companies were so close to the enemy they could hear the German NCOs giving their fire orders.

The CO, Lieutenant-Colonel John Sym, was hit in the neck by a rifle grenade but refused to evacuate. He requested tank support but was told they could not come up until morning. Throughout the desperate night, waiting for the tanks, casualties mounted. Stretcher-bearers took terrible risks moving the wounded out. Ammunition ran low and men risked their lives carrying fresh supplies up the ditch.

When the tanks finally arrived, a German 88mm came to life, forcing them back. Shortly before noon the CO, who had worked ceaselessly restoring and maintaining order on the line, collapsed from his wounds. Finally, Brigade sent up the order to withdraw. Major Hector ("Hac") Mackenzie, company commander with 5th Seaforths, saw his best friend killed trying to pass the message forward.

"The adjutant, Donald Monro, came over — he had grown up

just down the road from me, an eldest son — and he said, 'I've got to get up to the forward companies and give them the order to withdraw.'

"I said, 'Donald, you can't go forward. It's impossible.' But he insisted. 'The CO said I must.'

"Ten minutes later he came back on a stretcher. He'd tried to cross the road from one company HQ to the next and in the middle of the road he was shot."

The tanks returned, giving the battered battalion cover to withdraw. Their casualties after two nights' fighting were 94.

After so savagely beating back the Seaforth assault, the Germans were preparing to withdraw to their next defence position — a favourite tactic to unsettle the Allied advance, and one that was usually successful. In this instance, however, they were confounded by the fast action of two Black Watch battalions. Under a heavy bombardment by the whole corps artillery, the riflemen rushed the town.

"The infantry kept so close behind the barrage that they were in on the Huns before the latter knew what was happening," the division history recorded. "If ever an action was won by complete cooperation of gunners and infantry, it was this one."

Over 300 German prisoners were taken with barely any casualties. Major Landale Rollo interrogated a German officer shortly afterwards. "He told me, 'If you had been 10 minutes later you wouldn't have got us.' But we were so close behind the bombardment they were still all in the cellars. We got in just as it lifted. Another few minutes and they would have got away."

The 5th Seaforths' diarist had grudging admiration for the enemy's stern defence in the Reichswald battle: "The Germans who fought so well . . . and who were to cause us so much trouble before the battle was over were what Major-General Rennie used to call 'those bloody little Para-boys' — the hand-picked parachute troops, mostly very young, who were as good as anything the German Army had. They were tough and obstinate and they fought like fiends. When our flame-throwers were finished that day they were still shouting: 'Come and get us, you English bastards' through the trees at the Camerons. We did not like the Para-boys, but we respected them. They were good fighters."

On February 12, Montgomery signalled Field-Marshal Brook:

Enemy resistance against Veritable is becoming greater and
the operation is drawing up north most of the immediately
available German reserves. . . . We have made steady
progress. We now hold the road centre of Cleve securely
and own the whole of the Reichswald Forest and have
pushed the enemy well south of Gennep at which place
we are building a Class 40 bridge which will be ready for
use on Thursday morning. Our prisoners now total 5000
and our casualties total 1100.

Progress may have been "steady" but it was slow, painfully so.
Clearly, the flooding of the Roer dams and the subsequent postponement of Grenade were badly hurting the northern attack. Until
the Americans could launch their half of the pincer operation, those
"Para-boy" reinforcements would continue to make the Veritable
front hot.

9

The Outlook Seemed Bleak

Top Secret. Personal and Eyes Only for CIGS from Field-Marshal Montgomery, 14 Feb 45:
Enemy resistance is stiffening in the Veritable area and very heavy fighting has taken place today, chiefly east of the Reichswald Forest in the area of the Square Wood and further to the southwest about Kessel and Hommersum. Some savage counterattacks had been put in and these have all been beaten off with no loss of ground to ourselves and with some steady progress and gains. In the north 3 Cdn Div now have a battalion on the Rhine facing Emmerich.

THE OUTLOOK ON D-PLUS-SIX must have seemed bleak indeed to General Harry Crerar, Commander-in-Chief First Canadian Army. Unless Horrocks's 30 Corps broke out of the narrow, waterlogged bottleneck between the Maas and the Rhine, Operation Veritable would continue to be limited to a single corps attack.

Once they got south of the bottleneck, the Rhineland would open up to allow more divisions into the line. Until then, Crerar could not launch his long-planned phase two offensive: Lieutenant-General Guy Simonds's Operation Blockbuster, which would expand the offensive to a two-corps front. This important attack was to be staged on the enemy's last Rhineland defences: the Calcar Heights, Udem, and the Hochwald Forest. Only when these strongpoints were cleared could they forge a passage to the Rhine.

Not only was Crerar's army behind schedule by six days, but his line had not developed into that solid V-shaped battering ram with which he intended to drive through to Goch and Calcar.

A number of prime objectives had not yet been achieved. Goch

See Maps 4 and 5 (Appendix B).

had yet to be captured, and the vital high ground between Cleve and Calcar — Moyland Wood — had not been cleared. There still were few roads available to move up troops and supplies. The dream of an armoured breakout was still just that: a dream mired in mud. On all fronts, German fighting morale showed no indication of wavering.

True, some objectives at the periphery of the line had been reached. On the left (east) flank, Spry's 3rd Canadian Infantry Division had cleared the flooded west bank of the Rhine as far as Emmerich. On the right, Rennie's Highlanders had captured Gennep, on the Maas.

It was in the critical five- or six-mile stretch at the centre of the attack, however, that Schlemm — powered by von Luettwitz — had held back 30 Corps from reaching its targets. The 5th Battalion Wiltshire Regiment (43rd Wessex Division) had been stopped in its tracks south of Cleve, with 200 casualties including the CO and all but one of the officers. The 51st Highland Division was still held up at the Niers River. The 53rd Welsh Division had fought its way through the Reichswald but had run into furious opposition when it tried to break out of the forest.

Besides coping with the terrific pressure the Germans were exerting against his forces, Harry Crerar was also experiencing enormous pressures from his own side as well. He found himself in the usual squeeze play. His relationship with his boss, Montgomery, was far from comfortable. He was constantly having to hold the hand of his other boss — the Canadian Parliament. An irksome side issue was the persistence of the media of both countries in referring to the exploits of the "Canadians" of First Canadian Army in the battle, ignoring the high proportion of British troops involved.

On February 14, Crerar had lunch with his corps commander, Lieutenant-General Guy Simonds, instructing him to take over 30 Corps's left flank at noon the next day.

At 42, Simonds was the youngest general ever to command a Canadian corps in battle. His skill in improvisation during the Normandy battle had earned him widespread admiration — especially that of his commander-in-chief, Montgomery. He had effectively turned night into day and sporadic warfare into non-stop 24-hour action. By adapting Montgomery's tactic of bouncing searchlights off low-lying clouds to create artificial light, he enabled the troops to fight through the night.

To establish and maintain the line of advance of infantry and tanks onto their objectives in a night attack, Simonds marked the way by firing phosphorescent tracer ammunition from light anti-aircraft Bofors guns at regular intervals over the heads of the attacking force.

Perhaps his greatest contribution was devising the means of transporting infantry troops into battle swiftly and in relative safety. Simonds achieved this by removing the turrets and guns from armoured gun carriers, known as Priests, to create the incomparable Kangaroos. Each was capable of carrying a dozen infantrymen into action in its "pouch," in tandem with their supporting armour.

Throughout the Northwest Europe campaign, Simonds had proven himself an effective — and ambitious — corps commander. Since the onset of Veritable, however, he had been sidelined, waiting for the initial force to break out of its bottleneck. His divisions had been under Horrocks's command. Tantalizingly ahead was the opportunity that Operation Blockbuster would give him when he gained command of the 60,000 men from three infantry divisions, one armoured division, and an independent armoured brigade. Before he could unleash this powerful formation towards the Rhine, however, the objectives of the first phase had to be achieved, and these were still eluding the Allies.

Simonds did not tolerate delay charitably.

Top Secret. Personal and Eyes Only for CIGS from Field-Marshal Montgomery, 12 Feb 45:
I visited all the divisions of 9th army on the Roer front today and examined the problem in that area. The conditions in the river valley are appalling and Grenade is impossible at present. It may well be one week or more before we can launch it. Meanwhile Veritable must carry on alone and it is therefore bound to go slowly.

By the 13th of February — four days after the Germans detonated the Schwammenauel Dam — the flood levels of the Roer River had peaked at just over 11 feet (the mean depth being two to five feet). Ninth Army engineers at Siersdorf Castle anxiously scanned the charts updated hourly in the war room, waiting for a drop in the water level.

While the infantry and engineers geared up for the big assault, Ninth Army Intelligence and Reconnaissance Section worked intensively to detail the strength and skill of the enemy they would encounter. From close communication with British and Canadian intelligence units, I & R knew that the Germans had sideslipped their strongest units north, but they badly needed to know exactly which troops had been inserted into the line in their stead. The only way to discover the German defence buildup was to take prisoners.

As well, combat engineers sought data that would assist them in constructing bridges and detecting minefields. Patrols were dispatched nightly, taking terrible risks — often not returning — to capture prisoners and secure information essential to the success of Operation Grenade. They studied the streams, the currents, the terrain of the enemy banks, the sponginess of the ground, the locations of freshly laid mines and barbed-wire entanglements, and the positions of enemy outposts.

Patrol headquarters were set up in cellars of farmhouses deep in the front. The emphasis on creature comfort in many of these created a bizarre contrast to conditions awaiting the men on patrol in the bitterly cold and wet February nights. In one such room, a handful of GIs sprawled in overstuffed chairs reading Stateside magazines. Pin-up girls covered the walls. Bread, jam, and pickles were spread on a table next to some Dresden china and glasses.

"Company Fox has got so much glassware that it uses different glasses for every drink," Lieutenant Stanley Golub said. "The only reason some of the guys don't prefer it to a rear area rest center is on account of the patrols to the other side of the Roer."

Only a few hundred yards separated cozy niches like this from sodden dugouts under the noses of the enemy.

Three engineers on the 30th U.S. Division front were swept downstream and drowned when their pneumatic boat capsized. Mines took their toll. Lieutenant John Coester of the 171st Engineer Combat Battalion was seriously injured when he stepped on a schumine. The explosion alerted the enemy, who concentrated heavy fire on the minefield.

"It was midnight," the men later recounted. "The patrol had to lay flat but tossed first aid packets to Lieutenant Coester. The patrol leader, Lieutenant David Gibson of 309th Engineer Combat Battalion, cleared a way through the schu-mine field and got to Lieutenant Coester. He rigged up slings, using scarves, belts and even jackets, so the patrol could drag the wounded officer to safety because it was impossible to stand up." Coester was pulled out of the line of fire this way.

On another such patrol, 10 men, faces blackened, crowded sombrely into a dank cellar in the German town of Himmerich. It was a deadly cold night. Their mission: to cross a mile of enemy-held territory to the German stronghold of Hilfarth and probe its defence positions.

"Bring back prisoners," Captain Wallace Chappel, company commander with 134th Infantry Regiment, warned Staff Sergeant James Moore, leader of the small patrol.

The men studied the sand-table model representing the 1,500 yards of lethal terrain that separated the American lines from the enemy's. They noted the canal, the minefield, the barbed-wire traps, the water-filled anti-tank ditch, and finally, the town set into the west bank of the Roer River.

Chappel glanced worriedly at his watch. It was nearly midnight. A patrol that was due back at 2200 hours was late. "Hold your men until the others get in," he instructed Moore.

Finally, Moore's patrol left. Slithering, crawling, inching across the killing ground, they approached two rows of houses that marked the anti-tank ditch. They observed that Hilfarth was strongly fortified. Pillboxes were disguised as summer cottages, with walls of reinforced concrete, some even with simulated windows painted on them. The Germans, they noted, had brought up self-propelled guns to cover the Roer Bridge.

Suddenly there was a guttural yell. A German guard had spotted them. He lunged at the nearest American. In the struggle, Private Joseph Kelsoe was knocked out. Moore groped frantically for his knife and killed the German, but it was too late. The alarm had been sounded. Swiftly, the patrol broke up and made for their lines. Through the early hours of the morning, nine of the men trickled back to safety.

The young rifleman, Kelsoe, was taken prisoner. An SS officer interrogated him harshly, slapping him when he refused to divulge any information other than name, rank, and number. Later, he overcame his guard and crawled back to his own lines, under heavy enemy fire the whole time.

The information detailing the German defences that this small band brought back provided one more important piece in the intelligence puzzle.

One of these patrol units, Lieutenant Roy ("Buck") Rogers's daredevil Night Raiders of 407th Infantry Regiment (102nd Infantry Division), was to capture worldwide admiration. Staff Sergeant Rufus ("Bud") Wilkes was in that unit. His skill is reflected in his decorations: he was awarded the Silver Star, the Bronze Star cluster, the Purple Heart, and the Croix de Guerre in the European campaign.

"On my first patrol — that was before Rogers's Raiders was formed — we didn't get across. The boat sank about midstream and we had to scramble through freezing water.

"Shortly before the Grenade operation they asked for volunteers for this new patrol group. There were about 40 of us, under command of Lieutenant Rogers of Minneapolis — nicknamed 'Buck.' They sent us back for special training for a couple of weeks. Our main job was to make these forays over the Roer and infiltrate into enemy territory up to a mile or so behind the lines.

"We would steal over very quietly in darkness. The boats would hold three or four men, so we'd send one boatload for reconnaissance patrolling, and maybe three boatloads for combat missions. You didn't want to get too many boats at once across that river," Wilkes pointed out.

"Sometimes we were sent to bring back prisoners. One night — we were just on a recce — we ran into a bunch of Germans. We were going down a little road. There they were, in a dugout. Well, we lay still and doggone if they didn't come out and walk right down the road where we were. We let them get close enough and then we let 'em have it. A couple of them that we didn't kill we brought back.

"Other times we would be sent to find out the position and strength of enemy strongpoints. We would have to draw their fire on us deliberately in order to pinpoint the information. That was pretty risky stuff. That German in the MG nest — you'd be trying to get around him — you didn't know when the next step was going to be your last.

"But with all those patrols, not one of us was ever badly wounded. We were just so well trained and so close."

War correspondents assigned to 102nd Division wrote glowingly of their boldness. A key ingredient in their success was probably Rogers's painstaking preparation for each raid. "The boys all work strictly according to plan," he would explain quietly. "We don't take chances."

Seventy-five air photo-reconnaissance missions flown in February confirmed the findings of these frequent patrols on all fronts. Air recces in Cub planes gave infantry officers and artillery forward observation officers (FOOs) an opportunity to observe the ground over which the attack was to be made.

Clandestine traffic across the river was not all one-way. Having shifted the bulk of their defences north while the Americans were immobilized by the flood, the Germans were now desperate to discover when Simpson would re-stage the attack. Enemy patrol activity was reported almost daily. A reawakened Luftwaffe flew a number of reconnaissance and combat sorties.

To thwart the enemy from observing his buildup of forces, Simpson ordered that elaborate security precautions be undertaken. New code names were devised for road signs and telephone exchanges. Camouflage was emphasized. Troop movements were limited to nighttime. All unit identification had to be removed from men and vehicles.

The paper war continued. German leaflets were found in the 29th Division area. One featured three pictures: destroyed tanks, dead Americans, and general misery at the front. The reverse side carried a photograph of Manhattan at night featuring a can-can dancer. The caption: ''3000 miles afar from here . . . what a life!''

The Americans retaliated with leaflets dropped in bombs (4,500 in each bomb) or fired by artillery. Over 1,400,000 propaganda pieces were thus disseminated to German troops and civilians.

''Axis Sal'' — Arnhem Mary's propaganda sister — cooed out in daily broadcasts from Aachen that the Germans were ready and waiting for the American attack. But both sides were aware that while the waters of the Roer steadily rose, there would be no attack.

On Valentine's Day, D-plus-Six of Operation Veritable, four battalions of the 15th Scottish Division's 46th Brigade — 2nd Glasgow Highlanders, 9th Cameronians, 7th Seaforth Highlanders, and 10th Highland Light Infantry (brought in to reinforce the brigade) — launched an attack on von Luettwitz's forces in Moyland Wood. Water on the approaches had reached hedgetop height, creating small unprotected islands on which the troops were forced to advance.

Moyland was not the orderly state forest that the Jocks and Welsh had faced in the Reichswald. It was actually a series of pine-covered knolls, just over two miles long and one-third of a mile wide, extending southeast from Bedburg (below Cleve) towards Calcar. From the crests of these knolls, the Germans blocked all Allied attempts to advance south.

Von Luettwitz had chosen this narrow ridge on which to concentrate 47 Panzer Corps's main defences. From here, his three divisions — 6th Parachute, 15th Panzer Grenadier, and von Waldenburg's 116th Panzer — could fan out in several directions to block the Allied advance south. Securely dug in atop the high ground, sheltered by the thick trees and dense foliage, these crack units seemed impregnable. Their guns pounded at will at the vulnerable troops stuck out in the open below them. Across the Rhine, just six miles behind the line, their heavy artillery provided lethal back-up firepower.

No detail had escaped German attention. Booby traps were rigged, even to wiring the ID tags of their own dead. Trip wires and concertina wires were crisscrossed through the trees, some attached to tin cans hidden in the bushes. A machine-gunner, one hand on the trigger and one hand on the wire, was ready for any interloper who attempted to breach the black woods.

After some initial success the two lead battalions of the 15th Scottish assault — the Cameronians and Glasgow Highlanders — became engaged in close and bitter fighting and were pinned down by heavy fire from German units dug in on the crest. The next day, the Cameronians again launched an attack and met the same avalanche of fire.

In desperation, their CO, 26-year-old Lieutenant-Colonel Edward Remington-Hobbs, called in three Churchill tanks from his supporting armour (4th Battalion Coldstream Guards) to shoot the battalion forward. It was an unorthodox tactic. Tanks had seldom been employed in forest fighting over very soft and rolling ground because they carried the risk of becoming bogged down and disabled. This in fact became the fate of the first two tanks. The third, however, managed to get partway up the hill, providing sufficient covering fire for the troops of one company to reach the knoll. Isolated and without food or greatcoats, these forward troops hung on. "I ordered them to fight all night if necessary," the CO stated grimly. The men responded.

In the confused fighting that followed, enemy and friend were so intermingled that even battle-experienced men were baffled. "We fought as we'd never fought before," Lieutenant A.W. (Sandy) Waddell, the platoon commander, reported. "I saw men sit down and cry, not through fear alone but through frustration."

Meanwhile, 10th Battalion Highland Light Infantry battled to reach their objective on the eastern flank of the attack. Intense fire and savage fighting drove them back, but one company managed to hang on. "We were out there alone for three days," Lieutenant Robert Jackson (a Canloan officer) recalls. "The Jerries were on both sides of us, counter-attacking and bombing the hell out of us. The wireless was out. We tried to get a runner back and he was killed. Finally, as the Jerries were lined up coming at us, the Canadian Black Watch came up from behind and drove them back."

On February 15, the brigade came under command of 3rd Canadian Infantry Division, and the next day, the 7th Canadian Infantry Brigade took up the Moyland battle. The exhausted Jocks were pulled back.

"As the Cameronians left the battle area," a war correspondent recounted, "Lieutenant-Colonel Remington-Hobbs saluted his men."

On the eastern fringes of the Reichswald, von Luettwitz's 15th Panzer Grenadier Division was being pushed back, but they were not letting up in the stubbornness of their defence against the Welsh fighting their way out of the forest.

On the night of February 16, 7th Battalion Royal Welch Fusiliers put in an attack to clear the final 800 yards of woodland and break into open ground at the Asperden bridge. The Germans held the bridgehead and could not be budged. Later, the 7th RWF heard an explosion, which proved to be the enemy detonation of the bridge.

Standing outside the command post next morning, after spending an anxious night with the CO coordinating the battle, Captain Peter Dryland was wounded by mortar fire. He became the battalion's 70th casualty in this action. He later wrote to his parents about the awful guilt he felt in leaving his casualty-ridden unit:

Saturday, 17 Feb: Put on a stretcher, said farewell to the Colonel [Lieutenant-Colonel G.F.T.B. Dickson]. I could see him in his camouflage jacket, his face anxious behind his horn-rimmed spectacles. I could hardly face him, I felt so ashamed, I had let him down so very badly. He knelt beside me, took hold of my left hand and started to rub it gently. "It's all right old Peter," he said in his soft voice. "Don't worry." But I knew that we had already had 7 officers killed or wounded in a week.

On D-plus-Eight, February 16, 4th Battalion RWF sent out a fighting patrol to reconnoitre a house some 400 yards out of the forest. On reaching their objective, they were ordered to dismount and search a building.

"The Germans saw the men emerging from the forest and thought it was a major breakout. They opened up with everything," Major Bill Gaade recalls.

A red Very light signalled that the patrol was attempting to return. The battalion put down a large smokescreen to cover the withdrawal. However, overwhelming enemy fire from self-propelled guns, mortars, and small arms kept the patrol immobile. Three further smokescreens were laid down, but the enemy fire only increased in intensity. It wasn't until nightfall that the hapless band were able to filter back, leaving half their number sacrificed to the attack.

"Those men didn't have any cover at all," Gaade said. "They had a lot of casualties. It was a tragedy; they shouldn't have been dismounted as they were.

"However, by drawing all the enemy fire on us, it allowed the 43rd Division on our left to advance unimpeded."

In that spirit of cooperation, the four British divisions drove the Germans out of the Reichswald and its environs. Seven-eighths of the forest had now been captured by the 53rd Welsh Division and the 44th Royal Tank Regiment. (The remainder was cleared by the 51st Highland Division. Within earshot, the 43rd Wessex and 15th Scottish had swept across its northern edge and battled their way down the eastern boundary.)

The infantrymen and troopers had fought without relief for 10 days — and 10 nights turned into days by the ghostly illumination of artificial moonlight. Casualties soared. Nearly one thousand Welshmen became victims of the Reichswald, killed or wounded.

"It was not an exaggeration to say that the successful attack on the Reichswald Forest, under the weather conditions of the time, was an operation unique in military history," the 53rd Division history records with justifiable pride.

But it had been a miserable and ugly way to make history.

By February 11, the Highlanders, too, had fought their way out of the southern edge of the Reichswald towards the open tank country that Crerar had envisioned for his armoured breakout. But here, too, the February thaws and the enemy confounded his plan.

The two tributaries of the Maas — the Niers and, below it, the Kendel — were swollen to twice their normal 30-foot widths. The Germans were effectively provided with natural anti-tank defences that blocked the Allied forces from a clear advance to Goch and thence to the Rhine.

Goch, a town of some 10,000 inhabitants, occupied a strategic position as the pivotal point of the Germans' Siegfried Line defences. It seemed that the closer First Canadian Army got to Goch, the more determined was the opposition.

From the high ground above the river flats of the Niers and the

Kendel the enemy had the whole 30 Corps axis under observation. While the British owned the road, they still could not use it. Towns astride these rivers, like Gennep, Hekkens, Kessel, Viller, Asperden, Hervorst, Grafenthal, Hassum — normally of little import — became major enemy strongpoints imprinted on every Highlander's memory. Every yard gained was paid for with fierce counter-attacks and extremely heavy shelling and mortaring. It would require five more days of intensive fighting before the Highlanders smashed through these fortified villages, freeing up the road and breaking through to the outskirts of Goch.

Now that they were out of the forest, however, the infantry were no longer fighting it out alone. Every advance by the Jocks was preceded by massive bombardments that pounded the German fortifications. The new Canadian "land mattress," which fired hundreds of rockets at a time, pulverized the towns. Men fought through nights turned brilliant by the searchlights of artificial moonlight and by the raging fires. Typhoons roaring through the clearing skies unleashed their rockets on enemy strongpoints often just a few hundred yards ahead of the advancing Scots. The ground would not yet permit armour to join battle, but the infantry arm of the Guards Armoured Division — 32nd Guards Brigade — was fighting alongside the Highlanders.

The 5th Seaforths captured Asperden (a bare two miles northwest of Goch) almost unopposed, and then endured two days and nights of vicious shelling by the enemy. "It was not pleasant," they remembered. "But we drew solace from the fact that at least the Germans were pounding German houses instead of Dutch ones. It was good to see a wall with 'Ein Volk, ein Reich, ein Fuehrer' written on it slowly knocked to pieces."

At Hervorst, another village just north of Goch, a company of Camerons encountered enormous concrete pillboxes. These had walls three feet thick, camouflaged with a cover of earth and grass and with only a concrete entrance and gun slits showing. Each housed mutually supporting 150mm guns.

They dropped a grenade down one chimney, but its course was deflected. Then came retaliatory enemy Spandau fire, mortars, and rockets from the infamous Nebelwerfer. (This multiple-barrelled German mortar was known to the troops as the Moaning Minnie or Screaming Meamie, for the morale-shattering scream emitted by its bombs as they neared the target.)

Major Donald Callander, the company's commander, had a small army of armour under command: a troop of Churchill tanks, a troop of flame-throwing Crocodiles, a troop of AVREs capable of firing penetrating and destructive charges (petards), and a troop of Canadian 17-pounder anti-tank guns. Nevertheless, every attempt to capture the fortification was repelled. Two of Callander's men were killed, others wounded. Enemy infantry were seen forming up for a counter-attack. The AVRE officer suggested he fire a salvo of petards at the small steel embrasure on the side of the pillbox.

"An enormous explosion took place and the earth shook," Callander relates. "The Germans came out. They were half concussed. Some were bleeding from the nose and black from the dust and dirt of the explosion; three had been leaning on the wall where it was hit; they were dead."

One final objective — the escarpment overlooking Goch — remained before the attack on the town could be laid. This was assigned to Brigadier Essame's 214th Brigade (43rd Wessex Division), which was battling its way south out of Cleve. In a remarkable marathon of a little over 24 hours, the 4th and 7th Battalions Somerset Light Infantry (SLI), the 1st Battalion Worcestershires, and the 5th Duke of Cornwall's Light Infantry spearheaded the Wessex's 8,000-yard drive from their positions three miles south of Cleve to Goch, which erupted on that vital escarpment.

The initial advance swept forward 3,000 yards before nightfall on February 16. "The attack took the form of street fighting in small villages and house clearing," 7th SLI CO Lieutenant-Colonel Ivor Reeves wrote to his wife. "Every house, whether farm buildings, in villages or towns . . . has reinforced cellars, many of which are constructed so that their tops are just above ground level, where there are slits to fire from. Practically every house as we advance has to be cleared of enemy, which is a slow and exhausting process, but we go on."

Reeves singled out two factors that contributed to his success: "The cooperation of our tanks (4/7 Dragoon Guards) and infantry was excellent, and a high standard of tactical skill within companies was most noticeable."

A third factor, perhaps, was a canine morale-booster that accompanied them: an Alsatian dog "rescued just in time from the flames in a farm that was burning," the CO told his wife.

Essame then ordered 4th SLI to take up the chase. Half an hour after midnight, with the battalion's CO, Lieutenant-Colonel Christopher Godfrey ("Lippy") Lipscombe, himself laying the white tape to mark their FUP, the battalion surged forward.

"A night attack over country which had never been seen in daylight, and starting from ground only just captured, involved a step into an unknown bristling with incalculable hazards," Essame noted of the unique assault. "The enemy was completely taken by surprise."

Major Victor Beckhurst, commanding A Company, 4th SLI, pulled off a brilliant bayonet charge to capture one of his objectives — a farmhouse barricaded by stakes and a three-strand barbed-wire fence. The enemy was alerted to the attack and opened fire.

"I called forward a Wasp flame-thrower," Beckhurst recalls. "The chap pressed the button to release the flame. Unfortunately it didn't work — all that happened was that the flaming fluid came dribbling through the barrel, dropped onto the ground just in front, and lit up the whole area. My soldiers were silhouetted. Luckily, we sustained only a couple of casualties as I had to hurriedly order 'Back! Back!' "

Under cover of artillery fire called down by the CO, the men crawled forward and cut gaps in the wire.

"We were only 150 yards short and the artillery stonk was still going down. As soon as it finished I shouted 'Charge!' and with fixed bayonets we charged in and took three officers and about 37 German prisoners. The German officer who was commanding the enemy troops said he thought we were only a patrol as he had never known the British to attack by night."

By dawn of the 17th, 4th SLI reached the escarpment on a front of 1,000 yards dominating Goch. The ridge rose 60 feet, dropping sharply on the south side towards the town, only three-quarters of a mile beyond.

Now 7th SLI was ordered to consolidate the area. Again it was a running fight from house to house, with the tanks firing themselves almost out of ammunition. In one battle in the small village of Imigshof, the enemy surrendered only when every house in the town had been set alight. On 7th SLI's left, 1st Worcestershire and the 5th Duke of Cornwall's Light Infantry had also reached their objectives against equally strong resistance.

"By nightfall, they looked down on the chimneys of Goch on a front of 4,000 yards," Essame reported. It had been a major conquest in the hands of the inspired Westcountrymen.

For ten days the English, Scots, and Welsh had slogged their way south, launching attack after attack against an enemy who would at times lash back with lightning speed, or — eerily — simply vanish into the shadows.

The distance covered had been not much more than 10 miles. Ten miles in 10 days by a hard-punching, experienced force speaks volumes of the resistance they encountered.

"Fighting in that terrain was not dramatic," one platoon commander recalled. "It was more reminiscent of the static, slow-moving battles of World War I. There were no great battalion attacks, no very big butcher's bill, just fiddling on and on, wet and miserable. . . .

"Suddenly, all that changed. Suddenly, there was Goch."

10

Suddenly, There Was Goch

Top Secret. Personal and Eyes Only for CIGS from Field-Marshal Montgomery, 17 Feb 45:
In the Veritable area we are now closing in on Calcar and Goch and I think it is quite likely we shall have both of these places by tomorrow night. Southwest of Goch we have now captured Afferden and the woods east of it on the north side of the road. The prisoners are mounting and fresh formations are appearing on this side and it looks as if Veritable is going to draw in all the available enemy reserves. This will suit very well. The target date for Grenade is now fixed for 23 Feb and Cdn army will have to continue fighting alone until then, but the results should be that Grenade will have an easier task and go all the quicker. The weather has been very foggy and misty today and little air action has been possible.

AS THE EARLY MORNING MISTS lifted on the battle-torn escarpment overlooking Goch on D-plus-Ten, troops from two Scottish divisions massed to administer the death-blow.

It would be an epic conquest. The capture of Goch would mark a turning point in the Rhineland battle. It would secure the hinge for Montgomery's pivotal attack and — the Allies hoped — open up hard, dry tank country for an armoured sweep to the Rhine.

Goch and its environs would be Veritable's final battle for the 15th Scottish and 51st Highland. These two divisions — or what was left of them after the carnage of the Reichswald and the struggle to reach and capture Goch — would be pinched out of battle. They would play no further part in the Rhineland operation. Instead, it was to be their mission, for which they would train during the next four weeks, to help launch the armies of three nations across the Rhine.

Goch was a bustling road and rail centre, an attractive old town of some 10,000 souls. The Niers River carved a gentle U through its centre. Below it were the main housing estates and the large cobbled town square, where in happier days farmers brought their produce to sell at market, and children gazed wistfully at rows of sweets and savoury tarts in bakeshop windows.

All that was gone now. The townsfolk were gone, evacuated. The shops were gone, smashed by Allied bombs and shells. Goch waited silently for her invaders to make their final move.

General Schlemm was as aware as General Crerar of the strategic importance of Goch. The railway line and three important roads ran through it. The Niers River bisected it. The Siegfried Line fortified it. Goch was the heart of the Rhineland.

Schlemm had been counting on Goch as the pivot of *his* defences, too. The fortifications of the town had been hastily completed, although the RAF bombing raid on the night of February 7 had sorely disrupted the final construction. One hundred and fifty foreigners brought in for forced labour had been killed in the raid when bombs fell on two schoolhouses where they were quartered.

The Germans had dug two anti-tank ditches: the outer one sloped down some 20 feet and encircled the town on three sides, all but the southern periphery. The second, a thousand yards closer in, completely encircled the town. Concrete emplacements, barbed wire, and strategically laid mine belts had transformed Goch into a fortress. The embrasures of many of the pillboxes were of four-inch steel, mounted in two feet of concrete. Their approaches were covered by trip wires and mines. Even the cellars of houses had been reinforced. Machine-gun fire could sweep the streets through concreted slits.

The RAF had not succeeded in smashing these fortifications. Only the shops, houses, church spires, and factory chimneys had been reduced to rubble — providing additional protection to the defender. Here too, the Allied ''cratering is to be accepted'' decision was to backfire horribly on the infantrymen who fought there.

The German architects had made one error, however, that was to prove detrimental to their defence. Perhaps convinced that the ditches would keep out the tanks, they omitted to site anti-tank guns at each pillbox. The formula that the Highlanders had so successfully evolved to put such pillboxes out of commission — mask it with smoke, smash it with an AVRE, and flame it with Crocodiles — had consequently robbed the Siegfried Line of some of its bite.

On February 18, Schlemm and Commander of Army Group H General Blaskowitz met in the map room of First Parachute Army's

HQ in Xanten. The gloom of the day was only matched by the despondency on the faces of the staff officers grouped around the room.

Schlemm's gamble had failed. He had hoped that von Luettwitz's delaying actions would contain the Allied troops pouring south from Cleve and the Reichswald until he could move more units into his new defensive line south of the forest. But although 47 Panzer Corps had fought hard for a week, neither they nor General Straube's 86 Infantry Corps had been able to prevent First Canadian Army from reaching the outskirts of Goch.

Schlemm ordered General Eugen Meindl, humourless, sharp-eyed commander of 2 Parachute Corps, to take over the defence of the town, with Lieutenant-General Wolfgang Erdmann's 7th Parachute Division, Major-General Walther Wadehn's 8th Parachute Division, and the remnants of Major-General Fiebig's 84th Infantry Division under his command. Meindl was instructed to hold the line from Goch to Udem, a town partway between Goch and the Rhine. Von Luettwitz was assigned the defence of the line from Udem the rest of the way to the Rhine.

The 43rd Wessex's dramatic night advance had pre-empted Meindl's plans. When he arrived at his new headquarters the next morning, he learned that Goch was already under attack.

The plan for the capture of Goch called for a dual assault by the two Scottish divisions, each with two brigades up. The 44th Brigade would spearhead the 15th Scottish Division's attack on the sector of town north of the Niers on the afternoon of February 18. When the 15th Scottish had established a footing, 153rd Brigade of the 51st Highland Division would launch an assault south of the river just before midnight.

The 15th's original intention was to lay on a set-piece attack, including all supporting arms. Considering the ease with which their patrols had penetrated the outer defences, however, 44th Brigade Intelligence now wondered if the garrison strength was so minimal that the town could be rushed.

Patrols from 7th Battalion Somerset Light Infantry, penetrating beyond the outer anti-tank ditch, had reported little activity from the enemy. Brigadier the Honourable H.C.H.T. Cumming-Bruce, 44th Brigade's commander, and Lieutenant-Colonel the Lord Charles Tryon, commander of the Grenadier Guards supporting them, had gone forward on their own to make a reconnaissance.

Proceeding unmolested through enemy territory almost as far as the inner ditch, they also concluded that opposition was slight.

They shot back a change of orders. The lead battalion, 8th Royal Scots, was instructed to send one company forward immediately to charge the ditch and, if possible, to push forward into Goch. The inner ditch had a sheer 10-foot slope and was some 25 feet wide. The coup-de-main therefore depended upon the success of the AVREs in laying their bridges across the ditch so that the troops in armoured personnel carriers with their supporting tanks could swiftly penetrate the enemy line.

Immediately, the mission ran into difficulties. Instead of bursting into Goch, the infantry company became pinned down under heavy machine-gun and self-propelled gun fire. Major David McQueen, their commander, describes the difficult experience:

The bridge that the AVRE was carrying to span the anti-tank ditch — it was about 25 to 30 feet long — got stuck in the trees on the approach. We were able to free it, but it had been put off-centre somehow by hitting the trees. Consequently, while the bridge finally went down all right, its release jammed and it couldn't disengage from the tank. The APCs couldn't get across. By this time the opposition had come to life and had started to engage us. The lead platoon crossed on foot but couldn't get any further and was pinned down. The rest took up a company defensive position around the tank that had stuck.

While McQueen dug in on the near side, his platoon sergeant was isolated in a very unpleasant no-man's-land. Two enemy SP guns opened up.

"I had the whole of my platoon along that anti-tank ditch for the rest of the day while the others fought their way down the road to us," Sergeant James Cornwall recalls. "We were under fire from the Germans, who were in houses behind us, and then our own artillery began to fall on us."

Meanwhile, the brigade commander reverted to his original plan, launching a fresh attack in mid-afternoon. The 6th Battalion King's Own Scottish Borderers, following the Royal Scots, also ran into problems on the ditch, and it wasn't until nearly midnight that the two battalions penetrated the town and established small bridgeheads.

As Cornwall's platoon struggled over the last ditch and onto the railway tracks leading into Goch, they were pulled up short by a sharp command: "Who goes there?" an English voice challenged them. "We thought, 'Oh well, that's all right, it's only another of our platoons.' Then they let go with everything they had. It was a German post, and they killed three or four of my men, including my young Bren gunner."

On their left, 6th KOSB was engaged in a grenade-slinging match and was heavily counter-attacked. Casualties were high and two platoons, becoming isolated, were encircled by German paratroopers.

"We attacked and got three houses," Sergeant Alex Kidd, 6th KOSB, remembers. "Company HQ moved into one, but the Germans were in the next house not 30 yards away. They kept bazooking us all night. It cost us a lot in casualties."

The next morning, 6th Battalion Royal Scots Fusiliers joined battle; with the help of 4th Battalion Tank Grenadier Guards and a section of flame-throwing Wasps, the three battalions cleared the houses down to the river by evening. By boldly plunging into the core of the enemy defences, 44th Brigade forced the Germans into submission.

The German garrison commander, Colonel Paul Matussek, had transferred his reserves to try to stem the attack. Six hundred German POWs were taken, including almost all the men of 190th Fusiliers, reinforcements who were caught handily as they rushed in on bicycles.

"Our general was Tiny Barber — the tallest general in the British army," Kidd recalls with a grin. "He came up to our position in Goch the next forenoon and started talking to some of the lads. One of them — a little chap who used to sell newspapers outside of Wolverhampton Station before the war and had a very broad Staffordshire accent — he told General Barber he'd caught plenty of prisoners. 'Was it easy?' asked the general. 'Oh, yes sir!' he answers. 'I even got one with his trousers down!' General Barber had a good laugh on that one."

Then the 51st Highland swung into action. General Rennie gave 152nd Brigade the task of securing bridgeheads across the anti-tank ditch the night of February 18. Major Ian Murray, acting CO of 2nd Seaforths, had the satisfaction of duping the enemy.

"There were three main roads leading into Goch. The enemy expected us to use one of these. The 5th Seaforth was astride one and they were shelled very hard. We decided to advance up a small country road and we had hardly any shelling at all. The battalion laid on three separate company attacks — a technique that had been successful for us before — and was firmly on its objective with a bridge over the ditch within four hours of leaving the start line.''

In the early hours of the 19th, 153rd Brigade took over in the actual clearing of all the town south of the Niers. The lead battalion, 5th Black Watch, had as its objective the sector as far as the town square. The next battalion, 5/7th Gordons, would continue the attack to the railway line. Finally, 1st Battalion Gordon Highlanders would turn southwards and complete the clearance of the town and its outlying farmsteads.

At first, the Watch met only silence. The defenders were evidently not expecting an attack from that quarter. Coming in behind them, however, 1st Gordons soon found that the ''Hornets,'' as Company Sergeant-Major George Morrice had dubbed the German troops, had ''woken up'': ''We were being shelled to pieces. Our A Company commander, Major Arthur Thompson — he had just arrived the day before — looked out of his door and was shot by a sniper, along with several of his chaps. Our objectives were very strongly defended.''

''The rest of the day was perfectly bloody,'' Major Martin Lindsay, acting CO of 1st Gordons, noted. ''It was painfully obvious that first impressions were wrong and the enemy had every intention of defending the town. Resistance stiffened. The street was badly cratered by debris so we could not use tanks or Crocodiles, and any sortie by the bulldozer was met by aimed small-arms fire from snipers.''

Lindsay ordered two companies to form up for an attack on the enemy's left flank, laying on tanks and Crocodiles to support it, and smoke to conceal it. The attack was a complete success.

''For once we beat the Germans,'' Morrice gloated. ''They laid down a very heavy mortar stonk on our position, but we'd already left for the flank attack and they couldn't catch us. We went right into the town square and occupied buildings there. Shelling and mortaring were the heaviest we had experienced — it was only the excellent German cellars that saved us from having heavy casualties. I think Goch was one of the stiffest battles of the war — a real frightening time.''

Early in the morning of February 19, 153rd Brigade captured Matussek and his staff while they were eating their breakfast. (''But not,'' insists the 6th Guards Tank Brigade history, ''while they were in bed as reported in the *Daily Mirror*.'') Matussek had in his possession a pencilled note from General Erdmann, 7th Parachute Division commander: ''Blow the bridges and hold the line to the last.'' Matussek considered the order absurd. How could he hold to the last with a lot of uncoordinated troops and a Volkssturm battalion of five companies who tended to fade away?

By now, however, Meindl's reinforcements of seasoned troops were pouring in to bolster Goch's defences; half the town remained to be cleared. Supported by a weight of artillery and mortar fire, the Germans clung tenaciously to their positions. Bitter house-to-house battles ensued.

For the Jocks, house-clearing was a slow, dangerous, and exhausting business. Street by street, house by house, doorway by doorway they inched their way forward, skulking down back gardens or mouseholing through walls to elude enemy fire positions.

The scream of rockets and shells created disconcerting echoes. Piles of rubble and half-torn walls cast odd, almost human shadows. Was that a German sniper in the house ahead? Throw a grenade through an open door or window, wait for the explosion and charge — fast! — top floor first, Sten gun at the ready. . . . Check the window across the road, get that sniper! Then down to the cellars, a grenade tossed ahead to subdue opposition — round up the prisoners!

Up one side of the street, down the opposite side — they quelled each isolated pocket of resistance as they went. But, because they were Jocks, there was a moment for humour, too. ''Things had quieted down a bit next morning, just a few shells coming across,'' Colonel Thomas Landale Rollo recalls. ''Up the street comes a Jock, dressed as if he were going to a wedding, with a tail coat on. His 'bride' [a Jock] had a female dress on — right on the front line. What a real boost to morale!''

Confused fighting continued to rage for the next 48 hours. During that time, Lindsay was ordered to launch a company attack at Thomashof, a large farming complex on the southern outskirts of Goch.

Nothing was known of Thomashof. An aerial photo showed seven rather large outbuildings. Lindsay was deeply concerned. His two experienced companies were still fighting to hold the outskirts of the town. The only company he had available to take on the task was ill equipped to achieve it. Its commander, Arthur Thompson, had been killed that morning while talking with his second-in-command. The latter, Major Bill Kyle, was himself inexperienced and had been considerably unnerved by the incident. The only other officer, Lieutenant Charles Howitt, had had no combat exposure at all. One of the three platoons was commanded by a corporal, another by a sergeant.

As he had 10 days earlier on the Mook-Gennep road, Lindsay therefore elected to lead the attack personally. Just before dawn, the company silently crossed the open fields and dispersed without incident into several of the barns. At first light, however, the enemy came to life. The 18-set radio proved disabled, and Lindsay himself went back to organize reserves and coordinate tank support.

When he returned — delayed because all but one driver of the Crocodiles had been unwilling to cross the open ground — he found disaster. The company had vanished, its commander, Kyle, with it. A stretcher-bearer, who had been taken prisoner and escaped, reported that the Germans had been in hiding and had laid on several fierce attacks shortly after dawn. Howitt had been killed and the rest of his platoon scattered. Then the company was overrun.

The bodies of nine or ten of their number lay near the outbuildings. It was evident that these men had struggled manfully. But the capture of 43 soldiers with their commander told another sort of story. It was a tragic testimony to the demoralizing effect on men when led into battle by inexperienced commanders. Rudderless, they crumpled.

The simple farmstead of Thomashof was to extract even more casualties. Before nightfall, another Gordon company had 10 of its number killed in the quest for this objective. In the next days, both Black Watch battalions incurred terrible casualties before 5th Black Watch finally captured it in a midnight attack, taking 80 German prisoners.

"They found in a hay-shed a secret hidie-hole in the ground, full of Germans," the Watch history recorded. "The incident seemed to cast light on the experience of a Gordon platoon a day or two before which had disappeared after having captured a similar building. The technique was apparently to lie low until the attackers were lulled into the belief that the show was over, and then to emerge and catch them unawares."

Since the start of Veritable, 11 days before, the Intelligence Section had persisted in underestimating enemy strength. At Thomashof, on February 19, it outdid itself.

Top Secret. Personal and Eyes Only for CIGS from Field-Marshal Montgomery, 19 Feb 45:
We captured Goch today and the 15 and 51 divs are engaged in mopping up the town in which we have so far taken 400 prisoners. We have also now got the use of the road Goch-Calcar except at the Calcar end. Having captured Goch we have now got to fight for that ground which will enable us to use the road. I spent all today up in the Reichswald Forest area and visited most of the British divs and found the troops all in tremendous form and very well pleased with themselves. The total of prisoners captured in the Veritable Operation is now nearly 10,000 and we estimate that a total of 20,000 Germans have been put out of action. A very great many German dead have been buried by our troops. The recent dry weather has helped us in the road problem and the rivers are going down. Our total casualties in Veritable Operation are now 3,800 and all these are British except for 400 Canadians.

Even after the fall of Goch, the Germans were still able to plaster the Scottish front with intensive shelling. Casualties mounted. On the 21st, an enemy bombardment knocked out six lieutenants from 1st Battalion Gordon Highlanders, one of these killed by a direct hit on a command post. So heavy was the fire that a smokescreen had to be laid to allow British ambulances to evacuate the wounded.

Of the 203 casualties suffered by the 1st Gordons in Operation Veritable, 139 had occurred during the battle for Goch. Twenty-four men had been killed in action, 66 wounded in action; 49, including all the men of the ambushed A Company, were listed as missing (although believed to be POWs). Ten officers and 230 ORs (other ranks) were brought up to reinforce the battered battalion.

On the same day that German mortaring reached a crescendo, the men were assaulted from another, less predictable direction as well. Scottish troops noticed that the familiar drone of RAF bombers seemed louder than normal.

"We heard the RAF come nearer and nearer and next thing we knew, they dropped about ten bombs right down on our line," Colonel (then Captain) Bill Fargus, 8th Battalion Royal Scots, remembers. "We had no casualties, but the Argylls were badly hit."

In all, 23 men of 7th Argylls were casualties of this navigational blunder. Four men were killed and nineteen wounded. Most, including two officers, were from B Company. "Only about three of us got through; it wiped out most of my company HQ," Major

Harry Morton, commanding B Company, 7th Argylls, recalls grimly.

This tragic incident was far from isolated. On two separate occasions during the 1944 Normandy battle, RAF and USAF bombers misjudged their targets and inadvertently bombed First Canadian Army positions, killing or wounding over 700 men. In January 1945, 12 American B-17s on a bombing mission to Cologne dropped 365 bombs directly on the Division HQ of Major-General Terry Allen's 104th "Timberwolves" Division on the Roer. Twenty-four men were killed and 28 wounded. Major-General Rennie is reputed to have said that he refused to take part in any operation where the RAF was nearer then 40 miles.

At the battle for Goch, Major Alec Brodie preserved his record as being "the most perforated" — and droll — officer in 5th Battalion Black Watch. With a gash on his head streaming with blood, Brodie was insisting to his CO that he was quite able to carry on when he fainted dead away.

Stretcher-bearers were carrying him towards the regimental aid post when an unusually heavy stonk persuaded them to deposit the stretcher in a ditch at the side of the road and dive for cover. In due course, Brodie came to. Finding himself alone, he got off the stretcher, picked it up, and strolled back to the RAP.

The Highlanders were shocked to hear that the Commander Royal Engineers, Lieutenant-Colonel Ralph Carr, had been gravely wounded.

The engineers of all divisions — and at all levels — were fighting a war just as dangerous as that of the riflemen. Mines and poor roads continued to bedevil the Allied troops. In one month, the sappers had checked and cleared 54 miles of roads and verges for mines. They had loaded and placed by hand some 3,200 tons of rubble and 200 yards of corduroy road. Five bulldozers put in 780 hours of hard work.

War correspondent Victor Thompson of the *Daily Herald* quoted one 16-year-old engineer, Lieutenant A. Cowan of 53rd Welsh Division, as saying: "In one stretch of two miles Jerry had blown the road in seven places. The craters were huge, and there were more prepared charges which had failed to explode and which we had to remove gingerly. These charges were composed of a hundred pounds of TNT, six feet underground, with a layer of shells on top of that and a layer of mines on top of that again."

Getting the roads back into repair taxed the energy and ingenuity of the engineers. "We developed a very quick way of laying the roads," recalls the CRE First Canadian Army, Brigadier Geoffrey Walsh.

"We laid a mile or so a day. We bulldozed a road level and then we just laid logs as tightly as we could along it and dumped crushed stone on top. This acted as a binder. If we hadn't had the foresight to bring all the gravel and logs up from Belgium on trains we wouldn't have been able to do it. We couldn't use the trees — they were full of shrapnel. Every time one of our saws hit one, we not only got a casualty with the saw but we usually got a couple of casualties with our men."

Often, the handy little "tippers" or dump trucks from tipper platoons of the Royal Canadian Army Service Corps were up with the engineer assault troops in advance of infantry or armour.

Craters — the self-inflicted wound of the advancing troops — caused even more problems. There were two ways of repairing the craters: using armoured bulldozers to fill them with rubble, or bridging them over. Both methods required enormous amounts of material and — in the absence of the goods or of the roads with which to bring them up — ingenuity and round-the-clock work, as Lieutenant-Colonel George Lilley, CRE 2nd Canadian Division, recalls: "Bombed or shelled towns provided a much-needed source of material for road repair but it was not always possible for our trucks to backtrack against the traffic. In such cases, the nearest farm or roadside building was demolished to provide material. Full use was made of armoured bulldozers close behind the leading troops, but on at least one occasion a bulldozer was knocked out by enemy anti-tank fire."

The road crisis meant in real terms that the troops rarely saw those three vital morale-builders: hot food, dry socks, and mail from home. The Army Postal Service achieved miracles and took great risks in moving mail forward.

On a number of occasions, quartermasters had to resort to horse-and-buggy transportation to move the rations and supplies up to company areas. "A great deal of it went forward by hand," remembers Captain Ben Wilkie, quartermaster of the Royal Regiment of Canada. "We just loaded it onto people and they carried it."

In Goch, a wave of bitterness swept through the troops as never before," Captain Robert Woollcombe, a platoon commander of 6th KOSB, noted. "At last it was Germany: the thought never left you. Germany: it did not matter what damage we did." Revenge was profoundly felt by all the British troops whose comrades had suffered the humiliation of defeat and imprisonment at Dunkirk.

"Here in the enemy homeland, a grim satisfaction was the main emotion expressed," wrote one soldier. "Serves the bastards right! was the familiar comment."

Those "excellent German cellars" in Goch were yielding up more than just a secure shelter from enemy fire. While sporadic fighting persisted for several more days, occupation troops had the time, and certainly the inclination, to investigate the goods and chattels of their absentee hosts.

As they crossed the German border, the men were struck at the difference between the German and Dutch farms. "It was the difference between starvation and plenty," Major John Chaston, 2nd Battalion Monmouthshires, recalls. "The Dutch farmers' cattle — if they had any cattle — were skinny and ill fed, and the people had no food. The German farms were well stocked with animals. The farm houses had hams, vegetables, and bottled fruits."

Looting was officially prohibited — and universally prevalent.

Now that we were on German soil [one Welsh soldier wrote], we felt no compunction in looting, pilfering, or commandeering anything we fancied and felt a sort of rough justice in repossessing what the Nazis had taken from other countries since 1940.

What we were very surprised to discover was that practically every house was stacked with every sort of clothing and material, hidden away in cellars and stores.

Some of these luxury goods had been stolen by German soldiers posted to areas of Germany where civilians had been evacuated. It was a practice that the Wehrmacht abhorred. "The property of Germans who have been forced to leave their homes must be inviolate," a captured order sternly remonstrated. "Men found guilty are to be court-martialled at once."

The Allied authorities also tried to stem the stealing. General Eisenhower issued orders forbidding looting, the exception being weapons, or Nazi souvenirs such as flags and armbands bearing the swastika. Colonel Charles MacDonald notes that the order "sharply restricted the practice except in expendables like wine and schnapps which could be made to disappear — with not unpleasant results — before some conscientious investigating officer could check on its source."

Boredom with rations or sheer gluttony dissolved compunctions many troops might have had about helping themselves to food and wine. "Eating off the land" was tacitly encouraged and often was the only source of food for men at the sharp end.

There were shelves filled with every sort of bottled food, plums, pears, gooseberries, upon which we feasted with delighted greed [an infantryman described]. In one house there happened to be a piano which produced no sound when the keys were struck. On opening up to investigate, it was found to be stuffed full with bags of sugar! What vandals all soldiers become, surrounded by ruin and death and in the flush of victory far from the civilized constraints of home.

The resultant diarrhea from this gluttony of bottled fruit was noted in a number of war diaries for its debilitating effect on the fighting ability of the troops.

A company piper from 5/7th Battalion Gordon Highlanders, assigned to dig a latrine in the back garden of a house, uncovered an equally debilitating cache of six cases of spirits and liqueurs, which he generously shared with his mates. One company sergeant-major thoughtfully sent a crate of eggs to his battalion HQ. He didn't mention that it was just one of 20 crates he had "liberated" — or that he was feeling somewhat queasy from having downed 18 freshly cooked eggs in one sitting.

Pilfering was usually at a harmless level: like the two Jocks, borrowing German finery for a mock wedding . . . like the young private soldier billeted in a textile factory who couldn't resist sending a linen tablecloth home to his mom.

A company sergeant-major who had fought brilliantly on the approaches to Cleve thought he deserved a little "souvenir" of the occasion. Spying a large tapestry that had miraculously been spared in the shelling of the cathedral, he pulled out his knife, slashed it from its frame, and rolled it into his pack.

But there were also pockets of organized looting that prompted the CO of 1st Gordons, Lieutenant-Colonel Grant Peterkin, to protest: "From what I have seen myself . . . the discipline in the British Army will disintegrate rapidly unless something is done about organized looting. The scenes in Goch had to be seen to be believed."

The Ninth U.S. Army responded with similar vigour: "Religious articles found in wrecked or abandoned churches in occupied territory will be afforded the utmost protection possible to avoid damage, desecration or misuse by members of this command," a directive on February 18 stated.

When Lieutenant Ross LeMesurier, the Queen's Own Cameron Highlander platoon commander, was invalided back to hospital in Belgium, he was horrified to see Belgian children walking about in coats made from army-issue blankets and army-issue greatcoats. He was observing a thriving black-market business where Allied troops — mainly deserters — were selling British army issue at hugely inflated prices to the civilian population: "Bloody maddening when you think of the state of the greatcoats of some of the boys in the battalion," LeMesurier noted angrily in a letter to his father.

Men from a Canadian armoured regiment were reputed to have "stumbled on" a cache of diamonds in a safe in Cleve worth an estimated $20,000 (Canadian). An errant shell later disposed of it before the troopers could figure out a way to capitalize on their finding. Similarly, an infantry officer who had fought continuously throughout the long European campaign had been assembling, and periodically upgrading, a whole jeepload of "souvenirs." In the last week of the war he saw the whole collection blown to bits on a single mine.

The commandos — not having access to jeeps and tanks to transport their trophies of war — used baby prams. "I think the antique dealers in Brighton must have done rather well after the war," mused one army Commando lieutenant. Ultimately, the commandos vastly improved their means of travel. "We all finished up with cars," he noted. "I had a beautiful Mercedes; some of my men at the end rode magnificent racehorses."

POWs were ripe targets for loot. "I speak a few words of German," one junior officer quipped: " 'Where's your watch and have you got a decent pair of binoculars?' "

A platoon commander with 6th King's Own Scottish Borderers witnessed one of his NCOs' attitude towards two German staff officers who had just been captured.

Both were handled without ceremony and made to stand a long time with their hands up. [One of them] stood . . . as a man does who holds on to his pride under great humiliation. He had fought for his country . . . the hurt was plain on his face . . . but one of our sergeants in an ugly mood was soon at them, roughly searching them and stripping them of arms and papers. The sergeant . . . tore the Iron Cross from the officer's tunic. At this I took the Iron Cross . . . and gave it back to him. In English, simply, he said "Thank you."

For practical reasons, weapons were high on the hit list. Frontline officers and men soon learned to covet a number of German weapons that they believed were more battleworthy than their own issue. While the men had no compunctions about liberating such weaponry, they were leery of the consequences of being captured with German equipment.

A Schmeisser was a prize. This German machine pistol — an automatic, hand-held weapon — was very popular with the Allied troops who captured one whenever possible. Used at short range in close fighting, it was lighter and more rapid-firing than the American tommy-gun. It was also more reliable than the Sten, which tended to jam, or to discharge if dropped, inflicting many accidental woundings and sometimes death to the man who carried it.

One NCO relates how he had purloined a German Schmeisser and a pair of leather jackboots in Goch. For the most practical of reasons, he ditched them the next day: "We got word that the Germans had infiltrated our position. I didn't want to be captured wearing German boots or carrying a German gun."

The raw, wet weather of those days had its effect on the plundering. Troops built huge bonfires to warm themselves — and even to cook stolen chickens and ducks for their dinners. When the firewood ran low, they substituted tables and chairs, stripping many of the houses of furniture and art treasures. Be it a stout hand-hewn table of pine or a priceless rosewood antique — it made little difference to them. Both flamed brightly.

"I can distinctly remember in Cleve pushing a piano out of the third floor of a building just to see it hit the street," one sapper recalls. "A beautiful piano, right out of the goddamn third floor."

Not the least of the victims of Rhineland looting was the 16th-century Schloss Moyland, once the summer palace of Frederick the Great. During Operation Veritable, Wehrmacht units had commandeered the castle for a tactical HQ, finding that its castle turrets made excellent observation posts, its moats effective anti-tank defences, and its immense walls protection enough against enemy shells.

On February 21, the 5th Canadian Infantry Brigade's Régiment de Maisonneuve entered the castle unopposed, hearing, to their astonishment, strains from Rossini's *Barber of Seville*. Baronin (Baroness) Marie von Hahn received the Maisonneuves in her drawing room. Along with her family and nearby farmers and villagers she had been forced during the weeks of shelling to seek shelter in the castle's cellars. What she now witnessed was possibly more horrifying:

> In the principal bed-chamber, the curving walls embellished with paintings of flamboyant nudes, the cooking stoves of a French-Canadian company roared under pans of frying fat [the Maisonneuve history relates]. In the magnificently appointed bathrooms of the state apartment, groups of soldiers washed and shaved for the first time in a week.

One officer recalls, "A few of my men were having a great time parading around in top hats they found in the closets. Some of the troops were chucking furniture and paintings out the windows to make bonfires in the courtyard. It wasn't wanton. They were cold and they needed fire to cook their food." (In a recent letter to the authors, the present owner of Moyland Castle, Baron Adrian von Steengracht, writes: "Just now, big efforts are undertaken to restore the castle and transform it into a museum of modern art.")

Ironically, British plunder cost at least one British officer his life. Following in the wake of the combat troops, the Allied Army of Occupation was responsible for rescuing priceless documents and works of art and placing them in safekeeping. In Goch, Major Ronald Balfour salvaged three truckloads of valuable archives, including irreplaceable documents belonging to the registrar of landed property. He also discovered an abandoned lorry in the market square containing archival material from the Collegiate Church of Cleve. In Moyland he found priceless documents heaped up in the meadows surrounding the castle. All of these he stored in the Capuchin monastery in Cleve.

"The plundering is awful," he wrote a friend at Cambridge University. "Not only every house is forced open and searched, but also every safe and every cupboard. . . . All that I can do is to try and rescue as much as possible and put up signs of warning."

Balfour was killed by a stray shell as he was supervising the removal of land deeds and artworks — less at least one rare tapestry from Cleve Cathedral that now hangs sedately over a postwar hearth in Sussex.

11

Dan Spry and His Water Rats

Top Secret. Personal and Eyes Only for CIGS from Field-Marshal Montgomery, 18 Feb 45
It has been very wet today with rain and thickness and no operations have been possible. . . . Enemy resistance is thickening and I do not think we shall make substantial gains until the regrouping is completed and divisions are lined up in their battle fronts.

MAJOR-GENERAL DAN SPRY'S first task in Operation Veritable had been to clear the enemy from the flooded polders along the Rhine. Battle by Buffalo was a familiar theme for the Water Rats. His next objective — Moyland Wood — was more sinister.

"Clear the woods!" That was 2 Canadian Corps commander Guy Simonds's order to Spry on February 16. The Jocks had tried, valiantly. The 15th Scottish's Valentine's Day assault had been stopped midway by hard-hitting troops from von Waldenburg's Windhund Division. Now the Scots were exhausted. The job was handed to Spry's 3rd Canadian Infantry Division.

Until the enemy had been pushed out of Moyland Wood, Operation Veritable could not continue, and its subsidiary thrust — 2 Canadian Corps's Operation Blockbuster — could not begin. It was bad enough that the Germans had dug their heels into the strongpoint. Now Simonds had dug his heels in, too. Moyland *would* be cleared, and now!

Dan Spry inherited an inordinate challenge, but he had done that once before, in August 1944, on the troubled battlefields of Normandy.

See Map 6 (Appendix B).

Just a little over a week after Major-General Thomas Rennie took over the ill-commanded 51st Highland Infantry Division in Normandy, Daniel Spry found himself standing in Trafalgar Square, still in his bush shirt and shorts from the Italian front, newly promoted to Major-General and GOC of 3rd Canadian Infantry Division. The division had landed on the beachhead on D-Day with Second British Army. After a brilliant beginning, the 3rd — like the Highlanders — had begun to falter under what Corps Commander General Sir John T. Crocker called ''a lack of control and leadership from the top.'' In subsequent weeks, heads rolled and morale plummetted.

The final blow for the dejected unit came from friendly skies. On August 8, a searing midday sun blazed down on some 25,000 men of the 3rd Canadian Division and the Polish Armoured Division moving up with their artillery and tanks for the attack at Falaise. H-Hour was almost two hours away and the men were still well behind their lines, relaxing in vehicles jammed into the marshalling area.

At 1256 hours cheers rose as 492 bombers from the Eighth U.S. Air Force, attacking in support of the Canadians, crowded the airspace, heading for the German lines. Fifteen hundred tons of bombs smashed enemy targets just ahead of the Canadian front. But cheers turned to screams of pain and terror as one damaged Fortress released its load on the watching men. The remaining craft of the 12-plane group followed suit. Calamity followed calamity: the lead bombardier of the second group misidentified his target and led an attack on Canadian ranks.

Sixty-five men were killed and 250 wounded from the two divisions and their supporting units of the Canadian and British Royal Artillery. The 3rd Division commander, Major-General Rod Keller, who was severely wounded when his Tac HQ was hit. Spry was rushed up to replace him.

But where Rennie was a seasoned veteran, Spry's extreme youth (at 32, he was the youngest general officer in the Allied forces) did not always inspire confidence in officers of considerably greater years. And where Thomas Rennie came back to his division as an old and trusted friend, Dan Spry was thrust in as an unknown.

It was a curious coincidence that the three divisions that would clash so bitterly in the coming campaign — the Scottish Highlanders, the Canadian Water Rats, and the German Windhund — would within a few weeks of one another so traumatically lose their commanders.

The morale of a division can be badly jolted by such an event. Spry describes what he recalls was a "dicey time": "After a division headquarters has been bombed and its commander taken away on a stretcher, and part of a field regiment of artillery has been obliterated with its ammunition dumps blown up . . . the whole morale of the division became jittery.

"The principal staff officers recognized that I'd been battle-fighting for over a year in Italy and that I did know what I was talking about. They served me splendidly right from the beginning," Spry says. "But some of the subordinate commanders were dubious about me. I think they thought I was sort of a Johnny-come-lately. Who is this guy Spry coming up from Italy? What does he know about it? He hasn't been here for the last month. Guy Simonds had fired a number of infantry commanders in the first few weeks in Normandy. A lot of the new COs were walking tenderly — hoping they wouldn't make a mistake and have their heads cut off too.

"Fortunately, the first few engagements under my command (all three involving the troops in water-related actions; I coined the name 'Water Rats' for them) were very successful. Tails were really up; the men realized they were pretty damned good. We were ready — teed up, trained and prepared for what we had to do in Veritable."

Spry's liaison officers briefed him on the 15th Scottish Division's earlier struggle to break the German hammerlock on Moyland Wood. They had succeeded in pushing the enemy back from a large section of the forest but had not managed to dislodge his domination of the ridge.

"The Germans are experts at forest fighting," Spry summed up at a division Orders Group. "The troops will find it tough going; it will be up to the junior officers and NCOs to keep them moving."

Spry saw Moyland Wood as an offensive nightmare. Roads that were not hedgetop-high in flood water were mined and covered by enemy anti-tank and machine-gun fire. Getting vehicles forward on those mud paths, with essential cargos of weapons, ammunition, and hot food, would be a slow and formidable task. Getting the casualties out would be just as difficult. The surrounding open countryside, boggy and unfit for armour, was so restricted that units could only be committed piecemeal against a strongly centralized enemy.

As the Scots had discovered, there seemed to be only one way to take Moyland Wood: a frontal attack across wide-open ground up the wooded ridge — and dead into the teeth of the enemy guns.

On February 19, Simonds pondered the results of the first three days of fighting with growing impatience. Moyland was not going his way. Simonds desperately wanted to secure this prime objective. On a professional level, he realized it was of paramount strategic importance. On a personal level, he wanted to get on with Blockbuster — his baby, as it were. The fact that Montgomery had given command of Operation Veritable to Crerar instead of to him had been a terrible disappointment for the driving corps commander — a "heartbreak," as a fellow officer later observed. Now he would be back in command again, his corps front and centre in the coming Blockbuster action. It was unacceptable that its launch be delayed by failure at Moyland Wood.

Even the weather wouldn't cooperate. Rain and dense clouds had precluded vital air support from the Typhoons. Rain and thick mud had almost immobilized the armour.

For the next three days, the three battalions of 7th Canadian Infantry Brigade — the Royal Winnipeg Rifles, the Regina Rifle Regiment, and the 1st Battalion Canadian Scottish — fought doggedly, but intense mortar fire and belligerent enemy counter-attacks had blocked them from advancing beyond their initial objectives. Although they secured a launching pad to Moyland by capturing the open ground below the woods, all their subsequent efforts to penetrate enemy positions within the forest were repelled.

In the first wave of the attack, the Winnipeg Rifles achieved immediate success as they advanced in Kangaroos to seize the village of Louisendorf, southwest of the woods. (This would be the start line for the pending 4th Brigade attack to cut the Goch-Calcar road 1,000 yards to the south, which in turn would be the start line for Blockbuster.)

The Reginas had not fared as well. They ran into heavy fire from positions in the forest where the Germans had infiltrated, even after the area had been cleared by the 15th Scottish. Fresh enemy reinforcements from Major-General Hermann Plocher's 6th Parachute Division were being poured into the strongpoint. A Regina company was savagely counter-attacked and overrun as it attempted to enter the woods.

Despite incurring over a hundred casualties, the battalion managed to consolidate on their initial objectives. But here they were stopped, devastated by the extremely heavy mortar and artillery fire from across the Rhine and from the woods themselves.

One company (normally at a strength of 100) was reduced to one officer and 20 men. "High explosive projectiles coming into the wood were detonated by the trees," the battle summary noted. "This air burst made it unusually deadly."

"Further exploitation is impossible due to depletion in company strength," the Regina war diary reports. "Company commanders agree that the shelling and fighting in these woods have been just as bad as anything encountered in Normandy."

Meanwhile, the Canadian Scottish had advanced successfully to Heseler Feld. This 500-yard-square farm area rested on a small hill a bare half-mile south of the German-held woods — in direct observation of the enemy established on the ridge. The sparse clumps of trees and occasional farm buildings offered little shelter. The men dug their slits swiftly in the soft mud of the rain-soaked, ploughed fields. There they stayed, uncomfortably "under the eyes of the enemy on the higher ground," pinned down by relentless fire, snipers, and repeated counter-attacks.

In the Canadian Scottish command post on Heseler Feld, officers from Brigade, Battalion, and supporting artillery, each with signallers equipped with radio sets, crowded into a farmhouse cellar. Efforts to maintain communications with the forward companies had become "a nightmare of troubles":

Shelling and the constant movement of tanks successively cut every line which was laid from the CP to the companies [the Signal Platoon reported]. But since wireless reception was not always good the line crews worked day and night to keep repairing lines in the vain hope that some of them would not be cut. Each and every line was cut within a matter of one-half hour or less from the time it was laid down. More than eight miles of wire were laid during the action.

By the morning of February 19 there were fewer than 150 men of all ranks left among the three companies on Heseler Feld — half their normal strength. The Canadian Scottish renamed it "Slaughterhouse Hill" — a grim christening of what had become the burial ground of so many of their comrades.

Steaming down the Bedburg-Louisendorf road in his armoured Scout car — having administered a blistering dressing-down to his commanders — Simonds was stopped by a near-miss from a German anti-tank gun. A traffic jam on his way back, even more extensive than usual, did nothing to improve his disposition. Later that morning, Simonds chaired a hot meeting of his senior commanders. "Clear those woods!" he repeated.

"Simonds was pushing me and I was pushing the brigadiers and battalion commanders," Spry recalls. "He was very determined. Just by the glint in his eye and the set of his jaw you knew what he wanted. When he was angry, he became icy."

The Simonds "cold front" quickly found its way to the sharp end. The Regina Rifles reported bitterly: "By now Brigade HQ were screaming that the Wood 'should have been cleared by now and what were we going to do about it?' The huge casualties list was a mute answer."

Spry still believes that many of these casualties could have been avoided. "The people upstairs, Montgomery and so on, seemed to feel that the pace of the battle could be carried on regardless of the realities of the situation — regardless of the weather, of the reduced air support as a result of weather, of the flooding and the breakdown of the roads, tracks, and trails and of the ensuing supply problems.

"When troops are wet, cold, miserable, bloody-minded, scared, and tired, it takes time to move and assemble, re-assemble, and deploy them. Everything slows down. The longer the battle goes on, the worse that gets. People get more flogged, wetter, colder.

"These personnel, logistical, geographic, and weather problems were being partially ignored by the senior commanders," Spry relates. "They really didn't understand the sharp end of battle. They had a mental block; they'd never been there. If we had taken a little more time, even another two or three hours of preparation, of reconnaissance, of plotting and planning at various levels (perhaps even my own), we would have done better, without the staggering and unnecessary losses. We rushed our fences."

One of the by-products of this haste was the poor intelligence that hampered the Canadian effort. "The strength of the German defenders still holding the wood seems to have been seriously underestimated," the official Canadian historian, Colonel Charles Stacey, observes tersely.

The Canadian Scottish Regiment was up against the best. While the Reginas were struggling against Plocher's freshly reinforced 6th Parachute Division, the Scottish had run head-on against von Luettwitz's seasoned tank regiments — now refitted — of the 116th Panzer.

This division, in continuous action since it had come on the line the previous week, had in one week fought against four different divisions, as General Guderian recently recalled. They had encountered the 43rd Wessex and 53rd Welsh at Hau and Cleve; the 15th Scottish and the Wessex again on the roads around Bedburg; and the 3rd Canadian Infantry at Heseler Feld and Louisendorf.

Overnight on February 18-19, the Windhund Division was side-slipped a mile or so west to dig in against the pending attack to cut the Goch-Calcar road. Plocher, meanwhile, extended his front, inserting the newly arrived 18th, 19th, and 21st Parachute Regiments to augment his line. It was these seasoned troops, dug into Moyland Wood, that the Canadian Scottish attacked head-on on the morning of the 19th.

The battalion was ordered to advance out of Heseler Feld across an exposed roadway directly into Moyland Wood. Like its sister battalions, the exhausted Scottish had already been badly mauled after two days of enemy shelling and mortaring and continuous counter-attack.

This order, given by the brigade commander, Brigadier Jock Spragge, is therefore difficult to fathom. This highly regarded officer had been in the line throughout the Northwest Europe campaign. However, he had recently been recommended for a rest, and in fact Simonds was insisting that he be replaced. February 19 was his last day of command. The strain of being pressured from "upstairs," coupled with the weight of total fatigue, appears to have created unparalleled "fence-rushing."

"The brigade commander gave the 7th Brigade's task to the Canadian Scottish [Colonel Stacey reports], who were directed at the same time to improve their positions to the east and south by gaining more of the high ground overlooking Calcar. In these circumstances the attack against the wood was made by one weak company."

One weak company, sent into this proven force that had already stopped two entire brigades? And in a frontal attack over open ground against a strongly held enemy position? It is difficult to comprehend how such an attack could have been ordered. Even the Canadian Scottish's CO protested it, as its history noted.

To succeed, it would have needed at least some of the basic elements of offence: infantry strength at least five times that of the defender, overwhelming concentrated artillery support fire from guns and mortars to keep the enemy heads down, and armoured back-up. Instead, the attackers held none of these advantages.

The consequences were disastrous. Under sullen skies, with a fighting force of only 69 men, C Company launched the attack at 0730 hours. In 60 minutes the company was decimated. Only five men escaped unharmed; 16 were killed and 48 were taken prisoner.

"It was kind of a crazy idea anyway," ponders Major Harvey Bailey, second-in-command of D Company. "C Company had to go over a forward slope in broad daylight with a bunch of enemy paratroops waiting about a hundred yards in front. The Germans let them get in and then they cut them off."

Company Sergeant-Major C. ("Chum") Morgan, who was himself wounded slightly in the action, describes the disaster of the next minutes:

The lead platoons were forced to go to ground and to call for smoke from the supporting mortars to conceal further movement from the watchful enemy. Under its protection the Company crossed the road and carried on towards the certain fire of the defences at the wood. Just across the crossroad, Major R.H. Tye [the company commander] was hit by a burst of MG fire. He was unable to do more than crawl to a shell crater from where he directed as much of the remaining action as possible.

Only 15 minutes had elapsed. The lead platoons had disappeared over the crest of the ridge. Although himself slightly wounded, Morgan had taken over the company. Every effort to move to the aid of the forward elements was driven back by intense fire. Tye and Morgan decided to call down more smoke to give them cover. It was then that they discovered that their radio set had been pierced by machine-gun fire and was useless.

Twenty minutes later the pair watched with horror as some 50 Germans appeared over the ridge where the platoons had disappeared. Tye realized that his company had been wiped out as a fighting force. The position had been overrun — his men either killed or captured.

"Get back to HQ and tell the CO what has happened," he urged Morgan. The CSM called desperately to the remnants of the little band to follow him out. With three other men he made a dash back across the road, dodging a rain of MG fire until they reached the safety of their own line. Despite the prospect of certain capture, the company stretcher-bearer, Private Elder, refused to escape, insisting that his place was with the casualties.

Wounded and helpless, Major Tye awaited his inevitable capture by the steadily approaching enemy troops. The Germans rounded up the survivors and took them back for questioning. One man, Private Watkins, eluded capture by hiding motionless in a shellhole for 24 hours.

With the exception of this handful of men, the entire company was wiped out in less than one hour. Later, the battalion padre recovered 16 Canadian Scottish bodies dead on the ground over which they had attacked.

The remaining companies of the Canadian Scottish were also experiencing extreme difficulties on Slaughterhouse Hill. For 48 hours they unflinchingly endured every kind of abuse the Germans could devise, as one man later recounted:

> The ground was literally covered by a mass of singing lead. As we were in the folds of soft ground we dug in bloody fast. Casualties were mounting . . . we couldn't move one inch. The enemy MG and mortar fire was hellish.
>
> I ran about 200 yards to the platoon and had a sniper shooting at me all the way up. . . . It made our ears ring with every explosion. So close were the shells landing that it was hard to hear one another speak even when we were in the same slit trench.

The Scottish lost 11 stretcher-bearers in the Heseler Feld action: two were killed and several more were wounded while giving first aid to the wounded on the battlefield; one, Private Elder, was captured. Company Sergeant-Major J. Nimmo saw his company stretcher-bearer go out to help some wounded. "He was wearing a large red cross on his chest and back. The Heinie snipers started potting at him right away; it was still light and they could see him clearly. Finally he was hit."

The battalion's casualties in just these two days of fighting were 140, including 53 taken prisoner.

Three actions were to take the heat off the 7th Brigade assault at Moyland Wood. On February 19, the 4th Canadian Infantry Brigade attack to cut the Goch-Calcar road was finally unleashed. This gave right-flank protection to the Moyland battlers.

The second break occurred on the 21st — a break, finally, in the cloud-laden skies. For the first time in five days, the Typhoons could take up the attack; 84 Group RAF flew about a hundred sorties that day against enemy machine-gun and mortar positions.

Sergeant John Campbell of the Regina Rifles recalls a moment when his platoon was moving up in 1,500-cwt trucks. "My company commander said, 'Sergeant, get your men under cover. The Germans are in the bush over there and the Typhoons are coming in.' The next thing you knew, those Typhoons came in and, boy, did they ever smash the forest. The Germans hated them. If you'd take prisoners, all you'd hear was, 'Typhoons, Typhoons!' "

The third event took place that same day, when the Royal Winnipeg Rifles shattered the tenacious German hold on Moyland Wood.

Dividing the entire wooded area into 300-yard-wide sections, the 3rd Division artillery methodically pounded each section in turn as the Winnipeggers beat out the enemy. A miniature pepperpot provided by the medium machine guns of the Cameron Highlanders of Ottawa in addition to guns of the Toronto Scottish, the battalion's anti-tank guns, and all the available three-inch mortars in the brigade expended 100,000 rounds and 2,000 bombs in support of this action.

The RWR had never before used Wasp flame-throwers in forest fighting. Keeping six Wasps up with the forward companies and six back being constantly refuelled, the Winnipeggers were able to maintain this relentless pressure on the enemy without let-up. (General Schlemm aptly described flame-throwers as "the most terrible weapons of the war.")

Tanks from the Sherbrooke Fusiliers Regiment operated in close contact with the infantry, shooting them onto limited objectives. The Germans had mined the eastern exits to the woods with both anti-tank and anti-personnel mines, causing many casualties. The tanks were forced to withdraw temporarily. The CO, Lieutenant-Colonel L.R. ("Locky") Fulton, describes the serious difficulties that the withdrawal caused a forward platoon: "Immediately the tanks withdrew, about 25 of the enemy launched a wild counter-attack. Throwing grenades and firing Schmeissers from the hip, they charged our positions, yelling in English, 'Get your hands up.' At this critical moment, the Bren gun of the forward section jammed. The section's position was overrun."

Two more counter-attacks were repulsed before the battalion overcame the fanatical paratroopers and drove them out of the wood. The tanks were now brought forward to assist in consolidation.

The cost to the Royal Winnipeg Rifles in fighting from the 16th to the 21st was fearful: 183 men were casualties from the six-day ordeal. Of that number, 105 fell on the final day, 26 of them killed.

The Battle of Moyland Wood was over. The 15th Scottish and then the Canadians had fought for a total of eight days to acquire the two-mile-long ridge. Once again, the fighting men and their commanders in the field had been handed a hastily patched plan. Once again, by sheer bloody-minded determination and courage, they had salvaged it. Dan Spry and his Water Rats had pulled it off.

The "butchers' bill" was staggering. Four hundred and eighty-five Canadians, fully one-third of the fighting strength of 7th Brigade, had been killed, wounded, or captured. Almost that same number of the 15th Scottish Division were casualties as well in the grim Moyland fight.

The shattered companies of the Canadian Scottish were relieved by the Royal Regiment of Canada on the evening of February 21. As they moved out from Heseler Feld, the troops were met by pipers who led the exhausted and dejected men back into Bedburg. "The shrill, triumphant sound of the pipes gave something to the men that nothing else could," the regiment history noted with pride. "Almost automatically, the bone-weary soldiers began to march in step."

Captain Bailey remembers the galvanized moment: "When we brought the battalion out, there were only two officers and about 165 men left in the four rifle companies. I wasn't too badly off, I had about 60 men left, but C Company had five. They had been virtually wiped out. We started marching back and the piper called, 'What will you have, lads,' and they replied, 'Cock of the North'!

"The whole battalion pipe band met us and led us into town. As we marched back through the lines of the 15th Scottish Division, I can still remember some of the Scots shoving their heads out and saying, 'Who's there?' One of the boys yelled out, 'C'mon, stand back you guys, let the soldiers come in. It's the Canadian Scottish, or what's left of them!' It was a wonderfully cheerful sort of camaraderie."

Major William Matthews, second-in-command of the battalion, happened to be standing beside the 15th Scottish pipe major as the remnants of the weary battalion went by. Both men — the seasoned professional soldier and the youthful volunteer — were struck by the tragedy of young lives wasted by war.

"He was a big, tough ex-Scottish guardsman; I'll never forget him. He was standing there in the moonlight watching our companies come in, some of them with only ten or twenty men left. There were tears rolling down his cheeks and he turned to me, 'Makes you fucking think, don't it, kid.' "

12

The Goch-Calcar Road:
A Narrative of Battle

W.D. Whitaker:

"It was an ordinary enough narrow country road, hard-surfaced, dead straight, with barely space for two tractors to pass, connecting the market towns of Goch and Calcar. Four hundred men from 4th Canadian Infantry Brigade became casualties fighting for a mile-and-a-half section of that ordinary road.

"This is what I remember of the eight days of fighting."

D-MINUS-TWO
Royal Hamilton Light Infantry War Diary, February 17:

0630 hours: The CO held an "O" Gp re the forthcoming attack. In general 4 Bde was to attack and hold the high ground SW of Calcar on the main Calcar-Goch road with RHLI left, Essex Scot right and R Regt C [Royal Regiment of Canada] in reserve.
0900 hours: The CO with coy comds recced the FUP [forming up place] and SL [start line] but as the woods [Moyland] on our left had not been cleared as per schedule, the recce party came under heavy mortar and shell fire with the result that our operation was cancelled for forty-eight hours.
1400 hours: At rear Bn HQ the Asst Adj arranged for a cinema to be held at 1800 hrs.

See Map 6 (Appendix B).

D-MINUS-ONE
RHLI War Diary, February 18:

1130 hours: Bn "O" Gp held. The scheduled ops still postponed due to enemy resistance in the woods on our left
flank.
1230 hours: At Tac HQ it was observed that the usual
fare of compo was not present on the table, but rather lus-
cious fresh steaks and fresh vegetables made their
appearance.
2030 hours: The CO, Lt-Col WD Whitaker, and the IO, Lt
NW Bennett attended a coordinating conference at Brigade
HQ where a considerably increased artillery programme
was laid on. The objective in forthcoming ops was
switched 1000 yards to the right.

Lieutenant-Colonel Whitaker, Commanding Officer, RHLI:
"At the O Group, the commander of 4th Canadian Infantry Brigade,
Brigadier Fred Cabeldu, set down the objectives of the operation
to his three battalion commanders: Lieutenant-Colonel John Pangman (the Essex Scottish Regiment), Lieutenant-Colonel Dick Len-
drum (the Royal Regiment of Canada), and myself. As well, there
was Lieutenant-Colonel Mac Young, Royal Canadian Artillery commander 4th Field Regiment (in my opinion, one of the best artillery
regiment commanders in First Canadian Army); and officers of the
Fort Garry Horse (2nd Army Tank Brigade) and of the Toronto Scottish Regiment (MGs and Mortars).

"We were ordered to capture and hold the Goch-Calcar road as
a start line for Operation Blockbuster. The two battalions spearheading the attack were each supported by a squadron of 16 tanks of
the Fort Garry Horse. Kangaroos of the 1st Canadian Armoured
Personnel Carrier Regiment would transport the two forward
assault companies of the battalion. The remaining two would follow on foot, but with similar support by the Sherman tanks.

"Gazing southeast from Louisendorf, I could plainly see across
the stubbled brown field sloping gently upwards to the road 2,000
yards away. Dotted here and there were farmhouses and sheds.
To reach our objective my men had to cross that open stretch.

"But 'upwards' . . . I recall a disquieting thought: we were on
the forward slope. What lay over the top?

"I reckoned that if I could keep the enemy heads down during
our initial assault, our task would not be too difficult. I had tremendous confidence in our artillery, and particularly in Major Jack

Drewry of the 4th Field Regiment in controlling this. Two FOOs would be positioned with the forward companies to call down fire on known enemy positions and on targets of opportunity (enemy strongpoints not previously identified).

"We had an extensive fire plan involving the artilleries of the 15th, 43rd, and 53rd Divisions and the 2nd and 3rd Canadian Divisions. In all, 15 field and seven medium regiments, or 470 guns, all sizes, would support the attack — certainly sufficient fire to subdue the enemy during the advance."

RHLI War Diary, February 18:
2300 hours: Bn "O" Gp was held where all the latest details of the attack were passed on to company comds.

Lieutenant-Colonel Whitaker:
"I gave A Company, Major J.M. (Jimmy) Bostwick commanding, and B Company, Major Dunc Kennedy, the job of leading off the attack — A right and B left. They would be mounted on Kangaroos and would advance at tank pace — 100 yards in two minutes — under the cover of a rolling barrage at the same pace. I warned them that the success of the operation depended on their getting over the open ground and onto the objectives before the enemy recovered from our barrage. If they kept up to the barrage, the Kangaroos would deliver them to their company objectives.

"I reckoned without the rain. It continued through the night, making the ground boggy and treacherous.

"My two reserve companies — Major Joe Pigott's C Company on the left and Major Louis Froggett's D Company on the right — were following the lead troops on foot at a slower pace. Their main task was to mop up pockets of resistance bypassed by the first wave.

"My chief worry was that our left flank was wide open to the Germans, who still held strong positions in the areas of Moyland Wood and Calcar. We could hear the staccato sound of automatic weapons as the battle there raged on just a mile away. I hated to send my two companies on the left — Kennedy's and Pigott's — into this hot spot without extra support.

"For left-flank protection, I assigned Lieutenant Gordie Holder's Carrier Platoon with its Wasp flame-throwers. The carriers were augmented by medium machine guns of the Toronto Scottish. For the same reason, I assigned Lieutenant Bob Wight's Demolition Platoon to serve under command of Pigott's vulnerable C Company.

"One section of anti-tank guns was assigned to each of the forward companies, and the third was allocated to C Company on the left. The mortar platoon was instructed to neutralize on call targets of opportunity as well as some known enemy strongpoints. Their fire would be directed by mortar observation personnel assigned to each lead company.

"I hoped that these precautions would adequately protect my left flank. I believed my right flank would be well looked after by the brigade's right forward battalion, the Essex Scottish, who would themselves have their right flank protected by the 43rd Division.

"As I stood in Louisendorf studying the battlefield, I had of course no inkling of the frenzied activity that was taking place on the opposite side of the Goch-Calcar road.

"We had been alerted that we would be fighting German paratroops from General Plocher's 6th Parachute Division. However, our intelligence was not aware that Major-General von Waldenburg's 116th Panzer Division had been inserted in the line. By the worst of bad luck, this division, which had been fighting continuously for seven days, and most recently against the Canadian Scottish at Heseler Feld, had been brought up to strength on that very day.

"The advent of the Panzer Lehr Division was our second piece of bad luck. It had been moved up from the American sector and placed under the temporary command of First Parachute Army during the crisis as General Schlemm's last powerful reserve, to be used only in a counter-attack role but not for defensive tasks. A special counter-attack battle group, Kampfgruppe Hauser, was assembled under command of Colonel Baron von Hauser, commander of 901st Panzer Grenadier Regiment."

Lieutenant-Colonel Heinz Guderian, Chief of Staff, 116th Panzer Division:
"On the day of the Canadian attack, the 19th, our reconnaissance battalion and our engineers, who had stayed to repair our tanks, came back from the Eifel. Such a long time we had missed them. Then the Panzer Lehr came in with one Panzer Grenadier regiment, parts of the Tank Destroyer Battalion, and parts of the Tank Regiment. On our right was the 6th Parachute Division."

**Major Helmut Hudel, Commanding Officer, Panzer Lehr Regiment,
130th Panzer Lehr Division:**

"On February 18, the 130th Panzer Lehr moved into the concentration area. The hazy and rainy weather was favourable for the movement of the units, but because of the expected strong enemy air activity they were widely dispersed.

"The matériel of the 130th Panzer Lehr Division was still good. We had an adequate supply of weapons but the general lack of vehicles was clearly noticeable.

"During February 18 the 1st Battalion of the Panzer Lehr Regiment arrived and was unloaded at Marienbaum without enemy air interference. The battalion had two companies with 14 Panther tanks and one company with 14 Jagdpanther tanks.

"On orders from 47 Panzer Corps, the division command post was established at a forester's house at Nachtigall, along with that of the 116th Panzer Division."

One more piece of luck favoured the Germans. Captain Horst Hanemann, commanding the regiment's 1st Battalion, recounts his problems in just getting to Nachtigall. When the unit received orders to move up to the Goch-Calcar line, it was assembled in Krefeld, south of Wesel: "We discovered that there was no petrol with which to transport our equipment by road. We were directed to Marienbaum and we had to travel the 45 kilometres by rail. On arrival on February 17 we were fortunate in being able to obtain fuel for our 14 Panther tanks. We also took command of two Grenadier battalions, and this force was loosed as a counter-attack against the Canadians who had advanced 2,000 yards to cut the road in depth."

**D-DAY
RHLI War Diary, February 19:**

Weather this morning for the attack not very promising. . . . Quite cold with heavy clouds. . . . Road conditions bad making vehicle movement slow.
0945 hours: Our artillery commenced firing on known enemy positions to soften them up for the coming Bde attack to seize vital ground south of the Goch-Calcar road.

Major Hudel:

"On February 19 the 1st Battalion was reinforced by one company (Panzer Mark IV tanks) and four anti-aircraft tanks. . . . There were in all 22 tanks ready for action that day.

"Since early morning very strong artillery fire could be heard at the front. The expenditure of ammunition was extraordinary; no one had ever heard anything like it before. The terrain was reconnoitred during the morning of the 19th and early in the afternoon the Kampfgruppe Hauser was alerted."

Brigadier Fred Cabeldu, Commander 4th Canadian Infantry Brigade:
"H-Hour was set for 1200 hours. As the battalions crossed the start line, it soon became evident that the enemy had a screen of anti-tank defences, including many 88mm guns, along the Goch-Calcar road. On the left, in the RHLI sector, we had three Kangaroo and six tank casualties and, altogether, there were 11 tank casualties. Some of the tanks, particularly on the left flank, were knocked out by mines. While for the most part the Kangaroos were able to drop the troops near the objectives, these vehicles were unable to get right onto the objectives because of severe anti-tank fire."

Lieutenant-Colonel Whitaker:
"When the forward companies moved up in the Kangaroos, I followed in one of the Fort Garry tanks. I intended using a milk factory I had spotted on the Goch-Calcar road as my Tac HQ.
"I think that was the most frightening part of the battle for me. I never did like riding in a tank — no infantryman does. I was jammed with all my equipment into the narrow co-driver's seat of the squadron commander's tank (Major Harvey Theobold), peering out at the limited field of vision the slits provided. It was quite eerie to watch the enemy shells silently hitting the ground and exploding just a few yards away. You could hear nothing except the noise of the motor of the tank and the explosion of our own gun firing.
"I felt as though I were in a tin box that was going to be hit and brewed up at any moment. I had so much gear on me, I didn't think I could have ever gotten out if the tank were hit.
"The squadron's lead troop of four tanks went ahead of us. They came out from behind the protection of the milk factory and crossed the Goch-Calcar road into the open. Suddenly, two of the tanks burst into flame. Then the remaining two were knocked out by the same German 88 firing from the left flank."

Major Harvey Theobald. For Garry Horse:
"As we went over the little crest I glanced over to my left and saw the RHLI carriers up in flames. Then I saw the German 88s. Our

radio net was jammed — it seemed as if 75 people were trying for the same airtime! I was screaming, trying to get on the air to the fellows and warn them.''

Lieutenant-Colonel Whitaker:

''When the squadron leader saw the forward tanks being brewed up he yelled to the driver, 'Driver reverse! Driver reverse!' Two shots narrowly missed us. The driver quickly reversed behind the milk factory, out of view of the 88.

''That was my traumatic introduction to the battle of the Goch-Calcar road. It was a close call.

''It took my men just two hours to get on their objectives — but it took another seven days to fend off the determined enemy counter-attacks before we completely secured them.

''In those first hours I discovered the bad news that we would have no protection from either flank. We already knew that our left was wide open. Then we discovered that the British 43rd Division had not secured the right, and that consequently the Essex Scottish were being overrun. We were threatened with the same fate ourselves.

''I spent a week there in the milk factory with my CO's rep and firm friend, Jack Drewry. Hour upon hour we sat at a scarred wooden table in one room of the factory, transfixed to our radio nets, hearing the desperate voices of my men calling my radio code name, 'Sunray': 'Sunray, this is Dog Four. . . . We are being attacked by German paratroopers in area DF8. MIKE Target! Now!' 'Sunray, this is Dog Two. My Sunray wounded.' 'Sunray, four enemy Panthers heading for DF6. Need Big Brothers [medium artillery] fast!'

''We called down target after target of artillery fire, trying to knock out the tanks and enemy paratroopers; we sent our men to attack the counter-attackers until I had no more men to send. One by one my top officers were wounded or killed. After 36 hours, I could no longer stay awake. I lay down on the rough concrete floor, amid crates and ungainly metal milk containers, and for a couple of hours I slept.''

Joe Pigott's war, already into its fifth year, had just a few more minutes to go. He had fought in North Africa, in Normandy, and at the Scheldt Estuary in Holland. Casualties at the latter operation had been replaced by untrained reinforcements. (This travesty was denied at the time, and has continued to be denied by many historians up until the present. The fact is that the chief of staff of Canadian Military Headquarters in London, Lieutenant-General Ken Stuart, fudged the casualty figures and kept from the Canadian Parliament and public the acute shortage of trained infantrymen. The crisis, when it came to light, was exacerbated by Canadian Prime Minister Mackenzie King's political manoeuvring to avoid the controversial issue of conscription.)

Since November, Pigott's company had been in a static defensive role near Nijmegen — with the enemy's FDL just across the road. It had hardly been conducive to setting up battle training exercises for his men, although he had tried to do just that.

Pigott's last moments of war left a lasting — and bitter — memory.

Major Joseph Pigott, commander C Company, RHLI:
''At least 60 to 70 per cent of my company was composed of men who'd never heard a shot fired in anger. Not only that, the majority of them had not even joined the infantry — they were men from the service corps, ordnance or artillery transferred in. The fact is — as we at the front saw it — a bunch of frightened politicians in Ottawa reacting to a highly aroused public opinion in Canada saw this move as a solution to a very critical problem. Hundreds — perhaps thousands — of young Canadians who were moved up to infantry front lines as reinforcements died as a result. It certainly wasn't one of the more glorious episodes in Canadian history.

''God knows I was scared enough, going to the start line — even a veteran battleline infantryman like myself. I couldn't help but think what must be going through the minds of those poor devils, who had no idea what the hell they were in for, or how to cope with what they were going to experience. I have never felt so sorry for anybody in my life. For most of them it must have been a horrible experience.

''We had tried desperately to teach them elementary tactics prior to the battle itself, but they really were like lambs led to slaughter. To me the gratifying thing was the way they conducted themselves. Very few of them actually failed to stand up to it. They walked in and did their best and, for the most part, ended up dead. But they distinguished themselves in spite of their lack of training. They were up against tough-as-nails paratroopers, some of them really well trained and experienced, who not only knew what they were doing; they were defending their own homeland.

''The situation wasn't improved any by the fact that some of the bodies of the Winnipeg Rifles who had been fighting through there several days before hadn't been picked up off the ground. The troops were having to step over corpses to get to the start line.

"The Germans put in a counter-barrage just 100 yards behind ours and we were taking terrible casualties. We had three Sherman tanks in support. Halfway to the objective, I looked around to see where they were positioned, and the first one was just going up in flames. Seconds later the second one went, and as I looked for the third, it too got hit — all by a single 88, and all in the space of 40 or 45 seconds. The turret flew open and the crew was already bailing out.

"I had instructed my men — because of their inexperience — to watch me and do what I did. About 150 yards short of the objective we came under some very heavy machine-gun fire, and to my horror, some of our own troops started to go to ground and the advance faltered. I had lectured them that this was a surefire recipe for certain death.

"At this point, to my absolute delight, Sergeant Pete Bolus came up with three carriers carrying flame-throwers. He went through us, and attacked the objective with those flame-throwers going full blast. It was a really courageous thing to do because the amount of protection you have as the occupant of a carrier is about equivalent to being in a sieve! But the sight of those flame-throwers threw the fear of God into the enemy. It really demoralized them. It also triggered our troops to get on their feet again and make the final dash to the objective.

"At this moment, Sergeant-Major Stewart ("Pinky") Moffatt, who'd been with me for several months in that capacity, got hit by a sniper in the lower jaw, smashing it badly and knocking out his teeth. He was in agony. I then proceeded to do a very foolish thing for an infantryman. I picked him up with the idea of putting him in the hallway of a farmhouse I'd singled out for my company HQ, out of harm's way until he could be taken away to a hospital.

"Upon opening the door, I found myself face-to-face with a young German soldier, about six-foot-four, with a grenade in his hand. We stared at each other for a few seconds, and then he threw it. It landed on the body of poor Moffatt, whom I immediately dropped, and it then exploded on my chest.

"I was wearing a set of experimental infantry body armour. It saved my life. The grenade blew a great big dent in it — my chest was black and blue for about six weeks after that — but if I hadn't had that on, I certainly would have been killed. As it was, shrapnel from the grenade pierced my windpipe and I was severely wounded. I was blown back out into the farmyard. For me, that was the end of the war."

Sergeant Pete Bolus, flame section commander, RHLI:

"It was the most vicious battle I remember. They killed Gordie Holder — our carrier platoon commander — right at the start. Going through that field with the flame section through C Company we saw a hedgerow, a barn, and a house. Pigott hollered, 'There are Germans in that house! Go and burn the bastards out!'

"The fuel was a black jelly that stayed in a mass like a tube of toothpaste. You'd fire it on the ground — that damned stuff, it would crawl along the ditch and over the top. . . . It wouldn't break, it would stay in a mass until it dissipated itself — it would stick and burn and keep on burning. If you ever got it on your clothes you were a goner. It was devastating. You ran.

"At this first burst of flame, C Company got going again. We had burnt the house and barn, and the hedgerow was on fire when they captured it. Pigott yelled, 'Get back and get some more fuel for those sardine cans!' When I returned, he and Pinky Moffatt were wounded."

The men of C Company were extremely shaken at the loss of their much-respected commander. The combined force of the demolition platoon and the badly mauled C Company now had only one officer left: Lieutenant Bob Wight, sturdily build, youthful commander of the demolition platoon. Wight quickly rallied the remaining troops and continued the advance to the Goch-Calcar road with (as he recalls) "such excellent Pioneers as Hank Johnson, along with NCOs such as Art Kelly and Joe Hounan sticking right by my side through it all."

Lieutenant R.W. (Bob) Wight, OC Demolition Platoon, RHLI:

"Our objective was the crossroads, but there was still one more farm to reach before we could get there. A manned 88 stood near one of the farm buildings. Suddenly, a single Canadian tank appeared. I had no radio or any means of communication, but somehow, by running in front of and alongside the tank, I was able to direct cannon and machine-gun fire directly at the farm and the 88 gun, and at the same time indicate that we would rush the farm.

"The tanker apparently understood. It was now my difficult task to rally the men for an all-out assault on the farmhouse and the 88 gun. It occurred to me that with fixed bayonets, everyone might gain the courage needed for this sort of head-on attack. The presence of some of my own platoon, whom I had known and respected for months, helped me greatly. I started to sing the Demolition Platoon theme song, 'L'Amour, L'Amour, L'Amour.' The men took up the song. Getting close to the building, we charged and threw our grenades. Finally we took the farm and some 20 German prisoners.

"We reached our objective, a farmhouse on the road, and every man started frantically to dig in. The fire rained down on us, so no one had to tell the men to dig."

Just ahead of Wight, the RHLI's left forward company, Major Kennedy's B Company, was having an equally tough time trying to reach its objective: the Schwanenhof farmstead, 400 yards or so over the Goch-Calcar road.

Lieutenant John Williamson, commander of 10th platoon, B Company, RHLI:

"That particular battle, for my platoon, didn't start off very well. In the FUP we were practising getting in and out of the Kangaroos while we were waiting to start. The men were carrying No. 75 anti-tank mines on their belts. These looked like Johnson's Wax tins with a detonator on the top. One dropped on the floor. Someone stepped on it and it blew up in the vehicle, badly mangling the poor guy's leg. So that sort of shook the platoon before we started off.

"The Kangaroos stopped some 200 yards or so short of our objective. It was all across open ground, and the enemy was out on the flank, firing at us. My company commander, Major Kennedy, told me to organize my platoon to provide covering fire and lay down smoke with a two-inch mortar while he led the other two platoons across. It turned out we only had 13 smoke bombs, and by the time the company got to the objective the supply of bombs was exhausted. Then I led my platoon across. We came under fire from a machine gun. I was shot through the leg and fell or jumped into a crater. A stretcher-bearer put some sulpha powder on my leg and wrapped it up, so I carried on. In the meantime, of course, the platoon had kept on going and was on the objective when I got there.

"When we got into the farm area where we eventually consolidated, the other two platoons were dug in and the enemy was trying to infiltrate back. Some of my men were in the stable firing with rifles at Germans coming up a ditch 150 yards to the front. They had shot two or three of them when I arrived. The Germans were returning the fire.

"It was at this point that Major Kennedy got wounded. He and I were standing beside one of these machines that farmers use to thrash the skin off onions when a round hit the handle. The shot ricocheted off and hit Major Kenedy just below the belt. He was taken down to the basement of the farm, where he set up his company HQ, and although wounded he ran the battle from there.

"We were counter-attacked several times. The Germans were right in on top of us and, on a couple of occasions, were right in the same building with us! They ran in, threw a couple of grenades, and ran out again.

"Later, the counter-attacking became heavier. I got on the wireless to Battalion HQ to ask for artillery support. Being somewhat uninitiated to all the terminology, I asked Lieutenant-Colonel Whitaker for 'Big Brothers,' which of course I now realize meant 100-pounders (medium artillery). I intended to ask just for our mortars. We got the artillery on our position all right and it did the job, but it certainly surprised the hell out of me!

"Later that night, the Germans blew a hole through the end of the pigpen adjacent to the farmhouse with a Panzerfaust and started coming in through it. I had a tommy-gun — I'd got it from American airborne troops down at Nijmegen — and I let go with the whole 30 rounds out of the kitchen window and killed the first German officer who came through the hole. The others, I guess, dispersed and came under fire from the rest of the platoon.

"The weird thing I recall about that particular incident: I'd had a man posted out in the pigpen and I had just moved him into the parlour next door. I don't know whether he was leaning against or lying on top of a piano, but every time he fired his rifle you could hear the bloody piano tinkling."

Lieutenant-Colonel Whitaker:
"Two hours after the battle had commenced, at 1400 hours, my two forward companies were firmly consolidated on their objectives some 400 yards beyond the Goch-Calcar road. Behind them, Froggett and Wight also had their companies dug in. Battalion HQ was established in the milk factory on the north side of the road midway between and less than 100 yards from them."

Brigadier Cabeldu:

"RHLI had been quick in forming up and moving forward and, after heavy fighting, they managed to secure ground almost on their objective; on the right flank the Essex Scottish situation became obscure early in the battle because of communications casualties.

"At 1416 hours, February 19, the enemy made his first counter-attack on positions held by Essex Scottish. The counter-attack was made frontally and from the right with a considerable force of infantry supported by tanks; this was the first indication of the arrival of the 116th Panzer and the Panzer Lehr Division in that sector."

Major Charles Barrett, Brigade Major, 4th Brigade, 2nd Canadian Infantry Division:

"The Essex were being overrun because their right flank was exposed, due to lack of cover on that flank. On February 19 we had a liaison officer from the British at 4th Brigade HQ, and we asked him for the position of his troops. They were supposed to be coordinating their attack with us.

"After we'd launched the attack, word came back that the British hadn't moved, they hadn't gone into the attack at all. I remember, at the time, I was really shocked to hear this. We asked them why they hadn't moved, and their general or brigadier, or whoever it was that was in charge of that unit, said that he felt we could handle the situation on our own. But he never told us that he wasn't going to move. To my naive mind, I thought that was a terrible breach of conduct and discipline.

"We received word that Lieutenant-Colonel Pangman, CO of the Essex Scottish, had gone to ground, and that his HQ was being overrun by German tanks. It was reported that there were 400 Essex missing from the battalion."

Lieutenant-Colonel Whitaker:

"At nightfall, the Fort Garry tanks withdrew to replenish their fuel and ammunition. Our Allied tanks hated to be exposed in darkness when they were most vulnerable to enemy patrol attacks. The difficulty was that the German Panzer battalions did not share this apprehension, so we were often faced — as we were on the Goch-Calcar road that night — with enemy tanks attacking tankless infantry."

As it happened, another piece of horrible luck was taking place over the hill on the enemy side — in the form of a family reunion of German officers in a forester's hut. By sheer chance, two of the most experienced professional armoured corps and division commanders of the Wehrmacht were pooling their knowledge of the calibre of one battalion of Canadian volunteer soldiers — the RHLI.

Schwanenhof farm was their objective; Schwanenhof was where Dunc Kennedy, rugged features set against his severe wounds, was propped up in a cellar desperately trying to hold B Company together.

Lieutenant-Colonel Guderian:
"At 1630 hours the commanding general of the 47 Panzer Corps, General von Luettwitz, visited the CP of 116th Panzer Division by chance. It happened that the commander of 116th Panzer, Major-General von Waldenburg, was his cousin. Von Luettwitz stayed for supper. We spoke during the supper about the counter-attack planned that night by the 6th German Parachute Division and the Panzer Lehr. Kampfgruppe Hauser was alerted.

"We knew who was on the other side. We had all the battalion commanders' names but the names were not important. The quality of troops in each battalion was important. This we also knew."

A translation of the history of the Panzer Lehr Division gives this account of the action that night:

"At 2000 hours Kpfgr. von Hauser launched its frontal attack, on both sides supported: on the right by elements of 6th Parachute Division, on the left by 116th Panzer Division. As soon as the tanks rolled across the forward edge of the Canadians' position, their artillery fired barrages which made movement difficult and separated the German infantry from their tanks. Nevertheless, by midnight in the struggle for Schwanenhof, it changed hands several times. But the attack was halted at the Road Goch-Calcar, access to the area beyond it was denied by concentrated fire."

The crack 116th Panzer Windhund Division was beaten off by Major Louis Froggett's D Company on the right, but its Airborne Reconnaissance Regiment ("very tough, very brave," commented Guderian) managed to get across the road into the sector where the Essex were supposed to be.

Lieutenant-Colonel Whitaker:
"Back in the milk factory, we were swamped by reports from the FOOs and my company commanders about this extremely dangerous counter-attack. The Panzer Lehr attacked Kennedy's B Com-

pany at Schwanenhof from the south and the decimated C Company from the east.

"Jack Drewry and his gunner crew of two — the latter operating the 19-set from a half-track behind my HQ — swung into non-stop action that was to continue through the night. Jack was a big, bluff, good-looking, hard-drinking officer who never lost his cool. His gunners were an unlikely-looking crew, both characters: Steve Pinchuck, the driver, claimed to be the world's best half-track operator — and he was. 'Coop' Cooper, an excellent signaller, was an accomplished jazz player who had his own 4th Field Regiment band. His favourite tune was 'Pistol Packin' Mama' ('Lay that pistol down, babe'). Through numerous battles, those three men were responsible for saving many, many RHLI lives; the enemy laid many pistols down.

"Drewry had direct call on 24 guns of 4th Field (a MIKE target) and a call on all the guns of the three field regiments in 2nd Canadian Division when available (an UNCLE target). He called down many MIKEs and UNCLEs that night. It was a MIKE target Scale 5 artillery concentration (five rounds per gun fired rapidly in succession) that dispersed the enemy from C Company's HQ."

An impressed Gunner history reported: "In a hectic period of twelve hours, guns of the 4th Field poured 5,400 shells into one small area as they broke up determined German counter-attacks."

Lieutenant-Colonel Whitaker:
"The RHLI endured and fought off eight counter-attacks that night. My companies were being hard-pressed and our casualties were terrible. Around midnight I ordered my LOB reserves to reinforce the position (personnel 'left out of battle' to ensure battalion continuity). With some difficulty, Lieutenant Ken Dugall brought them forward."

D-PLUS-ONE
RHLI War Diary, February 20:
Weather this morning is damp and cold with visibility approx 400 yds. The condition of the roads has become steadily worse as a result of the rain which fell yesterday afternoon and evening.
0800 hours: At daylight this morning the enemy counter-attacked with tanks and infantry.

The disappearance of the Essex Scottish, who had vanished without a trace 24 hours earlier, was the cause of considerable concern. At first it was believed that the battalion had been annihilated.

Later it was learned that the Essex had been overrun. Fifty men were taken prisoner and 150 killed or wounded. During this time the CO, Lieutenant-Colonel John Pangman, was out of communication. Cabeldu sent the reserve battalion, the Royal Regiment of Canada, to restore the Essex area. It was not until 1400 hours on D-plus-One that Pangman was rescued from an empty cellar in a farmhouse where he had been holed up.

Gradually, as the day wore on, other individuals and small groups reappeared back at the start line. However, an entire company was still unaccounted for.

Several men who had been taken prisoner escaped and got back to the line. One such was Major Bruce ("Moose") MacDonald, OC A Squadron, Fort Garry Horse. His escape from careless guards and his hazardous return across 10 miles of enemy-held territory have become legendary in his regiment.

Because the Essex Scottish had not got on their objectives, D Company on the Rileys' (as the RHLI were called) right flank had no protection at all. Moreover, the Germans would have a clear swing at Battalion HQ if the company were knocked out.

In an impressive mix of gunnery skill and infantry tactics, Froggett collaborated with an anti-tank officer, Lieutenant David Heaps of C Troop, 18th Canadian Anti-Tank Battery, to destroy four enemy tanks headed for the RHLI HQ.

Major Louis Froggett, Commander D Company, RHLI:
"We could hear the Germans warming up their tanks in the woods about 800 yards out front. My company HQ was in a farmhouse forward of the Goch-Calcar road, less than a hundred yards to the right of Battalion HQ. The Germans had been shelling us very heavily and from what I could judge, they were going to attack across the field towards our positions. I had a pretty good idea where the anti-tank guns should be sited to meet the attack. So I went over and talked to the anti-tank officer and said, 'I want you over at D Company.' He agreed and we sited his 17-pounder right in behind a little building.

"We were absolutely determined that the Germans would be destroyed by our 17-pounder, especially if we could get them in enfilade. We explained to everybody in the company that it was important to wait for the tanks to come in. No matter how close they came, nobody was to fire until our anti-tank gun fired. That is exactly what happened. The anti-tank gun opened up and it knocked the tanks out: one, two, three, four. . . . The tanks fired up and Germans were jumping out of there — they were frying on the hot metal. We knocked out all their infantry too.

"If those tanks had gotten through D Company, they would have hit Battalion Headquarters and rolled up the battalion. They were stopped right in front of the milk factory, less than a hundred yards away."

Semper Paratus, the RHLI history:
Whitaker came barrelling up (from a Brigade "O" Group) in his jeep . . . and hit his brakes viciously when he noticed four Panthers in battle formation barely forty yards from the crossroads. "I was pretty upset until I noticed smoke coming from one of them, and realized that they were knocked out," Whitaker recalled. "A little farther down the road I met the gunner. You could tell he'd done it by the smile on his face."

RHLI War Diary, February 20:
1000 hours: During the course of the day all company positions were continually mortared and several counter-attacks were successfully beaten off with many enemy casualties. B Company (Maj Kennedy) seems to be bearing the brunt of these attacks but is standing up well, with everyone doing a remarkably good job.

At 1900 hours, Kennedy's beleaguered B Company at Schwanen-hof came under yet another counter-attack. Captured enemy documents confirm that von Luettwitz had issued specific orders to retake this position. Shells and mortar fire rained down as four Panthers and a company of Panzer Lehr closed in on the battered Rileys.

Corporal Eldrid Severin, 12th Platoon, B Company, RHLI:
"Major Kennedy had been hit pretty bad. The Germans brought their tanks into our front and then their infantry circled us on both sides. When we saw them coming towards us, Lieutenant D.W. Ashbury crawled out into the field with a PIAT and knocked out one tank. That slowed 'em but they kept on coming. They over-ran our company HQ."

Lieutenant-Colonel Whitaker:

''I received a call over the battalion radio net that the Panzer Lehr infantry had broken in strength into Kennedy's B Company position and had captured the company HQ. Lieutenant Williamson reported that the situation was desperate and they weren't sure how long they could hold out without help. I told him that all our troops were committed but I would do what I could.

''I called in Lieutenant Johnny Lawless — he commanded the scout platoon which was also the Battalion HQ protection platoon. Now it was to become our counter-attack force. Lawless had about 20 to 25 men. I told him to get over there and retake the position.

''The scouts moved silently across the field to B Company position and surrounded the company HQ house. Suddenly Lawless gave the signal and his men started yelling and making a terrific noise, throwing many grenades through the windows before rushing it. The operation was a complete success. Twenty-five Germans were killed or wounded and another 50 taken prisoner; our only casualty was Lawless, who was slightly wounded by shrapnel from one of his own grenades. B Company position was finally stabilized.''

D-PLUS-TWO

For 48 hours, Major Ken McIntyre of the Essex Scottish Regiment, and the battered remnants of his company, had been hanging on in total isolation, continuously surrounded by the enemy, before he finally decided to evacuate his men.

Essex Scottish War Diary, February 21:

At 0300 hrs A Coy under Maj KW MacIntyre . . . returned
from what was thought to be the land of the missing.
There was great jubilation and as the stories came out it
became evident that A Coy's stand ''because no order had
been received by them to withdraw'', had left them holding the battalion front with thirty-five men and several
wounded.

Major Ken McIntyre, OC A Company, Essex Scottish Regiment:

''We were taken up to our objective very successfully by Kangaroos. As soon as we hit the objective, things changed drastically. We came under immediate fire, which was a little unexpected because the intelligence we'd had said we weren't that close to the enemy.

"We had some tanks, but one of them burned up and there were some casualties with the other two. Through no fault of theirs, they were not too helpful. It really became a foot-soldier's operation. I'd issued orders previously that we were to dig in as soon as we got on the objective. Although we had several casualties (one of my platoon commanders was killed immediately), we were able to defend the position for a good period.

"So we held on. We weren't approached. Our casualties had occurred when we arrived. After that, all we had was some small-arms fire and occasional field-gun fire.

"The decision I had to make, knowing we were out of communication with Pangman, was whether to sit on that ground and do what we could — we could have held on, we felt — or get back to fight another day. We had a number of wounded by this time. I consulted with my two other platoon commanders and we agreed that we should try to get back.

"A corporal — a stretcher-bearer corporal, a wonderful little guy by the name of Ed — volunteered to stay with the wounded until we returned.

"We were occupying a farmhouse, and it had a good cellar where we were set up. The next thing that happened, a tank stuck its 88mm gun through the door of our building and blew it all to hell. We had a job getting out of the cellar, and we had to shore the thing up to protect the wounded. It was a difficult situation. We finally got back to our own lines with about 75 per cent of the company."

RHLI War Diary, February 21:
0900 hours: Today's sitrep from Brigade reported that our battalion had knocked out nine Panther tanks, three SP 88mm guns and two half-tracks.
1330 hours: The Adjt, Capt WO Avery visited Brigade re replacement of casualties and put in an estimate of 150 ORs and 6 offrs.

Lieutenant-Colonel Whitaker:
"When I visited the forward companies I found the men tired but still determined to continue to hold. They were proud of their achievements, despite the cost.

"The first clear weather the men had seen since the attack was launched allowed the Typhoons to operate again against enemy positions.

"That night, a rare mid-battle message came from General Crerar: 'Desire you convey to Lt-Col WHITAKER OC RHLI my congratulations on and admiration of the gallant and most successful fighting carried out by all ranks of the regiment he commands during last forty eight hours.'

"A pencilled note from the divisional commander, Major-General Bruce Matthews, concurred: '2nd Canadian Division is proud of the recent achievements of the RHLI. My congratulations to all ranks. You are making history — keep up the good work.' "

D-PLUS-FOUR
Lieutenant-Colonel Whitaker:

"The battle was far from over. Sporadic enemy counterattacks persisted. I thought the only way to secure complete control of the Goch-Calcar road was to clear out the German positions in a wooded area 500 yards to the south of us. I ordered Froggett's D Company to make a silent, unsupported night attack on the woodland."

Major Froggett:

"We were established in a farmhouse the first night of the silent attack and they counter-attacked us but only lightly with about . . . oh, half a platoon which we captured. An hour later, more Germans came at us, but we beat them off too."

Lieutenant Ken Dugall, platoon commander, D Company, RHLI:

"There was a hedge there, thick and thorny. As they tried to jump through the hedge we were shooting them. There were fellows lying there with their arms twisted, some shot through the knee and screaming blue murder. . . . Oh Jesus, it was terrible.

"The next morning the Germans put up a white flag. A young German officer and a German stretcher-bearer, who spoke quite good English, came over and told Sergeant Herb Prince that they wanted to pick up these guys who were lying just in front of the hedge, just about five feet away. There were about 35 wounded, mostly German."

Froggett, unarmed and accompanied only by his batman (and wearing an ordinary soldier's greatcoat without any rank badges), walked out in the field to meet the Germans.

Major Froggett:

"I decided that I might as well talk to their commander and see whether or not he might be ready to call it quits in this war. I met two of them, two paratroop lieutenants, both of them looked about six-foot-six. I insisted on the courtesy of my rank, which was very difficult to get, but I got it. I gave them a cigarette (they wanted to take the whole package), we had a chat, and finally it turned out that they'd decided I wanted to surrender. So I said to one lieutenant, talking through this first-aid fellow, 'You know, you can tell these officers that the war is over and they're going to be killed.' The reply came back, 'We will die for Hitler.' "

Lieutenant Dugall:

"Major Froggett said, 'Okay, pick up your wounded.' All of a sudden there must have been 20 Germans swarming about, all wearing Red Cross armbands. Obviously, they were trying to get a good look at our position.

"So we said, 'Okay, so we'll go over and have a good look at theirs.' Then this big guy with the paratroop helmet came over and said, 'Tonight we fix you. Tonight you're finished.'

"But that night another sergeant and myself were waiting, and as the Germans sneaked up, we heaved grenades at them. The next morning the big tall guy was lying there, wounded."

D-PLUS-SEVEN

For 72 hours Froggett clung to his precarious outpost, withstanding countless counter-attacks day and night.

He was told that 2 Canadian Corps was launching a major operation, Operation Blockbuster, through his line. "Hang on at all costs!" he was instructed. But his position was becoming desperate.

Major Froggett:

"We were almost completely overrun. There were tanks all around us, and my men were fighting hand-to-hand with the paratroops. It was the grisliest day of the war for me. Men were shouting, punching, heaving grenades, firing pistols, and swinging everything they could put their hands to.

"Lieutenant D.D. Edwards, my FOO, was with me in the little frame cottage when all of a sudden a tank started pushing the wall down. There were 40 or so German civilians in our cellar, all screaming. Edwards called down everything artillery could send directly on our position. The Germans were above ground and they got it. We were pretty well dug in.''

This dramatic action finally quelled the enemy opposition. Sergeant Prince, who was hit by a sniper's bullet later that morning, noted a strange and curiously humane finale to the vicious and inhumane fighting of the past eight days: ''The guy on the stretcher across from me [the RHLI history relates] was the young German officer I had met under the white flag only two days before. He smiled at me; I was so woozy that I couldn't smile back. But — just imagine! — he reached over and squeezed my hand. Here we'd just been through a scrap as bloody as Dieppe!''

In the battle of the Goch-Calcar road, the Essex Scottish incurred over 200 casualties, including 51 killed, 99 wounded, and 54 taken prisoner. The Royals lost 64 men.

The RHLI casualties were 125. (None were captured.) But they had, as always, held their objective and extracted a severe penalty from their German adversaries. Some 200 Germans had been found dead around D Company alone. The brigade took 275 prisoners. The 46 prisoners from Baron Hauser's elite Panzer Lehr battle group were a special prize for the Rileys.

Brigadier Cabeldu:
''All units have done an exceptionally fine job of fighting, and the RHLI 'fortress' is an outstanding example of a well-planned and executed operation and of the ability of our troops under good leadership and by sheer guts and determination to take and hold difficult ground against the enemy's best.''

13

Grenade! GIs Conquer the Roer

AT PRECISELY 0245 HOURS in the cold, dark, pre-dawn hours of February 23, two thousand Allied guns roared their angry message in an intensive 45-minute bombardment. And at 0330 hours, infantrymen of six American divisions seized 400-pound assault boats and wrestled them through oozing mud into the still-swollen Roer. Operation Grenade was on.

Committing this enormous force to battle had been a gamble born of desperation. On February 15 at Siersdorf Castle, a wave of suppressed excitement swept General Simpson's Ninth Army HQ. For the first time, the war room charts indicated a slight drop in the water level of the flooded Roer.

During the next five days, all attention was rivetted to the flood barometers. General James E. Moore, brilliant Ninth Army chief of staff, recalled those anxious days that led to taking the gamble. ''We were intently watching that waterflow. I remember General Nicholas [Brigadier-General Richard U. Nicholas, Chief Engineer, Ninth U.S. Army] — I was in his office five times a day — had observers all along the Roer.'' Finally, on February 21, the decision was made: the river, though still swollen, could be crossed and bridged successfully within two days.

The new invasion date was chosen in full knowledge that the Roer, though abating, would not by any means have returned to its normal banks. Ninth Army engineers deliberately took on a challenge of enormous and grave consequence — the challenge of moving men and building bridges over turbulent and treacherous waters — in order to achieve surprise.

If Simpson had waited until the river levels were safe, the enemy

---

See Map 5 (Appendix B).

would have been able to estimate, almost to the hour, when the attack would be launched. With the German guns ready and waiting, the troop casualties could have been disastrously high.

Intelligence reports indicated that there had been no significant shift south of the Wehrmacht armoured and parachute divisions. The bulk of the German line was still massed against the northern arm of the pincer movement, Veritable.

"[General Simpson] deliberately decided to take a few losses on the crossing to achieve surprise," Moore recalled. "I think we saved quite a lot of lives by doing it that way."

Simpson had a second surprise up his sleeve for the enemy. He had been intently studying the detailed intelligence reports and map overlays of the Siegfried defence lines between the Roer and the Rhine. Those defences would be hard to crack. He detailed the problems to his staff:

Beyond the Roer are well prepared defenses ranging in depth back to the Rhine. The first of these is a double line of trenches running south through Erkelenz to Linnich and east to the Erft canal. The latter part of this line commands the vital Linnich-Harff plateau. Some 5 miles further back is a second defense line covering approaches to Muenchen-Gladbach which includes fire trenches, belts of mines and wire and numerous heavily defended villages. Both these lines as well as other separate fortified areas face generally west and south but are more vulnerable on the east.

Simpson realized that an advance coming from the south would have the advantage of outflanking most of these defences. He wanted to get six divisions across the Roer on a 17-mile front and then pivot four of them north. On the right, 29th and 30th Divisions would be on the outside of the wheel. They would have to push hard to close the line with 13 Corps commander Gillem's 84th and 102nd Divisions. Then the four divisions would attack north and northwest behind the enemy's Erkelenz-Linnich defence line.

With the German defences rolled up, General John B. Anderson's 35th and 79th Infantry Divisions, 16 Corps, would be able to get across almost unopposed north of Linnich. Then the armour could break through the remaining defences. The Americans would link up with First Canadian Army, and the whole weight of three-quarters of a million men would turn east and head for the Rhine. "Relentless pursuit" — that was the key to success, Simpson stressed to all his commanders.

The soft-spoken Texan's plan was stunning. Wheeling an entire army — 300,000 men, with their vehicles and arms — was cumbersome and time-consuming. Wheeling it twice around (so that "it looked like the letter 'E,' " as newsman Wes Gallagher described it), and achieving this without pause, is audacious in the extreme and potentially risky. While Ninth Army pivoted north, its southern flank would be wide open to attack. Simpson confirmed with Hodges that two infantry divisions of his First U.S. Army — Allen's 104th Timberwolves and Major-General Bill Weaver's 8th Division — would force a crossing of the Roer at Dueren at the same time as the Ninth Army attack in order to secure that open flank.

To keep up the driving momentum that Simpson demanded, it was essential that vehicles, support weapons, and armour be transported over to the east-bank bridgehead as swiftly as possible. This meant bridges — and, before the bridges, boatloads of infantrymen and combat engineers to cross the murky waters and secure the immediate banks.

Even from the beginning, it was evident that there would be problems. The boats were a problem: there weren't enough, and those they had were needed by the engineers to be used as pontoons for the bridges. Lend them to the infantry, the engineers were told. Use them afterwards for pontoons.

The strong currents were a problem. Another trick was pulled out of the hat: drag underwater cables across to anchor the footbridges; stretch overhead cables so the men can pull themselves across.

The Germans on the opposite bank were definitely a problem. The solution: mask your operation with smoke. Keep their heads down with artillery bombardments. Knock out the machine-gun nests with patrols.

The 84th U.S. Division soon discovered that all these obstacles were very hazardous — and none of the proposed solutions entirely worked. Improvisation became the order of the day.

The 84th and 102nd Divisions (the two divisions of General Gillem's 13 Corps) shared the most northerly sector of the assault zone. Here the Roer spilled over onto flat, marshy banks. General Alexander R. Bolling, 84th Division commander, had ordered up a tremendous show of firepower, the greatest single artillery effort in the division's combat history.

"Everything we had, we fired," said First Lieutenant Robert

Truitt. "Besides the usual heavy artillery, there were all the .50- and .30-calibre machine guns, the tanks, and the self-propelled guns; they all opened up at that moment."

Tanks from the 771st Tank Battalion lined up hub-to-hub along the bank to add their weight to the fire plan. So much ammunition was fired that crews in the tanks became sick from the fumes and were forced to seek air to relieve their nausea. During one 15-minute period, one tank fired 75 rounds and another fired 60 — the equivalent to a basic load of ammunition for one day's combat.

The first wave of the 334th Infantry Regiment — 84th Division's narrow crossing site allowed only one regiment to spearhead the attack — made a textbook-perfect crossing. As each squad of infantrymen moved down to the water's edge, they picked up the heavy weapons stockpiled earlier by the bank. There they were met by an engineer guide who led them to the boats. Crossing in 15-man assault craft, the men were safely over the flooded marshland with no casualties in just over half an hour.

"I really don't know whether the enemy fired any shots at us or not," reported First Lieutenant Richard Hawkins. "Our own guns going off all around us in support of our crossing drowned out all other sounds."

Waiting to cross with 334th's 3rd Battalion, Lieutenant Kenneth MacInnis was still digging in with his platoon as the barrage began: "The sky seemed to split as 76s on the tanks barked, the heavy artillery rumbled, . . . and thousands of tracers streaked across the river."

It was daylight when MacInnis's turn came to make the crossing. The unexpected ease of the initial crossing was transformed into utter chaos. "Smoke and fog hung so thick over the water that it was impossible to see the other shore," he recounted. Leading his platoon to the staging area, MacInnis discovered to his chagrin that the boats that were supposed to have been recovered from the first wave's crossing were not there.

The engineers had badly underestimated the flow of the river. This created problems that were to have repercussions for all the subsequent troops. The strong current had deposited some of the boats of the first wave 75 to 100 yards downstream. It would be virtually impossible to recover them in the darkness. Other boats had been shot full of holes.

The Germans had by now recovered from the barrage: "[They]

began throwing in mortars and what seemed to be extra-big mortars or rockets. Some men were wounded while searching for boats or waiting their turn to cross," the platoon commander reported.

Of the original 70 craft, the battalion had only 20 to start with, and they ended up with no more than 10. Many of the boats were caught by the swift current. A wire cable that had been stretched across to assist in the crossing proved disastrous. Boats were swept against it and overturned.

"Men struggled in the river," MacInnis recalled. "Most managed to flounder back to their starting place. One whole squad was overturned and was unable to rejoin the platoon until late afternoon."

Finally, as craft were located, men were sent across in shuttles. As a result, it took over three hours for the hapless 3rd Battalion to complete the crossing. Then, because of their scattered arrival, it took additional time for them to reassemble.

At the crossing site, engineers worked at fever pitch to erect footbridges for the reserve troops waiting on the west bank to cross on foot. Then a new problem loomed out of the skies: "We saw our first German jet planes that day," Truitt recalls. "They were trying to get the bridges."

The Luftwaffe, which had been harassing the Veritable force at Goch, 45 miles north, now turned out aggressively on the Grenade front. No fewer than 97 sorties were flown by the Luftwaffe — including some by the startling new jets — in an attempt to knock out the American bridgeheads.

These German Me-262 jets were the first to appear on any front. Had their production not been stalled when Hitler decided to change their design from fighter to fighter-bomber, this new product of the still-fertile German inventiveness might have made a serious impact on the progress of the war. By February 1945, it was a case of too few, too late — but the sight of these super-planes was an amazing one for Allied troops.

Sergeant Philip Polozotto was astonished to see four fighter planes with American markings attacking his position. "At first we were very surprised that our own people would be after us. Then we realized that the Germans had captured the planes and started using them against us."

Finally, after enemy mortars had knocked out three attempts to erect a footbridge, one was completed just before noon. However, the treadway bridge for vehicle traffic was not finished until 2000 hours. "Fifteen minutes later," Major Jones of division engineers reported, "just as the lead vehicles were about to start across, more

German planes came over and strafed the bridge and knocked the pontoons out. This delayed our use of the bridge until about 1100, 24 February." Three men were killed in the attack on the bridgehead.

Meanwhile, the three battalions of the 334th had advanced so aggressively that they had out distanced their supporting arms. Their vehicles and anti-tank weapons were still isolated on the west bank pending the construction of a treadway bridge.

By evening of D-Day, the 334th found themselves in a dangerously vulnerable position. More than three miles forward of the whole corps, they were attacking the town of Baal, on the planning board as their D-plus-One objective. They were out of communication, both their flanks were exposed, and they had "nothing on either side but Jerries," as MacInnis recounted.

It was "a most ticklish moment," noted Lieutenant Clifton L. MacLachlan, assistant operations staff officer (S-3) of the regiment. "We still had no bridges capable of carrying more than a jeep. We had no anti-tank guns across, no artillery, tanks, or tank destroyers."

Simpson had said "relentless pursuit" and his men were determined to achieve it for him. Despite the dangers of sending them ahead of their supporting arms, the urgency of pulling off the breakout dictated the gamble. The situation was saved for the moment when P-47 fighters came tearing out of the skies, strafing the enemy in the woods and firing rockets.

Later that same evening the Germans laid on two counter-attacks supported by tanks that were finally repelled by the exhausted riflemen early the next afternoon.

"Enemy bullets began pounding the rear of [our] building," recalled platoon commander Lieutenant William Nelson. "Germans seemed to be everywhere but in the dark they could not be spotted. Machine gun and BAR [Browning Automatic Rifle] fire held the attackers back but our ammunition ran low."

Nelson had no radio communication. He sent runners to the company command post to call artillery on his position but the runners were cut down. Finally, artillery was brought down and the attack was subdued.

In pockets of desperate struggle such as this, the 84th Infantry Division fought on without armour or heavy weapons for 36 hours.

Two miles upstream, the two lead regiments of the 102nd Infantry Division, the 405th and 407th Infantry Regiments, were preparing to launch their assault at Linnich. Smoke had been released about 1,000 yards upriver as a diversionary action, drawing enemy artillery and mortar fire away from the actual assault area. In all, 980 smoke pots set in bunches 15 yards apart blanketed the region for more than two hours.

Thirty minutes before H-Hour, the extraordinary young patrol leader Lieutenant Roy Rogers, with his band of 16 men and two engineers of the 407th, put on a daring raid that crumpled the enemy's immediate defences on the far bank.

Rogers's Raiders had already achieved fame for their earlier patrols. But the next moments would justify their very existence. Rogers's mission: to knock out enemy machine-gun emplacements dug in along a low dike on the far shore that threatened the success of the operation. Even before they pushed off, three of the men were wounded by shrapnel from an exploding German mortar bomb. Rogers himself was nicked in the eye (an injury that was later to cause temporary blindness).

The Raiders paddled furiously against the racing current. A German machine-gun opened up not 50 yards away, barely missing them. Ashore, the men scrambled hastily up the slippery slopes, and, with the precision for which Rogers's operations were renowned, fanned out purposefully on their objectives. Tossing a grenade into each machine-gun nest, they leaped upon the survivors, killing the rest in fierce hand-to-hand fighting. Four such MG nests were destroyed.

Minutes later, as the 407th's assault battalions crossed, a fifth nest — one that Rogers and his crew had spared — came to life, shooting from a camouflaged Red Cross aid station. It was angrily silenced.

In that savage half-hour of action, Rogers's Raiders cleared a 200-yard front, knocked out six automatic weapon positions as well as the MGs, and killed or captured 23 Germans. (Later that night at Field HQ, Rogers was awarded an immediate Silver Star by 102nd Division Commander General Frank A. Keating himself.) With the opposition thus partially quelled, 1st Battalion 407th Regiment crossed with only light casualties. On landing they captured 25 shell-shocked prisoners whom they persuaded to guide them safely across the minefields.

The barrage had undoubtedly killed and maimed many of the defenders, and demoralized those who survived the torrent of fire. The division chaplain observed a pitiful parade of German prisoners in the early hours of the battle. He reported that they all seemed numb and shell-shocked, and that many of the younger ones were shaking and crying.

When the barrage ended, however, subsequent waves of the assault troops met with havoc. The CO of 2nd Battalion, 405th Infantry Regiment, Lieutenant-Colonel Buford Bryant, led his men to the staging area and found just two boats moored on the shore and no engineers to guide them. After considerable confusion, more boats were rounded up.

"It was every man for himself," Bryant reported angrily. "We had to grab any boat that came along." Fifty of Bryant's men were swept downstream. (These men later found their way back to the line.)

The 407th's 2nd Battalion was equally unlucky. Its CO, Lieutenant-Colonel John Wohner, termed the crossing "disorganized," again faulting the engineers who had let the infantrymen down badly. Private First Class John Emerich, part of this second wave, echoes his commanding officer's criticisms.

"Our engineer crawled in behind a bank and wouldn't come out so we paddled the boat across ourselves. It was so packed, there were only about two inches between the water and the gunwale. A lot of boats swamped. We hit a current in the middle and the boat just twirled around and hit the near shore twice. The third try, we finally got across. But we lost more people from drowning than we did from the enemy rifles." An attempt was made to send three loads of LVTs (landing vehicles tracked, such as Alligators or Buffaloes) across, but the current was too swift and the far bank too muddy to land.

If the engineers were criticized for their ferrying procedures, they were resoundingly praised for their efforts in just about every other field of operation. Combat engineers of the 102nd crossed with the initial waves and set to work clearing minefields, repairing roads, and filling shell craters. When bulldozers could be taken across, the engineer operators worked tirelessly making the crossing sites and roads usable.

More teams of engineers struggled to put in infantry support bridges. At H-plus-20 hours, two were completed. An out-of-control LVT knocked out the first before it could be put to use, sending the bridging material crashing downstream. Work was immediately begun to rebuild it.

This became the recurrent theme for all the divisional engineers during the first 24 hours of the assault. Just as a bridge would be completed, enemy mortars or aircraft would smash it, or the other major foe of the day, the currents and floating debris, would sabotage it. Some of the first narrow footbridges snapped their cables and were swept downstream under the weight of the troops. Rubber pontoon bridges became punctured by enemy fire.

Until these bridges were erected, the tanks, tank destroyers (TDs), and heavy artillery pieces could not cross to support the vulnerable forward troops. Even when infantry support bridges were completed, the long line of TDs waiting impatiently to cross often had to yield to trucks hauling the rubble that was so urgently needed to repair the shell-torn and rutted roads. Rolls of steel mesh were used to keep vehicles from sinking to their axles.

The fragile bridgehead was in serious peril as ominous reports came in of enemy counter-attacks.

Late on the afternoon of D-Day, 405th Infantry Regiment was consolidating its position in the town of Boslar. The day had turned warm and sunny with the first stirrings of spring. Lieutenant Joe Lane was actually playing football with his platoon (using a cabbage for a ball) when the counter-attack came in. Twenty self-propelled guns of the German 341st Assault Gun Brigade and two infantry companies attempted to encircle the village. The attack was stopped, but two or three of those dangerous guns managed to break through into the town.

At 2200 hours a second attack was made. Throughout the night the intensity of the counter-attacks increased as the enemy stubbornly hammered at them. Seven times, German tanks and infantry dug in at the outskirts of the hamlet pounded at the beleaguered force.

"On the fourth try, enemy tanks and infantry succeeded in penetrating the town," Lieutenant-Colonel Eric Bischoff, CO of the battalion, reported. "The night was very dark, so that the Americans in the houses had difficulty spotting the Germans roaming the streets and shooting into the buildings."

Sergeant Roddy Parker knocked out three of the enemy tanks with a bazooka, one shot of which was fired from the door of a building being used as the battalion CP (Parker was wounded by rifle fire later that night from one of the tanks he had disabled. He died the next day.)

Desperately, Bischoff called down artillery fire on his own position. The Americans huddled in the houses while the shells fell around them. The night was "the worst I ever spent," Bischoff recalled. He felt that at any moment his battalion would be over-

Lieutenant-General Eugen Meindl, Commander 2 Parachute Corps. (BAM)

Lieutenant General Bill Simpson, Commander 9th U.S. Army, and Major General Charles Gerhardt, Commander 29th Infantry Division, plan the Roer assault. (USAMHI #RS4195)

Schwammenauel Dam on the Roer. (Courtesy: USAMHI)

Major-General Siegfried von Waldenburg, GOC 116th Panzer Division. (BAM)

Lieutenant-Colonel Heinz Guenther Guderian, Staff Officer (Ops), 116th Panzer Division: "We did not fight for the Nazis, we fought for the Fatherland."
(Courtesy: Lt-Gen Heinz Guenther Guderian)

Major-General Dan Spry. GOC 3rd Canadian Infantry Division (left), confers with Major-General Chris Vokes, GOC 4th Canadian Armoured Division, at the Hochwald. (Jack H. Smith/DND/Public Archives of Canada/PA-145746)

Infantry vehicles mired in floods in Kranenburg. (IWM #B14536)

Planning Operation Veritable: Lieutenant-General Brian Horrocks, Commander 30 British Corps; Field-Marshal Bernard Montgomery; and Major-General "Tiny" Barber, GOC 15th Scottish Division. (IWM #B14869)

Traffic jam in the rubble of Calcar, March 1945. (K. Bell/Public Archives of Canada/DND/PA-137452)

Front row, left to right: Field-Marshal Montgomery and Generals Eisenhower and Bradley; back row, left to right: Generals Crerar, Simpson, and Dempsey. (Barney J. Glosten/Public Archives of Canada/DND/PA-136327)

Drowned Churchill tank near Kranenburg. (IWM #B14657)

General Alfred Schlemm, Commander of the First German Parachute Army. (BAM)

Major-General Thomas Rennie, GOC 51st Highland Division. (IWM #B41578)

The 5/7th Gordon Highlanders drive through the Reichswald. (IWM #B14412)

German Jagpanther with 88mm. (Ken Bell/DND/Public Archives Canada/PA−145729)

Simpson and Montgomery view the ruins of Juelich. (USAMHI #RS4195)

An armoured bulldozer halts at a ruined church at Udem. (Donald I
Grant/DND/National Archives of Canada/PA-170262)

*Heavily damaged German town submerging:
Middleaar, Germany, February 14, 1945.* (Barney
J. Gloster/DND/Public Archives of Canada/PA-145755)

*Major-General Heinz Fiebig, Commander 84th
Infantry Division.* (BAM)

An AVRE Churchill tank with bridge and piscine: the "Funnies" to the rescue. (IWM #B14582)

Infantry troops cross an anti-tank ditch at Udem. (IWM #B14937)

Cleve: "Cratering is to be accepted." (IWM #B14617)

run and annihilated, so much so that he removed all his regimental insignia and documents, preparatory to destroying them. One enemy tank was disabled near the CP and its motor ran all night, adding to what the CO remembered as indescribable confusion. Finally, after a night of horror, the counter-attacks died away.

Seventy-four Americans of the 102nd were killed securing a bridgehead over the Roer. Another 493 were wounded, and 31 were reported missing. One hundred and thirty Germans became prisoners.

The two divisions of Major-General Raymond McLain's 19 Corps — Simpson's southernmost corps in his pivot force — faced even more severely swollen waters and swifter currents than those downstream.

The 29th Infantry Division also faced the Citadel at Juelich — a confrontation they had been dreading these many months. The 400-year-old fort had great walls of stone and earth 144 inches thick and 150 feet high. Its ramparts were honeycombed with an intricate system of interconnecting tunnels. On February 20, an American bomber raid pounding the Citadel with 1,000-pound bombs scored eight direct hits on a corner of the fort. Still the Citadel stood.

The Germans were determined to keep the fort inviolate. Its approaches were liberally sown with mines and obstructed with barbed wire. A normal amphibious infantry assault would surely fail.

Major-General Charles Gerhardt, flamboyant commander of 29th Division, knew he had to gamble. Gerhardt was an American answer to the German "Watchmaker" Straube: no detail was too minor for his attention. The combination of verve and precision had worked well for this successful division commander.

Gerhardt's hope was that as the river was narrow at Juelich, and the banks high, his engineers could erect a footbridge prior to the massed infantry assault. This would mean that the construction would have to take place with almost no protection from enemy fire on the far bank except a small vanguard of patrol troops. His gamble was that the engineers would be defiladed from enemy fire because of the high banks.

With a footbridge in place, the infantry could then race across, quell the opposition, and establish a firmer bridgehead so that vehicular bridges could be built. The scheme worked, but with terrible casualties.

Thirty minutes before H-Hour, two 27-man patrols from 175th Infantry Regiment pushed off in assault boats. They had orders to take up positions on the far bank and defend the bridge-builders.

The patrols immediately came under heavy enemy fire. The first never reached the bridge site across the river. Led in two boats by Second Lieutenant Ralph Howland, the men were swept downstream. One boat capsized. The remaining men landed and tried to work their way back but ran into barbed wire and anti-personnel mines. Some, including Howland, were later picked up and evacuated by other units. The rest were drowned or wounded.

The second patrol also came under fire from automatic weapons. The men fired tracer ammunition at the Germans, marking the enemy positions. Supporting tanks opened up with machine guns and 76mm guns to silence the enemy. On the far bank, the patrol leader, Lieutenant Warren Snyder, spread his men out to defend the crossing site.

Promptly at H-Hour, under cover of smoke, troops of the 121st Engineers waded into the river in high rubber boots to begin construction of the footbridges. Working frantically, the engineers completed a footbridge in less than an hour. A boat crashed into it, knocking it out. It was swiftly rebuilt. At 0600 hours the first riflemen of the 175th Regiment crossed on a dead run, footboards clattering under their heavy boots.

The infantrymen surrounded the Citadel, pouring machine-gun and rifle fire on it. Unfortunately, the explosives they had brought to blow the only gate in the wall had been lost when the assault boats overturned. The tanks and flame-throwers designated for the final annihilation of the defenders of the Citadel were still stranded on the other side of the river. When they finally arrived, on D-plus-One, the Germans had withdrawn.

At other 29th Division crossing sites, the dense minefields took a severe toll on riflemen from both the 175th and 115th Infantry Regiments. The virtually undetectable plastic Topf mines, containing 12 pounds of explosive, created many casualties.

The problem of medical evacuation became imperative. The 115th's history relates that "wounded men spent most of the day in exposed positions with their wounds untended because the medics were unable to reach them."

Just manhandling heavy stretcher cases across the river was an exhausting job. Often, small canals or branches of the river would compel the stretcher-bearers to load the casualties on boats, unloading them and reloading them several times before they finally reached the west bank. Under fire, the procedure was impossible. Battalion surgeons moved ceaselessly where they could among the frontline companies, treating wounded who could not be evacuated.

It was a miserable time for all the troops. Soaked from the icy waters, their equipment wet and heavy, they huddled shivering in mud- and water-filled slit-trenches.

At the south end of the wheel, the 30th Infantry Division also found that a major crossing by assault boats would be impossible because of the swift currents. Like their sister division, the 29th, they sent small support units across — using LVTs instead of the less reliable assault boats. Their task was to protect the engineers as they constructed footbridges.

The 30th had developed a high level of technical skill in combat river crossings, having participated in a number of them during the Northwest Europe campaign. Major-General Carrol Dunn, CO of the 105th Engineer Battalion in support of 119th Infantry, terms the project "an outstanding success under very extreme conditions." Working under cover of smoke and artillery screen, Dunn's engineers had a footbridge installed before the last shells of the barrage had fallen. "We had previously stretched an underwater cable across the river which provided an anchorage for the footbridge," the engineer explained.

But there was a second obstacle to overcome: across the river was a 25-foot drainage canal that separated a flat spit of land from the mainland. Just 48 hours before the attack, an engineer patrol had slipped over in darkness to examine it. They reported to Dunn that the canal's depth was 10 feet — too deep for fording. The assaulting troops would be trapped on this exposed spit under direct enemy fire. Dunn came up with a solution.

"We fashioned some wooden duckboard footbridges. Our men towed these in sections behind assault boats and laid them across to bridge the canal banks," Dunn explains. The scheme was a success.

The 119th's sister regiment, the 120th, was forced to attempt a crossing by cable ferry. Clambering into inflatable rubber boats, a company of some 100 infantrymen tried to pull themselves hand-over-hand along the cable. The current was too strong for them; only 30 reached the far shore. Finally, two companies got over in LVTs.

The men dismounted at various points along the bank and started out through a woods to reach their assembly area 200 yards inland. On the way, they ran into a "perfect hell" of booby traps and anti-personnel mines. Trip wires had been attached to hand grenades and to cement blocks filled with explosives and bits of steel. Seventy-five men were injured.

The combination of enemy fire and strong currents destroyed four footbridges put in during the next hours by the engineers. By the time the fifth was completed, night had fallen. The engineers persisted through the night, and in 20½ hours (rather than an estimated 36) a vehicular bridge was constructed.

Like the aggressive 84th, however, the infantrymen of the 30th had to spend the entire first day of the attack isolated on the enemy side of the river, without armoured support. Once across, the 30th pushed hard for their objectives, feeling the pressure of being on the outside of the wheel as the Ninth Army began its massive pivot to the north.

"We managed to surprise the Germans," the division's operations officer, Lieutenant-Colonel Harold Hassenfelt, remembers. "When we made that turning movement after we crossed, we went in behind enemy lines and caught them looking in the opposite direction. Their defences were well organized, but they faced the wrong way."

The commander, Major-General Leland Hobbs, decided to keep going through the night. Night fighting was "one of our real weaknesses," as U.S. Army historian Charles B. MacDonald recently stated. With the exception of 104th division, the American soldier was not trained for night operations.

Using artificial moonlight, the 119th's reserve battalion was ordered to advance through Hambach Wood to capture the German garrison of Hambach, some 1,000 yards inland. The area was heavily defended by permanent gun emplacements in log-buttressed dugouts, each crowned with a revolving steel turret and armed with a .30-calibre machine gun.

In daylight, under the muzzles of these guns, the assault would have been suicidal. By night it was merely terrifying. First Lieutenant Donald Ward noted that night fighting caused the men to be jumpy. Control was harder to maintain, and the troops had difficulty identifying their own units. (The 102nd Division wore white armbands for this purpose.)

Captain Victor Salem, a rifle company commander with 119th Infantry Regiment, was moving into Hambach Wood when he experienced a graphic demonstration of the men's nervousness:

"It was the first time we had put in a night attack. Our colonel had said, 'It's a breeze.' But the men found it very frightening.

"Suddenly the whole company just stopped — froze. They wouldn't go through that forest at any cost. We were getting some small-arms fire, nothing much. But they thought that every tree had a German behind it.

"I said to them, 'Now look — I'm going to take my platoon runners, my radio and telephone men, and go in ahead of you. I'll show you it's safe. Then I want all of you to start moving.' I went through about 100, 120 feet. All of a sudden I could sense without looking back that the company got up. We went safely through the forest and into the town."

Despite these many difficulties, both regiments got on their objectives by the conclusion of D-Day. In ten hours, 30th Division had pulled off a difficult river assault and established a bridgehead 5,000 yards wide and 2,500 yards deep. The 30th Division was well out in front, living up to its nickname of "Workhorse of the Western Front."

On its left, 29th Division was still engaged in the battle for Juelich. But in this first momentous day the four assaulting divisions of Bill Simpson's Ninth Army had had only 100 men killed in action.

The final two infantry divisions to cross on D-Day were the 104th and the 8th, both in 7 Corps of General Courtney Hodges's First U.S. Army. It was Corps Commander "Lightning Joe" Collins's task to protect the exposed southern flank of Ninth Army. The southern tail of the 17-mile Grenade force endured Grenade's most intensive fire on its open flank. The 8th Division, on the right, was in the most precarious position of all.

Like the other assaults, this crossing was cloaked in a dense curtain of smoke, produced by smoke generator and chemical mortar battalions. Captain Frank Hallahan, a company commander with the 104th, recalls that the smoke caused a disquieting incident — harmless, as it turned out, but quite capable of causing dangerous confusion to the already nervous troops, many of them inexperienced, waiting to attack: "We were late joiners in the European theatre and at first we used to carry an awful lot of equipment — we were overburdened with it. Gradually, as we got into combat situations, we shook down. It happened that just before the Roer assault we had elected to dump our gas masks so we could move about a little more quickly. When they put down some smoke, one of the men in an OP gave the gas alarm.

"For a minute there, utter confusion took place. Our gas masks were back on the trucks. Fortunately it turned out to be the smoke — but it gave us a bit of a scare."

The infantrymen and engineers experienced even more serious problems of flood and enemy resistance than those confounding the divisions a few miles north. Crossing at the shattered town of Dueren, they encountered currents up to 12 miles per hour, which caused many of the boats to overturn, spilling the men into the chilly 49-degree waters.

The 8th Division experienced the toughest D-Day of them all. They managed to get only one battalion on its objectives that day. In one instance, all 140 men of one of the companies swamped and overturned. Despite their heavy gear, they somehow managed to reach the far side of the river. With only 30 rifles left among them, they swung straight into action.

On 8th Division's 28th Infantry Regiment front, all the motors for the assault boats failed, and most of the crossing was made by paddling the boats — a difficult feat against so strong a current. Many of the craft dumped. One company, launched upriver near a blown bridge, lost all 10 of its assault boats. Every one of them was sunk either by accurate mortar fire or by the swift current.

The banks on the east side were as high as 15 feet. Its shores were thick with minefields running back to a trench system that commanded the river. Major Hugh L. Carrie, operations staff officer (S-3) of 415th Infantry Regiment (104th Division), described an ingenious device for dealing with the mines: "Eleven men in the first wave of each company carried cordite nets, each 18 inches wide and 12 feet long. When areas were reached which had been sown with schu-mines, these nets were unrolled over the area and then detonated, thus providing a safe pathway through the minefield."

Both divisions were given the task of clearing Dueren. The city had been completely shattered, with only the bronze statue of Bismarck standing in the square. The largest carpet-type operation of the war had employed heavy bombers of the USAF and the RAF to devastate the town. "We dropped 9,000 tons in two hours," reported Major-General Elwood R. Quesada, USAF.

A war correspondent, Graham Miller, described the carnage: "There's not a house, not a tree, not a blade of grass. . . . [Dueren] is the most completely smashed town I have ever seen in this war."

Resistance to the infantry attack was uneven; a number of counter-attacks were fended off. The 8th Division's 13th Regiment, which captured two strongly defended barracks, suffered 134 casualties in the action.

Major Frank J. Flette, S-3 of 414th Infantry Regiment, recalls an attack put in by men of the 414th against a pocket of Germans entrenched securely on top of a slag pile. "They defied our men to come and get them. One of them shouted in English, 'The hell with Roosevelt, I'll die for the Fuehrer.' He did."

By midnight of D-Day, the 104th had eliminated every enemy position along its sector of the Roer. During this 21-hour period the division artillery fired 18,346 rounds and Ninth Air Force flew 17 missions of eight airplanes each in close support of the assaulting infantry.

Throughout the night of February 23-24, First Army engineers, often working under intense artillery and mortar fire, threw bridges across the Roer. By midnight, two infantry support bridges and one treadway bridge had been completed. Shortly after midnight the supporting weapons and heavy traffic began to roll forward.

Now only 15 miles from Cologne, Major-General Terry Allen's 104th Division "Timberwolves" would strike out aggressively in a 53-hour non-stop drive that spun out headlines across the United States with every bold advance. The Washington *Evening Star* termed the advance "one of the most spectacular night operations of the campaign."

Despite all the adversities experienced by the six assaulting divisions of the Grenade strike, by midnight of D-Day 16 battalions had been established on the east bank of the Roer. Eight miles of the major road to the north was in their hands. Within 48 hours, 19 new bridges would be erected, including seven for tanks. The infantry force would double in strength, with each unit supported by tanks and heavy weapons.

Three new infantry divisions joined battle in the next few days. The 83rd Infantry Division was temporarily attached to 29th Division. Major-General John B. Anderson's 16 Corps, comprising the 79th and 35th Infantry Divisions (and the soon-to-be-unleashed 8th Armored Division), went into action on February 25.

The 35th Infantry Division took heavy casualties at Hilfarth when they encountered vicious fire from automatic weapons and thickly planted mines and booby traps in the town. However, the vital bridge over the Roer was saved by the daring action of two young engineers. The pair managed to slip through enemy automatic fire, cut the demolition wires, and remove the charges before the Germans could detonate the bridge. The corps then made an unopposed crossing on this northern flank. By D-plus-Three, the Grenade bridgehead would be enlarged to an area 20 miles wide and 10 deep.

An elated Montgomery was able to report:

Top Secret. Personal and Eyes Only for CIGS from Field-Marshal Montgomery, 23 Feb 45:
GRENADE. This op was successfully launched at 0330 hrs today and 9th army has now 23 bridges across the Roer river with 4 Class 40 bridges. Juelich is clear of the enemy and we hold the lateral road from that place northward to Rurich. 700 prisoners have been taken. Casualties to our own troops have been generally light. On my right, the left corps of 1st US army attacked this morning and my latest news is that 8 battalions are over the river on either side of Dueren and fighting is going on in that place.

Fifteenth Army commander General Gustav von Zangen noted the first suggestion of a northward pivot by the U.S. 84th Division, breaking through the outer crust of his defences at Erkelenz. He desperately hoped that this would prove a secondary effort to the main attack due east to Cologne. If he was wrong in his assessment, if in fact Ninth Army was part of a giant pincer movement with Canadian Army to the north, Zangen realized it spelled defeat for his Fifteenth Army. The entire south wing of Army Group H would be crushed in its vise.

Meanwhile, General Alfred Schlemm also watched the Grenade attack unfold with grave concern. The parachute commander had moved First Parachute Army HQ back from Xanten to Saalhoff, near Rheinberg. He too was alarmed at the mounting threat, conjecturing that the Americans would destroy von Zangen's Fifteenth Army and then turn north and attack First Parachute Army in the rear.

"It will be impossible to form a new defence front on the east bank of the river," he informed Field-Marshal von Rundstedt worriedly.

On February 25, D-plus-Two of Grenade, 220 German planes attacking in twos and threes made a last-ditch effort to knock out the bridgehead. Eighteen were shot down.

That same evening, von Rundstedt informed Hitler that unless there was a general retreat across the Rhine, the entire western front would collapse. The appeal was ignored. The aging Commander-in-Chief West again interjected. Would Hitler at least agree to his adjusting Fifteenth Army's line?

Ridiculous! Hitler retorted angrily, confirming his refusal with a personally signed letter. Withdrawal was not even to be considered. For the third time in the war, von Rundstedt's career was in jeopardy.

Resignedly, von Rundstedt pulled those reinforcements that he could divert from the First Canadian Army front and rushed them south again. These included two of his strongest Panzer divisions — the Panzer Lehr and 15th Panzer Grenadier divisions.

In what proved to be a "futile attempt," von Zangen sent his 338th Infantry Division to Erkelenz on the night of the 25th to intercept the 84th's swing to the north.

"Erkelenz was the key," Emerich recalls. "That's where the last anti-tank ditch was located. When we took that, the 5th Armored Division moved their tanks up next morning and took over."

Top Secret. Personal and Eyes Only for CIGS from Field-Marshal Montgomery, 25 Feb 45:
GRENADE. Good progress has been made today. The Roer river is falling rapidly. We now have good bridges over the river and the leading brigades of armoured div began to cross the river tonight. The prisoners captured by 9th US army on 23 and 24 Feb total 3,000 and total casualties are under 2,000.

Bill Simpson and his commanders had gambled on the date of the attack. They gambled on its direction. They pioneered new river assault tactics and the hazards of night fighting. They risked moving infantry forward without tanks and other supporting arms.

The cost for that day's work was minuscule compared with the size of the force: of some 375,000 men, just 1,447 were casualties (158 were killed, 1,193 wounded, and 96 missing).

The reward was vast: before them stood a wide-open, firm-footed plain that swept all the way to the Rhine. The armoured breakout was on.

February 26: The Grisliest Day

THREE DAYS AFTER the Ninth U.S. Army launched Grenade across the Roer, Operation Blockbuster also commenced its drive to the Rhine.

When mild, myopic Major Louis Froggett and his battered Rileys were beating off the last of the savage German counter-attacks on the Goch-Calcar road, he thought that the battle was over. He thought that February 26 — his "grisliest day of the war" — had done its worst. Froggett was wrong.

February 26 had only begun to unleash its havoc. From the first pre-dawn savagery to the final vicious exchange of grenades under a restless moon, that bleak Thursday maintained its momentum of butchery. On that one day, 214 young Canadians were killed. Only on three other days, all in Normandy, was the fatality rate higher.

The Rileys' final struggle to fend off a defiant German horde after their hard-won gains on the Goch-Calcar road overlapped by an hour the opening salvos of Operation Blockbuster. The finish line for the exhausted Royal Hamilton Light Infantry became the start line for this fresh Canadian offensive.

In the 19 days thus far of Operation Veritable, Crerar's divisions had clawed a passage of between 15 and 20 miles from their original positions south of Nijmegen. They had reached the halfway point. The objective of this next operation, Blockbuster, was to open the rest of the way to the Rhine.

It was a cursed time for the 65,000 men at the sharp end. In the 13-day struggle to execute this objective, from February 26 until

---

See Map 3 and 7 (Appendix B).

March 10, there was never a moment when they were not rain-soaked, cold, and afraid, or when the threat of defeat did not hover over them.

The Canadian operation would not be the sizzling breakout that Simpson's forces were achieving at the Roer bridgehead. Instead, Blockbuster was destined to be a miserable rerun of the previous two weeks' struggle, its outcome salvaged only by outstanding efforts on the part of the men who were handed the job.

Only the first day — February 26 — lived up to the expectations of the operation. At senior command level, plans were still rational and coherent; on the ground, hope and confidence still prevailed. After that day, the confusion brought about by deplorable roads and non-existent communication — the blight that came to be known as the "fog of war" — would settle on weary shoulders for the remainder of the ill-conceived operation.

As one tank officer explained the "fog of war," it was as if a dozen men on a playing field were trying to score a goal without any one of them having the slightest idea of what the others were doing. That is a fair description of the events of Blockbuster.

At a convent near Cleve on February 21, General Crerar had issued orders for the continuation of Operation Veritable. Horrocks's 30 Corps — temporarily an all-Jock force, with the 52nd Lowland Division and the "Scottish Horse" (a medium artillery regiment) in the line — would form the right flank. The 15th Scottish and 51st Highland Divisions would continue the attack south from Goch until squeezed out of battle to prepare for the Rhine assault. The 3rd British Division would relieve the 15th Scottish on February 27. Further south, the 53rd Welsh were advancing towards Weeze. In reserve, the Guards Armoured Division continued to stand ready, as they had since February 8.

Lieutenant-General Simonds's 2 Canadian Corps would launch Operation Blockbuster on the left, using the Goch-Calcar start line. He would exploit in a southeasterly direction to the Hochwald Forest and, beyond it, the Rhine.

Simonds may have coined the wistful tag of "Blockbuster" because the operation's added weight in manpower and tanks gave it hope of an armoured breakout. In execution, however, it was to prove as hampered as Veritable had been by the same wretched conditions, created by the same February thaws: rain, mud troughs up to five or six feet deep in the few available roads, and cloud cover that prohibited any air support during the critical first two days of the operation (and only limited support for much of the rest of the time).

Simonds had augmented 2nd and 3rd Canadian Infantry Divisions with supporting armour from 2nd Canadian Armoured Brigade. In addition, he had under command the 43rd Wessex Division and two fresh armoured divisions: the irascible Major-General Chris Vokes's 4th Canadian Armoured Division and Major-General G.P.B. ("Pip") Roberts's 11th British Armoured Division. It was, observed British historian Major-General Hubert Essame (who commanded a Wessex brigade in the operation), "Napoleonic" in magnitude.

The same writer leaped forward a century in his metaphors to describe Blockbuster's outcome as "reminiscent of the muddy fields of Passchendaele and the shell-torn slopes of Vimy Ridge, a struggle to the death between Canadians and Germans of equal valour, attack and counter-attack."

The Passchendaele reference is not misplaced. A total of 3,638 Canadians would be killed or wounded opening up Blockbuster's 16-mile corridor to the Rhine.

In a mammoth shift to re-position his various divisions for this new thrust, Simonds made the mistake of immobilizing the bulk of his units for four days. Once again, General Schlemm was given breathing space.

Schlemm took advantage of the lull to stabilize his front. Forced back from Moyland Wood by the 46th Scottish Brigade and the 7th Canadian Infantry Brigade, and from his hold on the Goch-Calcar road by 4th Canadian Infantry Brigade, the German parachute commander had set his next strategic defence line along a horseshoe-shaped escarpment stretching from Calcar to Udem. Von Luettwitz and Meindl — his corps commanders — were instructed to anchor the head of their defences at the north end of the escarpment in Calcar and their tail in the fortified town of Udem to the south, with a strongpoint entrenched midway along the Calcar-Udem road at Keppeln. The German rear defence line extended east to Xanten, the gateway to the Rhine.

Once more, the Canadian troops were presented with a near-impossible task. As was the case at Moyland Wood, any approach across the flat open farmland broadside to the six-mile ridge committed them to the close scrutiny of the enemy. This became Major-General Spry's task for his Water Rats, the 3rd Canadian Infantry Division.

Attacking the ridge head-on seemed equally suicidal. But that became the shared task of 2nd Canadian Infantry Division, under Major-General Bruce Matthews, and 4th Canadian Armoured Division, under Vokes.

The action was to be launched under a massive artillery program. More than 700 guns from six divisional artilleries and six AGRA regiments were allotted to the support plan. Five salvos (1,527 rounds) were fired by 1st Canadian Rocket Battery. With the aid of artificial moonlight, the attack would advance in continuous waves until it was completed — with luck, within 24 hours.

Having gained this objective, Simonds then intended to thrust his armoured divisions into the next phase. As men had run the gauntlet in medieval days, so the 4th Canadian Armoured Division would run its gauntlet dead east for some five miles in an armoured thrust through a narrow and strongly defended corridor known as the Hochwald Gap, between the German-held Hochwald Forest and Balberger Wood.

It was hoped that these flanks — the two forests sandwiching the gap — could be secured in time by the 2nd and 3rd Canadian Infantry Divisions. Given the proven German skill in forest fighting to date, however, it was perhaps optimistic to expect that all strongpoints and infiltrations could be so swiftly and simultaneously eliminated prior to the armoured breakout.

A prime objective was the Goch-Xanten railway embankment that traversed the gap. To ease the supply crunch that had plagued Veritable since D-Day, Simonds had devised a unique plan. He proposed that the instant the line was captured, his engineers would tear up the tracks on the rail line and build a single, one-way road to Xanten.

Traversing a raised corridor under the muzzles of German guns is not the stuff of which infantry and tankmen's dreams are made. The reward, however — should they pull off long odds and achieve it — would be home plate: the final, eight-mile sprint downhill to Xanten and thence to the Rhine.

Essame's guns are levelled at First Canadian Army planners for selecting this battlefield venue, instead of looping around to the south of the gap and bypassing it:

Why Crerar elected to make his main effort with 2 Canadian Corps in the north where the enemy was strongest has never been satisfactorily explained. Whether the southern approach was ever considered is not known. It may well be that the fact that

2 Canadian Corps was already in the northern sector decided the issue. So far, most of the fighting by the 1st Canadian Army had been done by UK-based troops: it would be invidious, however, to suggest that the wish to ensure that the Canadian divisions got their share of glory influenced Crerar's decisions in any way.

To suggest that the choice of venue for the major Blockbuster battle was motivated by the pursuit of "glory" may be overly harsh. However, Simonds did have two viable (if unappealing) alternatives to the Hochwald scheme. He could relinquish command of the main thrust to Horrocks, who did have the expectation of a good axis south of the forest. He could also — in light of the success of the Operation Grenade assault on February 23 — hedge his commitments in the expectation that the German strength would be diverted and their position weakened.

To be sure, Simonds was ambitious — but he was also too shrewd a commander to back a loser. He must genuinely have believed that the need for a supply axis to the Rhine was sufficiently urgent to justify the gamble of forcing the gap. He was obviously convinced that his plan was a good one. Given the close relationship and pipeline of communications between them, Montgomery clearly shared his confidence and supported the scheme, possibly over Crerar's head.

Spry's 8th Canadian Infantry Brigade — comprising the Queen's Own Rifles of Canada, the Régiment de la Chaudière, and the North Shore Regiment — was given the task of opening up the approaches to the Calcar-Udem escarpment. The 1st Hussars Regiment added armoured support to the action. The 9th Brigade would move through them later in the day to seize Udem.

The initial objective for the Queen's Own Rifles was a scattering of three farmhouses in Mooshof, a small hamlet near the Calcar-Udem road where the German forward defence lines were strongly entrenched.

At 0345 hours, February 26, the darkness was shattered by the flash of thousands of shells and tracer fire. The entire 2 Canadian Corps artillery erupted.

In driving rain, the men of the Queen's Own Rifles groped sleepily in the icy blackness for their kits as they rose to battle. The inevitable tot of rum was passed around along with steaming coffee and sandwiches; the inevitable pre-attack nerves and stomach-clutch caused each man to wonder if he would see another dawn, another meal. The rum was swiftly downed.

The troops moved forward from the FUP, following the white tape laid to guide them through the inky night to the start line. Suddenly, beams of four huge searchlights — bounced off low-lying clouds — illuminated the sky; artificial moonlight transformed night into day. With it came the first inkling of disaster.

"It backfired," Major H.E. Dalton, second-in-command of the Queen's Own Rifles, concludes flatly. "It did us more harm than good. In that kind of hand-to-hand fighting to clear houses, you didn't need light.

"There was no element of surprise whatsoever. The Germans were waiting. Some of the POWs that we captured told our fellows that they saw us coming before we got anywhere close to the start line. One company lost 11 men before they even got to it."

At 0430 hours, Major Ben Dunkelman of the Queen's Own Rifles advanced with his men to their first objective in Mooshof. Dunkelman had been a searing force with his battalion since D-Day. Now he commanded a company and was as committed to the men he led as he was vengeful to his Nazi enemy.

"Ben was one of the best officers I had," his CO, Lieutenant-Colonel Stephen Lett, remembers. "He didn't want to do anything else but fight. I said to him, 'You'd better take it easy!' and he pulled out a dog tag and showed it to me. 'It says right here, Hebrew,' he answered. 'You know what's going to happen to me if they catch me.'"

Dunkelman remembered the enemy's frequent tactic of pulling back to a second line of defence when attacked and then lacing the attackers' position with pre-ranged artillery. He yelled to his platoon commanders to spread out and dig in well away from the captured German positions.

In the confusion and noise, one platoon — 16 Platoon — failed to heed the warning and came under heavy fire.

"The Germans were waiting for us," Rifleman Norm Selby remembers. "We were lying in shell holes. They had MG-42s upstairs in the barns. God, they were wicked guns."

"I went through the most horrendous artillery fire I had ever experienced," Rifleman Don Chittenden of the same platoon adds. "It was extremely accurate. . . . It winkled the guys right out of their slit-trenches. We had terrible casualties."

One of Chittenden's best friends was shot dead by a German

Spandau gunner. "I just stood there, stunned, staring down at Fraser's body. I was shocked because he was the first one of the guys I'd been close to."

By now, Dunkelman's company was in desperate trouble. The Germans had infiltrated 16 Platoon's position, killing its commander and one entire section of seven men. Then, regaining their original buildings, they laid on a fierce counter-attack, threatening 17 Platoon. Sniper fire was so intense that one rifleman had the handle of a stretcher blown off in his hand when he tried to rescue one of the severely wounded men.

"The whole area is turning into a shambles," Dunkelman wrote at the time. "Bodies of wounded, dead, and dying lie everywhere you look."

Meanwhile the platoon sergeant, Aubrey Cosens, had been trying to get one of the 1st Hussar tanks forward. At 23, Cosens was an "old man" in the eyes of many of the green and often guileless teenaged soldiers he led. In a sense, he had been gearing up since boyhood for this moment. He was easily as strong, fit, and fiercely aggressive as his enemy.

Courage and determination were ingrained early on in Cosens. Exploring Temagami's lakes and forests — his Northern Ontario backyard — the young Aubrey became imbued with a mental and physical toughness and steel-edged resourcefulness that only wilderness survival and solitude can engender.

He tuned his muscles by wrestling and weightlifting and his mind by tests of will. A loner by inclination and a leader by nature, Cosens could prowl the isolated forests for week on end — but still enjoy lifting a pint with his pals in Porquis Junction on a Saturday night. When the air rang with ribaldry, his broad face would break into a wide, ingenuous grin.

Now he was battle-seasoned. His skills had been honed by war's kill-or-be-killed atmosphere. On February 26, he would need these qualities.

"I thought he was just damned, damned good," Chittenden recalls. "He came running over to me yelling, 'Chit, get your ass out of here. You're going to get shot.' He grabbed Fraser's body by the collar and the straps and dragged it to one side. 'A tank is coming up this way,' he said. 'I don't want it to crush Fraser's body.' "

It was at this point that the 1st Hussars tank, commanded by Sergeant C.R. ("Andy") Anderson, approached the battle scene. Running across the open ground under a hail of mortar and shellfire, Cosens reached the tank and directed its fire on enemy positions, breaking up a second German attack. "There was heavy sniping coming from the farm buildings," Anderson said. "We fired 75mm shells into the building."

"The Germans tried to pick him off with tracer fire," Chittenden describes. "It was just like bloody rain bouncin' off that tank. He stayed out there in the open with his Sten while the tank knocked out the farmhouse."

"Cosens asked if we could ram the building with the tank," Anderson recounted. "We did so and knocked a hole in the wall, through which Cosens entered the building."

Rifleman Selby, one of the handful of survivors of 16 Platoon, believes that their lives were saved by Cosen's actions that morning: "There were only four of us by then; we needed a leader, somebody to say, 'OK, let's go.' We realized that if we stayed there we were going to get killed or taken prisoner.

"Cosens was screaming at us at the top of his lungs from the tank, 'Follow me!' So we got behind the tank and ran in behind to give him fire support. The tank rammed into one of the houses and bashed the hell out of it, firing its turret gun into the house. Cosens jumped off the tank and tore into the house and the Krauts started coming out the other door. We got them all corralled."

Cosens personally killed more than 20 Germans and took as many prisoners. "When we had cleaned out the last farmhouse," Selby recalls, "Cosens said, 'OK, take up defensive positions. I'm going to find the company commander and report to him.' Then he started off. I guess he got about 8 or 10 feet from me and plink! Down he went — that was it. Where that sniper came from I don't know."

Aubrey Cosens died almost instantly, shot through the head. The time was 0830 hours; four hours had passed since the men of the Queen's Own Rifles had crossed their start line. In that short time, this human dynamo from the backwoods of Northern Ontario — this "old man" of 23 — and his brave little band of young soldiers broke the core of enemy resistance at Mooshof.

For his actions on February 26, attacking across a sodden Rhineland pasture, the quiet Canadian was posthumously awarded the Victoria Cross, Britain's highest award for gallantry.

Dunkelman later wrote:

The price was dreadful. At the end of that gruesome day, there were only 36 fighting men left in my company, out of the 115 who had crossed the start line. I was the only officer to come through unwounded, along with only one NCO. I was exhausted: sick in body, and even sicker in spirit. . . . For all my exhaustion, I did not sleep well that night.

"The next day we were ordered to clear the Hochwald Forest," Selby remembers. "There weren't many of us left in the company and Major Dunkelman protested. We thought, Jesus Christ, haven't we done enough?"

At 0830 hours on Feb 26 — the exact moment, by chance, that Aubrey Cosens was killed — the Régiment de la Chaudière surged into battle. Fifteen minutes later, the third battalion of 8th Brigade, the North Shore Regiment moved out.

Keppeln, the North Shore objective, was just another farming hamlet on the Calcar-Udem road — harmless, they thought. The CO, Lieutenant-Colonel John Rowley, had been informed that there could be no support tanks; all available armour had been committed to the Queen's Own Rifles and the Régiment de la Chaudière. No problems, however, were anticipated.

"We had been led to believe that all the German fortifications were at Udem, two miles farther down the road," remembers Major Jim Currie, commander of one of the lead companies. "From the aerial photographs and intelligence reports Keppeln appeared undefended."

"We had an open stretch of about 500 yards, maybe more, with a slight upward grade. A narrow, paved road ran right into the middle of Keppeln. Both sides of this road were wide open; I took the left-hand side and young Billy Parker, Major of B Company, was on the right."

For the first 45 minutes of the advance there was no sign of trouble. When the lead platoons reached the rise, all they could see was the first building of the town, an innocent-looking barn. But the next moments revealed a cunning ambush. "The Jerries let us get well up before they cut loose," Currie said. "We ran up against a strongpoint, more heavily defended than anything we'd encountered before.

"A big gun firing from one of the windows of the brick building at the edge of the village was really knocking the lead troops down. I crossed the field and got the machine-gunners to concentrate on that window."

Devastating crossfire from concealed trenches laced across the open ground, cutting Parker's and Currie's men to pieces. Enemy tanks appeared from behind the outbuildings. Two 88s, camouflaged behind the barn, opened up.

The North Shore flame-throwers went into the attack; all but one were blown up by German mines or shellfire. The surviving Wasp, led by Sergeant Horace Boulay, drove wildly through the deadly rain of fire and flamed the barn.

"Never in the war had I seen such small-arms fire," Currie remembers. "We went to ground. With those 88s dug in there we couldn't move." The two company commanders worked their way back to Battalion HQ to report their predicament to the CO. Casualties are heavy, they told John Rowley. We must have tank support.

It was on their return to their companies that Parker was killed. "Harry, this is my last go," he had said the previous day to his friend Lieutenant Harry Nutter. "I tried to kid him but he just smiled at me," Nutter remembered sadly.

It had been a morning of nasty reversals for the battalion. A senior commander and many of his men had been killed. Two companies were pinned down. Rowley realized that the attack was going to fail unless he got the men back on their feet. Tanks were the answer.

John Rowley, known to his men as the "Good Shepherd" for the long staff or "thumb-stick" he habitually carried, coolly revised the battle plan. C Squadron of the 1st Hussars, having put in a tough morning's action at Mooshof with the Queen's Own Rifles, was ordered to replenish its fuel and ammunition and move up in support of the beleaguered North Shore companies. All anti-tank weapons in the company were also taken along. Rowley set H-Hour for the renewed tank-cum-infantry attack at 1415 hours.

"I was instructed to place my platoon on the tanks, which were to be under my command, and attempt to break through the enemy lines and occupy Keppeln," Nutter recalled.

"We made up a force of 42 men, infantry," the lieutenant related. "To say I was scared to death does not describe my condition. I spread a map on the back of a tank and said to my sergeant, 'What do they want us to do? Win the war?' "

Nutter and his platoon clung fiercely to the outsides of the tanks as they charged at full speed through the torrent of fire towards the enemy. Midway, they had to swing off the road to avoid running over the dead and wounded of their comrades of the two lead companies while they bore down on the German trenches, "shooting like mad."

"Two German tanks were dug in behind a house just beyond the trenches and our tanks blasted away at them as they could not swing their guns enough to fire back," Nutter reported.

By now, Nutter's platoon was approaching the town. "Some of our tanks blew up on mines. The rest, including the one I was on, went as fast as possible, swinging out around the town. A German tank dug in behind the church began picking off the first tanks. . . . I could see my men jumping off as the tanks were hit and I beat my tank commander over the head with a Sten gun to get him stopped. We jumped off and I gathered Corporal [Jack] Tree and four other men. No others were in sight. Only six of our fourteen tanks had survived."

Having battled his way to the outskirts of Keppeln, Nutter and his band were now isolated deep in enemy territory. He was relieved to see a line of North Shore troops approaching up the road.

"I told my men to follow me and we would attack enemy trenches at the edge of town. We ran into town, shooting at any Germans we saw, had luck all the way, and kept booting prisoners back towards our advancing troops. . . . We were firing up the main street of Keppeln when our troops finally arrived."

By nightfall, Keppeln was firmly in their grasp. The tally was grim. Twenty-eight North Shore infantrymen were dead; 61 were wounded and three missing in action. Harry Nutter's tiny "army" of 42 riflemen had been reduced to nine. Yet they had "won their war."

After the town was taken, a North Shore platoon commander, returning from Company HQ, was hugging the wall to escape fire from the still-active enemy mortars when he came upon Lieutenant-Colonel Rowley.

I met the "Good Shepherd" . . . walking alone in the open on the road. He was in super-fine battle dress with brass glittering, binoculars on his chest and map-board by his side. He began to talk about the possibilities of a counterattack, as if he were standing in a railway station, while I felt the most dangerous place in the world right then was the centre of the main street in Keppeln.

John Rowley was awarded the DSO for his inspired actions in conducting the Keppeln battle. Sergeant Boulay, who had performed so courageously with the Wasps, received the Military

Medal. The commander of the 1st Hussar tank — on the outside of which Harry Nutter had clung so tenaciously during his wild charge through enemy lines — was decorated with a well-deserved MC for bravery.

Nutter was also put up by the North Shore Regiment for an MC, but the quota of medals for brave young infantry lieutenants appears to have been filled that day. The recommendation was returned, the request denied. Nutter's actions at Keppeln were deemed by officialdom as "not beyond the line of duty."

Despite Canadian Military Headquarters' protests to the contrary, decorations often appear to have been issued strictly on a ratio system. For every decoration awarded to men at the sharp end (and these were allocated on a monthly or quarterly basis), a proportionate number would be made to headquarters-based men at brigade, division, and corps level and to supporting arms such as the Royal Canadian Artillery, the Royal Canadian Corps of Signals, and even the Dental Corps.

The British appear to have been equally cavalier. Of 12 men of 153rd Brigade (51st Highland Division) recommended for decorations in the Reichswald/Goch battle, none received a medal.

Less than half a mile away, the Régiment de la Chaudière was running into equally determined opposition at Hollen. This small village was to form the start line for an attack on Udem later in the day. The situation was critical; the Chaudières had been thrown back twice.

Hollen had become a "scene from the Inferno." The sky was black with the thick smoke from crashing shells, the worst of them coming from Keppeln, where the North Shore Regiment was still pinned down. A company of Chaudières saw a white flag and thought that the enemy was surrendering. Three German Panthers opened up on them, causing heavy casualties and forcing a withdrawal.

The CO of the Stormont, Dundas & Glengarry Highlanders, Lieutenant-Colonel Roger Rowley, was deeply worried about the delay. Until Hollen was taken, the SD&G attack on Udem could not be launched. As reports of strong enemy resistance all along the line filtered back to his HQ, Rowley became more than professionally concerned. It was his brother, John, who was the Good Shepherd prodding his North Shore flock to keep up the attack a few miles away at Keppeln.

"I knew that John was fighting nearby. We both had our hands full that day so there was no time to worry about each other — that's what being brothers in wartime meant. In an attack, all you can let yourself think about is the next thousand yards ahead of you.''

What Roger Rowley was thinking about was in fact three thousand yards ahead: the German strongpoint of Udem. ''I didn't like the look of Udem at all,'' Rowley remembers. ''It was surrounded by an anti-tank ditch and was heavily fortified. I called Rocky [9th Brigade commander Brigadier John Rockingham]: 'This is supposed to be a daylight attack. Now, because of the delay, it's going to be a night attack. I've got to get going!' ''

Darkness descended on the stricken Chaudières. At 1900 hours the battalion secured its final objective, 10 hours after crossing the start line; ''a long day,'' company commander Captain B. Atkinson remembers. Seventeen men of the Chaudière were killed and 51 wounded; 224 Germans were captured.

At 2100 hours Rockingham unleashed his 9th Brigade attack on Udem. He bisected the wedge-shaped town down the middle, assigning the western side to the SD&G and the eastern portion to the Highland Light Infantry of Canada. The North Nova Scotia Highlanders would move through these battalions and secure positions on the Goch-Xanten railway for the start of Simonds's proposed new roadbed.

The town was surrounded by an anti-tank ditch, which was heavily mined. Pioneers lifted many of these but some that were missed took their toll.

''We had carriers going up like popcorn,'' said Major Ray Hodgins, second-in-command of the Highland Light Infantry, whose Balmoral tam acquired extra ventilation from a bullet that whistled past his ear as he advanced on the ditch.

Midnight in Udem saw the two 9th Brigade battalions embroiled in confused fighting within the town, but by dawn the North Nova Scotia Highlanders had been brought in and the last enemy counter-attacks beaten off.

Lieutenant-Colonel E.P. Thompson, CO of the Queen's Own Cameron Highlanders of Canada, did not live through the carnage of February; he did not even survive one hour of it.

Tommy Thompson was shot by a sniper as he led his battalion forward in battle on the Calcar Heights. He was 23 years old, the youngest battalion commander in the Canadian Army. The ink on his official DSO Citation (for his command at the Battle of the Scheldt) was barely dry: his decoration had been presented at 2nd Canadian Infantry Division's Tac HQ at Bedburg by Montgomery three days earlier.

The groundwork for the capture of the Calcar Heights had been done at the battle of Moyland Wood, and at the Goch-Calcar road, which formed the start line for this attack. The climax was a mobile blitz at 0345 hours by two Canadian infantry brigades — the 5th and 6th — supported by tanks of the Sherbrooke Fusiliers, 1st Hussars, and the Fort Garry Horse. Moving up beside the Camerons, the South Saskatchewan Regiment (Lieutenant-Colonel Vern Stott in command) and Les Fusiliers Mont-Royal (under Lieutenant-Colonel J.A. Dextraze) reached their objectives without undue opposition.

Because of the mud and mines, the Camerons had to divert their approach and consequently lost the protection of the barrage. Anxious about the delay, Thompson wanted to talk to the commander of the next tank.

"Instead of using the wireless," his signals officer, Captain R.G. Elliot, relates, "he climbed out of the hatch of his tank to walk over. The Germans had their snipers in a church where we stopped, and that's when he got it."

When Thompson was hit, a paralyzing shock flashed through the battalion. The impetus of the attack was retrieved by the quick thinking of one of Thompson's company commanders, David Rodgers (newly promoted to major in February), who swiftly stepped in to stabilize the situation:

Single-handed [the battalion history relates] he cleared two houses of enemy snipers who were blocking his company's advance, and taking over the battalion headquarters he personally disposed of a third houseful of Germans whose fire was sweeping the headquarters area.

Rodgers's actions on the morning of February 26 were remarkably similar to those of Sergeant Aubrey Cosens — who at almost the same moment was single-handedly clearing three houses of Germans just a mile away. Both men were recommended for the Victoria Cross. Rodgers's recommendation, complete with eyewitness accounts and maps, was endorsed all the way up the line as far as corps commander. Montgomery picked up his pen and stroked out the designation of "Victoria Cross," scrawling in instead, "Approved for immediate DSO for gallantry."

The quotas for VCs would seem not to have been working for brave young majors that day, either.

To get his battalion on the objective, the CO of the Régiment de Maisonneuve of 5th Canadian Infantry Brigade, Lieutenant-Colonel Julien Bibeau, experienced (as the Maisonneuve war diary describes it) "the dubious thrill of being shot at close range by snipers and MGs."

The trouble began at dawn. Crossing an open field, the forward platoons of D Company came upon a heavy line of German dugouts 100 yards from their objective. They were pinned down by fire. No tanks were available to the battalion. The reserve platoon, commanded by Lieutenant Guy de Merlis, worked its way forward along a small road hugging a woods. De Merlis saw dugouts, some evacuated just moments before with candles still lit in them: "A few of the houses had pictures of Hitler, which were boobytrapped — I guess they thought that if we saw a picture of Hitler, we'd want to tear it off the wall.

"I got to the first house at the edge of the wood. We were pinned down, as were the other two platoons 15 or 20 yards away. It was house-to-house, practically hand-to-hand combat. Some of our men had been taken prisoner. The wounded had taken refuge in a house that was still occupied by the Germans. I had a medical orderly with us. He made about six trips getting our wounded out of there until finally the Germans refused to let him go any more. There were a number of our officers lying on the road. Twelve men were killed, two died of wounds, and 79 were wounded.

"Later in the afternoon Lieutenant-Colonel Bibeau himself led the relief. He came up with flame-throwers. I went with him to the edge of the house. I remember him directing their fire into this house, and I can still see, to this day, this German in the door of the house, caught by the flame."

Top Secret. Personal and Eyes Only for CIGS from Field-Marshal Montgomery, 26 Feb 45:
VERITABLE. 2 Cdn corps attacked this morning and have captured objectives according to plan against very determined resistance and some very heavy fighting took place on the Calcar-Udem ridge. Our troops are now firmly

established on the northern end of that ridge and are moving southwards along it towards Udem. Operations are continuing all through tonight so as to give the enemy no time to recover and will go on all tomorrow without stop. . . . If we can bring it off and write off or capture the bulk of the Germans west of the Rhine and cut off their escape, there will be all the fewer Germans to oppose us on the east bank of the Rhine. But this converging operation with 2 large armies is a tricky business and I have got to keep a pretty tight grip on the battle to ensure it goes the way required. We are planning the maximum activity of air forces on the Rhine by day and night to make the enemy getaway as difficult as possible.

Meanwhile, a battle group of Vokes's 4th Canadian Armoured Division, comprising three armoured regiments, a motor battalion, and two battalions from 10th Canadian Infantry Brigade, attacked southeast between the 3rd and 2nd Infantry Divisions. Brigadier Robert W. Moncel commanded "Tiger" Group. The force, itself divided into five sections for the attack, successfully penetrated the highest point of the Calcar-Udem plateau.

On Blockbuster's first day, the complex interactions of many units jelled successfully. In demonstrations of personal courage, few days in World War II can match it.

Major Ray Hodgins insists, "The corporals and lance-corporals — the men at that level — they really did a job. Those guys made the first contact. Once you launched them, it was pretty hard to influence very much until they consolidated. It was their fight. They carried us. I'm just so thankful for good types up front."

The objectives of February 26 — the first day of Blockbuster — had been met. The cost had been terrible.

15

Lulu Goes to War

LULU, ALLISON, BEEBE, Caraboo, and Rookie — and a host of like-named tanks from the Allied armies — took on the German Panzer regiments and battered a way through the last Siegfried defences to the Rhine. They were less massive warriors than the Panthers and Tigers they confronted, and less potent in firepower, but with spunk and sheer numbers they could out-fight and out-manoeuvre the enemy giants.

Two types of tanks, with variations, were employed in the Rhineland fighting. The 45-ton British Churchill, with its wide tracks, was the only armoured vehicle capable of movement in the Reichswald fighting. The Churchills continued to perform yeoman duty both in traditional roles and as one of the varieties of Funnies with other capabilities such as bridge-laying or flame-throwing.

The Americans and Canadians preferred their lighter and more manoeuvrable 35-ton U.S. M-4 Sherman tank, with its 75mm gun. The Firefly, a later design, mounted the potent British 17-pounder gun.

Each squadron (comprising four troops with four tanks each) had at least one troop of Fireflies. This tank was often used for "quick-lifting" infantry into battle — always a rough and dangerous ride for the men "making fingernail dents" on its hull.

There were usually five men in a Sherman tank (four in a Firefly): the commander and a crew of four — driver, co-driver, gunner, and loader-operator. The driver and co-driver shared the bow seats.

The driver's job was one of almost unrelieved fatigue (as is described by one history), "wrestling with two clutches and sluggish controls, bouncing around in his tiny compartment, peering through the slit trying to reconcile what little he could see with the never-ending babble of instructions from the commander."

"A good driver was the key to manoeuvrability," says Trooper

Arnold (Tommy) Boyd. "If a German Panther or Tiger attacked, you had to hull-down pretty damned fast, find some dead ground, maybe a hollow where they couldn't get a bead on you. Or you'd zigzag reverse out of his line of fire — behind a wall or a tree."

Behind the driver and co-driver in the tight confines of the turret, the gunner and loader-operator sat elbow-to-elbow. The fighting compartment was ringed with shells. In this narrow space, the loader-operator had to grab a shell quickly from its bracket, ram it into the breech, and then be ready immediately to snatch a fresh shell when the gun was fired. He was also responsible for operating the machine gun and the wireless.

Besides his obvious tasks, the gunner was sometimes put upon to "sit on the floor with the old cooker going" (strictly forbidden) and brew up a cup of (illicit) tea. "The tea was marvellous when you got stuck, but it would be absolutely wicked for you if you were caught," smiles Brigadier M.J.P. O'Cock of 2nd Battalion Irish Guards.

The tank commander usually stood behind the gunner in the open hatch, ignoring the periscope. He reckoned that the risk of having his head blown off was a fair exchange for 30 seconds' warning of danger from the menace of an enemy 88mm or the German "bazooka boys" closing for an attack. "A tank with hatches closed was like a blind monster at the mercy of a fast, sharp-eyed enemy," recalls one commander.

"Many tank commanders were killed with a single bullet through the head," points out Brigadier-General E.A.C. (Ned) Amy (then a lieutenant-colonel, and CO of the Canadian Grenadier Guards). "It was one of the hazards, particularly in close country and built-up areas."

The troop leader was under even greater pressure, as the Grenadier Guards history notes:

He [had] to guide his tank, make full use of the ground, keep in constant touch with his infantry, scan the landscape for the enemy, direct his gunner on to targets, position his other tanks, pass messages back to the squadron leader over the air, and at the same time be on the alert for all the unexpected situations which might arise.

The job was that much tougher in the woods, where trees sheltered enemy snipers and bazooka men and at the same time obstructed the tank's traversing gun.

None of the Allied tanks had the firepower of the German armour. Sergeant R.E. Rogge, who served in both the Canadian and American forces, observed that "in a tank-against-tank battle we were decidedly mercenary and bet on the Jerries, unless our tanks outnumbered them something fierce. A Tiger could sit all day just like a chunk of solid steel, soaking up the punishment, and then blast off one 88 and put 'paid' to the pestering Sherman, or whatever. One Jerry, with five Tigers, shot up a whole British armoured division. Of course, he was Michael Wittman, the Tiger 'ace' who had about 141 confirmed tank 'kills.' "

However, Brigadier Robert Moncel, who commanded 4th Canadian Armoured Brigade, points out that "the real and proper role for tanks was to get in among the cooks and butchers and spread chaos and destruction — not to fight enemy tanks. In this role the Shermans were better than the heavy German tanks; they were reliable, faster, more manoeuvrable, more agile — and the 75mm gun was ideal for this purpose."

Ideally, then, tanks should be employed in massed formations, over hard open country, to break through and disrupt the enemy in their rear areas — the classic German *Speerpunkt und Aufrollen* (break through and roll out) tactic.

With two magnificent arms with which to wage war, the infantry and the armour, senior Allied army staff too often failed to exploit them by fully marrying up their combined talents in such massed attacks. The most successful operations depended upon such employment, and on a high level of cooperation between these two vital arms.

In many cases, infantry mistrusted and misunderstood the role of the tanks. They called tanks "mobile dungeons." The twin fears of being closed in and flamed up persuaded most riflemen that they were better off on their own two feet:

I would rather have been an infantryman than a tankman any day of the week [a rifleman wrote]. It might feel safer inside so long as nothing happens, but you couldn't hope for a pleasant death if anything did happen, shut up in a blazing steel room that was rapidly becoming white-hot and filled with an infernal symphony of fireworks as your own ammunition caught fire and added to the horror.

Tankmen saw it from a different perspective: they felt safer. The armour protected them from rifle and machine-gun fire and, to some extent, from mines. The troopers made friends with their vehicles. They named them for girlfriends or wives; they pampered their engines and polished their armament with the same care and pride that aircrews gave to their planes.

Trooper Al LaRose recalls, "I was glad for the security of my tank. I remember being in an anti-personnel minefield in the Hochwald. There were a lot of wounded foot-soldiers lying on the ground and it was terrible. I could hear their voices, even with my earphones on: 'Stretcher-bearer! Stretcher-bearer!' Those guys screaming, you can't forget that."

Major John Munro, a squadron leader with the Canadian Grenadier Guards, believes that "good radio communication and the ability to throw smoke added to our sense of security. However, we were very aware that the tanks were not heavily armoured against the big German guns."

There were perks to life in a steel box. Major Ivor Crosthwaite, with the British 4th Grenadier Guards, remembers, "We were very comfortable in tank fighting; we were infinitely better off than anybody else. When we stopped for the night, our ammunition and petrol would come up. We had our own rations and our own stoves — even a stovepipe. We carried all our blankets with us. Every night, after we'd cleaned the guns and completed the maintenance on the tanks, we would dig a hole under each tank big enough for four or five people to sleep in. We felt very safe there; that helped a lot. And we slept, which is perhaps the most important thing of all."

In the Rhineland, however, the ground was often too boggy to allow the men to sleep under the tanks. There was a very real risk that the tanks would sink on them.

There were detractions, too, to life in a tank. There was the noise, the discomfort of jamming five men into the equivalent of an American Chevy (each wedged into his narrow little compartment) — and the smell of gasoline fumes and sweaty humanity. Five men jam-packed into one small compartment could require a lot of forgiving, some days.

When caught in an intense bombardment, it was suicidal to get out. "You got out of the tank to take a leak and you were a dead duck," one trooper said. "We used our damn helmets and dumped them out of the turret." Empty shell casings likewise came in handy.

A steel box it might be, but the Sherman was not — as its crew was only too aware — inviolable. Schmeissers and Spandaus could not penetrate its armour, but the high-velocity shells of the dreaded 88mm could slice the casing as if it were paper, killing or maiming any obstacle they encountered on their course through the tank and out the other side. Lieutenant-Colonel H.A. ("Snuffy") Smith, CO of the Canadian Grenadier Guards (commanding "Snuff Force" at the Calcar-Udem ridge), suffered first-hand experience of this when his tank was holed and his leg was irreparably shattered.

Some of the Shermans had spare track welded on the outside to provide extra protection against enemy fire, but it wasn't enough. "Sherman tank — cheese!" sneered one captured enemy bazooka man.

Most dreaded were those bazooka boys: German infantrymen who infiltrated among the tanks armed with Panzerfausts or "one-shot wonders," as the Allied troops termed the bazookas. This incredible short-range German anti-tank rocket weapon was so light and cheap it could be thrown away after it had fired its single shot. The damage it inflicted — and the fear it engendered — was awesome.

How the troops hated the bazooka [a regimental history records]. Enemy infantry so armed could nip swiftly from one position to another, making it often impossible to locate them. . . . They would lie in wait by the roadside or near a roadblock and with one discharge from their cheap single-shooters could immobilize or destroy a tank.

"You always hear about the 88mm being so dangerous, but you never seem to hear about the bazooka," Trooper Alex Graham says. "I thought it was the worst. An 88mm would go right through the tank and out the other side. If you happened to be in the way, you might be hurt. But when the bazooka hit, it made a hole and exploded inside. It fired from such close range that there was no way the tank could swing the gun around to defend itself."

"If the tank was hit below the turret ring, it brewed," Tommy Boyd notes. "That's where all the ammunition and gasoline were stored; it was bound to hit something."

Many tanks caught on fire — "brewed" was the tankmen's vivid term — or were blown up by mines and shells. Some bogged in mudded ruts and had to be abandoned, their parts later cannibalized to eke out another few miles for another tank.

Trooper James Love of the Sherbrooke Fusiliers was the only crew member to escape injury when his tank was attacked at Calcar. "The Germans had wisened up. They let the 75mm tanks go through and waited for the Firefly. Just at dawn we got hit by a bazooka. The commander of the tank, Captain Gary Gould, got about four shots away before he was wounded. We had to bail out. Our co-driver was killed, George Harvey got his hand taken off with a Schmeisser, Trooper MacDougall was shot in the shoulder — I was the only guy that got out without a scratch."

Bogging down could be a very frightening experience. It happened to Boyd at Calcar. "The Germans were shelling something fierce. We were struggling to put the cables onto another tank to pull us out and I thought, 'This is it! This is the way I'm going to get it!' But we got them on OK. Then we went about 20 yards and both tanks bogged down. We had to stay there till daylight — we were sitting ducks."

The horror of being burned alive in a tank festered in every trooper's subconscious. The Shermans were dubbed "Ronsons" by the troops — because they "lit every time." With the same black humour, the Germans called them "Tommy cookers."

"When our tanks were replaced we were always worried we might get gasoline engines instead of the newer diesels," Trooper Jim Jones, a loader-operator with C Squadron, Sherbrooke Fusiliers, said. "With a diesel at least you had a chance it would just smoulder when you were hit. You would have time to get out. A gasoline tank blew up."

You had just three seconds to bail out of a flaming Sherman before its 90 gallons of fuel or some of its 125 high-velocity shells exploded. Five men — or those of the five who survived the explosion — would dive for the hatches, praying the metal hadn't buckled in the searing heat. Even when the tank was only disabled, it was a sure bet that the enemy gun had its range and within a few seconds the next hit would set the tank on fire.

These were thoughts that a tankman tried to block out, but inevitably, fear found a chink and forced its way into the consciousness. For LaRose, the bad moment came before the battle. "Before we jumped off, everybody was keyed up. Once you started to move you got busy and forgot about being afraid. But if you were pulled out for a rest, even the thought of going back made your stomach squirm."

General Simonds may have devised the means in Normandy to

move infantry forward with the armour, but he had not come up with a formula for their firm working partnership. There were a number of obstacles to a successful alliance.

In the winter and spring of 1945, both arms were hindered from fulfilling their roles by inexperienced and ill-trained reinforcements, by bad weather, and by terrible terrain.

They were not comfortable bedmates. Tankmen feared the dark; infantrymen often clung to it to achieve surprise in an attack.

Many infantry did not understand or symphathize with the terrible vulnerability of the tanks against bazookas or self-propelled guns — especially at night or in close fighting. They believed that armour ran scared under fire. The riflemen tended to short-fuse when they saw the tanks disappearing from battle at dusk to refuel and replenish ammunition. They figured that "maintenance" was merely a euphemism for getting a hot meal, a good night's rest, and an escape from battle. They were almost equally resentful when the tanks would return at dawn in a great cloud of dust and noise, giving away the riflemen's position and drawing enemy fire.

Major Donald Callander of the Queen's Own Cameron Highlanders ran into German Panzerfausts in the Reichswald. "They fired at our first tank and hit it. They didn't do much damage, but the tank went into reverse, the others followed, and we never got them up again. From then on it was just infantry fighting." Major Martin Lindsay had problems getting the flame-throwing tanks to cross an open field and come to the aid of his beleaguered company of Gordons in Thomashof; just one finally agreed to come — too late to save the men.

Riflemen tended to want the tanks to remain up front to defend them against counter-attacks by enemy tanks. However, as Brigadier Moncel maintains, "the best tank killer was the well-sited, bravely served, dug-in SP anti-tank gun."

At the Goch-Calcar road, Major Louis Froggett proved the point when his collaboration with Lieutenant David Heaps of the 18th Canadian Anti-Tank Battery knocked out four German Panthers.

Because he had been an infantryman before he joined the armoured brigade, Brigadier-General Sidney Radley-Walters (then a major and squadron commander, Sherbrooke Fusiliers) did not agree that the armour's disappearing act was necessary when the riflemen needed their support: "It's a lot of BS that tanks have to pull out on the infantry to go back for maintenance. As long as you can keep the damn thing filled with gasoline and ammunition, those were the only two important priorities.

"I tried my best to stay with the infantry all the time, for the simple reason that every time we moved, we didn't suffer but the poor old infantrymen got shelled to hell," Radley-Walters recalled. "In most cases, when the petrol truck got up — oh, within a couple of hundred yards or as close as he could to us — we'd get out some ropes and pull the damn diesel jerry-cans into the back of the tank and load there, just to keep the dust and noise level down."

In a sense, the riflemen's bias had some foundation. Tank commanders were very concerned with self-preservation.

A veteran of Dunkirk, Grenadier Guard Major Ivor Crosthwaite was an infantryman before he switched to tanks. He evolved a tough but realistic approach to armoured combat. "We had just two priorities: to help the infantry and to avoid getting killed ourselves. Anyone who doesn't say that is a fool," Crosthwaite declares.

"Whenever the infantry got stuck and couldn't get forward, our troop commanders would put the tanks behind cover and shoot the infantry forward. We avoided casualties ourselves by keeping out of sight. We never appeared at all unless we were moving and unless we were firing. We never hung about in the open, because the Germans would bring up a self-propelled gun or tank or they'd stalk you with a bazooka.

"But we never left the infantry without protection. We hung on right up front until our own anti-tank guns were completely dug in against any counter-attack. We'd stay up there until the last moment of daylight and if necessary we'd even leave one tank up there during the night."

There were other problems between the two arms. "Infantry-cum-armour cooperation was awful!" insists Lieutenant-Colonel G.P. Wood (then a platoon commander with 7th Battalion Argyll & Sutherland Highlanders). "How many infantry formations were trained intimately with armour — living together, eating together, and so on? Yet there was no other way to achieve the necessary rapport."

Not surprisingly, when the men of the two supporting arms not only learned more tricks of the other's trades but even shared a meal and a joke, efficiency increased enormously, and jealousy vanished. This was demonstrated by the Guards Armoured Division, and it worked superbly, as Lieutenant-Colonel Roddy Hill, CO of the 5th Battalion Coldstream Guards, recalls: "We had each armoured squadron working with its own infantry company and they became a well-trained team — and very close friends."

Simpson's Ninth Army, like the British Guards, used a system of tank-infantry cooperation that proved highly effective. Major-General Lunsford E. Oliver, GOC 5th Armored Division, describes it:

> Within each combat command area, two task forces were in existence. Within each task force the similarly lettered tank and infantry company were paired off in "married" companies. Within the companies the individual platoons worked together, and within the platoons each squad worked with a specific tank. These "married" companies lived, worked, trained, and fought together. As a result, the tankers and infantry knew exactly what was expected of each other and it is believed that the maximum efficiency resulted.

But, as Captain Ray Latvamaki of the 701st U.S. Tank Battalion pointed out, like any marriage, there were the odd foibles too. Cannibalizing was his pet peeve. "I wish the hell the infantry would leave our knocked-out tanks alone," he grumbled. "Usually the .30-calibers are gone and the radio too. They leave only the hull."

Few formations reached the state of wedded bliss described by Oliver, although a guarded courtship was attained within other armoured units. The 4th Canadian Armoured Division, for example, had one armoured brigade and one infantry brigade. The armoured brigade had three regiments plus a recce regiment that performed as a fourth armoured regiment. The infantry brigade comprised three infantry battalions plus a motorized infantry battalion. At the sharp end, then, where a smooth working relationship often determined the success of the operation and the lifespan of its participants, the 4th Armoured had nine squadron commanders who would have to work with no more than 15 infantry company commanders.

However, problems erupted when independent armour and infantry formations were cast in a mix-and-match situation, as many were in Operation Blockbuster. There, Simonds attempted to meld sub-units from the 2nd Canadian Armoured Brigade (Sherbrooke Fusiliers, Fort Garry Horse, and 1st Hussars) with units from two infantry divisions. In this brand of frontline tactics, nine squadron commanders might have to get to know and work with 72 infantry company commanders. It was often an unworkable ratio.

"Difficulties occurred when strange tankers worked with strange infantrymen and the two married up for the battle only hours (and in some cases minutes) before crossing the start line,'' Ned Amy noted.

Radley-Walters recalls a number of such difficulties: ''Communication was not that good. There were many cases when we'd be told to go over with a particular battalion — it might be 3 a.m. and black as hell — and quite often you wouldn't know the people. It became a matter of hopping out of the tank and talking to the platoon or company or battalion commander.

''If we had known one another,'' he points out, ''we could have worked out little drills: the burst of a Bren gun with some tracer could identify a target, or letting off a smoke shell. But that takes preliminary getting together. When men work together, fight together, get drunk together, they develop confidence and respect for each other.''

The riflemen were frustrated by their inability to communicate with the tanks of the independent formations. Field infantry commanders were not on the tank radio net.

In order to disseminate intelligence to the tank commander (who might be just 20 shell-swept yards away), they had to radio some distance back to Brigade on an infantry 19-set and ask HQ to transmit the information forward on the tank net — a cumbersome way of relaying essential information.

The alternative, as Captain Robert Hemmingsen, Canloan company commander with 7th Battalion Seaforth Highlanders, remembers, was to brave the bullets and talk directly with the tank commander — if you could: ''Near Calcar, we came under some pretty heavy fire and I was trying to indicate the German positions. The Churchill tanks had a telephone on the outside but they never seemed to listen to it. I finally wound up beating the hell out of the back of the tank with the butt of a rifle trying to get them to pay attention to me.'' This tactic created a very real risk of getting shot, as happened to Tommy Thompson when he climbed out of his Kangaroo during the Calcar attack to confer with the tank commander.

The marriage may often have been rocky, but the inescapable fact was that each partner needed the other. Amy cites an incident when one of his tanks knocked out an enemy tank that was moving directly towards a soldier: ''When the tank blew up, the soldier got off the ground and ran towards the Sherman, which he patted, and exclaimed: 'You big cast-iron son-of-a-bitch: I could kiss you!' ''

A dramatic example of armour helping infantry occurred when a British Grenadier Guard tank boldly entered a field of schu-mines where a number of riflemen were severely wounded.

"My tank commander exploded the mines as he went in," Crosthwaite remembers admiringly. "And then all his crew went in along his tank tracks. They managed to bring out 17 wounded, and every one of those men had one or both legs blown off."

But there were equally dramatic incidents where roles were reversed. Colonel John Chaston, then a major and a company commander with 2nd Battalion Monmouthshires, describes a situation where infantry bails out armour: "When a tank has blown up on a mine, an infantryman might have to go and clear a path for other oncoming tanks. He'd have to crawl forward on his stomach, probing for the mines with a bayonet — being damned careful, because there also could be schu-mines there — afraid to stand up or he might get shot at."

Tanks also depended on the riflemen to flush out the enemy opposition. Brigadier-General Gordon Wotherspoon, commanding the South Alberta Regiment, makes the point: "In order for the tanks to be effective — particularly at night — you had to have good infantry protection to keep the bazookas away.

"The infantry never failed to support us, and I hope we never failed to support them. We never pulled back to refuel. We sent our trucks up to refuel where they were. I can still see some of my tanks busy firing, when the echelon would come up with a truck loaded with ammunition and petrol. They would get on top of the tanks and load them with ammunition and petrol with the Germans still shooting."

On February 26, the armoured units of three nations were thrust into the Rhineland battle alongside the infantry. How they fared depended to a large extent on lessons learned by both partners of the union since Normandy — and on the manner in which they were committed by the senior planners.

16

Valley of Death

Top Secret. Personal and Eyes Only for CIGS from Field-Marshal Montgomery, 27 Feb 1945:
The fighting today in the Hochwald Forest area has been
very fierce and the enemy is resisting strongly this
advance towards Xanten and Wesel. The total prisoners
taken by Cdn army since Veritable started is now 15,000.

"I MUST HAVE A ROAD through which the momentum of the advance can be fully maintained to its conclusion," Lieutenant-General Simonds insisted at the start of Blockbuster. Getting Simonds his road was to be an exercise in frustration and futility, costing many more hundreds of casualties than the possession of that two-mile passage seemed to warrant.

The Goch-Xanten railway line — Simonds's proposed new road — was built on an embankment. It traversed a narrow corridor — the Hochwald Gap — which cut through two elevated forests: the Hochwald Forest and the Balberger Wald. The gap, some two miles long, varied in width from 250 yards at its neck to one mile at its eastern shoulders.

Reconnaissance had indicated that the line was free of mines and that it had not been demolished. It would be relatively simple for engineers to tear up the track and develop the roadbed for one-way traffic.

The alternative route to the Rhine was a good road that skirted the woods some three miles to the south. However, it would have had to be shared with Horrocks's 30 Corps. Simonds feared that this route might become too congested to support all the supplies needed for the forthcoming assault across the river.

See Map 8 (Appendix B).

Two British divisions (temporarily under Simonds's 2 Corps command) were assigned major roles in the Blockbuster offensive. The 43rd Wessex was responsible for protecting the Canadian left flank between Moyland and the Rhine. Blockbuster's south (right) flank was entrusted to Major-General Pip Roberts's 11th British Armoured Division.

General Crerar recognized that whichever of his two corps opened up the most efficient road to the Rhine should spearhead the major attack. His directive to Simonds and Horrocks on February 25 had stated that if by D-plus-One of Blockbuster (February 27) 2 Corps's armoured breakthrough to the east had not been achieved, "the weight of the Canadian Army effort will then be transferred to 30 Corps."

Both corps were driving southeast on parallel courses: Simonds on the left and Horrocks some ten miles farther south on the right. Between their positions lay the second German Siegfried defence system, known as the Schlieffen Position. Both commanders realized that the defence line would constitute a replay of the obstacles the troops had struggled against in the Reichswald sector: anti-tank ditches, belts of trenches two to three lines deep, and bands of barbed wire — all under enemy gun sights.

Both Horrocks and Simonds must have realized that the terrain they faced — low, soggy, and traversed by numerous small waterways — promised monumental difficulties for their armoured units. Yet both apparently felt that tanks would be indispensable in dealing with the enemy defences.

The weather, as in Veritable, had turned wet and cold again, precluding air support for the first two days of the operation. The rain exacerbated the terrible road conditions, creating near-impossible going for the tanks. Deep ruts of mud caused even the 20-foot-long Sherman to wallow "like small craft caught in a Channel blow."

Of the two men, Simonds seemed to have taken on the less promising line of attack. With his gaze fixed determinedly on the railway line, he appears to have shrugged off the negative features of forcing the Hochwald Gap. There were many.

The approaches to the gap were across a sodden, treeless valley under direct scrutiny of the enemy. The railway's high embankment was similarly exposed. The entire area — gap and approaches — was too narrow to allow manoeuvrability for tanks. Underpasses would allow German armour to harass the infantry and tanks and then retreat back to safety. A knoll (Point 73), always a difficult objective to capture, was astride its entrance. The Germans had had ample time to mine the corridor heavily and range their guns on it.

Clearing the two forests that flanked the Hochwald Gap could be a slow, slogging operation. Von Luettwitz had amply proven the skill of his troops in defending forests. His recent six-day defence of Moyland Wood was reminder enough of that. It would not be the 24-hour zip Simonds anticipated.

Should the Canadians surmount these obstacles, capture the Hochwald Gap, and convert the rail line to a road, there was another problem: the Sherman tanks, noted for their high profiles, would be skylined on the embankment "like a row of ducks in a shooting gallery," as a number of troopers soon discovered.

Nevertheless, under pressure from this threat of Crerar's to denude his operation and give the main thrust to Horrocks, Simonds urged Major-General Vokes to strike eastward through the gap with his 4th Canadian Armoured Division, seize its rail line, and continue on to Xanten. At the same time, he instructed 2nd and 3rd Canadian Infantry Divisions to clear out the enemy strongpoints in the two flanking woods.

For six days and nights, the tanks of the 2nd Canadian Armoured Brigade and 4th Canadian Armoured Division gamely supported the infantry of three divisions in the Battle of the Hochwald and the death trap of the Hochwald Gap.

The problems that these divisions faced in conquering the Hochwald and its gap were the mud, with the resulting road and communication chaos — and the senior Allied commanders who so grievously miscast them for their role in Operation Blockbuster.

Half a league, half a league,
Half a league onward,
All in the valley of Death
Rode the six hundred.
"Forward, the Light Brigade!
Charge for the guns!" he said.
Into the valley of Death
Rode the six hundred.

Major-General Vokes had divided the 4th Armoured Division into two groups for Operation Blockbuster: Tiger Group, commanded by Moncel, and Lion Group, under Brigadier J.C. Jefferson. Each of these two groups was then divided into five complex sub-units.

221

The Tigers had achieved their objectives on the Calcar Heights on D-Day. Now it remained for the Lions to force the mouth of the gap. The Lions (the Algonquin Regiment supported by a troop of tanks of the South Alberta Regiment) initiated the attack on February 27, D-plus-One, on Point 73 — the small hummock at the western end of the gap.

At the same time, the South Albertas were ordered to support the Algonquin Carrier Platoon in an attack that was so speculative it evoked a protest from the regiment: the small attack force was commanded to make a "diversionary" right hook through a narrow underpass beneath the railway line, deep into enemy territory.

Their misgivings were justified; the mission was jinxed from the start. "The success of this show depended on the cover of darkness and surprise," the South Alberta war diary recorded. Because their designated FUP had not even been cleared of the enemy, the column was eight hours late in starting. They lost the darkness — and they lost the surprise.

Moreover, the woods on the left and right of the attackers had not yet been secured by the 2nd Division, who were held up at the edge of the Hochwald, or by the 3rd Division, still fighting their way through Udem to the Balberger Wald. Despite the determined efforts of the two divisions, these flanks would not be finally cleared for five more days. In fact there was never the remotest possibility that they would be cleared to protect the flanks of the 4th Division. The battle of the Hochwald Gap was fought throughout with open flanks.

It was soon evident that the Germans were ready and waiting. An unparalleled concentration of mortar, shell, and rocket fire from enemy defence lines in and beyond the forest — and even from across the Rhine — effectively hammered the attackers from three sides. The fire from the German guns eight miles north across the Rhine (where the river forms a U) was actually coming in from behind the advancing Canadians.

Major George Cassidy, second-in-command of the Algonquins, recounts: "One expected fire to come from the front, or even from a flank, but when it came in over one's shoulder, it was unsettling, to say the least."

"They amassed a hell of a lot of guns from somewhere," puzzles Major George Hale, squadron leader with the Canadian Grenadier Guards. "They had a lot of their mediums and heavies over on the other side of the Rhine and we were a pretty easy target, well within their range."

"We could concentrate our fire against the small gap," Major-

General Guderian recently commented. ''We had ammunition in those days and some Sturm-Tiger [mortar]. We were reinforced by Parachute Regiment 24 and the Army Weapons School of First Parachute Army under Hauptmann von Huetz. He defended Udem and fought with us around Louisendorf.''

Without waiting for permission from Berlin, General Schlemm had diverted fifty 88mm guns to the Hochwald front. First Canadian Army Intelligence estimated that during the first week of March the German First Parachute Army had available to it 717 mortars and 1,054 guns. POWs from 86th Werfer Regiment revealed in interrogations that there were at least 54 projectors of 15cm and 24cm rockets: the discordant screams of the fearsome Nebelwerfers, or Moaning Minnies, added to the pandemonium.

By sheer grit, the Algonquins and their supporting South Alberta armour inched along the valley towards the knoll but got no farther than 500 yards beyond the entrance to the gap. Counterattacking Germans with tanks virtually encircled the troops. Casualties piled up; under the heavy fire, wounded men lay in the battlefield for 24 hours before they could be evacuated.

The right-hook assault fared even worse. Disaster struck without warning as the column of South Alberta tanks advanced at dawn into the underpass beneath the tracks. Suddenly the silence of the mist-shrouded morning was shattered by a deadly hail of shellfire. The enemy had formed an ambush on both flanks. Coolly, the Germans picked off the lead and two rear tanks. The crippled vehicles lurched and flamed. The remaining tanks and the Algonquin carriers were trapped. One by one, the anti-tank guns knocked them off.

Enemy infantry with bazookas moved in for the kill. Of all the vehicles — nine tanks and 12 carriers — only one carrier escaped the ambush unharmed. Their bewildered crews — some 40 men who had managed to avoid being killed or captured by bailing out — dug into the verges and watched the annihilation with horror.

''Forward, the Light Brigade!''
Was there a man dismayed?
Not though the soldier knew
Some one had blundered:
Theirs not to make reply,
Theirs not to reason why,
Theirs but to do and die:
Into the valley of Death
Rode the six hundred.

It was now February 28: D-plus-Two of Operation Blockbuster. Crerar's warning that he would shift the weight of the attack to Horrocks's command on the right was being curiously ignored. Essame has suggested that the reason Montgomery refused to call off the ill-fated struggle in the gap and stage a full-scale attack elsewhere instead was to avoid "an Anglo-Canadian breach of confidence." More likely, Simonds, determined to see his plan through, bypassed Crerar's command by using his direct pipeline to Montgomery.

Whatever the reason, the folly continued. On this last day of February, yet another attacking force was flung into the gap. Before dawn on the 28th, the Canadian Argyll & Sutherland Highlanders moved forward with another squadron of South Alberta tanks to continue the attack. By first light they were dug in at the eastern end.

Von Luettwitz had been anticipating the attack "with great anxiety." The 116th Panzer Division had incurred many casualties, including almost 500 of his men taken prisoner on February 26 (the majority by 8th Canadian Infantry Brigade). Now, von Luettwitz spirited fresh troops from 8th Parachute Division (including the battle-sharp 24th Parachute Regiment) into the line alongside his armoured division.

At 0645 hours the first German counter-attack set the pace for a day that was to become "a nightmare of terror and blood and sudden death and slow death" for the Argylls.

The story of one company of that battalion typifies the Canadians' dogged resistance. At dawn, the company — Captain L.V. Perry's B Company — had dug in around its objective: a house on the edge of the wood at the far end of the gap. The Germans counter-attacked savagely a number of times and the company became isolated and out of communication with the rest of the battalion. Casualties mounted, and finally Perry was the only officer left. Eight times during that desperate day he sent runners back to HQ to inform them of the critical situation. None survived to make the report.

The enemy overran the defences in front of the house. A German tank commander stood up in his turret and arrogantly demanded the surrender of the small garrison. Perry's single remaining PIAT spewed back a furious reply: the German was killed. The Argyll history reports the events of the next hours:

Capt Perry's flaming spirit had communicated itself to his men, by now a mere handful of effectives who, feeling themselves abandoned by all, had resolved simply to sell their lives as dearly as possible. The little band of half-crazed men continued to hold their position after dark; about 2000 hours, Capt Perry, who had heard nothing from any Canadian force all day, and whose position had been subjected to barrages both by their own and by enemy fire, decided to try himself to contact headquarters.

Perry left his senior man in command: a blinded lance-sergeant. He made his way back to the battalion CP. Lieutenant-Colonel Fred Wigle, who had been striving to control the battle from one of his forward company positions (and had twice been wounded), organized the relief. Of the hundred attackers, only 20 men survived — five of these severely wounded.

The Lincoln & Welland Regiment was slated to attack through the Argyll position at noon the same day. Impossible ground conditions delayed the arrival of the armoured support. The CO, Lieutenant-Colonel Rowan Coleman, recalls: "Every tank was stuck. You couldn't even dig them out."

When finally the men moved up to launch the assault, "both units came under the crushing weight of the heaviest enemy artillery and mortar concentration that any of us had seen on the Continent so far." Cassidy describes: "Caught above ground, with no hope of cover, with scores of casualties, the attack withered and died."

The next plan for an assault down the Hochwald Gap was even more stunning in its obliviousness to the reality of the situation. Notwithstanding the disastrous outcome of the day's attack by the Algonquins and the South Alberta Regiment, who had been driven back even before they reached the mouth of the gap, and by the Argylls and the Lincs, who had been pinned down, the Canadian Grenadier Guards were coolly directed to lay on a fresh assault. Lieutenant-Colonel Amy, CO of the Grenadiers, was "amazed" at the objective he and the Lake Superior Regiment were jointly given: Xanten. It might as well have been the moon.

As even securing the gap seemed a near-impossible challenge at this point, the prospect of achieving this and *then* advancing another eight miles to the Rhine at Xanten seemed totally unrealistic to the men at the sharp end.

"I still wonder," Amy reflects even today, "on the basis of what information the senior commanders were directing troops in the Hochwald."

Looking at the map on that bitter night, seeing the forbidding mass of the Hochwald and Balberger Wald, with the slim corridor of the gap snaking through, he was prompted to make a comment that was uncomfortably prophetic:

Gerry Chubb, the CO of the British Columbia Regiment, said, "You'll never make it to Xanten." I said, "Not to worry, Gerry, we'll get stopped here" (and I pointed to the gap). "Then *you* will be ordered to pass through." His response was, "Son of a bitch."

Vokes had decided that the time had come to put Simonds's railway-cum-road theory to the test. Earlier attempts by the Sherbrooke Fusiliers to bridge the Hochwald Gap by using the rail line had been a disaster. "It was a death trap," one trooper remembers. "We was silhouetted against the skyline and the Germans were firing from both sides. There was no getting off; finally we had to reverse out."

"Part of the rail line was on a high embankment with practically no place to get off," Major John Munro of the Canadian Grenadier Guards recalls. "All that the Germans had to do was to pick off, say, the tenth tank. Then they could just systematically go up and knock off the others.

"It was an obvious area for bombardment; we were very much out-gunned. Fighting was very intense. Tanks were roaming around and at any point there might be an 88 poking through a hedge or in a hull-down position up on a hill.

"Meanwhile, the wireless was cracking out orders saying, 'Get moving.' "

Ned Amy, small and spunky and quite unruffled, was regarded by many as the "heart of the Grens." With their CO severely wounded the previous day, he was now also their commander. Moving up to the start line of the attack the next morning, he was concerned about exploring the best way to conquer the Hochwald Gap. He sent his recce troop to assess the possibility of advancing up the railway track. The troop leader's report convinced him that for a number of reasons it was not a viable route.

The line went through a cutting — ripe ambush territory for the enemy — and then along an embankment where the troops would be exposed. Furthermore, the line was swarming with Germans; the British 11th Armoured Division was at that moment engaged nearby in a furious battle on the south side of the wood.

"The track literally ran down the flank of the German formation opposing the Brits,'' Amy describes. ''I directed the lead group to find another route. Vokes was displeased with my decision not to use the railroad approach and aparently considered putting me under arrest.''

Vokes is reputed to have threatened next, in the heat of the moment, to put the entire regiment under arrest. He cooled off considerably in the next days and wrote, finally, a congratulatory letter to the regiment for their ''terrific efforts'' in attempting to surmount ''this difficult obstacle.''

While the argument raged, an enemy bombardment opened up again, catching his men without protection and wounding Amy. The barrage effectively nullified the attack — and ended, once and for all, any further thought of attacking under fire up Simonds's rail line.

The combination of mud, rain, deteriorating communications, unexpectedly ferocious enemy fire — and the unrealistic decision-making from high command — had by now produced chaos.

''The battle . . . deteriorated into more or less isolated actions,'' Cassidy stated. ''The 'fog of war' was at its thickest. For a spell the Algonquin felt like . . . the Lost Tribe of Israel, wandering about in circles, trying to find a spot to light down.''

Communication between units and sub-units had become almost non-existent. Even the 4th Canadian Armoured Brigade commander, Moncel, was in the dark. ''I often only knew the situation 50 yards around me — sometimes it was 50 feet!''

''It was a real shambles,'' Brigadier Gordon Wotherspoon confirms. ''There was a definite lack of coordination. When some unit was supposed to capture an objective and failed to do so, other troops were not advised of the fact. This happened on any number of occasions.''

Intelligence reports were often misleading. An intelligence officer in 3rd Canadian Infantry Division attributes this to the climate of war in 1945. ''Senior staff only heard what they wanted to hear. They had already made the plan; what they wanted was substantive back-up from the 'I' guys. If you didn't agree with them, you found yourself out in left field minding the transport echelon.''

The tactical deployment of Canadian tanks in such conditions was a travesty. In postwar analysis, both Canadian and German commanders were sharply critical.

''When you're assholed in mud and you can't get off the road, the role of tanks becomes rather obscure,'' asserts Major Hale. ''The biggest problem, as far as my squadron was concerned — and it was a bigger obstacle than the enemy — was keeping the damn things moving. It just wasn't moving weather; our tanks got bogged. I would suspect we outnumbered the Germans substantially in guns and manpower but we were moving and they were sitting.''

The struggle had sorely depleted the armoured strength of the Canadians. The 1st Hussars Regiment had 82 tank casualties during the operation. Following the Calcar-Udem ridge struggle on February 26, the Grenadier Guards had only 31 tanks of their original 66. By D-plus-Four (March 2), the count of Grenadier tanks was down to 21.

The recovery of damaged tanks from under direct German observation and fire was an exercise in boldness, lightning speed, and skill. The 54th Light Aid Detachment of the Royal Canadian Electrical and Mechanical Engineers, under Captain P.C. Neil, managed to salvage many of these tanks. They were swiftly repaired and returned to action.

Nonetheless, Major Curtis Greenleaf, second-in-command of the Grenadier Guards, was outraged at the waste: ''There was simply no justification for putting more tanks in there because all that was going to happen was that they would get bogged down or knocked out. One of the principles of war that we were taught was, you don't reinforce failure; you reinforce success. Obviously, we were having no success moving the tanks through.''

Brigadier-General Radley-Walters agrees: ''At division level up they didn't know what the hell was going on. Instead of going forward to find out what was happening, the senior staff made their decisions from sitreps [situation reports].''

Lieutenant-Colonel Rowan Coleman, commander of the Lincoln & Welland Regiment and fresh from the ''straightforward'' battlefields of Africa and Italy, was ''halfway up the wall.''

''I thought, 'Good God, how mixed up can you get?' I was really wild with impatience and anger, as anybody who was with me will attest.''

No one was more surprised at Simonds's tactics than the Germans themselves. ''They didn't concentrate their attack on any one front on the same day,'' Guderian, chief of staff of the 116th Panzer Division, notes critically.

''They attacked one battalion here . . . one battalion there. . . . We could put ourselves sometimes here, sometimes there. We could hold up the whole Canadian Army for weeks. But if they had attacked on one front I believe we could not have stood it for long."

General Plocher, the GOC of 6th Parachute Division, concurs. He wonders why — instead of the costly and slow forest slogging — the Canadians didn't concentrate all of their tanks and artillery at either end of the Hochwald and simply go around it.

Instead of gambling on a frontal attack on the obstructing woods, Simonds could have bypassed the trouble spot by hooking just a few miles around, ultimately rolling up the German defence. Defending a wood, as he well knew, took much less strength than attacking into (or out of) it.

Or he could have diverted his attack two miles to the south, as Crerar had outlined, and handed over the bulk of his divisions to Horrocks's command.

Just as Veritable had faltered on D-plus-Three, so Operation Blockbuster was in similar peril on its fourth day. All five of Simonds's divisions were losing their momentum.

Efforts by 4th Armoured Division to break out of the Hochwald Gap had been stalled. The Canadian infantry had not secured its flanks. North of the Hochwald, 43rd Wessex had taken Calcar unopposed but had not been able to advance much farther. South of the gap, Spry's 8th Canadian Infantry Brigade (supported by 1st Hussars) was still striving to help both the Canadians and the British 11th Armoured Division forward by clearing enemy strongpoints from the high ridge on the Balberger Wald that overlooked their positions.

A First Canadian Army Intelligence summary of March 1 reported: "The operation was three days old, but the initial progress, which had held promise of early success, was for the moment slowed up. . . . The enemy had now been able to stabilize his line . . . he had succeeded by hard fighting in keeping his ground losses to a minimum."

Nor was the advance of Horrocks's 30 Corps any more galvanized. His four divisions were struggling against the same terrible combination of determined enemy opposition, impossible ground conditions, and reduced air support that were daunting 2 Canadian Corps's advance.

Fatigue had become an ugly and omnipresent factor in eroding the battle efficiency of the Blockbuster force and in slowing down the advance right across the front. A CMHQ report noted, "Due to the close fighting, very little sleep was possible, and the nerve-racking strain of innumerable schu-mines, causing constant casualties, combined with lack of food quickly reduced the drive of the attack."

"After three weeks we got our first wash and real sleep," an officer from the 53rd Welsh Division recounted. "My sleep during that period had averaged two and a half hours out of each 24. The men were simply magnificent. Almost exhausted, they sometimes fell asleep when talking."

The fact that much of the fighting was taking place in wooded areas only exacerbated the problems. Snipers nested in the treetops and airbursts from the torrent of enemy mortars and shells caused untold casualties.

Fatigue had no respect for rank. From private soldiers fresh on the line to seasoned and senior officers, the same appalling conditions had to be endured. Like the men they commanded, senior officers sweated out enemy bombardments, ducked sniper bullets, crawled on their bellies to reach forward units, slept standing up, and saw their friends taken off the battlefields, dead or seriously wounded.

"The time element cannot be judged by ordinary standards in woods fighting," a 3rd Canadian Infantry Division report stated. "Time and distance should be multiplied by four."

No one at the rear echelon was doing any compassionate multiplying in those pressure-filled days. The commanding officers — men who were the "heart and brains" of battalions, brigades, and divisions — were expected to meet objectives despite the conditions of the battlefield. Adding to the pressure was the frustration of not being able to meet deadlines. They were finding that the impossible took a little longer.

"We'd been fighting for over a month, steady," Queen's Own Rifles CO Lieutenant-Colonel Stephen Lett remembers. "We were getting pretty ragged by those days."

The Rhineland operation gave truth to the adage that everyone has his limit of endurance. The British addressed the problem by giving reliefs to their senior officers with frequent temporary rotations of command. In the Rhineland, British second-in-commands shone. The Canadians gave their commanders no leaves during combat periods — unless they were "eased out" with one-way passes to England. As in Normandy, when the battle faltered, heads rolled. A notable example of this bungling was Simonds's decision to replace one of his most astute commanders when the Hochwald Gap operation soured: Major-General Dan Spry.

Nor were the life-givers and life-savers spared from the perils of combat. Casualties rescued from the field — at great personal risk — by the padres and stretcher-bearers were taken back to the regimental aid posts. Those requiring immediate treatment (other than the severely wounded, who were rushed back to casualty clearing stations) were then moved by field ambulance to the field surgical units and field transfusion units.

Over 20,000 wounded were evacuated by DUKWs through the flooded polders to Nijmegen during Operation Veritable, reaching a peak of 500 a day during the first week of the Hochwald fighting.

The forward medical units moved ahead as the battle progressed. During the Hochwald fighting they were set up near Bedburg, "dangerously close to the fighting," as the Royal Canadian Army Medical Corps history notes. Casualties to the medical officers — some of them fatal — resulted.

A mud-caked schoolhouse basement near Bedburg, readied as a field surgical unit, became the target of German mortar bombs when searchlights used to produce artificial moonlight were located nearby.

"The enemy was trying to knock out the lights but the near-misses got us," Captain Fred Sparling, 12th Field Dressing Station, RCAMC, recalls. "We lost a couple of men, and we all had to work fast to get the operating room back in shape for the operations." Despite working under the handicap of crude facilities, the swift treatment given by these forward MASH units considerably lessened fatalities.

The Germans continued to dominate the gap for two more days, despite the efforts of armour and infantry to break through the bottleneck.

Ironically, the success of the Ninth U.S. Army's drive from the south had made it seem increasingly urgent to Schlemm that he maintain his bridgehead against the Anglo-Canadian attack in the north. He had to keep an escape avenue open across the Rhine for his divisions. That escape was through the bridges of Wesel. His biggest concern was that First Canadian Army might desist from battling the Hochwald head-on and instead mass an attack around the flanks.

The Lake Superior Regiment — the motorized infantry arm of

the 4th Canadian Armoured Division — had reinforced the weak grip that the Argylls and the Lincoln & Wellands had on the eastern shoulders of the gap. Just beyond, but still an elusive target, they could see the neck of the corridor opening out into the Rhine plain.

Squadron commanders like John Munro recall the regiment as having "all sorts of battle courage": "The Lake Sups were an efficient, fast-striking force of skilled infantrymen. They were heavily tracked — their carriers looked like battleships — and they had every weapon they could get on them. They were over-sized, over-strength, and very tough guys — just great to work with."

On March 2, the Lake Superior Regiment — like the rest of the 4th Division troops — had been fighting hard for four days with little sleep. Their last hot meal had been 48 hours before. Nevertheless, a fresh assault was laid on that day by the tireless planners of the corps and division staffs.

The new plan ordered the exhausted Lake Superiors, with a squadron of Grenadier Guards in support, to attack forward on Kangaroos one thousand yards beyond the end of the gap to a small stream (Hohe Ley) in the direction of Xanten. Then one company of Algonquins with the tanks of the Governor General's Foot Guards would advance through them over a flat saucer of land to a woods a further thousand yards. One key ingredient of the plan — and one that backfired badly — was flank protection. The 3rd Canadian Infantry Division, assigned to secure the high ground on the far side of the rail line before midnight preceding the attack, had been held up and had not even launched the assault. The right flank of the attacking force was wide open.

The most ambitious aspect of this highly ambitious battle plan was that the attack was to take place under cover of darkness. Moving diverse units of infantrymen and vehicles forward in split-second coordination through the quagmire of the Hochwald Gap had already proven to be a near-impossible task.

Inevitably, the mud took its toll; the troop carriers were delayed and the assault did not take off until dawn. What followed was sheer disaster. The Lake Sups seized the cluster of farmhouses on their objective. But in the growing daylight they were pinned down by vicious enemy fire from anti-tank guns and tanks.

All of the forward supporting tanks from the Grenadiers either bogged or were wiped out. Emboldened by the destruction of the tanks, the German parachute troops attacked the Lake Superiors.

"It was bitter, close-range fighting," the regimental history relates. "Germans and Canadians struggled, shouted and screamed. . . . Grimly the Lake Sups held on."

Meanwhile, riding the only four Governor General's Foot Guards tanks available, Captain Johnny Jewell led two platoons of the Algonquin company to a point just beyond the Lake Sups. Here, they too were stopped by small-arms fire and the deadly 88s. (The remaining platoon, following on foot, was caught up in the midst of the Lake Superiors' struggle.)

"In the fog of battle," the Canadian official historian, Colonel C.P. Stacey, relates, "erroneous reports came back that the company had reached the wood, and spurred by frequent urgings from Brigade HQ, the remaining Algonquin companies strove desperately to get forward in relief."

The company spearheading the relief was itself hit heavily by enemy fire and pinned down in isolated groups, unable to move and with heavy casualties. Soon a third company was cut down by the deadly fire.

Then the Governor General's Foot Guards, completely exposed to direct enemy fire as the early-morning mists lifted, requested permission to pull back into the shelter of the gap and support the infantry from long range.

"Permission granted if the infantry commander agrees," Brigade replied, apparently not registering that the forward infantry company was cut off and its wireless set had ceased to function.

Shortly after 0745 hours, the tanks withdrew. At that instant, the fog of war — the breakdown in communications between armour and infantry — was to work horribly against the men on the field. The Germans, realizing that the Algonquins now had no tank support and were virtually defenceless, closed in around them.

"Whether or not Captain Jewell sanctioned their withdrawal cannot be known now," Major Cassidy reported, "but it is unlikely that he did so, considering his urgent message later."

At 0830 hours, Jewell ordered two men to try somehow to get back and summon up help, especially heavy support and tanks. Moments later, he was killed. The garrison was overrun. Of the 37 Algonquins in the tiny band, 32 were taken prisoner. Fifty more from the battalion were casualties.

The Battle of the Hochwald Gap was over — dismally over. When the 5th Canadian Infantry Brigade relieved the battered survivors the morning of March 4, the Germans had withdrawn.

The Lake Superiors left 36 men, wounded or killed, on the battlefield. Sixteen more were seized by the enemy. In the division's 24-hour ordeal, 268 men had become casualties. (Guderian claims 14 Canadian tanks destroyed, 66 prisoners of 4th Canadian Armoured Division taken: "Hohe Ley Brook was not reached by the Guards.")

It was 116th Panzer Division's last encounter with the Canadians. Orders from General Schlemm came the night of March 3-4; the division was to proceed south immediately to form a new defence line near Wesel.

The Battle of the Gap had been a "shattering experience" to the division, as the Lake Superior diarist noted. The morning after the battle, a burial party from the regiment went to the area. From the position of the dead men found there, it was possible to piece together some of the story of the struggle:

> There was unforgettable courage recorded here. . . . Pte Yanchuk, G, . . . was within a few yards of an enemy position, lying on his back with a grenade clutched in his hand, killed as he charged. At his side . . . Pte Middlemiss, WR, . . . was sitting in a shell-hole in a life-like position. He had been with Yanchuk when a burst of small-arms fire in the abdomen stopped him. He crawled into the shell-hole, sat there and died. An unknown Canadian made the enemy position. With arms locked around a German he was burned to a crisp by a mound of hay which caught fire alongside the slit-trench in which he fought hand-to-hand. Sgt Lehman, TM, was lying a few yards away, struck down as he brought in the platoon.
>
> Ahead of the Lake Sup positions five men of the ALQ R [Algonquin Regt] were found: four ORs and an Officer. These had been killed by mortar or artillery. The officer had lived long enough to put a shell dressing on one of his men and was crawling to another when he died.

Cannon to right of them,
Cannon to left of them,
Cannon behind them
Volleyed and thundered;
Stormed at with shot and shell,
While horse and hero fell,
They that had fought so well
Came through the jaws of Death,

Back from the mouth of Hell,
All that was left of them,
Left of six hundred.

The Battle of the Hochwald Gap can only be likened to the Battle of the Huertgen Forest: the wrong troops used in the wrong place at the wrong time . . . a battle that never should have been.

In their fight through the mouth of hell, those gallant tanks — Lulu, Allison, Beebe, and the rest — had been reduced to "relative impotence as fighting machines."

"Only as morale stiffeners were they of any value" was the Lake Superior diarist's sorrowful assessment of their efforts.

A senior commander has bitterly denounced it as the Charge of the Light Brigade. Who can argue that the Hochwald Gap was indeed the Valley of Death.

The Obstinate Canadian

Courage is a queer thing which we all have in a greater or
lesser degree and men react to different stresses and
dangers in different ways. If there is one single common
denominator amongst VCs . . . it is a degree of obstinacy
— a refusal to be beaten or pushed around.
Brigadier the Right Honourable Sir John Smyth, Bt, VC, MC

ON THE WESTERN EDGE of the Hochwald, one man epitomized the
spirit that finally won the forest and opened the way to the Rhine.
He is Fred Tilston.

Major Frederick Albert Tilston's obstinate five-year drive to get
to the front line was almost as intense as his struggle — on the
morning of Thursday, March 1, 1945 — to stay there. It began in
Windsor, Ontario, in 1940, shortly after war was declared, when
the determined Canadian pounded in vain on recruit depot doors
across the province. No one, it seemed, was actively recruiting at
that point in the standstill war. And in any case, the mild-
mannered, affable, 34-year-old University of Toronto and Ontario
College of Pharmacy graduate was not, perhaps, the firebrand the
forces were looking for. For one thing, he was too old.

Finally, by "adjusting his age backwards," Tilston left his job
as a pharmaceutical sales manager to join the Essex Scottish Regiment as a second lieutenant.

His next challenge was his health. In England he was wounded
in training and later, on a midnight mission during the Normandy
fighting at Falaise, his jeep ran over a mine. The explosion resulted
in superficial burns and shrapnel slivers in one eye (he was later
to lose the eye) — and yet another sojourn in an English hospital.

See Map 9 (Appendix B).

Tilston fought his way back from these setbacks to rejoin his unit, where he found himself still frozen, now as a captain, in the administrative job of adjutant of the battalion.

Adjutants performed many essential tasks, acting as right-hand men to the commanding officer, with responsibility for a multitude of administrative matters, so that the men on the ground could fight with maximum effectiveness. Because of the importance of keeping the battalion wheels running smoothly, they were usually LOB (left out of battle) in operations. It was not a job that Tilston relished.

"Fred was always at the CO to let him command a company," the Essex Scottish medical officer, Dr. Clifford Richardson, recalls. "He wanted to see some action. He felt that he hadn't seen any because as an adjutant he was always LOB."

In January 1945, just prior to Operation Veritable, Tilston's persistence paid off: he was made second-in-command of C Company. To his disgust, in the battalion's next major action — the Goch-Calcar road battle — he was again LOB (although when the CO was out of communication with his battalion during the battle, Tilston as senior ranking officer actually had temporary command for 12 hours).

Severe casualties to the company and its commander finally gave him his chance. On February 22, Tilston was given command of C Company with the rank of acting major. On March 1, after a week of frantic reinforcing of the badly mauled company, he led his men into action for the first time.

Even at the outset, he realized that the company wasn't battle-ready, as Tilston recalls even now. "Two-thirds of the 100 men of my company were new. After Goch-Calcar, we were out four or five days until we could get reinforcements and replacement of weapons and equipment. The reinforcement situation was horrible; there just weren't enough trained men available.

"Some of our new men had been remustered from other services that had become redundant. Others, the NRMA [Canada's conscripts, named for the National Resources Mobilization Act], had originally volunteered for service only in Canada and had just been sent over. The NRMA men were well trained; the ones who had been remustered had been given only basic infantry training. But they all lacked battle experience. Of my three officers, two were brand new. I had them for just a week when both were wounded."

On the night of February 28-March 1, the Essex Scottish Regiment moved forward to its forming up place for an attack on the

German Siegfried defences at the edge of the Hochwald Forest. A reconnaissance patrol had reported the enemy established in strength 200 yards ahead. The patrol noted defences of barbed-wire entanglements and an elaborate trench system covered by machine guns and mortar fire.

"About midnight," Tilston relates, "the colonel told us to bog down for the night and we did the best we could, which isn't very good when you're digging where water is one foot below ground surface. We had maybe an hour and a half's sleep when Major Paul Cropp and I were called to Battalion Headquarters. Our orders were to lay on the two-company attack before daybreak: my C Company on the left, and Cropp's D Company on the right.

"My company had excellent cover. At the actual start line there was a substantial farm, with a nice wooded area. There was no harassing fire; I think we were unseen. The original start time was about 5:30 a.m. It would have been dark. Fortunately for us, there were several delays. Finally the time was set for around 7:30 a.m. when there was reasonable light.

"We had an excellent artillery barrage of 72 guns," Tilston continues. "Unfortunately, a couple of guns were off target, and fell on the two forward platoons. Well, naturally the men scattered and there was considerable confusion. The NCOs were mighty good, they got the men back into position. There were a couple of serious casualties but the stretcher-bearers did their excellent work. When the barrage lifted, we broke through the hedge, which was part of our cover, and started off. The tank support which we were to have had did not materialize because the ground was too wet and soft."

Citation for Victoria Cross: Maj F.A. Tilston
Across approximately 500 yards of flat open country, in face of intense enemy fire, Maj Tilston personally led his company in the attack, keeping dangerously close to our own bursting shells in order to get the maximum cover from the barrage. Though wounded in the head he continued to lead his men forward, through a belt of wire ten feet in depth to the enemy trenches shouting orders and encouragement.

"Halfway up to the woods," as Tilston recalls it, "we encountered trip wire supported roughly 10 inches above ground. The

238

mesh of the wire was just sufficient to allow you to put your foot through. It was very fortunate for us that the H-Hour had been delayed, because had this been a pre-dawn attack, I'm afraid it would have been a shambles. We would have got our feet entangled in the wire. However, seeing the wire, the boys simply stepped on it, and that way we covered it.''

Cropp recalls Tilston's eagerness: ''This was Freddie's first attack as a company commander. He came over to me and said, 'Where does a company commander go in the attack?' That was how much he knew about it! I gave him a suggestion that — since we were going up close behind an artillery barrage — he might travel just behind the two forward platoons so that he could control anything that was necessary. It turned out, of course, that he went ahead of everybody. He was just so anxious to get going that he was the first one into the German lines.''

Citation:
When the platoon on the left came under heavy fire from an enemy machine-gun post, [Tilston] dashed forward personally and silenced it with a grenade; he was first to reach the enemy position and took the first prisoner.

Tilston recalls the moment: ''The wire was also covered by a machine-gun post and the platoon — commanded by Charlie Gatton, a good and experienced officer — was being held up with machine-gun fire. It was obvious there was only one thing to do and that was to get rid of the post. I went over and tossed in a couple of 36 grenades. The effect of a 36 grenade exploding in close quarters is most shattering. We had no more trouble.

''The commander of one of our forward platoons was wounded. I remember that I went to him and saw this little German stretcher-bearer whose position we'd overrun looking after him.''

So far, Tilston's determination to achieve his objective had overcome a multitude of problems: an inexperienced fighting force, strong enemy defences, misfiring guns, and a lack of armoured support. Now he faced still more critical hazards.

As he approached the woods, he suddenly felt a sharp sting in his head and noticed that his ear was bleeding.

''Further on, I got hit by a piece of shrapnel, a good-sized piece that made a four-inch gash on my hip. It knocked me to ground.

While I was lying there I felt something wet. I reached around and my reaction was, 'Damn it all, there goes my water bottle' — except that it was filled with rum. The shrapnel had gone right through it.''

Now twice wounded, Tilston reloaded his .303 rifle and forced himself back into the battle. Moving up, he found that his forward platoon was reduced to eight men:

''The one concern I had was losing such a large number of men. When you find your platoon, which comprised over 25 men, now had only eight men left, it's not very encouraging. Far from it. However, there was no point in leaving them isolated so far forward, so I pulled them back. But it did not occur to me to withdraw. We were now stretched out in a long straight line along the enemy trenches at the edge of the forest.

''In the meantime, the Germans came down with counter-attacks, accompanied by intense machine-gun fire and excellent mortar work.''

Citation:
An elaborate system of underground dugouts and trenches was manned in considerable strength and vicious hand-to-hand fighting followed. . . . Two German Company Headquarters were overrun and many casualties were inflicted on the fanatical defenders.

The enemy counter-attacked repeatedly, supported by a hail of mortar and machine-gun fire from the open flank. Maj Tilston moved in the open from platoon to platoon quickly organizing their defence and directing fire against the advancing enemy. The enemy attacks penetrated so close to the positions that grenades were thrown into the trenches held by his troops.

Under the weight of the counter-attacks, casualties mounted alarmingly. ''We had no shortage of weapons,'' Tilston relates, ''but we did have shortages of men and ammunition. Battalion Headquarters inquired if we wanted reinforcements, and I simply said, 'Well, if we have more men we could sure cover a lot more ground.' But we didn't get them.

''When we found we couldn't evacuate the wounded, we got them safely into one of the captured enemy company command posts. The one we were occupying was the closest to the main road. It was quite large — about 10 feet square, and lined with wood.

It had a dugout and was very comfortable with a table and a couple of chairs.''

Then Tilston learned that the carrier bringing up the reserve ammunition had been knocked out.

''We were short of ammunition and now we found that we would get no more. There was only one thing to do, and it's sad to have to say, but we had to strip our dead for their ammunition. It is hard to think that these boys we'd been living with, laughing with, and even kibitzing with — now all the use they were to us was how much ammunition they had. I then decided to go over to D Company to see if they had any.''

Tilston managed to get through the bullet-swept and cratered ground to Cropp's D Company position, a hundred yards or so on the right, returning with a case of ammunition and some 36 grenades. Then fate dealt yet another blow to the obstinate Canadian: it began to rain.

''Our Brens got wet and became jammed. We were in terrible trouble. Boy oh boy, you talk about your heart in your boots, that was the moment! But the next thing I knew, our NCOs had got our wounded men in the dugout busy cleaning guns. There were about 15 of them at that point.

''They had the table to work on and they were using everything they could lay their hands on. Of course that four-by-two-inch piece of flannel we were issued didn't last long. The boys were using their shirts, their underwear — but thank God they kept us supplied with workable guns. When a gun jammed, there was a clean one lying beside us, and the jammed one would be reserviced and put back into use.''

Fresh trouble arose from a second enemy post. ''Charlie Gatton came up with an idea. He said, 'Let me put a PIAT bomb into it.' Charlie did exactly that, and that ended that problem.

''It was now about one o'clock. I counted the men. There were just 27 of us left of the original one hundred. Things had quietened down considerably, and Major Alf Hodges, commanding B Company, came through and went forward.''

Hodges still remembers the encounter: ''I had lost about half my company before I got up to Fred's position, because the Germans still held their right flank. When we got to the woods I saw Fred Tilston. I had lost my three signallers on the way in — they'd all been hit. Fred had one signaller left, so I borrowed his set.

''Fred quipped at me as I came through, a classic line that is still repeated today: 'Keep going, Alf. All they've got is rifles and machine guns!' Just after I left him, one of those mortars or rockets landed right at Fred's feet. My company sergeant-major was the one who picked Fred up.''

''It was shortly after Alf went on that I decided to go over again to D Company, to bring back some more ammunition,'' Tilston remembers. ''Between our position and that of D Company there was a huge bomb crater. As I went through it, a shell or a mortar bomb exploded within six feet of me.

''I knew I was through right then and there. I just made myself as comfortable as I could. I undid my webbing, gave myself a shot of morphine, and I think I became unconscious intermittently, because not too long afterwards when the stretcher-bearers were around I heard them yelling 'Hey! There's another one over here,' and I was it.''

Citation:
[Tilston] made at least six of these hazardous trips, each time crossing a road which was dominated by intense fire from numerous, well-sited enemy machine-gun posts.

On his last trip he was wounded for the third time, this time in the leg. He was found in a shell crater beside the road. Although very seriously wounded and barely conscious, he would not submit to medical attention until he had given complete instructions as to the defence plan, had emphasized the absolute necessity of holding the position, and had ordered his one remaining officer to take over.

Tilston's friend Major Ken McIntyre, OC of A Company, had been watching the events of the morning through his binoculars: ''It was a fairly misty morning, but still daylight enough that I could see the attack. I actually saw him carry out these jobs that won him the Victoria Cross.

''He had one leg blown off and the other badly mangled. I was about to go out to him when I saw a stretcher-bearer there. They got him back to the regimental aid post and one of the stretcher-bearers, a little over-anxious, put a blanket over his head. The padre — we had a wonderful padre at that time — thought he saw some movement under this blanket. Thank God he did. Fred was living — just barely living. They got him back by aircraft to England and tried to save the other leg. Eventually, because of multiple shrapnel wounds, the surgeons just had to make a decision to take it off.

"It was a bloody battle," McIntyre recalls. "Afterwards, my company moved into the Hochwald. Fred and his incredibly fine men had softened the thing up to such an extent that we didn't have too much trouble after that."

Citation:
By his calm courage, gallant conduct and total disregard for his own safety, he fired his men with grim determination and their firm stand enabled the Regiment to accomplish its object.

Freddie Tilston, obstinate to the end, had refused to let anyone push him around. He had made it to the front, and — for one decisive day — he stopped the German army.

Breakout!

MUD — COUPLED WITH an unrealistic strategy that dissipated the potential strength of the armour-infantry partnership — had stalled the British and Canadian advance in Operation Blockbuster.

Fifty miles south, however, where the topography was suitable and mud was not a factor, a brand of electric warfare was being waged right across the Ninth U.S. Army front. Here, tanks and infantry were massed into a dynamic force powerful enough to strike through the enemy defences.

On the evening of February 26, the fourth day of Operation Grenade, General Bolling, GOC 84th Infantry Division, called a staff meeting at his forward HQ. The exhausted officers — bleary-eyed from operating on two or three hours' sleep a day for the past four days — straggled in. "The staff could hardly stay awake," noted Lieutenant Clifton MacLachlan, assistant operations staff officer (S-3) of the 334th Infantry Regiment.

General Simpson's "relentless pursuit" mandate was putting the pressure on his field commanders. They had been directed to create opportunities that came their way, not merely to exploit them. Bolling's proposed operation did all of that. It was, in plain words, a sizzler.

The plan was designed to exploit the enemy's obvious disorganization — the by-product of Ninth Army's wide pivot to the north, which was so effectively achieving its purpose of catching the Germans by surprise. Simpson's massive wheel had propelled the powerful American force on a diagonal cut north and east across the Cologne Plain. The distance was doubled, but the risk was

---

See Map 5 (Appendix B).

244

worth taking. In the flat open country and on the extensive road systems, the tanks could chew up the miles.

Montgomery's great armoured breakout, at this moment literally floundering in the mud on the Hochwald front, would finally come to life in Operation Grenade. When Ninth Army linked up with First Canadian Army, the jaws of Montgomery's trap would snap shut.

The outcome of Bolling's meeting, formally set down in Letter of Instruction No. 15, dated at 1800 hours, 26 Feb, was the formation of Task Force Church, a motorized, armoured column that could move "like greased lightning" through German lines. Its commander was the volatile assistant division commander, Brigadier-General John Church: "One hell of a fine little soldier . . . absolutely fearless," remembers his chief of staff, Lieutenant-General Lewis W. Truman.

The task force was a unique combination of all arms. It was an army in miniature — a marriage of infantry, armour, artillery, engineers, reconnaissance, anti-aircraft and tank destroyer units, and a medical outfit, all closely liaised with the tactical air force in a ground support role. The result: a formation "strong enough to slash through any possible opposition, fast enough to cover the maximum ground in the shortest time, self-sufficient enough to hold out alone if the rest of the division was held up, flexible enough to attack, defend, ride, walk, smash through or slip through."

The 334th Regiment was assigned the infantry task. This was the regiment that had led the division's assault across the Roer and smashed through the defensive crust as far as Baal. It would now be committed to "go like hell," in the words of its commander, until the scheduled disbandment of Task Force Church at 1800 hours, February 28, two days hence.

These riflemen, tankers, engineers, and gunners knew the terrible risks of penetrating deep into German lines. They would be completely vulnerable to attack on unprotected flanks and wide open to being cut off and slaughtered.

The first reaction of many of the still-groggy officers to this new scheme was one of doubt. "Without G-2 [Intelligence] knowledge, Task Force Church looked foolhardy," MacLachlan remembered. "We had no knowledge of any other breakthroughs."

Yet the breakout concept was so dynamic that fatigue and fear were quickly shrugged off. These were men who had endured the horrors of the battle of attrition in the Huertgen Forest in November, where sheer exhaustion had reached a new dimension. Then, whole companies and battalions had been wiped out. In the seemingly endless weeks of futile, exhausting slogging, death was almost better than the misery of life in those God-forsaken woods.

For too many months, maximum effort had produced minimum results. Now it would be reversed. Objectives that only too recently had been measured in yards were now viewed in miles.

"In November we beat our way to the Roer, sometimes, it seemed, almost with our bare fists," Lieutenant-Colonel Glover Johns observed. "This time we have the stuff we need — tanks, tank destroyers, artillery — and we have them in the quantity we need."

At 0650 hours on February 27 (D-plus-Four of Grenade), Task Force Church advanced over the start line. Infantrymen of the lead company clung precariously to hulls and turrets as the three tank companies of the 771st Tank Battalion pushed to the head of the column. It snaked out eerily for miles, its tail vanishing into the grey and misty half-light of early morning.

A *Time* magazine reporter described the awesome spectacle of an armoured column in action:

From the air in a Piper Cub the tank drive was a thing of the sheerest military beauty: First came a long row of throbbing tanks moving like heavy dark beetles over the green cabbage fields of Germany in a wide swath — many, many tanks in a single row abreast. Then, a suitable distance behind, came another great echelon of tanks, even broader, out of which groups would wheel from their brown mud tracks in the green fields to encircle and smash fire at some stubborn strongpoint. Behind this came miles of trucks, full of troops, manoeuvring perfectly to mop up bypassed tough spots. From the flanks sped clouds of tank destroyers, cutting across the landscape in wild swoops that hit the enemy and cut off communications with bewildering speed.

In the first 90 minutes the task force bounded ahead five miles — an achievement dazzling to the men after their snail's pace in the first four days of Grenade. They passed through village after village along the broad plain, penetrating far behind enemy lines.

"It was just a wild ride from one town to another," Lieutenant-Colonel Jack Childers, commander of 771st Tank Battalion, remembered. "This was our first opportunity to act as armour should act: in massed attack. It was a fine infantry-tank action."

Tankers fired away at everything that moved. "Any target that looked suspicious — haystacks, machine-gun positions, and possible obstacle points — was fired on," said Lieutenant-Colonel David Smith, CO 771st Tank Destroyer Battalion.

Surprised German troops, some still sleeping or eating their morning meal, were summarily disarmed and sent unguarded and on foot to rearline POW cages. "We were not interested in prisoners," the 771st noted. "No time for them."

The task force's mandate was to charge ahead, bypassing opposition whenever possible, stopping for no one — not even their own casualties. Pockets of enemy were left to the 333rd and 335th Infantry Regiments advancing in their wake. Consequently, the rear areas remained somewhat "warm" for the next six to eight hours.

"Everyone was on wheels," remembers First Lieutenant Robert Truitt of 333rd Infantry Regiment. "When we ran into enemy pockets we would drop a battalion off to mop up. Like the armour, we tried to get around the pockets rather than take them head on."

"Our flanks were way out in the breeze but we disregarded them completely," the 84th Division after-action report noted. "Our leading tanks were very aggressive. In one place the Germans put two wagons hitched to two horses across the road. The leading tanks simply smashed into them."

Roadblocks formed the first major obstacles. Wagons, carts, and large tree trunks were piled up at intersections. Vehicles stopped by the blocks were fired on by German bazookas rigged by electrical remote control. Engineers and bulldozer tanks advancing alongside the infantry soon cleared them.

The realization swept over them all: "It was working. We were breaking through. It seemed too good to be true." But they roared on, sometimes at more than 35 miles an hour, with the column whipping along behind, throwing out fire here and there. So fast did they advance that on occasion the Germans did not even have time to man their guns.

"We captured brand new 88s," Lieutenant Beckwith, the 84th Division operations staff officer, reported. "I saw one which had not fired a single round and was in a brand-new emplacement in cement. I think we captured eight to ten of them."

Later in the afternoon, organized resistance at the village of Steeg forced the column to hesitate while the infantrymen quelled the strongpoint. Major-General Church decided to drive up in his jeep and see for himself what the holdup could be.

A German in a ditch 10 feet away suddenly started shooting at Church and his staff officers. As they sped past, eight more guns opened fire. "General Church reached for his pistol and the fire was thick and fast," Lieutenant Beckwith, who accompanied him, reported. "All this time we were speeding along. We cut loose on them."

As they progressed, another pocket of 15 or 20 more Germans started firing. Church decided to turn back in case an even heavier ambush awaited them. On the return sprint, fire came alive from both sides of the road. General Church's car was hit. The commander and his driver, Private Technical Class 5 Kyser Crockett, were both wounded.

"I've lost my arm!" Crockett yelled to the general, slumping back in the seat of the lurching vehicle.

"Keep your foot on the foot feed!" Church ordered.

"Lieutenant Norman Dobie, the general's aide, leaned over from the back and steered," Beckwith continued. "The general was shooting all the time and got three Krauts himself. Their bullets hit the jeep and fragments hit the general below the eyebrow, five or six around the knees, but the worst one was in the ankle."

Crockett suffered a complex fracture of the forearm. Church, bandaged up, returned to his HQ. "Twenty minutes later he was cussing us out for not moving," his ops officer said with a grin.

By the end of Task Force Church's first day of action, it had advanced a searing nine miles, overrun 54 villages and towns, and captured or destroyed a substantial amount of German equipment. An estimated 50 enemy were wounded and, in a reversal of the usual casualty proportions, 100 were killed. The 334th had taken almost as many prisoners on this single day — 1,249 — as they had in five weeks' continuous fighting on the Siegfried Line or four weeks in the Ardennes.

The Army newspaper, *Stars and Stripes*, wrote glowingly that the 84th Division's infantry regiment had "even outrun the tanks."

"Actually," the divisional history retorted caustically, "the 84th's tanks outran all other tanks."

Top Secret. Personal and Eyes Only for CIGS from Field-Marshal Montgomery, 28 Feb 45:
GRENADE. Good progress has been made today in this sector. The 19 corps area, 2nd Armored Division is in the Glehn area and has been directed northward towards Krefeld. They have been followed by 83 Div which has

been directed on Neuss while 29 Div will deal with
Muenchen-Gladbach and 30 Div will protect the right flank
on the line of the Erft River. In 13 Corps area, 102 Div is
masking the western exit of Muenchen-Gladbach and 84
Div is in the Waldniel-Merveck area and 5th Armoured Div
is moving on Viersen and will then be directed on Krefeld. I
visited the forward areas in 9th Army today. The army has
gained a great victory with very few casualties and this
has raised morale to a high level.

On D-plus-Five, February 28, Task Force Church crossed the inter-army boundary from General Gustav von Zangen's crumbling Fifteenth Army sector into General Alfred Schlemm's First Parachute Army defence zone.

German resistance immediately stiffened with the infusion of tough, battle-hardened paratroop and Panzer divisions hastily diverted from the British-Canadian front farther north. These were to prove much better soldiers than those of von Zangen's army, with little inclination to surrender as the earlier defenders had done.

It was in the little village of Berg that the 125 men of Company G in the 2nd Battalion of the 334th took on a battle that would be remembered as one of the bloodiest of the entire campaign.

The force that opposed them were elements of the 8th Parachute Division, described by combat troops as "fanatical paratroopers who fought like savage maniacs, and died while still fighting." Of 50 enemy, only two were taken prisoner.

The Jerries had perfect reverse slope defences [men of the company related shortly after the action]. Company G worked up so close that the Germans couldn't use mortar fire for fear of killing their own men, yet their machine-gun fire kept us down. The only way we could get Jerries was by standing up and taking quick shots at helmets on the other side of the slope, about 25 yards away. There was a force of about 50 Germans supported by machine guns, and the whole force had to be wiped out to the last man. We had to dig out Jerries with grenades, bayonets, and hand-to-hand combat, and only two prisoners were taken.

The company then jumped off to attack Eicker. Staff Sergeant Artis Britton, squad leader, worked his way up to within a few yards of a machine-gun position, rushed it alone, and threw in a grenade.

Company G received a Presidential Unit Citation for the action. They lost 40 men: every platoon leader and platoon sergeant and most of the squad leaders. But they never gave ground.

The action typified the dogged defence put up by these elite German troops. All the battalions of 84th Division had a strong dose of it. In contrast with the euphoric charge of the previous day, their pursuit had slowed to a deadly crawl gaining a bare two miles in 12 hours.

Running into the same tough opposition, Company K, in the 3rd Battalion of 333rd Infantry, on foot in a mopping-up role, lost one man in every four who went into battle in less than six hours — the equivalent of a full platoon.

The company had marched 25 miles since the Roer crossing and the men were sore and exhausted before the battle even began. The German paratroopers waited silently until the men advanced across an open field before they opened up the ambush with lethal machine-gun fire. "The fields were crisscrossed with bursts of mud kicked up by interlocking bands of fire," described Captain H.P. Leinbaugh.

The promised American tanks that could deal with the machine-gun posts were bogged and hadn't shown up — but the enemy tanks had, with 88s blazing.

The company fought fiercely, but the Germans were well entrenched and many of the Americans were caught in the open. "We were all pinned down," remembers Technical Sergeant George Pope. "It was flat as the floor. There wasn't a blade of grass you could hide under. I'm yelling, 'Shoot, you sons-of-bitches!' That was a tough time." Later, the men found periscopes the Germans were using from their emplacements and burp guns with bent barrels for firing around corners.

As darkness closed on the last day of February, the disbandment of Task Force Church was imminent. And John Church was thinking hard. "The Krauts wouldn't expect us to attack them at night; they know the American Army never attacks during the night. So that is a good reason for doing so," he said to Childers.

The 771st Tank Battalion's commander agreed. Although it was an unorthodox move, there would be a great advantage to launching an armoured attack at night. "We can't see the enemy, but neither can he see us."

The dissolution order was changed verbally and Task Force Church was extended. One hour before midnight, the three battalions of the 334th and their armour jumped off for Boisheim, a key road junction that was blocking the American advance. The town was asleep. A child at a farmhouse directed them to the anti-tank guns that defended it. Even these were not manned.

"The attack was a complete surprise," Beckwith reported. "Everyone was on foot except the tanks. We cleared the towns as we went through. We literally had to wake up the Krauts from sleep and kick them out of bed to take them prisoners. Some POWs had their girls with them. The girls refused to leave."

Once alerted, the rest of the German garrison at Boisheim had to be prised out from behind barricades in houses and shops. When he found one door firmly locked, Lieutenant Kenneth MacInnis smashed through a side window with his carbine. A German raised his pistol to fire. MacInnis shot him and then leapt over the windowsill to capture the rest.

"On the way in [to Boisheim]," the redoubtable MacInnis noted, "some of the boys found a baker who was just taking his first batch of bread from the oven. They all picked up a loaf of fresh bread, and dug up some jam. . . . Some of them flushed houses with rifle in one hand and bread and jam in the other. One private found a keg of beer which was enjoyed by the platoon before they settled down for a short rest."

Top Secret. Personal and Eyes Only for CIGS from Field-Marshal Montgomery, 1 Mar 45:
GRENADE. The most sensational results have been achieved today. Our troops are now fighting in the outskirts of Neuss and our line runs from there northwest . . . to Venlo. The enemy seems to have lost all grip on the battle in this area and his command organization seems to have broken down. We have captured static back area units who are quite unaware of the situation and at one place we captured a complete armoured column of tanks moving westward from Neuss toward Muenchen-Gladbach which was very astonished at being captured. . . . All HQ are moving forward and the distances for liaison are becoming great and I shall be on the move myself very shortly and back to the caravan life in the fields.

By 0600 hours on March 1, the Ninth Army had passed the halfway point from Roer to Rhine. In its 20-mile advance thus far, combat command units from six infantry and three armoured divisions were bursting out across the hard, dry roads of the Cologne Plain towards the Rhine. No fewer than 1,394 tanks were used in the breakout. Mile upon mile of tanks rumbled through the night. The 84th Division had captured 2,876 prisoners. Altogether, 13 Corps (84th Division, 102nd Division, and 5th Armored Division) had bagged 6,444 POWs, and Ninth Army claimed over 11,000.

Now 13 Corps wheeled sharply to the east again, its target set 20 miles away on Uerdingen — and beyond it, the enemy's last line of defence, the Rhine.

South of 13 Corps, Major-General Raymond McLain's 19 Corps (29th and 30th Infantry Divisions and 2nd Armored Division, reinforced by 83rd Infantry Division) formed combat command units of infantry and armour that smashed through on a line northeast of Juelich, heading for the Rhine towns of Neuss and Oberkassel.

In a strenuous, week-long pursuit, 29th Division swept a path 4 miles wide by 25 miles long containing some 40 towns, the final and largest being the textile centre of Muenchen-Gladbach, with a population of over 300,000.

It wasn't all swashbuckling. Many GIs crossed from Roer to Rhine the hard way, on foot. The only way to advance in the open country of the Rhineland Plain was "a steady slow walk," as Major Theodore Franke, 3rd Battalion, 406th Regiment, remembers. "The method of moving by bounds, as taught in the service schools, is exhausting to the men and affords no protection in flat open country. Two of the battalion's company commanders were lost during the advance."

"They could see you coming for miles," agrees Corporal Dan Callahan, an engineer with 104th Division. "It was difficult work."

One of the toughest battles involved the 116th Infantry Regiment at the little village of Stetternich along the Juelich-Cologne highway. It was a minor action, affecting just a single battalion. It never warranted much space in the after-action reports — except a reference to its being "a piece of cake."

To First Lieutenant Norvan Nathan, it was a bitter concoction: "We were told that we would use marching fire — that is, we would fire our weapons from the hip at the target as we charged. It was something we had never heard of. They explained how it worked, how it kept the enemy's head down. But it did seem sort of strange to us, didn't make much sense because our big problem on the other side of the Roer was that the country was like a tabletop.

"There were around 137 men in my company, good men — all pretty experienced. Almost every one had been wounded at least once before, had come back; I had been wounded twice," Nathan recounted.

"When we debouched from the woods we had to cross a large open field that seemed to go on for miles. There were a lot of German trenches running through it. Then we started getting enemy rifle and machine-gun fire.

"We suffered badly. We were just falling left and right. We were told, don't stop to pick up anybody. I got hit, got a bullet through the neck. It came out my spinal column. I jumped into a shell crater and crawled along the trench back to the woods. The rest of the company, what was left of it, continued along with the company commander. They got stuck under fire and had to lie out on this flat tabletop field for the better part of the day until the tanks came along. It was a very bad casualty day for us — 31 or 32, just from my company. That is the action that has always been depicted as being a piece of cake."

Overwhelming as the armoured strength was, a handful of infantrymen could still be potent agressors. At Titz, four GIs and their sergeant stopped a counter-attack of six German tanks. The men adopted the German tactic of holding their fire until the last moment.

"The tanks were close enough to spit on when the men let loose with their bazookas, rifle grenades and small arms," the 29th Division's newspaper (*29 — Let's Go*) recounted. "They knocked out the lead tank, crippled two others and forced the three rear ones to retire."

As the men advanced across the Rhineland Plain, the months of bitter cold gave way to the first stirrings of warmth and the promise of spring. And the ravages of war gave way to the first stirrings of a civilization unscarred — whole towns intact and inhabited, houses still standing, beer in pubs, fresh warm bread in bakers' shops, tramcars still running, lights gleaming through lace-curtained windows.

The sight of stray dogs and cats in the streets again made the men realize with a pang that not even pets had survived the devastation of the villages in the battle zone.

After advancing through enemy opposition in a succession of towns, Staff Sergeant Harry Jenkins was surprised on the second day to encounter one village that was utterly quiet. "It was 1300 hours and the civilians were cooking dinner."

The owner of an imposing château in Putz offered to barbecue a pig for the advancing troops of the 117th Infantry Regiment (all the while making derogatory remarks about Hitler). In Krefeld, where one-third of the normal population of 100,000 was still living, the phones were fully operative. Military police encountered a local citizen nonchalantly telephoning a German field officer who was behind enemy lines to reveal the disposition of American troops in town.

A sergeant and a corporal from 111th Field Artillery Battalion tossed a grenade into the cellar of a house in a newly captured town and went cautiously down the steps to check it out for enemy troops or booby traps. They found, instead, a five-week-old baby. "They found no deficiencies," their history records, "other than a leaky radiator, so they bundled up the kid and started down the street with him until they located the frantic mother, a Polish woman."

"The civilians were scared to death," Lieutenant Beckwith reported. "They saw the soldiers put their hands over their heads so they did too. There was a continuous stream of them."

"*Nicht schiessen, nicht schiessen!*" (Don't shoot!) was the common cry of many who, bordering on hysteria, believed that the firing squad was their destiny.

"Some were stony-faced, some had tears in their eyes," observed Lieutenant MacLachlan. "I fell asleep in a ditch . . . I was awakened by a German woman carrying a baby, stumbling over me to get out of machine-gun fire." MacLachlan was amazed to see "people expelled from their houses, leaving things cooking on stoves, old men pulled in wheelbarrows, wounded Germans lying by the side of the road."

Men of the 102nd Division reported civilians lining the streets waving white flags and singing. The women kept crying "*Gott sei danke!*" (Thank God!) They discovered that many of these people were displaced persons — foreign workers from Poland, Russia, and France brought in as slave labourers — who regarded the Americans as their liberators.

In Lintfort, 660 slave labourers were found in an underground factory. The screening of these civilians — some of them choking the roads to escape being swept up into the conflict — was almost impossible. To add to the confusion, enemy troops who traded uniforms for civilian clothes to escape capture mingled with the normal populace and the displaced persons.

Food shortages created immediate problems for the Military Government units charged with the responsibility of coordinating the civilian population. In all, 35,000 displaced persons were found in the Ninth Army sweep. Thousands were evacuated. In major centres, the civilians were resettled in large buildings and food teams were set up. Health units became alert to outbreaks of typhus, diphtheria, and scarlet fever.

The sick and wounded were treated through army medical channels and the dead were buried by burial parties. In Erkelenz, one officer was even pressed into delivering a baby.

By March 15, more than 40 Military Government detachments were operating in the sector, addressing enormous problems of sanitation, transportation, housing, and resettlement. Loudspeaker trucks cruised the streets, alerting the populace to each regulation. At first, civilians were curfewed and allowed out of their homes for just one hour a day to shop or attend their businesses. This time limit was gradually relaxed.

It was a dynamic week, and the news media were out in full number to record its momentous events. The 29th Infantry Division alone had 34 accredited newsmen accompanying it.

After four days and nights of savage fighting to clear the southern flank of Simpson's assault, General Joe Collins's 7 Corps reverted back to First Army command on February 27. In its role of anchoring the Ninth Army's exposed right flank it had not been required to pivot north, but the corps had had to drive 13 miles east of Dueren, beyond Elsdorf, to secure the flank. In doing this they endured some of the toughest resistance. The ruins of Dueren itself held up the two infantry divisions, the 104th and the 8th, for most of two days. The German 10th Panzer Grenadier Division put up a strong fight at Hambach Forest on the uncompleted Aachen-Cologne autobahn. On February 26, Collins could finally unleash his armour. After stiff fighting, the six combat task forces of the 3rd Armored Division secured Elsdorf and went on to establish bridgeheads over the Erft River.

This left the remaining and most northern corps — General John B. Anderson's 16 Corps — to forge some 40 miles northwest and link up with First Canadian Army and Second British Army at Venlo. The united force would then thrust shoulder-to-shoulder eastward to the Rhine and close the jaws of Montgomery's pincer movement.

On March 1, Colonel B.A. Byrne, commanding Task Force Byrne (320th Infantry Regiment of 35th Infantry Division, reinforced as a combat command with armour from the 784th Tank Battalion and other supporting arms), spearheaded a ''shootin'-tootin' 23-mile northward slash, rolling up the Siegfried Line defences from the rear.''

As dusk fell on the first day of the blitz the task force liberated the joyous Dutch population in Venlo, a major centre on the Maas just inside the border of Holland. The next day it shot forward another 15 miles until it ran into stiff resistance at Sevelen.

The force entered the town in a midnight attack and became trapped when the Germans detonated a bridge, isolating their forward units. The *New York Times* headlined the Associated Press dispatch "Negro Tank Outfit Repeats Bastogne." The inexperienced troops of the 784th Tank Battalion killed 53 and captured 207, "mauling German parachute units in savage street fighting while cut off for eighteen hours."

This was a special vindication for the black troops of the 784th. The battalion had been activated in 1943 despite strong objections from the Armored Force, who felt the best employment of black troops was "as chauffeurs, janitors, firemen, cooks, basics and bandsmen."

As the Ninth Army approached the Rhine, sporadic opposition gave way to a resistance as fierce as any seen in the campaign. The men were exhausted.

Keeping the rapidly advancing units supplied with essential goods was a major challenge. The half-tracks bogged down in the mud. The 5th Armored Division noted that their Combat Command was running low on ammunition, but with the congested roads it took the trucks three hours to bring more up — a trip that normally should have taken just a few minutes.

A fleet of 14 fuel trucks and 13 ammo trucks supplying 36th Tank Battalion rolled into Lintfort just after dark one evening and discovered that the town had not yet been cleared of snipers. A single incendiary grenade is the stuff of nightmares for men driving service vehicles. Their drivers took terrible risks to bring fuel and ammunition to the men at the front and replenish them, usually in darkness during brief halts. "It takes guts to jockey a truckload of gas or ammo past a corner you know the Krauts have zeroed in."

Captain Clinton Basler recalls one such incident: "What a spot! No cover, the trucks lined up like ducks, a full moon lighting things up like day, and us with about 70 tons of ammo and 10,000 gallons of gasoline. Then the stuff started coming in. Screaming Meemies and light artillery. I remember hoping to God it wasn't observed fire [deliberately aimed], and evidently it wasn't, because they never hit a thing.

"Most of us hadn't had any rest in about 60 hours and we were too tired to be scared. My belly was hard and cold, though, and I wasn't as hungry as I should have been."

The maintenance platoons were frantically busy all through the drive to the Rhine. They worked on the run, making repairs, recovering vehicles, and keeping the supply of parts coming up.

Motor transportation was at a premium with the pressure of keeping supply lines apace with the rapid progress of the attack. Support troops from all arms made huge — and sometimes unorthodox — contributions. 110th Field Artillery Battalion noted that black troops engaged in hauling extra ammunition had fallen into the habit of lugging the ammunition boxes right up to the guns, then of opening them. Soon they were preparing the ammunition for firing and finally they were taking positions in the gun crews — welcome help for regular crews who were working a 20-hour day firing and continually moving forward.

Medics were constantly on the go, roaring up and down the combat columns, often as much under fire as the men they were treating. So fluid was the battle that aid stations had to be hastily set up in fields or streets adjacent to the ongoing battle. Yesterday's frontline became today's rear.

In one town, house-to-house fighting disclosed a cellar full of German propaganda material: leaflets warning the Americans that the Roer Valley defences were "impregnable." In less than two weeks the Ninth Army had driven approximately 53 miles across that "impregnable" valley.

The combined U.S., British, and Canadian forces were closing down the length of the Rhine — but they were a long haul from getting over that formidable barrier. The race for the bridges was on.

19

The Nine Bridges of
General Schlemm

IN THE EARLY DAYS of March 1945, the Allied effort to capture an intact bridge to the Ruhr front became intense. One man stopped them: General der Fallschirmtruppen Alfred Schlemmn, commander of First Parachute Army.

There were nine Rhine bridges in his sector, nine of the largest in Germany. Schlemm had been made personally responsible for them. If they could not be kept for use by German troops, they would have to be demolished. If a single bridge were captured, Schlemm would forfeit his life. Hitler had decreed it.

"Special courts [are] ready to judge immediately the responsible person in case he lets a bridge fall undamaged into enemy hands," Schlemm reported bitterly to his staff officers. "Every dereliction of duty is to be punished by death."

However, execution was also the fate of any commander who detonated the bridges too soon. Each bridge must be maintained until the last possible moment to ensure an uninterrupted flow of reinforcements and supplies to the combat troops.

So, Schlemm mused caustically, he was damned — and dead — if he did . . . or didn't. With nine chances to fail he assumed his life expectancy was not very great.

The Para leader designated an officer to be responsible for each bridge, with sufficient troops and engineers under command to ensure successful demolition. Their orders: fight to the last man.

"You will be in direct radio communication with me," he directed

_____

See Maps 3 and 9 (Appendix B).

them. ''I reserve for myself the authority to order the demolition of each bridge.''

On a moonless night on March 2-3, a handful of men moved cautiously across the shadowed struts of a bridge. Below, the murky waters of the Rhine mirrored the pyrotechnics of the artillery war overhead.

The three-span Adolf Hitler Bridge at Uerdingen was as formidable as the reputation of its namesake. It stretched 1,640 feet and was wide enough (65 feet) to carry an armoured column on attack. It was a prize that the Americans badly wanted. The Germans were equally determined to detonate it before it was captured.

For over 15 hours the 92nd U.S. Armored Field Artillery Battalion had kept up continuous fire over the bridge to keep the enemy from destroying it. The Germans returned it with equal ferocity. The 2nd Armored Division, with two battalions of infantry, had attacked the structure earlier in the day but had been beaten back. A 13-foot crater at its western end now formed a formidable tank barrier. Only the infantry could get through, but they were pinned down by the heavy fire.

Captain George Youngblood of 17th Armored Engineer Battalion was told to lead a small band of volunteers over the bridge to check it for explosives. It was a hazardous mission:

We approached the bridge from the south, passed under the ramp and walked up about 30 steps on the north side of the bridge. I dropped three men off at the west end . . . to discourage any Krauts away from our rear. The remaining six men were split equally on both sides of the bridge with one man out in front.

We checked each column, all joints, suspension members and other critical points in the superstructure of the bridge. We cut every wire that we could lay our hands on. We didn't find any dynamite charges but we did find a small wood box which contained a detonator. The latter was not connected up.

The patrol returned after two and a half hours of perilous work, satisfied that the wires had been cut. Their efforts were nullified when German engineers tested the wiring shortly afterwards. Assuming that artillery fire had pierced the lines, they worked feverishly to repair them. At 0730 hours, the Americans heard a series of mighty explosions and the great bridge thundered into the river.

An even stealthier attempt to snatch a bridge from German grasp was attempted the same day by a task force of the 83rd Infantry Division, comprising elements of 736th Tank Battalion, 643rd Tank Destroyer Battalion, and 330th Infantry Regiment. Disguising their tanks to look like German Panthers, with infantrymen following behind on foot, they boldly advanced through enemy lines for 15 miles until they reached the outskirts of the river town of Oberkassel.

German-speaking American troops riding the lead vehicles successfully averted suspicion until an enemy soldier passing the column on a bicycle gave the alarm. The tanks charged the bridge but they were too late. As the lead tanks got astride its western end, the Germans blew it up.

In such a succession of dramatic last-ditch actions, Schlemm had already ordered the detonation of seven bridges to prevent such American coup-de-main seizures.

"At the Adolf Hitler Bridge in Uerdingen the demolition wires were shot out by artillery fire," he summarized for his staff. "At Rheinhausen, damage was insufficient; further demolition had to be carried out under enemy machine-gun fire. At Homberg an Oberst [colonel] of Fifteenth Army forbade the bridge commander to carry out the order for demolition issued by me, since he wanted to bring over more vehicles from the west bank."

By March 3, First Parachute Army was almost completely encircled by its enemy, its 50,000 troops in danger of being trapped. First Canadian Army now had two corps thrusting towards Wesel on the Rhine.

With two armoured divisions (4th Canadian and 11th British) and three infantry (43rd Wessex, 2nd Canadian, and 3rd Canadian), 2 Canadian Corps was maintaining steady pressure on the left. The Wessex had advanced southeast along the Rhine's flooded banks almost as far as Marienbaum, four miles short of Xanten. The Canadians had finally broken out of the Hochwald Forest and the Balberger Wald. After very stiff fighting, the 11th Armoured Division (on the Canadians' right) was within a mile of Sonsbeck.

On the right of 2 Corps, Horrocks's 30 Corps forces had fanned south and east from their line between Goch and the Maas. The 1st Commando Brigade, the 52nd Lowland Division (relieving the 51st Highland), the 3rd British Infantry Division (relieving the 15th Scottish), and the 53rd Welsh Division had been given the task of clearing the enemy strongholds in the towns such as Weeze, Kervenheim, Kevelaer, and Winnekendonk. They finally joined hands with Simpson's Ninth Army on Veritable and Grenade's mutual boundary line.

Goch had not, as expected, marked the final musket shot for the Jocks. The Highlanders were required to open the country southwest of Goch as far as the Kendel River — directly in the teeth of General Eugen Meindl's newly formed line of strongly armed and supported troops of 2 Parachute Corps. Hamlets bearing the names of Boeckelt, Blumenthalshop, Siebengewald, and Boyenhof became hard-won conquests in the coming days.

Meindl had strongholds on a ridge and wooded area running down to the Niers River just east of Goch. It had been the task of 15th Scottish Division's 6th King's Own Scottish Borderers to drive them from this vantage point. At a historic and crumbling castle in the woods, Schloss Kalbeck, the 15th Scottish Division and its supporting armour, 5th Coldstream Guards, had battled for another five days. Both divisions were withdrawn on February 25 and 26 to train for the Rhine crossing.

Despite the terrible ground, 30 Corps fought on. The 1st Commando Brigade, assigned the task of clearing the Maas valley, had swept south as far as the river town of Wells. Second British Army immediately began construction of a bridge there.

The 53rd Welsh Division, after mopping up the last pockets of enemy resistance in Goch, had been assigned the task of capturing Weeze, some four miles south of Goch. On March 1, St. David's Day, the division went into battle with the leek — the national emblem of Wales — proudly tucked in the camouflage netting of their helmets. "Operation Leek" embroiled them in a week-long campaign as bad as any that the division had encountered to date.

In one action of 2nd Battalion Monmouthshires against 7th Parachute Division, only 40 men of a company of 120 reached the objective (Starfish Wood). Eight counter-attacks were beaten off. A squadron of the 13th/18th Hussars lost 14 of its 18 tanks to mines and anti-tank fire on a single day. The battalion had 118 casualties in three days of fighting. The *Daily Herald* reported, "They were still at it on this day of the Welsh. . . . Some of them found leeks and wore them and went into action and died."

Fighting their way north, American troops had formed a 30-mile front, with solid possession of the Rhine's west bank from Duesseldorf to Krefeld. On the outskirts of Geldern, a shattered inland market town of 7,000 souls midway between the Maas and the Rhine, a historic meeting was taking place that would seal the hinge

of the Allied pincer attack. The Americans and Welsh collided —
with a bang.

At 1435 hours on March 3, Lieutenant-Colonel Dan E. Craig
moved forward to a creek on the outskirts of Geldern with his unit
and supporting armour (1st Battalion 134th U.S. Infantry Regiment,
with tanks of 784th Tank Battalion). "The small-arms fire . . . was
joined by automatic and mortar fire and Screaming Meamies from
across the creek, and the unit was pinned down," Captain Donald
G. Rubottom, operations staff officer (S-3) of the battalion,
described.

At 1530 hours an unidentified column came in view. The American tanks took aim. A forward observation officer with the 134th
shouted: "Wait! They might be Allied troops!"

The 1st East Lancashire Regiment of 53rd Welsh Division with
4/7th Dragoon Guards in support — and one slightly nervous war
correspondent from Associated Press in tow — were scrambling
to find a scrap of cloth that was still white after three weeks of mud-
slogging.

"When we reached the canal we saw the Americans,"
Lieutenant-Colonel Frank Brook relates. "They did not know we
were British and opened fire. It was only when one of our officers
went out under a white flag that the mistake was rectified and we
joined forces."

With German bullets still crackling overhead, the British met
Major John E. Davis (Craig having been wounded moments before).
The long-awaited juncture between the First Canadian Army and
the Ninth U.S. Army was achieved.

Just before dawn on March 4, the Welsh attacked through the
American positions and secured Geldern without resistance. The
Geldern-Wesel road was thus cut. That same day, Meindl, commander of 2 Parachute Corps, informed his army chief that the town
was lost.

"At 0100 hours I heard through my open window the sounds
of enemy machine guns from a southerly direction," Meindl told
Schlemm. "I established contact with 190th Infantry Division in
Geldern. At daybreak we retired our command post. All secret
documents were burned."

On March 5 a special courier from the Commander-in-Chief West
of the German army, Generalfeldmarschall Gerd von Rundstedt,

relayed a message to First Parachute Army Tac HQ. Schlemm scanned the contents incredulously.

"Hold!" he muttered. "They want me still to hold the west bank! But how can they expect me to defend the east bank of the Rhine if my army is completely destroyed in the west?"

Schlemm was informed emphatically that the supply of coal to the North Sea naval ports depended on keeping the river open for barge traffic on the stretch of the Rhine between Orsoy and Wesel. The west bank of the Rhine must be held "at all costs."

His bafflement was understandable. Three days earlier he had alerted the Army Group H commander, Generaloberst Johannes Blaskowitz, that the Americans now virtually dominated Rhine shipping. Gain after gain by the British and Canadian forces on his northern flanks and by Ninth Army on the south had shrunk his bridgehead. His army's line of defence was now far too extensive for its diminishing forces.

Schlemm confided to his staff his grave concern that the American forces would turn to the north and attack him from the rear. "If they act quickly and hurl their powerful armoured forces boldly and unhesitatingly along the Rhine to Wesel, the left bank of the river will be lost, and Army will be cut off from a retreat over the Rhine." There would be no time to destroy completely the final bridges. It would be impossible to form a new defence on the east bank of the river.

Schlemm's Tac HQ had been moved twice: first from heavily bombed Xanten to a village near Rheinberg and finally across the river to a site near Wesel on the east bank. At a staff meeting later in the day the parachute commander drew a sweeping 15-mile-long semi-circle on the army tactical map to delineate his new defence line: the Wesel Pocket. The pencilled line curved around a pocket of land formed by a U-shaped bend in the Rhine at Wesel. The line started in the north at the old Roman town of Xanten. Then it curved inland along the Boenninghardt Ridge — the last high ground before the Rhine — and circled back to the river near Rheinberg on the American front.

"Everything depends on our holding Wesel," the parachute general said grimly. "Its two bridges and the free running of the ferries across the Rhine are our only communication line — and our only means of salvaging what is left of First Parachute Army.

"Our new bridgehead will be anchored in the north at Xanten.

General von Luettwitz's 47 Panzer Corps, with 6th Parachute Division, 116th Panzer Division, and 180th Infantry Division, will defend the Xanten-Sonsbeck line against the Canadians and British,'' he ordered. ''I want fresh reinforcements and substantial reserves of ammunition and armour directed there.''

Schlemm assigned the middle sector of the bridgehead to General Meindl. ''The ridge at Boenninghardt is of utmost importance. From this high ground we can defend against any attack from the west. If we lose it, however, the British will gain total observation of our entire bridgehead. [Meindl's] 2 Parachute Corps will hold the Sonsbeck-Issum line along the western boundaries of the ridge. Under command will be 7th and 8th Parachute Divisions and 84th and 190th Infantry.

''63 Infantry Corps has been pushed back towards Rheinberg by a powerful U.S. armoured spearhead. General Abraham will direct 2nd Parachute Division, Panzer Lehr Division, and 15th Panzer Grenadier Division to contain the Americans on the Issum-Orsoy line.''

Although Hitler was insistent that not a single man or piece of equipment be evacuated across the Rhine without his specific permission, Schlemm had been able to wrest some concessions from the commander-in-chief of Army Group H, Generaloberst Blaskowitz. Schlemm was concerned that the narrow bridgehead had become so congested by surplus vehicles, weapons, supplies, and administrative staff that troop movement and combat actions would be hopelessly confused. On March 2 he had received permission to withdraw these surplus units to the east bank. Special staff was set up at all available ferries and bridges to conduct an orderly evacuation. Moving stealthily at night to avoid observation by the British and American tactical air forces, 50,000 vehicles and their supplies crossed the Rhine. They were immediately deployed for east-bank defence.

Schlemm noted that his huge reserves of artillery were mainly intact, despite the counter-battery efforts of the Allies. Without even consulting Hitler, the Para commander had evacuated 50 batteries of 88mm dual-purpose (anti-tank and anti-aircraft) guns to the east bank. These he immediately repositioned and sited with ample ammunition to cover Allied positions across the river. He also ordered General der Infanterie Erich Straube to withdraw across the Rhine and prepare a defensive front on the east bank. The Watchmaker's 86 Corps had been driven back from the Goch-

Geldern line by British troops. After a month of continuous fighting, its usefulness there was over.

Schlemm's luck was holding out. Despite the poor flying weather, the RAF staged a major raid focussed on the two Wesel bridges that very day. Forty-eight aircraft unloaded 183 thousand-pound bombs aimed at the road bridge; 41 more bombers dropped 164 bombs on the railway bridge.

"The attacks were unsuccessful," Schlemm told his relieved command staff. "The bridges are intact; our columns of vehicles were evacuated without damage."

If the German High Command's lack of realism confounded Schlemm, he himself had no illusions that he could stem the Allied advance indefinitely. Schlemm's hope was that by inflicting heavy casualties on his enemy and demonstrating an unbending German resistance, he could force the Allies to negotiate more favourable terms of peace. His 11 divisions had been reduced to one-half and in some cases one-quarter strength. But by careful deployment of them, Schlemm reckoned that he could continue to hold out for a limited time at least. The advantage, he well knew, was on his side as the defender.

The parachute commander swiftly bolstered his new line. He ordered all his infantry weapons retrenched into fixed positions covering specific or expected target areas. His troops, too, would be safely dug in and protected from heavy enemy artillery bombardments. Patrols were sent out to probe enemy positions and discern enemy intentions. Prisoners were interrogated. Then Schlemm set up his anti-tank weapons to cover any likely tank approaches.

Artillery weapons were in good supply (although every round of ammunition expended had to be accounted for). The fifty 88mm guns he had conjured from under Hitler's watchful eye were transferred to the front. His supporting arms — mortars and rockets — registered every possible target so that FOOs could call down artillery on any map reference where the enemy advanced. To compensate for his depleted tank force, the general deployed flak units with self-propelled guns in depth throughout the sector.

His engineers tirelessly dug anti-tank ditches, laid minefields, cratered roads and streams, and prepared bridges for demolition. These were tactics of delaying and withdrawing that Schlemm had picked up and polished in the Russian and Italian campaigns.

Schlemm was openly scornful of the Allied tactics which, he

265

insisted, "never surprised us": "We could determine from the kind and location of artillery fire and from the assembly positions of the tanks where and when the attack would take place. This gave us time for counter-measures. We seldom noticed exploitation of favourable opportunities, swift pursuit of the retreating enemy, surprise attacks by infantry at dusk or at night without the support of artillery and tanks."

This Allied strategy allowed the Germans to string relatively weak outposts along their front while holding in readiness a strong second line on which to fall back. A mobile reserve such as 116th Panzer Division stood ready to "firefight" any danger spot. With these tactics, the Germans had been able to maintain a steady defence, often breaking out of almost complete encirclement to withdraw and organize further resistance.

The concentrated Allied artillery fire (termed by Schlemm a "very impressive technical achievement") was at times so intensive that Schlemm was amazed any German soldier could live through it: "Two qualities are necessary if the troops are to stand this 'hell fire': energy and resistance. Deep and narrow foxholes for one or two men have to be dug. The men have to have nerves of steel."

Still, he was livid to hear that 250 men from the Panzer Lehr Regiment had surrendered after a vicious tank-infantry battle with the 1st Lincolnshire Regiment and the 3rd Battalion Scots Guards. The Germans had fought fanatically in hand-to-hand combat and then suddenly had given up. Later, the British discovered the extent of the strongpoint: four 88mm and at least two SP guns, six dug-in 50mm anti-tank guns, and "a haul of Spandaus and infantry weapons of all kinds." (The young Scots Guards officer who administered much of the punishment that so demoralized the Germans that day, Lieutenant Runcie, is now the Most Reverend Robert Runcie, Archbishop of Canterbury.)

The morale of the German troops remained — with these few exceptions — high. Colonel Hugh Rose of 7/9th Battalion Royal Scots remembers them as being "incredibly brave." "Four boys lying over their Spandaus in front of a farmhouse held up the battalion on my left for some time — just four young boys holding up an entire battalion of men."

Fear was a powerful weapon in maintaining a stubborn defending force. Two young parachutists captured on March 2 confessed under interrogation at 2 Canadian Corps's POW cage that "they were elite troops and were warned not to get captured. Anybody about to surrender was to be shot by his comrades."

A captured document signed on March 5 by Blaskowitz confirmed this: "Soldiers . . . away from their units . . . will be summarily tried and shot. To this end HQ Parachute Army is creating as many mobile courts-martial as possible, which will be positioned at bridges and ferry sites in particular."

Like so many spokes in a wheel, the Americans, British, and Canadians converged angrily on Schlemm's new defensive line. Each thrust was aimed from points around the semi-circle towards the hub: Wesel.

From the south 16 U.S. Corps was pushing hard towards Rheinberg. From the North, 2 Canadian Corps were driving east towards Xanten. And from the west, Horrocks's 30 Corps was punching a hole through the Schlieffen defences to reach Boenninghardt. From Geldern and Weeze, the 53rd Welsh attacked forward another three miles to Issum and were now barely six miles from the Rhine. As they closed in, they ran into unyielding resistance from the German 21st Parachute Regiment. On March 4-5 the 30-year-old CO of 7th Battalion Royal Welsh Fusiliers, the gentle, unrufflable Lieutenant-Colonel G.F.T.B. Dickson, went ahead alone to advise one of his forward companies of a delay in launching an attack. On his way back, Dickson was mortally wounded.

This was the last engagement of Operation Veritable for the battalion; one major confrontation awaited its sister battalion, 4th RWF. The 53rd Welsh Division had been in the line under active combat longer than any other British unit in Veritable. In that month they had foot-slogged 40 miles, fired 1,000,000 rounds of machine-gun ammunition alone, built 12 bridges, manhandled 1,040 three-ton loads of rubble for road repair, erected 75,000 signs using 3,500 gallons of paint — and drunk 1,228 gallons of rum.

Against murderous small-arms fire and continuous shelling and mortaring, 4th Canadian Armoured Division, still hurting from its five-day ordeal in the Hochwald Gap, now plunged into renewed battle to capture the villages of Veen (a "miniature fort") and Winnenthal. For four days, the Assault Battalion of 6th German Parachute Division held them back, inflicting terrible casualties.

An entire company of Argylls was trapped, with only a handful of survivors able to fight their way out. Thirty-two were taken prisoner. The battle was taken up by the Algonquins and the Lincoln & Welland Regiment, supported by tanks from the South Alberta and British Columbia Tank Regiments. The B.C. commander, Lieutenant-Colonel Gerry Chubb, fulfilled Ned Amy's prophecy at the Hochwald Gap that it would be Chubb who would end up with the task of attacking towards Xanten, and it would indeed be a "son of a bitch." Infantry casualties alone amounted to 311.

At the very beginning of the operation, Horrocks had put Major-General Alan Adair's Guards Armoured Division (5th Guards Armoured Brigade and 32nd Guards Infantry Brigade) — his break-out force — on standby. They were to have burst out of the initial bottleneck and captured a bridge at Wesel in a couple of days. Cratering and mud dampened that plan. Now, almost a month later, the complete division finally came on the line (although its infantry arm had already been fighting in support of the 51st Highland Division).

At Hamb, just west of the Boenninghardt Ridge, an officer from 3rd Battalion Irish Guards (32nd Guards Infantry Brigade) put Schlemm's defence theories to the test. The "Irish copse party" on March 5 was Lieutenant R.H.S. O'Grady's first battle, and a boisterous one it was. The young Irishman had joined the army straight out of school, "a new boy, full of zest, rather more so perhaps than some of my compatriots who knew more about it."

The "Micks" were given the task of capturing the village of Hamb. However, when they got there they found it abandoned. The CO, Lieutenant-Colonel Giles Vandeleur, was veteran enough to realize that if the enemy position in the high ground overlooking Hamb were not cleared, the Irish group would come under direct and devastating fire. O'Grady, who commanded an infantry platoon in the 32nd Guards Infantry Brigade, and Lieutenant Neil Whitfield, his "partner in crime," a troop commander in the 2nd Irish Guards of the 5th Guards Armoured Brigade, were ordered to advance before dawn to seize the ridge.

By dawn the force had reached an open field, when they suddenly came under intense small-arms and self-propelled fire from all sides. Seven tanks were knocked out. The Germans had obviously pre-registered the target area and were waiting in ambush: "We were pinned down and had lost at least half the platoon," O'Grady remembers. "We had about eight men left, not many more, and the rest were lying dead in the field or very badly wounded. Our one object was to get out of that field and up to the objective a half-mile away. When we got there we found the enemy in bunkers. I managed to throw some grenades at them and my guardsmen attacked with Bren guns, capturing the Germans."

For the next 24 hours, the small band was pinned down under shellfire and small-arms fire. The remaining tanks came up in hull-down positions to support them, and by the next morning, the situation was improved.

Seventy casualties resulted from the O'Grady-Whitfield operation, but a foothold had been gained on Schlemm's vital five-mile Boenninghardt Ridge. The hold was expanded in the next days in bitter fighting by other regiments of the Guards Armoured Division: the 4th Grenadiers and 5th Coldstream Guards. The final strongpoint, Boenninghardt village, fell, with 200 troops from Meindl's 8th Parachute Division put in the POW cages.

Cold, grey days, March winds, and sleet storms marked the last days of winter. On Sunday, March 4, pale sunlight struggled wanly through a cloud cover that had begun to seem almost permanent to the miserable and tired troops beneath. Driving along a wooded trail in his Sherman tank, Major A.M.H. Gregory-Hood of 2nd Grenadier Guards emerged into a clearing. He suddenly caught a glimpse of something so English, so peaceful, that for an instant the war must have seemed very far away. In a dank corner of these God-forsaken woods, Gregory-Hood saw a patch of yellow daffodils.

That same Sunday, the Massed Pipes and Drums of the 15th and 51st Divisions sounded retreat before a distinguished group: Prime Minister Churchill, Field-Marshal Montgomery, Field-Marshal Sir Alan Brooke, and Generals Crerar and Horrocks.

The pibroch's eerie lament, "Flowers of the Forest," died on a parade square whipped by raw wind and rain. Four thousand men stood sombrely, oblivious to all but the haunting wail that recaptured flashes of the 24 days in quite unlovely forests and boggy plains that many would rather forget.

The two commanding divisional generals addressed the men. Major-General "Tiny" Barber, his giant frame leaning over the familiar shepherd's crook, proclaimed, "I salute you all on your great deeds," and promised every officer and man in the 15th Scottish Division a 48-hour pass to Brussels. Major-General Rennie hailed the Highland achievement as "one of the finest of the Fifty-First."

"The end is at last clearly in sight," he assured his Jocks. Those were strangely weighted words. Thomas Rennie had a premonition.

Later that day, Montgomery, wearing a green sniper's jacket, and the Prime Minister toured the front, visiting Simpson's and Crerar's headquarters and lunching with General Simonds.

As the entourage moved on to the Siegfried Line, Churchill emulated the Jocks in giving the historic gesture of contempt for his enemy, the prospect of which he had been savouring throughout the long years of war. It was thus described:

The Prime Minister climbed out of his car and walked solemnly to the line of "dragon's teeth." Unbuttoning his fly, he turned to the assembled officers.

"Gentlemen," he said sonorously. "I'd like to ask you to join me. Let us all urinate on the great West Wall of Germany." He wagged a finger at the photographers, who were aiming their cameras, and called out, "This is one of those operations connected with this great war which must not be reproduced graphically."

Brooke stood next to the prime minister. "I shall never forget the childish grin of intense satisfaction that spread all over his face as he looked down at the critical moment."

The puckish PM was not done with tomfoolery for the day. At one point on the tour, dispatch riders were seen approaching the column of VIP vehicles at great speed. A signal of great importance from the British Cabinet, the onlookers guessed. Only a handful saw the PM reach out of his Rolls-Royce for the box, slip it open, and, with the ghost of a smile, pop in his missing dentures.

On March 5, a message of considerably more bite reached General Simpson at Ninth Army HQ. At 1230 hours that day, Simpson had held a staff conference with his engineers. The subject: a proposed immediate surprise crossing of the Rhine by McLain's 19 Corps. Simpson's personal diary noted the engineers' conclusion: "The crossing was viewed as completely possible against minor opposition."

At 1330 hours the dramatic request was referred to Field-Marshal Montgomery. Less than an hour later, the reply was given. Simpson's suggested crossing was in the "wrong tactical locality." Further, there was not sufficient bridging equipment for both this and the "big crossing" — Montgomery's Operation Plunder, set for March 23. The field-marshal said no.

Simpson's request was a curious reversal of his judgment a month before when rising flood waters had persuaded him to cancel the

Roer assault. Then, it had been Simpson himself who feared that his assault unit could be cut off from reinforcement and supply and annihilated. Now, with another river assault in contention — the Rhine — it was Montgomery who voiced the same argument: a premature crossing, he said, was not worth the risk of heavy American casualties.

Had they been able to read the mind of General Schlemm, neither commander would have hesitated to commit his forces. The Germans had not yet had the opportunity or resources to mount any significant defences on the east bank. In fact, the Rhine could probably have been "bounced" with ease that day. Whether, however, the bridgehead could have been held is still under debate.

"I can get across if they'll only turn me loose," Colonel Glen Anderson, CO of 5th Armored Division's Combat Command Reserve, had implored, voicing the bitter frustrations of many American commanders in those edgy days of March as they neared the Rhine.

Historian Chester Wilmot believes that Monty's insistence on a "tidy battle," with masses of logistical supply to back up every move, was at this point in the war unrealistic, given the situation of a crumbling enemy. "[Monty] did not appear to realise that American 'untidiness' and improvisation, however dangerous when the enemy was strong, could now yield great dividends."

Two weeks later, Schlemm's defences would be mounted. The Rhine assault would be a different — and much more costly — affair.

The sun rose crimson over Rheinberg on March 5. The battlefield that day was to become as scarlet as the sky.

From a small hill overlooking the flat approaches to the town, Schlemm watched intently from the command post of Generalmajor Siegfried von Waldenburg's 116th Panzer Division as a seesaw struggle unfolded.

The attack on Rheinberg by the American 8th Armoured Division had been expected. The Para commander had prepared a hot reception for his enemy. On the night of March 3, Schlemm had ordered von Waldenburg to withdraw 116th Panzer Division from the Canadian front under cover of darkness. Without pause, the Windhund Division was assigned a new line at Rheinberg where the southern defences of the Wesel bridges were anchored.

The division had been engaged continuously since February 10 against First Canadian Army. Casualties in tanks and infantrymen had depleted its strength. Fuel was scarce and ammunition in short supply. Nevertheless, they could not be given time to rest and refit. ''Strong enemy movements . . . made us expect the American attack March 5,'' the 116th's history notes. ''The division formed two task forces. There was still a weak task force of the Panzer Lehr Division in the southeast of Rheinberg.''

The troops waiting in ambush did not require a large force to wreak havoc on the attackers. They were dug in and armed to the teeth with automatic weapons and Panzerfausts. Interlocking defences comprising 88mm anti-tank guns, supported by 20mms, were strung closely together around the periphery of the town. In addition, 150mm heavy artillery had pre-registered every promiment feature of the approaches.

Curiously, Combat Command B of 8th U.S. Armored Division had no such knowledge of its enemy. Its commander, Colonel Edward Kimball, had been ordered to advance on Rheinberg and its environs and then push ahead to seize the bridges at Wesel, seven miles to the north. Unaware that Schlemm had slipped his trouble-shooting Panzer forces into the line, American intelligence indicated that Rheinberg was defended by approximately 300 disorganized and demoralized troops, supported by a few self-propelled weapons and anti-tank guns. No preliminary air or ground reconnaissance had been ordered; no preliminary artillery barrage was prepared.

Two task forces, neither with any real battle experience, were assigned the job: one composed largely of infantry to take the town (Task Force Roseborough) and another comprising mainly armoured units from 36th Tank Battalion to rush the bridges (Task Force Van Houten). The latter's commander, Major John Van Houten, had no inkling of opposition. ''We thought it was to be a road march,'' he recalls.

Lieutenant-Colonel Morgan G. Roseborough, 49th Armored Infantry, led the advance. In the confusion, Roseborough's infantry force had taken a wrong turn earlier and become separated from Van Houten's task force. ''We were barrelling along against minimum resistance when we ran out of maps and intelligence,'' he explains.

The tanks were ordered to proceed alone. ''Our armour just ploughed headlong into a prepared defence that the Germans had put in to protect the Wesel bridge,'' Roseborough recalls. ''They had a number of their dual-purpose 88 anti-aircraft and anti-tank guns ringing the town, and they had a field day with us until we could recover.''

March 5 was to be a day of grim gratification for the German commanders on the hilltop — and a day of annihilation for the Americans. From 0800 hours until dusk descended on the flaming battlefield, and even through the long evening hours, Schlemm and von Waldenburg sat transfixed, with headsets on. Through the intercepted radio net they could track the course of the American tanks as they approached Rheinberg.

The chatter was from the Shermans. "The U.S. tanks radioed often and openly," Schlemm noted. Before his eyes, "a wedge-shaped formation of several hundred tanks with little dispersion approached the German position," he recorded in his war diary. This tantalizing concentration of armour generated wistful thoughts in the Para commander: "If only I had ammunition of a larger calibre or a few Luftwaffe fighter units."

The German troops crouched in silence, bazookas ready — and waited until the tanks lumbered unsuspectingly into their midst. Then the radio crackled. Schlemm heard the furious roar of tanks flaming and the screams of men wounded and dying.

"With no accompanying infantry to root out the German infantry or anti-tank guns nor any air or artillery fire to hold them down, the tanks . . . offered easy targets," Combat Command B reported.

"We lost about 50 tanks in about five minutes that day," remembers Major Henry Rothenberg of 8th Armoured Reconnaissance Battalion. "They caught us between the water and the hills — then all hell broke loose. The tanks couldn't move. They were just sitting ducks."

The verges were honeycombed with mines, and they were at the mercy of the 88s — and the dreaded bazooka boys. Captain Kemble ("Cowboy") Tucker, leading one armoured column, had his tank knocked out twice. Each time, he dismounted under fire and boarded another.

"The tank battalion and company officers called in vain for infantry support throughout the day," the CCB noted. "All we could do was sit there and sweat," recalled Sergeant Vernon McLean. "We were hemmed in. We couldn't turn."

Tucker collected the crews of other disabled and burning tanks and directed the battle on foot, attempting with only sub-machine guns to clear the area of German Panzerfaust teams. Fatally wounded, he was shouting encouragement to his men as he fell.

Leading another column into the slaughter, Captain David B. Kelly charged single-handedly into the town square at Rheinberg and wheeled around the church, guns blazing at a bazooka nest, before he was forced back by heavy fire. He organized his surviving tanks to return the fire. With the help of infantry from 3rd Battalion, 137th Infantry Regiment, which had moved up by dusk, the small band drove the enemy from the town.

In its first major fight, 36th Tank Battalion had almost its entire armoured strength wiped out. Of 54 tanks, 41 were destroyed. Casualties to the battalion and its supporting 49th Armored Infantry Battalion totalled 343: 92 were killed, 31 missing, and 220 wounded. That evening, the survivors of the mayhem wearily consolidated in the battle-scarred village.

From his hilltop vantage point, Schlemm still held his vigil, dreading a renewed attack. When his defences of Rheinberg crumbled, he had expected to see a fresh column of tanks racing to cut off his army at Wesel. But even in defeat, the victory was Schlemm's. His forces had devastated the American attackers and stalled an advance that could have been dangerous.

Incredibly, the final two bridges of General Schlemm remained intact.

On March 8, Lieutenant-General Guy Simonds's 2 Canadian Corps was given operational control over all of Montgomery's forces for the final thrust to the Rhine, with the divisions of 30 British Corps and 16 U.S. Corps temporarily under his command.

Montgomery explained the move to CIGS:

The enemy is resisting desperately in the Xanten-Wesel bridgehead. 2 Cdn Corps takes over operational control in the bridgehead tomorrow and I think things will go better with one man running that battle. The Americans are pushing up from the south and are within 2,000 yds of the crossroads southwest of Wesel.

The pocket is slowly being squeezed in but it is tough going and many enemy paratroopers refuse to surrender, even when they have run out of ammunition and have to be shot and several instances of this have occurred today. If we could get 2 days of good flying weather, it would be a great help but we have not been able to operate the fighter bombers for several days.

The badly missed Typhoons materialized only briefly. During the first week of March, heavy casualties to 84 Group RAF and continued bad weather prohibited close air support.

However, Schlemm's ever-dwindling bridgehead was now a small nodule of land a mere eight miles in width that was sandwiched on two sides by the Rhine. His escape hatch at its head was through the city of Wesel. The key towns of Xanten, Alpon, and Ossenburg anchored his final line of defence.

At 0530 hours on March 8, a massive artillery barrage heralded the attack on Xanten from two directions by two brigades: the 4th Canadian Infantry and the 43rd Wessex's 129th. Ninety-eight per cent of the historic city — the legendary birthplace of Siegfried — was destroyed as the Germans fought savagely to maintain their last foothold on the west bank. The Royal Hamilton Light Infantry lost 134 men, with two company commanders killed and a third — the indomitable Major Froggett — taken prisoner. The Essex Scottish casualties were 108 men.

The German paratroopers fought with such tenacity that when the battle finally wound down, Brigadier Joe Vandeleur, commander of 129th Brigade, saluted the German survivors as they were marched away to POW cages.

Schlemm evacuated the staffs of 116th Panzer Division and his own Parachute Army that night, placing all remaining combat units under command of General Meindl. The latter's report was dismal. Schlemm scanned the list. He could almost picture his corps commander's white eyebrows winging up in alarm: "Serious lack of ammunition for artillery and mortars . . . no supply coming forward . . . concentric fire by enemy artillery into bridgehead, enemy in possession of the heights which gave him an insight into the positions right up to the Rhine . . . the only traffic possible within the bridgehead was by motorcycle with sidecar during firing pauses . . . telephone connections could not be maintained . . . flame-throwing tanks demoralizing the infantry who felt themselves powerless against this weapon. . . ."

Meindl warned Schlemm that unless his men were evacuated by 1700 hours on March 9, they would be doomed. And Schlemm — "brilliant, impulsive," and determined to save his army — decided to defy Adolf Hitler.

"We *must* withdraw," he urged his chief, Blaskowitz. "It is only sheer luck that the bridge at Wesel has not yet been hit sufficiently to destroy it. If the bridge is destroyed there is no other escape route for my men trapped on the west bank of the Rhine. If this force of fighting men is lost, there will be no experienced troops left in this area to prevent an Allied crossing of the Rhine. I see no reason to sacrifice the last remnants of First Parachute Army west of the Rhine," he declared.

Then Schlemm gambled with one final challenge to Hitler: "If the Supreme Command in Berlin do not believe me, let them send a representative to Wesel. They will see the situation themselves!''

It was a shrewd move. Hitler had ridiculed von Rundstedt's persistent requests to withdraw. He did not trust official reports. ''They are made only to throw dust in our eyes. Everything is explained and later we find out that nothing happened,'' he complained. ''We have to get a couple of officers down there — even it they only have one leg or one arm — officers who are good men, whom we can send down there so that we get a clear picture.''

A stubborn 29-year-old Scottish major and an ambitious 42-year-old Canadian corps commander played a strange role in getting the Fuehrer his ''clear picture'' — and expediting the end of German resistance on the west bank.

The final key to the Wesel bridges was the hamlet of Alpon. The town sat astride the main road running down the steep reverse slope of Boenninghardt Ridge to the Rhine. The river was less than three miles away; Alpon was the last German strongpoint. Simonds shot off an urgent order to the 52nd Lowland Division commander, Major-General Sir Edmond Hakewell-Smith: ''Get Alpon!'' Hakewell-Smith directed his 156th Brigade to put in the attack immediately.

There was little information on the sector, and no time for reconnaissance. Moreover, because the Guards Armoured Division was still fighting in Boenninghardt, one mile to the southwest, the Lowland attack had to be put back two hours.

Then the BBC reported on the 9 p.m. news that Alpon had just been captured by the American Ninth Army. The report was untrue, but artillery support for the Lowland operation was cancelled for fear of hitting American units moving up on the far side of the Alpon road. The British maps proved unreliable; defence overprints did not disclose a 50-foot drop at the foot of Boenninghardt Ridge that would prevent the passage of tanks. It was classic Simonds fence-rushing: without artillery or armoured support, in the face of protests by the brigade commander, the attack was ordered in.

The plan called for a flanking assault by two battalions of 156th Brigade: 7th Battalion Cameronians and 4/5th Battalion Royal Scots Fusiliers. The 6th Battalion Cameronians would guard the flanks. Major Jack Holland, commanding a company of 6th Cameronians, was ordered to move forward during the night so that he would be in a position to intercept retreating German prisoners when the attack went in at dawn. ''Get over the railway line and dig in before first light," he was told. "Do not cross the main road on your right; the Americans are moving up in that sector."

Just before midnight on the night of March 8-9, Holland moved off. He had to attack across the raised railway embankment and was involved in several skirmishes with German patrols on the way, but he was on his objective at 0600 hours.

What worried Holland was the growing suspicion that he was dangerously behind German lines. A troop of enemy reinforcements, rifles slung, moved up the road towards them; Holland took their rifles and stashed the prisoners in a cellar, leaving one of his Jocks sitting on the trap door. Off in the darkness he could hear the clunks of tanks, probably in lagger for maintenance, he thought.

"Obviously, the Germans hadn't dreamt there was anyone so far behind their positions. Brigade had not attacked yet. No other of our companies had got beyond the railway line. We were on our own," Holland recalled.

"We only had about three-quarters of an hour to dig in before daylight — and you don't get a company properly dug in in that time. If I'd had time to reconnoitre, I would have said 'To hell with the Americans,' and I would have gone across the road. It was about four feet higher than the ground we were on. The only way to be safe was to dig in on both sides."

Two soldiers came running down the other side of the road. Holland couldn't make out their identity. "I shouted to my men, 'Don't fire! Don't fire! They might be Americans!' Suddenly they stopped and their mouths fell open: they were German paratroopers. As quickly, they realized by the shape of our tin helmets who we were. We killed them. After that the tanks came clunking out: Panthers.

"They shot up all our defences. I put down smoke and they just put in a round of mortar. I hit them twice with a PIAT and they knocked both the PIATs out.

"I radioed back to Battalion HQ for tank support but the tanks couldn't get through. I had my FOO with me, and I asked for artillery cover, but they wouldn't give it to me because they said I'd asked for it on my own positions. I said, 'Well, I'm in a slit-trench and the Germans are not. It will do them more damage than it will do me!' Then the Germans shot out our wireless set. We had an hour of silence.

"It was during that period that I saw a German staff car coming up the road, obviously not realizing we were there. It was an irresistible target and our Bren guns opened up. The car stopped right in front of us and because the road was high up, I could see the space between the road and the bottom of the car, and I saw this figure dive out on the other side. I fired but he got away.

"Then more paratroopers came down the road. By 10 o'clock in the morning, I was looking down the barrel of a Schmeisser." Twenty-seven men were killed and wounded in the action. The remaining 60 were captured.

It was some time later, after being seized and walked across Schlemm's bridge at Wesel ("But I never put my hands above my head"), after his 50-mile route march across Germany, his imprisonment at Oflag Brunswick, and his subsequent release after VE-Day, after talking to historians and survivors — that Jack Holland had a glimmer as to the identity of the officers in that staff car.

Holland believes that these were the observers Hitler had sent to the front line to get that clear picture. He reckons these officers misunderstood an attack by one company isolated behind the lines, thinking they represented a major force. He knows from German interrogations that the officers ultimately reported to Hitler that Alpon had been taken and that the Wesel bridges were about to be overrun.

Holland concludes that the ill-considered plan to rush Alpon that annihilated his company had one good result: it ensured that Schlemm would receive Hitler's permission to withdraw across the Rhine the following night.

Meindl's deadline was fast approaching. By 1700 hours on March 9, his ultimatum still had not been acknowledged. The corps commander had prepared the abandonment order on a precise timetable. He had consulted with his engineers about traffic control on ferries and bridges. Two liaison officers from each division had been rushed to Staff HQ by motorcycle and had been pacing now for three hours, waiting for approval to release the order.

"At last, about 1900 hours, consent arrived," Meindl recorded. "At 1905 hours, the special missions officers [left] by different roads to the respective divisional artillery and combat groups, having instructions to report personally the passing on of the order. At 2000 hours already those units nearest the bridge were on their way."

All through the night and the following morning tens of thousands of German troops and vehicles poured east over the Rhine. The remnants of 116th Panzer Division were among them: "Exhausted and debilitated, overtired and full of alarm for the future," the division had lost close to 3,000 men in the campaign.

March 10 dawned with fog and a wet drizzle that was welcomed by the escaping men, and the evacuation continued without fear of Allied air interference. Meindl had covered his tracks: ''Rearguard units had received their instructions to hold out for a further 24 hours and mislead the enemy to believe that the old line was still manned.'' Lieutenant-Colonel Guderian, the last officer of his division to leave, crossed by storm boat two kilométres south.

At 0700 hours on March 10, Alfred Schlemm stood at the Wesel bridge in the fine rain and watched the last of his evacuated units cross to the east bank. His defending force, begun as a single reinforced infantry division on February 8, had swollen to a peak of 11 divisions during the course of the Rhineland campaign. Now his enemy had achieved its objective; Veritable and Grenade were concluded. But First Parachute Army had achieved its objective too. It had stemmed the tide of battle for 31 days.

It had inflicted 15,634 casualties on the British and Canadians of First Canadian Army during the month-long battle and 7,300 on Ninth U.S. Army in its 17-day campaign. The cost to the Wehrmacht had been devastating: over 50,000 Germans had been captured. An estimated 40,000 more had been killed or seriously wounded.

Schlemm would wonder if Hitler's stubborn insistence to fight the battle of the Rhineland — instead of making his stand on the Rhine's east bank — had been worth the cost: 113,000 young men from both sides of the hill had paid the price.

Now, Schlemm had one final order to give. At 0700 hours he gestured wearily to his signals officer: the final two bridges of General Schlemm were demolished.

20

The Power of Plunder

WHILE GENERAL SCHLEMM was beating off the Allied power play to capture his bridges, one of the most improbable crossing points along the length of the Rhine became the scene of a stunning coup.

On March 7, Hodges's First U.S. Army — still on the sizzling advance that had begun with the Grenade force at the Roer — approached the crest of a hill overlooking the Rhine town of Remagen. Amazed, they peered down through soft rain at the magnificent vista far below: the Rhine in all its might, dark waters coursing powerfully between steep volcanic cliffs. Spanning it, teeming with the traffic of fleeing troops of General von Zangen's Fifteenth Army, was the Ludendorff railroad bridge. Incredibly, it was intact.

The commander of 9th Armored Division's Combat Command B was hoarse with excitement. "Grab that bridge!" Brigadier-General Bill Hoge shouted over the radio.

An infantry platoon tore down the hill to the town, encouraged by the white flags of surrender hanging from windows. "The bridge is going to be detonated at 4 p.m.!" gasped a German prisoner. They glanced at the time: 45 minutes to go.

The men raced for the entrance to the bridge. A mighty explosion erupted, releasing a cascade of rubble. The bridge is down, they thought. But when the dust settled they realized that the Germans had only blown an anti-tank crater on the near side. There was still time to get across and prevent them from carrying out any more sabotage.

The riflemen hesitated. It was 10 minutes before four. What if it was a trap, they worried, and the Germans were waiting until

---

See Maps 1 and 11 (Appendix B).

they got on the bridge before they detonated it. They would all be killed.

Just then, they heard another explosion.

One thousand feet away, on the east side, the German commander of Ludendorff Bridge had been watching desperately as the American troops neared the bridge. He was trapped between two fears: the fear of losing the bridge to the enemy, and the fear of being court-martialled by Hitler's edict for detonating the bridge without higher authority. Finally, von Zangen's operations officer gave the order. Cautioning his men to stay down, the commander turned the key to set off the 60 charges wired to the struts of the bridge. Nothing happened. The circuit had obviously been cut by American artillery.

"Get out there and ignite the manual charge," he snapped to one of his NCOs. A sergeant darted forward. Moments later, the explosion finally came.

As the Americans watched helplessly, the bridge shuddered and seemed to rise in the air, suspended in a great pyramid of dust and smoke. This time it's really down, they thought. But to their amazement, when the smoke subsided they saw that the bridge was still intact.

"Let's go!" yelled company commander Lieutenant Karl Timmerman as he plunged across the bridge. The men followed nervously, ducking bursts of small-arms and machine-gun fire from the twin stone towers at the opposite end — not daring to look down at the turbulent water 80 feet below where they might tumble at any moment.

The gamble paid off. Resistance was quickly overcome and by 4 p.m. the bridge was theirs. Twenty-four hours later, 8,000 American troops were crammed into the narrow bridgehead, and within three days the number had more than doubled, with six heavy pontoon and treadway bridges replacing the damaged but still intact Ludendorff Bridge.

The Americans had breached the greatest water obstacle in Western Europe — and the last defence line of Hitler's western armies. It was a dynamic demonstration of the special skills of the U.S. military in grasping and exploiting the unexpected opportunity.

"It just doesn't fit in with the plan," was the dismaying reaction of Eisenhower's assistant chief of staff when he heard the news.

Although no one disputed the courage and initiative of First Army in seizing it, the best thing that the Ludendorff Bridge at Remagen seemed to have going for it was its availability. Eighty-five miles south of Wesel, the Ruhr gateway, Remagen was in near-impossible terrain for the massive armoured breakout that the Allies needed. Consolidating their position in strength would be difficult. Expanding it would be a herculean effort.

A high outcropping of sheer rock dominated the eastern exit of the bridge, giving the Germans an effortless vantage point for their ack-ack gun positions. (The cliff was quickly renamed ''Flak Hill'' by the reinforcing troops who came under its deadly cascade of fire.) A quarter-mile-long tunnel through the rock emerged into the Westerwald, a densely treed mountainous forest. The roads on both sides of the river were poor. Seven miles beyond, to be sure, was the escape hatch of the Ruhr-Frankfurt autobahn, but — as the Huertgen Forest, the Reichswald, and the Hochwald had shown — traversing a wooded area with armour could be a slow and costly effort.

Eisenhower, lukewarm to the potential of the bridgehead, was reluctant to weaken Operation Plunder, his long-planned Rhine assault at Wesel two weeks hence, by diverting forces or equipment south. He ordered Bradley to commit no more than four divisions to developing the Remagen bridgehead and to limit his advance to 1,000 yards a day.

Montgomery, however, immediately saw the advantages of the American bridgehead as a diversionary tactic to his major crossing.

Top Secret. Personal and Eyes Only for CIGS from Field-Marshal Montgomery, 8 Mar 45:
A complete infantry division is now over the Rhine at Remagen and a pontoon bridge has been made. The plan is to extend this holding to a bridgehead from Bonn to Andernach which would be held by 4 divisions. I was consulted by Eisenhower by telephone this morning as to my opinion on this matter and said I considered it to be an excellent move as it would be an unpleasant threat to the enemy and would undoubtedly draw enemy strength onto it and away from my business on the north.

It was a bitter disappointment to the heroic captors of Ludendorff Bridge to have their achievement taken so lightly, but it did not drain their enthusiasm. The Germans finally retaliated with desperation measures, including frogmen with explosives, floating bombs, jet attacks, and V-2 rockets — the only time in the war that Hitler allowed either of his V missiles to be used as tactical weapons. Even when the cumulative effect of all this abuse finally sent the bridge toppling 10 days later, the American bridgehead, now fully reinforced and with replacement bridges, thrived and expanded.

The Americans would have been gratified to discover the dramatic impact the capture of Ludendorff Bridge was having on the Germand High Command.

Hitler was enraged. Although 120,000 of his best fighting men had been taken prisoner during the recent Allied sweep, he still refused to comprehend that he himself had exacerbated the Allied threat by insisting that his armies stand and defend the Rhineland. His double-edged threat of court-martial to his bridge commanders had only resulted in the demoralization of his Wehrmacht officers — and the loss of a vital bridge to his enemy.

Hitler used the storming of Ludendorff Bridge as an excuse to fire the commander-in-chief of his western armies, von Rundstedt, whose persistent urgings to draw back over the Rhine had merely irritated him. It was the third time during the war that the aging warrior had been given the sack; this time he retired to his home in Bavaria and thankfully hung up his uniform.

Hitler further demoralized his military staff by initiating court-martial proceedings against the "cowards and betrayers" of Remagen who had not blown up the bridge in time. On March 18, four German officers of the Remagen affair — one of whom had not even been present — were executed by order of summary court-martial.

"The 'shock of Remagen,' as it was called, kept many of the responsible men in a state of terror until the end of the war," Albert Speer, Hitler's brilliant architect and minister of war productions, said of the executions.

That same day, Hitler initiated his "scorched earth" policy. He issued orders that all essential goods and services be destroyed, leaving "a desert" for the advancing enemy. The *Volkischer Beobachter* newspaper parrotted his propaganda:

Not a German stalk of wheat is to feed the enemy, not a German mouth to give him information, not a German hand to offer him help. He is to find every footbridge destroyed, every road blocked — nothing but death, annihilation, and hatred will meet him.

The list was comprehensive: power lines, gas and water pipes, food supplies, factories, monuments, churches, even civil records

— all would be destroyed. Farms would be razed, cattle killed, roads torn up, bridges blown.

"If the war is lost," he told his shocked ministers, "the German nation will also perish. There is no need to consider what the people require for continued existence." Only Speer's quiet intervention with Hitler prevented the order from being carried out.

On March 11, von Rundstedt's successor, Generalfeldmarschall Albrecht von Kesselring (known popularly as "Smiling Albert"), met with Blaskowitz, commander of Army Group H, and Schlemm at First Parachute Army HQ near Wesel. Although the final evacuation from the west bank had been completed only two days before, defence restructuring was feverishly under way and the army commanders expressed optimism.

Schlemm, who would again head up the defence of the retrenched German line, explained reassuringly that "First FS Army succeeded in withdrawing all its supply elements in orderly fashion, saving almost all its artillery, and withdrawing enough troops so that a new defensive front [can] be built up on the east bank." Those 50 artillery batteries that he had managed to evacuate from Wesel were to become vital to the east-bank defences.

The wily Para commander expected a major attack across the Rhine, guessing that the focal points would be Emmerich and Rees. He also reasoned that the Allies would attempt an airborne assault.

Against this threat, Schlemm strengthened his anti-aircraft defences in the obvious potential drop zones near Wesel. A total of 814 heavy and light anti-aircraft guns bolstered the defence line. Farmhouses were turned into concrete fortifications; innocent cottages became defensive posts with all-round trenches and sandbagged windows. Specially trained mobile anti-airborne forces covered all likely drop and landing areas. Gunners had to sleep fully clothed at their posts.

Schlemm gave General Straube's 86 Corps the task of defending Wesel. The Watchmaker positioned 84th Infantry Division (still under command of the defender of Cleve, General Fiebig) at the northern edge of the Diersfordter Wood, the high wooded ground overlooking Wesel. General Eugen Meindl's 2 Parachute Corps was responsible for the sector on Straube's right, from Emmerich to a point opposite Xanten. Meindl set up headquarters for his three divisions — the 6th, 7th, and 8th Parachute Divisions — at Bocholt. The corps had 10,000 to 12,000 fighting men. The weakest corps of First Parachute Army, General Erich Abraham's 63 Corps, guarded the sector south of Wesel. For the moment, Schlemm held his key troops — those of von Luettwitz's 47 Panzer Corps (116th Panzer Division and 15th Panzer Grenadier Division) — in reserve.

In addition to First Parachute Army's regular divisions, eight battalions of Volkssturm had been rushed to the front. This hastily recruited unit of the "people's army" — judged to number 3,500 — comprised civil defence men, boys of 16, and weary 60-year-olds. Despite the poor quality of this group, which he shrugged off as "not of combat value," Schlemm expressed confidence in the ability of his army to stave off the attackers, "if it were allowed at least another eight or ten days to re-equip, prepare positions, bring up supplies, and rest."

Appointing Kesselring was a last-ditch attempt by Hitler to stem the Allied invasion. "My orders are categorical," the field-marshal stated: "Hang on!"

Schlemm would get his extra days — 12 of them. The Allies were preparing a massive three-nation, three-army, million-man assault on the Rhine. Codenamed Operation Plunder, the attack could not be coordinated and mounted until March 23. Montgomery, commander-in-chief of 21st Army Group, issued the orders. Combined American and British forces would secure a bridgehead on the Rhine between Rheinberg and Rees.

In the original plan, a single corps of Ninth U.S. Army was ordered to serve under command of Lieutenant-General Sir Miles Dempsey's Second British Army for the Rhine assault. By not allowing Ninth Army to spearhead its own crossing, Montgomery finally found the boiling point of the previously unrufflable General Simpson. The latter strongly protested against Ninth Army's being left out of the historic crossing. Even the Canadians argued against being left behind.

Monty promptly backed down. In a revised plan, both Ninth U.S. Army and Second British Army would launch assaults (under 21st Army Group command); a Canadian brigade would also be included. The combined force, including the breakout units, would include twelve American, eight British, and four Canadian divisions, in addition to two airborne divisions and a Commando brigade. (Of those, Plunder's actual assault force would comprise two divisions each from the American and British forces plus the Commandos, the airborne, and the Canadian brigade.)

Montgomery was content to gamble in giving the enemy a little more time to retrench. He badly needed that lead time too. His objective was an armoured breakout by a massed Allied force deep into the heart of Nazi Germany. He was determined to build up such a level of training and logistical strength that his bridgehead would not falter or be driven back. The Germans had managed to slow up the Veritable operation and stall Grenade. Montgomery was resolved that no amount of last-minute scrambling by the enemy would be able to withstand the power of Plunder.

Although clearly under pressure from his more impatient American counterparts to expedite an assault over the Rhine, Montgomery refused to be hustled. Even the success of Remagen farther south did not convince him that a full-scale assault would succeed against the much more stoutly defended Ruhr sector unless it was fully prepared. Simpson seemed to agree. On March 21, after a meeting with 21st Army Group staff, he noted in his personal diary:

Resistance: The Field-Marshal foresaw [it] would be light in the south — 9 Army zone — and grow progressively heavier to the north flank. The Ninth Army crossed in a zone held by only one German div, while the 2nd British crossed into an area held by three German Para Divs — tough eggs.

The diverging opinions about the best time and place for the invasion were prompted more by practical motives than by vainglorious ones. Freshly trained American troops were pouring into Europe every day. Britain, however, was almost bereft of manpower. Montgomery was well aware of the consequences: a precipitous attack would risk the success of the operation — and the lives of ill-trained soldiers on the line.

"Our men were not sufficiently well trained at this stage in the campaign to be able to exploit against the professional German soldier in a hasty impromptu crossing," points out Major-General John Graham. "We couldn't overcome the shortage of leaders. By that time in the war the experienced corporals and sergeants had disappeared, been killed, and we were left with people who were really privates who had been promoted. (It still seems absurd that I was 21 and a major.) I think it would have been a pretty unwise commander who launched them into battle without the most thorough preparations."

So complex was Plunder that it begat five separate major operations under the umbrella plan: Flashpoint, Turnscrew, Torchlight, Widgeon, and Varsity.

The rail and road centre of Wesel was the focal point of the assault. Simpson's Ninth U.S. Army, comprising the same three corps that had starred at Grenade (Gillem's 13, Anderson's 16, and McLain's 19), had the responsibility for the crossing on an 11-mile sector of the Rhine south of Wesel. His assault divisions were 79th Division and the dependable "Workhorse" of Ninth Army, the 30th. Codenamed Flashpoint, this attack would be launched from two points near Rheinberg in the early hours of March 24.

It was judged that the assault would be less hazardous than the earlier one over the Roer. "A large river, slow of current, with ideal launching and landing sites, in which a mass of assault craft could be employed was to be preferred over a small, narrow, swift moving river," Simpson was advised by his planning staff.

Beyond the Rhine, the inferior roads in the American sector and two raised rail embankments could cause problems for the armour. Simpson arranged to send a corps through the British sector when it was cleared.

Second British Army would cross on a 12-mile front extending from Wesel north to Rees. (The Lippe River would be the inter-army boundary.) Lieutenant-General Sir Miles Dempsey — like Crerar, a craftsman in coordination and planning — was given command of this operation. The Jocks would spearhead the assault. Dempsey planned his attack with two corps — Horrocks's 30 Corps on the left at Rees and Lieutenant-General Sir Neil Ritchie's 12 Corps on the right at Xanten: these were Operations Turnscrew and Torchlight.

Turnscrew, the assault at Rees by 51st Highland Division, would be the first to jump off, at 2100 hours on the 23rd. Canada's Highland Brigade — the 9th CIB — was under command for the operation. Following the assault force, 43rd Wessex Division, 3rd British Division, and the armour (the Guards Armoured Division, 6th Guards Armoured Brigade, and 8th Armoured Brigade) would advance through and enlarge the bridgehead.

The reduction of Wesel required special tactics and a specialized force. One hour after the 51st launched their assault, 1st Commando Brigade would make a silent river crossing behind Wesel and — pausing at the bomb line while the RAF laid on a heavy raid — seize the town. This operation was named Widgeon.

While this was in progress, 15th Scottish Division would assault at 0200 hours on March 24, from Xanten, midway between Rees and Wesel. For Operation Torchlight, General Barber's two assaulting brigades were the 44th and the 227th. The 11th Armoured Division would move across for the breakout when a Class 40 bridge was erected.

The most unorthodox element of Plunder was the final phase of the strangely named miscellany of operations: Varsity. Thirteen hours after the infantry and commando forces had launched their Rhine assaults on March 23, some 14,000 airborne troops would be dropped or glided onto or near the high ground north of Wesel.

Their prime tasks were first to knock out Schlemm's gun emplacements overlooking the Rhine and then to deepen the bridgehead with all possible speed so that Second British Army and Ninth U.S. Army could link up and surge out across the German industrial interior.

Under the command of Major-General Matthew Ridgway's 18 Airborne Corps, two divisions — 6th British Airborne and 17th U.S. Airborne — were given this vital objective. To avoid the carnage of Arnhem and the confusion of Normandy, the assault would take place in daylight, directly on enemy targets, with artillery and ground troops already established nearby in support.

The vehicles and supplies necessary to equip a million and a quarter men for a river assault were of staggering quantity. By D-Day, over 250,000 tons of supplies had been amassed on the west bank for the two armies. The British alone had stockpiled 60,000 tons of ammunition and 30,000 tons of engineer stores. General Simonds's hard-fought-for and controversial one-way road-cum-rail line through the Hochwald Gap was put to good service.

Every shed, barn, and backyard along the river was crammed with goods, camouflaged to deceive the enemy (who were supposed to think the attack was coming from the north at Emmerich or from the south towards Homberg). Concealment was a major problem for the planners because the riverbank was under direct observation — and direct fire — from the east bank. All dumping had to take place behind the bunds, or flood dikes, that ran along both banks of the river. These were as much as 20 feet in height and 70 feet in depth.

While they offered protection, the dikes' steep sides also blocked the passage of the Buffaloes and amphibious duplex-drive tanks (DDs) that were an essential part of the operation. These powerful new swimming tanks were successfully pioneered at the Normandy invasion. They were actually Shermans with inflatable air tubes that could make them amphibious for water crossings. The troops called them Donald Ducks.

Sappers were delegated to ''gap'' the west bunds and ''carpet'' a route the night before the invasion.

A continuous 66-mile smokescreen — the longest in history —

masked the Allied buildup. Likened by British soldiers to a London fog, it was lifted just twice to allow assaulting commanders to make a brief reconnaissance of the crossing places (although with an unexpected shift of wind, one officer recalls it was more of a "watery-eyed squint"). More reliable recce was achieved from air photos and from models of Sorbo rubber or other composites that were created in amazing precision "down to the last telegraph post."

"Every single man right to the last private soldier in my battalion had at least 20 minutes looking at the most wonderful model of Bislich, our objective," recalls Brigadier Charles Richardson, CO of 6th Battalion, King's Own Scottish Borderers, 15th Scottish Division. "He knew exactly which five houses he had to take."

Over 5,000 guns had been assembled; the British had 3,411 artillery pieces, the Americans had 2,070. To get maximum range, they were stealthily moved up as far forward as possible during the night of D-minus-Two. The gunners were so close to the front that a number of them became ill from the chemical smoke.

The need for speed was imperative. To avoid injuring the airborne troops, it had been reluctantly agreed that the artillery barrage would cease entirely during their drop or landing. Commanders therefore felt extra pressure in capturing as much ground as possible before that deadline.

They had just 12 hours to move four divisions of men across the river and onto solid bridgeheads before the fire support was lost. Their first objective was to get the assaulting brigades onto the east bank "on a jeep and carrier basis" by first light. A subsequent objective was to have the amphibious tanks follow as soon after that as possible, to give early armoured support to the infantry.

A final objective was bridging the river. It took the first Rhine assaulter — Julius Caesar (c. 55 B.C.) — ten days to complete the construction of a bridge on which to cross the river. The Ninth U.S. Army engineers did somewhat better; they erected a 1,152-foot treadway bridge nine hours after the attack was launched. In anticipation of this vital task, a company of the 17th U.S. Armored Engineer Battalion trained intensively from March 9 until D-Day.

The force employed some 9,000 sappers or engineers. Three thousand of them, with a thousand truckloads of equipment, would converge on each divisional crossing site for bridging duties at H-Hour. The Royal Engineers were responsible for bringing up not only all bridging equipment, but also all storm boats and rafts, tugs, LCVs (landing craft vehicle), pontoons, anchors, and winches. The naval units of both countries were also involved in Plunder, providing LCVPs (landing craft vehicles and personnel) and LCMs (landing craft medium) to the assaulting forces.

Controlling the movement of all the troops and vehicles from the marshalling areas down to the banks required special Bank Control Units of hundreds of officers and men. Every vehicle due to cross within 48 hours of H-Hour was given a serial number in order of priority. Every unit and every vehicle was then called up in strict rotation and timing on the night of the assault.

The weather had turned warm and sunny. While they waited for Plunder to be launched, the troops of three armies enjoyed a few days' respite from war.

Dugouts safely out of range of enemy shells took on a strange glamour. "The dugout I took over was sheathed inside with beautiful wood," an officer of 3rd Canadian Infantry Division wrote. "Those German officers certainly had the best possible quarters. The roof was steel, laid with logs and covered by five feet of solid earth . . . nearly everyone had some fancy furniture, chesterfield suites, lovely mirrors hanging from trees, pianos, clocks, huge brass beds. . . ."

The Toronto Scottish Regiment enjoyed several elaborate mess dinners. "It was unbelievable, absolutely marvellous," Major William Whiteside of the Canadian Argyll & Sutherland Highlanders remembers. "They had rigged up a marquee to keep the rain out. Inside they had a dining room table, comfortable chairs, and a sofa. The corporal who handled the meal was in a white pea jacket and the table was laid with a white linen cloth. Platoon commanders were coming in and out, soaking wet from the rain, and here was the company commander drinking wine and enjoying his supper."

Food was plentiful; the farms and fields were full of it, although consuming it was officially disallowed. Major Joe Corcoran, company commander of 7th Battalion Argylls, had a call from his CO. "If you look out of your window you will see a pig being led towards your company area on a lead. Please see that it is released when it reaches you." Corcoran — who had been looking forward to that pig all morning — reluctantly concurred. Many another Jock who gazed longingly at a fine fat pullet or a plump pig had to practise self-denial.

Men of 5th Battalion King's Own Scottish Borderers were ordered to round up all the cattle, which were then to be returned to Holland and Belgium. "Each company had its own rodeo, working in the artificial fog," the battalion history noted.

However, SHAEF Intelligence warned the units to beware of certain enemy foods: "Information recently received from captured German saboteurs indicates that the Germans either are contemplating preparing or have prepared poisoned Nescafe, sugar, German cigarettes and German chocolate. German brand of chocolate Sarotte was especially mentioned."

On March 12, CIGS Field-Marshal Sir Alan Brooke piquantly recorded in his diary: "12:3:45!! It is sad that this date will not return for another 100 years! It looks so nice!"

That same day, intense training for the assault was begun. The men were drilled until they dropped. "The normal crew, 14 men, could barely carry the boats up the steep incline at first," a 79th U.S. Infantry Division after-action report commented. "After practice the difficulty was overcome."

The troops from both armies had day and night rehearsals in boat training. Lieutenant Hubert Campbell of 5th Battalion Black Watch recalls the confusion of the night rehearsal. "We hadn't seen the Buffaloes before and we hadn't had much practice in the dark. In the fog, we got turned around and landed downstream on the same bank we started from."

As there were not enough Buffaloes to carry all the assaulting troops, the lead British battalions would have their use and the reserve battalions were assigned storm boats. These boats gave considerable cause for concern. They were powered by Evinrude outboard engines that had a reputation of being hard to start and undependable.

The Scots established a miniature harbour where the boats could be started and warmed up ahead of the assault. The Americans went one better: "We wrapped each motor in chemical heating pads that we got from our medical people," explains Major-General Carrol Dunn, then a battalion commander of the 105th U.S. Engineers.

The commander of 1st Commando Brigade, Brigadier Derek Mills-Roberts, went right to the top with his criticism. The storm boats were "unreliable, high revving monstrosities," he complained to General Dempsey. Even after his Royal Electrical and Mechanical Engineers personnel had taken all the engines to pieces and tested them, lavishing "work, care, and blasphemy," they were useless. Dempsey went for a trial run. To Mills-Roberts's quiet delight, the army commander ended up adrift in the middle of the stream.

Troopers of 44th Royal Tank Regiment discovered that they were to man the amphibious tanks as the DD Regiment for the crossing, although they noted that "none of us [had] ever seen a DD, let alone travelled in one." They spent 10 intensive days learning how to navigate them in water and then how to service and fight them on land.

Ferry-craft had to do all the transport work until the bridges could be built. Vehicles were pre-loaded with essential supplies for the assaulting brigades, ready to be ferried over on call. As well, provision had to be made for evacuating casualties and enemy prisoners. With considerable ingenuity, American engineers pre-cut lengths of bridging material for the treadway bridges and staged rehearsals in assembling and installing them swiftly.

Security was tight. As part of the elaborate deception scheme, Ninth Army ordered that all shoulder patches and unit identifications on vehicles of the assaulting divisions be removed. Special deception units adopted these identifications and established dummy command posts with mocked-up installations farther south to mislead the enemy. Units from other corps sectors were required to duplicate any obvious movement of equipment or troops that could not be camouflaged. Patrolling was intensified to keep enemy infiltrators from discovering ammunition and bridging dumps. Ninth Army intelligence listed one final and extraordinary precaution: "Only specially selected men, who would not talk if captured, were used for reconnaissance across the river."

The 52nd Lowland Division was holding the west bank of the Rhine on the 15th Scottish front. (The 3rd British Division held the 51st Highlanders' start line.) So secret was the troop buildup that even the CO of 7/9th Battalion Royal Scots (52nd Lowland Division), Lieutenant-Colonel Hugh Rose, was amazed to see old friends from his sister battalion, 8th Royal Scots, moving up for pre-battle reconnaissance. (It was not uncommon to find battalions of the same regiment dispersed among several different brigades, often not even fighting in the same campaign or country.)

One of the 8th Royal Scots officers, Captain Bill Fargus, asked the Lowlanders in amusement: "What are things like down here?" "They said, 'Oh, it's desperately boring! Absolutely nothing happening here!' They had no idea there were about three divisions all piled up a couple of miles behind them, and that the biggest artillery barrage that war had ever seen was about to come down in six hours' time."

One of the tasks of Captain John McVie, signals officer with 7/9th

Royal Scots, was to locate German gun positions across the river by taking bearings on their gun flashes. Accomplishing this sometimes required extreme measures. "There was one occasion when the carrier platoon sat revving up their engines and yelling and screaming to try to get a bit of German gunfire going so we could spot it."

Miles of line was buried by signallers in the soft mud flood banks along the river to supply the vast Bank Control communications system. The Jocks used Weasels to get through the mud; in one case, the Americans commandeered a tractor and plough for the job. The moment the assault was launched, the lines would be hooked up across the river.

An important preliminary to Plunder was the Allied air forces' heavy bombing program. During the previous month, 7,311 sorties by Allied aircraft had dropped 31,635 tons of bombs on the road and rail systems of the Ruhr. On the final three days before Plunder, the bombers concentrated on German airfields and barracks.

On March 22, General Alfred Schlemm was working late into the night at his Tac HQ, trying to pull together his defensive forces against the expected Allied invasion. He glanced up from the pile of administrative orders on his desk to hear the familiar air-raid siren. Another bombing raid, he thought tiredly. Then an explosion rocked the room as a direct hit shattered the building.

Schlemm, severely wounded, was pulled out of the wreckage. He continued the command for another two days before he collapsed and was admitted to hospital with a fracture of the skull.

The noted Para commander's war was at an end. He had been in conflict almost as often with his own leader as with his enemy. Despite Hitler's erratic and unrealistic orders, Schlemm had maintained a brilliant holding action against the powerful Allied Rhineland operation and had achieved a disciplined withdrawal. General Guenther Blumentritt was rushed in to take command.

At 51st Division HQ, Major-General Thomas Rennie held an Orders Group on March 22. Major Thomas Landale Rollo, 7th Battalion Black Watch, remembers the close rapport Rennie had developed with his commanders. "By this time we had got to the stage that a lot of the planning was done automatically. General Rennie hardly said a word. He'd nod to our brigade commander: 'Jim, you'll do a thing here, and So-and-so, you'll do a thing there.' "

The Highland Division GOC was strangely uneasy about the coming operation, as General Horrocks later recalled: "I always thought Rennie had some foreboding about this battle. . . . I had never seen him so worried as he was over this Rhine project. He hated everything about it and I couldn't understand why. Like so many Highlanders, I believe he was 'fey.' "

A few miles to the south, General Eisenhower strolled among the waiting and nervous GIs, imparting cheerful wishes for success on the mission. Major-General Gerhardt, GOC 29th Infantry Division — one of Ninth Army's follow-up divisions — spotted one of his men wearing a Navy knit wool cap.

I flagged him down and spoke to the man, because we had very strict uniform regulations that required all personnel to wear helmets at all times. I asked this man what the idea was. He looked me in the eye and said, "General, what do you care what kind of hat I wear. We are going to cross the river and take that town for you." Giving no answer to this, I wished him well and told him to go ahead about his business. This man was killed in the assault.

For his part, Field-Marshal Montgomery, who hated having anyone peer over his shoulder when he was at work, was busily arranging just that. A letter from Brooke urging him to invite Churchill to view the Rhine assault had given him no option:

Now as regards the PM, do not take this matter too lightheartedly. In his mind you stopped him before Overlord . . . you tried to stop him in Normandy . . . I can tell you he is determined to come out for the crossing of the Rhine and is now talking of going up in a tank! . . . The best thing is to find some reasonably secure viewpoint (not too far back or there'll be hell to pay) to which he can be taken.

The 1,600 men of 1st Commando Brigade had learned their trade at Achnacarry, on the desolate slopes of Scotland's Ben Nevis Mountain.

"My sergeant-major used to say, 'The training at Achnacarry is far worse than any battle,' " recalls Captain J.A. Clovis, who fought with and finished as an instructor to No. 6 Army Commando. "I believe it.

"The commandos were hand-picked from other services, volunteers. I think they were 100 per cent better than anybody else. They'd do anything. If you said, 'Climb up that wall to the roof,' they'd do it. Nothing was impossible when you got in that frame of mind, because they'd been trained like robots.

"You started off with road work — 10, 20 miles — and then you'd go to the top of Ben Nevis and bivouac there for the night with one blanket per man.

"All our exercises were done with live ammunition. No blanks. And then we had karate, but it wasn't karate in those days. It was 'unarmed combat.' We had milling contests where you filled a boxing ring with about 30 chaps. The one who stood up at the end was the winner.

"We were all qualified paratroopers. When we were down at Brighton with Mills-Roberts we trained in landings day in and day out. If you didn't do it properly you went back again and again. You'd be wet through. The next morning you had to be on parade with everything shining."

At one minute before 2200 hours on March 23, the first Buffaloes — already loaded with green-bereted men of No. 46 Royal Marine Commando — lumbered clumsily over the dike. At 2200 hours they roared over the shingle banks of the Rhine into the murky water. Operation Widgeon was on.

A three-quarter moon filtered through the acrid screen of smoke that shrouded the battlefield. It was eclipsed by the darting beams of artificial moonlight and the brilliant flashes of tracers and gunfire. The men hunched anxiously down in the wallowing craft cast ghostly shadows.

The staccato explosions of 5,000 guns erupted in a single, solid roar. Shells bursting over the eastern bank screamed like so many freight trains rushing through the night. The fire seemed to blanket the entire shore; it was hard to imagine how anything could stay alive on the other side of the river.

The Buffaloes coursed against the heavy current, submerged with only a foot of freeboard. In just three and a half minutes they had crossed the 300-yard-wide river and were nosing up the grey banks of the enemy shore. A phosphorus mortar hit one Buffalo and flames shot 15 feet into the air. Several men struggled out, wounded and burning. Nine were killed. Trained never to hesitate, the Commando swept past the carnage and swiftly overran the German trenches and their gun emplacements in the houses beyond.

Mills-Roberts, commanding 1st Commando Brigade, crossed with the first wave. He had deliberately chosen this improbable mud flat as a landing site. Wesel, a town of 24,000 inhabitants, was strongly held. A frontal assault was impossible. He therefore planned to slip in from the side and surprise the German defenders. With luck, the entire brigade of 1,600 men could be ashore and deployed to the outskirts of the city in 45 minutes, before the enemy artillery woke up to the fact.

Next to cross was No. 6 Army Commando. Their job was to move through the bridgehead and lead the remaining three Commandos — Nos. 46 and 45 Royal Marine Commandos and No. 3 Army Commando — into Wesel. But No. 6 Commando had drawn the storm boats, which were at their temperamental worst that day. One, as the CO, Lieutenant-Colonel A.D. Lewis, recalls, got in serious difficulties: "One boat was overladen. When the driver took off, the thing dove straight into the water. Many of the men had their rucksacks still on their backs (instead of loosening them as they were meant to once they got aboard), and some were drowned with the weight of them.

"My second-in-command happened to be in that boat. Fortunately, he had taken off his rucksack so he was rescued. He used to wear a monocle quite frequently, so the *Daily Mirror* came out with a headline: 'Monocled Major Swims the Rhine.' "

Many boats were hit by enemy fire, and there were also casualties to the engineers who launched the craft. Regimental Sergeant-Major Woodcock had three boats shot from under him before he managed to effect a crossing.

Nevertheless, No. 6 Commando was across within 15 minutes of the launching of the assault, and Buffaloes transported the remaining two Commandos without mishap. The time was 2230 hours; just half an hour had elapsed.

The brigade paused. Overhead they could see the leading RAF Pathfinder flying low over Wesel as he dropped his brilliant red flares to mark the targets. Two hundred and fifty Lancasters followed. In a remarkable demonstration of precision bombing, Bomber Command dropped 1,100 tons of high explosives on the town, while the waiting Commandos crouched little more than half a mile away.

"For fifteen minutes nothing could be heard but the shriek of the descending bombs and the terrible explosions as they burst . . . only a thousand yards away," the Commando history reports. "The whole town looked as if it had been picked up and dropped down again," remembers Lieutenant David Ward. "It was totally on fire."

German prisoners were commandeered to carry some of the equipment. Mills-Roberts overheard two Commando soldiers comparing the merits of the POWs as they plodded towards the town. '' 'I've got a fine big bugger 'ere, 'e's doing grand,' one soldier said to his pal. His companion grudgingly agreed, 'My little bugger isn't doing too bad neither.' ''

Mills-Roberts had perfected a method of advance and infiltration by night that had already been used successfully in Normandy: the entire brigade moved forward in single file, following a trail of white tape laid by the lead Commando team.

''It was a major operation, laying 5,000 yards of tape,'' Lieutenant-Colonel Lewis recalls. ''The tape was on reels. As we moved forward in single file, the man ahead carried the reels on his back. The soldier behind him would pull the tape out and stamp it in the ground.

''Seventy men were involved, some protecting the tape party and some being the tape party. One of the major problems was that, being in the lead, we had to cope with enemy opposition while at the same time staying on direction with map and compass and laying the tape.

''Luckily, the opposition was fairly feeble. The Germans were stunned. All the fight had been taken out of them by the aerial attack. I can remember going down to a cellar to establish my HQ and finding 17 German soldiers down there, all lying in their bunks. There was no sort of control or command at that stage. The people fought as individuals.''

The Commandos arrived in Wesel at midnight. Fighting patrols fanned out over the town and small battles erupted everywhere. The 13th-century Hanseatic city was in ruins.

''The streets were unrecognisable,'' Mills-Roberts recalled. ''Many of the buildings were mere mounds of rubble. Huge craters abounded and into these flowed water mains and sewers, accompanied by escapes of flaming gas.''

By dawn, 400 prisoners had been taken. No. 45 Royal Marine Commando was firmly established in a large factory (''full of hundreds of thousands of lavatory pans!'' Ward recalls). A brigade signals group — ''swinging from girder to girder several hundred feet above the Rhine, under spasmodic fire'' — managed to lay a telephone line across the river.

By chance, Lewis's headquarters was across a small garden from the headquarters of the garrison commander, Major-General Friedrich-Wilhelm Deutsch, GOC of 16th Flak Division. A patrol from No. 6 Commando, led by Woodcock, discovered the general and his staff in their underground shelter. "Deutsch became very aggressive, quite dangerous," Lewis remembered. "He had to be shot."

A map revealing all the German flak dispositions was discovered in the HQ. This would be of inestimable assistance in knocking out the installations prior to the airborne drop. The details were relayed back immediately over the Royal Artillery signal net.

Later in the morning, the counter-attacks began. "It got a bit rough towards 9:45 a.m.," Ward figured. "Our airborne were coming in at 10:00 a.m. so at 9:50 our artillery had to stop. We weren't even allowed to fire a two-inch mortar. And that is when the Germans came back."

"At 1:30 p.m., down came the long-awaited artillery support," Mills-Roberts said. "This was the turning point in the whole battle and now I felt that the brigade was secure in Wesel."

The assault moved "like clockwork" on all fronts. "The firepower was awesome," recalls Lieutenant-Colonel Harold Hassenfelt, operations officer, 30th U.S. Infantry Division. "The Germans that we captured came back mumbling; they were just stunned."

Sergeant William L. McBride of the American 311th Field Artillery Battalion snatched a moment to scribble "300,000" on a shell, marking the 300,000th shell the U.S. artillery had fired off in the space of one hour. Forty thousand men were employed in the task. During the artillery preparation, mortars fired 1,000 rounds on the far shore to detonate mines.

For the Americans, Operation Flashpoint was a triumph of organization and of cooperation between the infantry; the artillery, who lifted the barrage with pinpoint accuracy as the riflemen reached the enemy shores; the navy, who operated the boats; and the engineers, who handled the loading and landing.

Nothing was left to chance. Both the 30th and the 79th Infantry Divisions had sent patrols across to reconnoitre the terrain in detail. Tracer bullets were fired over the heads of the troops of the first wave to direct their way. Then red, green, and blue flashlights and luminous markers were set in place to guide each company by colour to its exact landing place.

"We were not to land until we saw two white phosphorus shells land in front of us," recalled First Lieutenant Whitney Refvem, who commanded one of the assault companies of 117th Infantry Regiment. "That would be the signal for us that the [artillery] preparation was being lifted.

"There was no real fight to it. The artillery had done the job for us. It was timed perfectly, timed so as to lift just in front of us as we advanced. After climbing out of the boats the leading platoons ran from the river to the dike, hitting some trip wires which ignited trip flares of all colours. That was the signal for enemy mortar fire, most of which fell behind us.

"We captured a German soldier at the dike and used him as a guide through the minefields. We reached the town without encountering any mines, [taking] prisoners as we went."

Only the boats were uncooperative. The assault battalions used 54 storm boats powered by 25hp motors and 30 double assault boats with 22hp motors. Shells, currents, and overloading dumped some. Others stalled and were swept downstream.

"On the way over, my boat sank and the Colonel picked me up," recalled Captain John Potts, S-3 of 315th Regiment, 79th Division. " 'Colonel gathers staff as he crosses Rhine' would make a good headline," he added wryly.

Before dawn on the 24th, both American divisions had crossed the Rhine and were wiping up the German coastline defences with ease. "Our assault companies went so quickly they overran enemy positions without discovering them," Potts noted. "When our reserve company came up they found an underground concrete bunker that contained a good many civilians. On investigation, 15 German soldiers were discovered, some of whom were forward observers."

Casualties in the two-hour crossing were the lowest on record for a major American operation: they totalled 31, including several cases of exposure from tipped boats.

The all-time record for bridge construction under combat conditions was established by the 2nd U.S. Armored Division. At H-Hour, division engineers launched into action. Working under enemy fire, they constructed two rafts for ferrying vehicles across. The long-planned 1,152-foot treadway bridge was then built and open to traffic by mid-afternoon. Three hours later, a raft with a tank aboard smashed it. Undeterred, the engineers set to again and had the bridge rebuilt by 0200 hours the morning of March 25.

In a message of congratulations, Major-General I.O. Inglis, CRE, 21st Army Group, signalled Brigadier-General Richard U. Nicholas, Corps of Engineers, Ninth U.S. Army: "Successful operation of boats and rafts and completion of six bridges by D-plus-Two permitted the establishment of 5 divisions by D-plus-Four, I believe astonished the world."

"Opposition was so light that hopes were running high among the American men and officers that they were engaged in the war's last campaign in Europe," wrote United Press staff correspondent Clinton B. Conger, who crossed with 79th Division assault troops.

In the north, the 51st Highland Division, leading off first in Operation Turnscrew, also completed a swift — although more costly — Rhine assault. The division's objective was to establish a bridgehead at Rees. Here the river varied from 300 to 450 yards wide. The old meanders of the Rhine had created a number of islands that became obstacles to the assaulting force.

Pipers led the Cameron Highlanders forward to the marshalling area. General Rennie moved among his Jocks with a reassuring word. They were about to make history in the epic crossing, he told them proudly. But Major Rollo did not leave the history-making to chance: "My job was to cross and be the beachmaster, so I was in the first wave. I had our signaller with me — we were on a DUKW. I said to him, 'The moment this DUKW touches the other side, you give a message that 7th Black Watch is first across,' and he did that. Three minutes after we left, the message went back to Battalion and then to Brigade, Division, and Corps: We were the first!"

The lead Highland battalions crossed in Buffaloes: "Soft stuff, right enough," commented one Scot, recalling the canvas craft of his previous assaults. As the first Buffalo hit the water, the "slick, lovely Scottish machine" (as one admiring Jock described it) went into action. Into the first craft piled sapper delousing parties bent on clearing the enemy shores of mines, and signalmen hauling submarine cable to connect up communications with the far side. The Bank Control officers began calling the serial numbers that alerted the battalions when they could pass through. Medical aid units were moved in.

The follow-up battalions were forced to clamber aboard the despised storm boats. Within half an hour of starting, only a dozen of the 30 storm boats originally available were serviceable. As each boat took only 10 men, the riflemen were delayed by as much as two hours in crossing. Fifty sappers were killed or drowned ferrying them across.

Foremost in the lineup were gun crews of 545th Mountain Battery, specially trained for the Rhine assault. Their 3.7 Howitzers — the only guns that could cross by Buffalo — and the intrepid men who hauled them up and down stairs and over rubble in the ensuing battle were the heroes of Scotland that day. It was Goch revisited: brutal, hand-to-hand street fighting and town-clearing, only this time in a succession of towns clustered near the river named Rees, Speldrop, and Bienen.

Every house was fought for, one by one. It was the Highlanders' bad fortune that von Luettwitz had been ordered — over his strong protestations — to split his corps, sending his 116th "Windhund" Panzer Division to stop the American assault on the Ruhr, and the 15th Panzer Grenadier Division to block the Jocks in the Rhine fortifications.

In Speldrop, the Black Watch were counter-attacked by seasoned 15th Panzer troops with 88mms and self-propelled guns. One platoon became trapped. The Highland Light Infantry of Canada, under temporary command of 51st Division and hence the first Canadian battalion to cross the Rhine, was ordered in to the rescue. The HLI battled throughout the next day and on into the night, with the Canadian North Nova Scotia Highlanders joining in one of the toughest struggles any of the Highland troops could remember.

In their operation, called Torchlight, the 15th Scottish met softer resistance. They made their assault from Xanten, six miles upstream. Here, too, the storm boats caused problems. Lieutenant-Colonel Richardson of 6th King's Own Scottish Borderers submitted a strong report afterwards. "I recommended that the storm boat not be used again. A lot of my men had to paddle with their rifle butts or hands, landing hundreds of yards downstream." Fortunately, Richardson's objective, Bislich, was landmarked by a prominent white house. His men had no problem making their way back to it and taking their objective.

"About halfway across the engine packed up and the driver could not get it started again," remembers an assault soldier in another battalion. "We cursed and swore at him but of course it did not help. By this time we were getting scared, the current was very strong and we were being swept downstream. . . . Luckily for us, the very wide awake driver of a DUKW saw our predicament and came to our rescue."

With bullets whizzing overhead, the craft finally landed. First out, to the young rifleman's astonishment, was a photographer. "He took his pictures which appeared on the front cover of the next edition of *War Illustrated*, much to my parents' astonishment. . . . I admired his courage, taking all these risks just for a few photographs.''

(Photographic units were with all leading elements of Ninth Army in the Rhine crossing, too. During the first four days, 79 radio photos were sent from London to New York, receiving front-page coverage in the New York papers. Ninth Army Press Camp had 39 accredited correspondents. They filed 226 stories totalling 74,510 words, including broadcasts.)

The next day dawned fine and clear. Four divisions of Scottish riflemen were safely over the Rhine and — with the exception of 154th Brigade — had consolidated swiftly on their first objectives. Casualties had been slight in most sectors, and morale was soaring. The scene that greeted the weary men was ''more like the Henley regatta'' than war:

The banks were crowded with men and vehicles [44th Brigade's history records]. The storm-boats, rafts and Buffaloes plied backwards and forwards with their loads, every moment landing more stuff on the east bank; and the DD tanks, like strange canvas boxes, dived into the water and swam slowly across, emerged on the far bank, shook themselves, deflated, and then miraculously appeared as Sherman tanks again.

At 7th Black Watch HQ, General Rennie, who had crossed the Rhine with his men, warmly congratulated the battalion on being the first over. As he climbed back in his jeep and moved away, a concentration of mortar bombs came down. Rennie's vehicle received a direct hit.

''Are you all right, sir?'' his aide-de-camp asked. There was no reply. Rennie died almost immediately. After 45 days of almost continual action — and over five years of continual war — this spirited Scot lost his life leading his division onto its final objective of the Rhineland campaign.

''The General's dead.'' Word of the tragedy reached the battalion commanders. ''You musn't tell anyone yet,'' they were admonished. ''Not until this business is over.''

The battle raged on, but the keen elation of victory was dulled.

Top Secret. Personal and Eyes Only for CIGS from Field-Marshal Montgomery, 24 Mar 45:
Op Plunder was launched successfully last night and by dawn this morning 2nd Army had 5 infantry brigades over the Rhine and 16 US corps of 9th US army had got 13 battalions across. The commando brigade is complete in Wesel and is mopping up that place. About 1200 prisoners had been taken by dawn. Resistance during the night was not very great but it began to stiffen somewhat at dawn and several counterattacks were put in.

As 10 a.m. approached, the guns fell silent. It was H-Hour for Operation Varsity, the 18 Airborne Corps assault. All eyes turned westward as the great sky train appeared on the horizon.

21

Winged Soldiers

THE ARMADA FILLED the airspace, its birds of conquest wheeling in beautiful and terrifying formations. The sky, moments before blue and benign, became dark. Ten thousand aircraft plunged through the dense curtain of smoke. Many never returned.

The scramble to create and meld this vast column had been a herculean effort. At 18 U.S. Airborne Corps HQ near Paris on a raw morning on February 9 — the day after Operation Veritable was launched, and the day before Grenade was postponed — Major-General Matthew Ridgway had learned of his mission. With barely six weeks to formulate a plan, he was ordered to organize and mount an airborne assault across the Rhine. The veteran parachute leader's mandate in devising Varsity was to neutralize or destroy the German gun positions on the east bank of the Rhine.

Montgomery was convinced that an early cessation of the war depended on the combined Allied forces cutting through the enemy's Rhine defences and breaking out onto the Ruhr plain. The enemy firepower was potent enough to delay or even endanger the Rhine assault by ground troops. Swift deepening of the bridgehead was essential, so that tanks could be brought into the fight.

Just getting a foothold on the bridgehead was not enough. The enemy could contain the attack for precious days or weeks, as he had on the Normandy beaches. Without the rapid and deep expansion of the bridgehead that only an airborne assault could provide, the ground troops on the Rhine could be similarly stalled.

Ridgway learned that the enemy controlled a high ridge running along the heavily treed Diersfordter Wood, some four miles inland from the eastern banks of the Rhine. It would be from this ridge,

---

See Map 12 (Appendix B).

with its clear view of the Westphalian plain sloping down to the marshy riverbank, that enemy artillery spotters could call down fire on any assaulting troops attempting to cross the Rhine. And from those shadowy woods, well-entrenched and camouflaged enemy guns and infantry would be capable of inflicting terrible damage and holding off any invaders trying to advance inland. The delaying tactics that had hampered the Allied advance through the Rhineland could not be allowed to occur again.

Ridgway and his deputy commander, Lieutenant-General Sir Richard Gale, conceived a daring scheme. A force of over 14,000 airborne soldiers would be committed in a single, simultaneous massed daylight attack, virtually on top of the waiting gun positions of trained German anti-airborne troops.

The 6th British Airborne Division and the 17th American Airborne Division, two units of General Lewis Brereton's First Allied Airborne Army, would mass this greatest air armada in history. Ten thousand aircraft — reconnaissance, bomber, fighter, paratroop carrier, tug aircraft, and glider — would cram the airspace over the Rhine. In barely two hours, this mammoth combat force would land troops, tanks, transport vehicles, fuel, ammunition, and heavy equipment on an area less than six miles long and five miles wide.

The lessons of Normandy and Arnhem could not be ignored. Ridgway had learned the importance of keeping his forces intact and in close proximity both to the enemy and to the supporting Allied infantry and artillery. In Normandy, where the airborne made a night drop, 75 per cent of the men were missing for a considerable period. In Arnhem, airborne troops had been landed in stages, well behind German positions. In the confusion of the landings, they became separated from one another and from their supplies, and still had an exhausting 10-mile forced march before encountering the enemy — or linking up with the landborne assault. As well, the gliders' designated landing zones were so distant from the parachute drops that the paratroops were unable to provide much support. This led to carnage of the trapped airborne division when the infantry and armour failed to drive through to the rescue.

Borrowing from the past, Ridgway strove to ensure the best chance of survival for these Anglo-American parachutists and glider troops, while achieving a swift and sure victory. His concept broke new ground. A frontal, daylight airborne attack could effectively eliminate enemy opposition. But the danger in plunging this vast horde of men into such a confined area concerned him deeply. They would have none of the advantages of surprise that had marked previous nighttime airborne assaults. Nor would the parachutists' DZs (drop zones) and the gliders' LZs (landing zones) be a safe distance from enemy strongpoints.

To counter the danger to his men created by an opposed assault — attacking directly into the muzzles of the German anti-aircraft defences — Ridgway relied heavily on the combined air strengths of the American and British bombers to smash the ack-ack guns. In the three days prior to the assault, the RAF (83 and 84 Groups) flew 1,500 sorties with their Spitfires, Hurricanes, and Typhoons over enemy territory, dropping some 10,000 tons of explosives and firing the lethal Typhoon rockets on all known enemy gun positions, airstrips, bridges, and supply lines. Over 2,500 heavy bombers of the Ninth and Fifteenth U.S. Air Forces similarly pounded areas that menaced the drop.

To avert confusion with so many varied air force units involved, Group Captain Paul Davoud, a Canadian commanding 83 Group RAF, was given overall command. "I had complete operational control of over 600 fighters and fighter bombers in the Rhine crossing," he recalled.

The airborne troops' greatest safeguard lay in a dramatic reversal of their traditional role. Instead of spearheading the invasion, to be followed in hours or even days by ground troops, the airborne men would land after the initial commando and infantry river crossing had been launched. Further, the DZs would be within range of Allied artillery, offering the initial support of the barrage prior to the drop, and subsequent support in blasting out nests of enemy opposition. Ridgway hoped the German land defence would thus be silenced.

It would also be blinded. A dense smokescreen would be maintained in a continuous 66-mile line along the river to mask Allied movements of troops and vehicles and their artillery dispositions.

A total of 889 aircraft from the British and American tactical air forces would escort the great air train to the Rhine. Another 2,153 fighter aircraft from RAF Fighter Command and the Ninth U.S. Air Force would blanket the armada on its approaches over the Rhine and sweep the skies in a 50-mile radius. It would be virtually impossible for any German predators — even the new Messerschmidt-262 jet fighters — to penetrate that screen and attack from above.

The coordination and timing of this huge operation had absorbed Ridgway's France-based staff for four weeks. Now it was time to transfer the plan from paper and engrave it indelibly on the minds of the men who were to take the ultimate responsibility for its success.

Early in March, Major-General William E. (''Bud'') Miley, commander of 17th U.S. Airborne Division, and his counterpart Major-General Eric Bols, recently appointed commander of the 6th British Airborne, were given full particulars of the operation for the first time. And on March 6, at the 6th Airborne HQ on blustery Salisbury Plain, the commanders and support personnel of the six British parachute and three airlanding glider battalions committed to the operation were briefed.

As they examined a full-scale model of the divisions' attack zone, with detailed maps and blown-up aerial photos of the DZs as a backdrop, the objectives of the drop and its revolutionary plan of attack were revealed to the astonished commanders. A daylight attack, jumping directly on enemy gun posts — in startled silence, the veteran leaders' first reaction to the complex undertaking was one of dismay. But as they grasped the full impact, they recognized the advantages of being able to see their DZs, of identifying landmarks, and above all of having the massive support — far more potent in daylight — of ground and air weapons and infantry backup. This outweighed the threat, however ominous, of being a visible target for the waiting German guns during the descent.

The concept was dazzling. Wing tip to wing tip, two divisions flying abreast in ''nine-ship elements'' (nine aircraft wide) stretched back some three miles in aerial length. Over 14,000 men and all their equipment would drop or be landed in gliders, all in less than an hour.

The parachutists would lead the attack. Those from the 6th British Airborne were assigned the task of clearing the enemy from designated landing areas before the ungainly gliders made their wobbling descents. The 17th U.S. Airborne glider troops would, however, clear their own LZs. Then, both glider and para men would attack critical strongpoints and bridges located within five to ten miles of the Rhine, holding them until ground troops could fight their way east from the river to relieve them.

Impressed by the detail of the operation and the confidence of the men commanding it, the commanders felt their doubts dispelled. It could work, they reasoned — and by God, they would make it work.

The aerial photographs revealed a horseshoe-shaped pocket of land formed by a bend in the fast-flowing waters of the Rhine on the west and south, and by the Issel Canal and Issel River on the east. Within this pocket were a number of wooded areas interspersed with small fields. It was hoped that these clearings, although of minimal size, would provide adequate landing and drop zones for the glider men and paratroopers.

However, there were several major obstacles posed by this five-by-six-mile tract. In the centre of it rose the Schneppenberg Rise, the 150-foot-high ridge controlled by the enemy in the Diersfordter Wood. Several of the meadows selected for the drop were encircled by outcroppings of smaller woods. In some cases, the breadth of the paratroop transport planes in the fly-in was actually greater than the width of the drop zone. The danger of having men land in the trees seemed almost inevitable.

The Issel River and its connecting canal flowed from the village of Hamminkeln southwest to Wesel, on the Rhine, four miles away. These water barriers were important tactical objectives. They also posed dangerous landing obstructions to parachutists and gliders. Until the Issel bridges were secured, the entire infantry and armoured breakout would be stalled.

The 194th U.S. Glider Infantry Regiment under Colonel James Pierce was given the task of attacking and holding three of the bridges. It would not be easy. After the spring thaw, the Issel's width was swollen to some 60 feet of swiftly moving water. The 6th British Airlanding Brigade, Brigadier Hugh Bellamy in command, would land specially trained coup-de-main bridge-raiding forces at Hamminkeln with orders to capture the town and seize its bridges intact.

Finally, three additional hazards would plague the invaders in their attack: the sandbank of a still-unfinished autobahn that ran broadside to the river, a rail line, and a high-tension power line on 100-foot pylons.

The complete drop of the four British and American parachute assault units with their weapons and ammunition, plus their support force of signallers, engineers, artillery FOOs, mortars, machine-gun and anti-tank units, medics, and even padres would take a mere 10 minutes. Their first task would be to knock out the flak guns defending the LZs of the incoming gliders to ensure safe landing of the essential glider cargo of equipment, arms, vehicles, and troops.

The Allied airborne planners were confident that they knew the disposition of the German troops — but what about their guns?

Enemy anti-aircraft fire was considered to be the most serious threat to the success of the assault.

Extensive aerial photographic reconnaissance missions were sent out. An anti-flak committee of 83 Group RAF plotted the disposition of these dangerous ack-ack guns on flak maps. Fighter and bomber attacks were subsequently laid on, up to the very moment of the parachute fly-in.

However, the Germans countered this by continually changing and adding new gun positions to their defences. Allied planners then scrambled to add these to the defence overlays (the map captured by the commandos from General Deutsch's HQ in Wesel was a valuable contribution) — and even by radio communication directly to the gunners up to the last minute — but the enemy batteries never were fully catalogued. And they were never even remotely close to being silenced.

An after-action report stated: "An estimate of the number of AA guns . . . on 17 March was 153 light and 103 heavy. Less than a week later, just before Operation Plunder began, the figures had risen to 712 light and 114 heavy."

The gun positions were so numerous that the best the American and British artillery could do was to spread their fire around so that at least all the targets were covered, if only sketchily. A fire plan of more comprehensive "milk round" stonks (concentrations of artillery on a single target) was impossible. Moreover, some enemy batteries were beyond range of all but a few guns.

A key part of the anti-flak protection was a 30-minute pounding on the menacing German ack-ack guns scheduled immediately prior to the para drop. The timing of the fly-in was therefore critical.

Allied intelligence assumed — with the complacency that had often been its trademark during Operation Veritable — that after the bitter Rhineland campaign, the German forces that had escaped across the Rhine would be shattered, with severe losses of arms and vehicles and lowered morale. "The enemy morale allowed chances to be taken," considered Major-General Bols, GOC 6th British Airborne Division.

However, elements of General Schlemm's First Parachute Army had been identified in enemy dispositions. In particular, the order of battle included Meindl's 2 Parachute Corps with Erdmann's still-potent 7th Parachute Division, Plocher's 6th Parachute and Wedehn's 8th Parachute, forces that had so vigorously opposed the Scottish and Welsh advances from Goch to Weeze. These units had been reinforced and re-equipped since the Rhine evacuation.

It was dangerously optimistic to believe that the indomitable spirit of these German parachutists might falter now. They had, after all, been pushed back across the Rhine only after 31 continuous days of heavy fighting.

In a postwar interrogation, Lieutenant-General Gustav Hoehne, commander of 2nd Parachute Division, confirmed that "morale was fairly high and this was especially true in the Fallschirm [parachute] divisions." He noted, however, that material losses and lack of equipment hampered Army Group H to a very great extent. "At one time Army Group H had 50,000 men for whom there were no weapons."

The significance of the fact that the coming clash would pit paratrooper against paratrooper was not remarked upon. Yet the elite German parachutists, now fighting in an infantry role, would be especially alert to all the parachute and glider combat tactics. They knew all the tricks; they had been the route themselves just a few months earlier in the Ardennes.

They knew that it was the hulking, swaying gliders that made a rich, irresistible — and virtually foolproof — target for the defenders. A German officer, Major Sepp Krafft, had made a detailed examination of the bullet and shell holes — and even the bloodstains — found in crashed Allied gliders at Arnhem. "Gliders are most vulnerable between casting off and landing," he stressed, urging his artillery units to concentrate their fire on gliders because they were "larger and slower targets."

His advice was carefully followed. His gunners had to sleep fully clothed at their gun posts in readiness for the attack. The gliders never had a chance.

While the enemy steeled himself for the ordeal to come, the Allied combat troops in France and England laboured hard to master all the details of the operation.

Within the camps, briefing at all levels became intense. Each man was required to recite his objectives and identifying landmarks of his RV (rendezvous) to his fellows.

"It is never a very pleasant thing to be pitchforked out of the air into the unknown," noted Brigadier Bellamy, Commander 6th Airlanding Brigade, "if you are not confident in what you are going to do."

Above all, these men were confident. This was to be the third operation of the war for troops of the British 6th Airborne Division, which comprised eight British battalions and one Canadian

Major Louis Froggett of the RHLI views the German Panther tank that his company knocked out on the Goch-Calcar road. (Courtesy: Mrs. Hugh Arrell)

German 88mm on the Goch-Calcar road, February 19, 1945. (Courtesy: Mrs. Hugh Arrell)

German prisoners at Calcar, February 26, 1945. (J.H. Smith/DND/Public Archives of Canada/PA-145761)

Sappers of RCE lift rails to create road from Goch to Xanten. (Jack H. Smith/DND/Public Archives of Canada/PA-145745)

Aerial view of the Hochwald Gap. Note the railroad track through the cutting. Point 73 at the entrance was an Algonquin objective. (Wilfrid Laurier University Archives)

Sherman Tank destroyer in forest near Xanten, March 9, 1945. (K. Bell/Public Archives of Canada/DND/PA-137463)

A tall Story? British Guards meet U.S. allies. (IWM #B15232)

Sergeant Alexander Drabik of 9th Armored Division, U.S. 1st Army, was the first man to cross the Rhine River at the Remagen railroad bridge. (Courtesy: USAMHI)

The bridge at Remagen. (NA)

RCAMC stretcher-bearers load casualties at Sonsbeck. (Jack H. Smith/Public Archives of Canada/PA-113872)

Shermans of Governor General's Foot Guards at Sonsbeck, March 1945.
(Jack H. Smith/DND/Public Archives of Canada/PA=113682)

Private Eddie Gagné, Régiment de Maisonneuve, drinks tea outside Schloss Moyland. (Michael M. Dean/DND/National Archives of Canada/PA-170265)

Dinner time: the Argyll & Sutherland Highlanders of Canada at Veen. (Jack H. Smith/DND/Public Archives of Canada/PA-145739)

Canadian troops gloat over captured Nazi flag in Xanten, March 1945. (K. Bell/Public Archives of Canada/PA=137461)

Major Fred Tilston VC: an obstinate Canadian. (Public Archives of Canada/PA=132827)

Mail from home, read in comfort. (Public Archives of Canada/PA-137456)

Looking out from the Hochwald at a captured anti-tank gun position where Tilston won his VC. (Public Archives of Canada/PA-113683)

Brooke, Churchill, and Monty view the airborne assault over the Rhine. (USAMHI #RG4195)

Devastated Wesel: note the numerous shell craters. (US Air Force #56831A.C)

Glider troops of the 1st Allied Airborne Army leave their gliders and prepare for enemy resistance near Wesel — part of the greatest airborne invasion in history. (Courtesy: USAMHI)

HRH Princess Elizabeth and Brigadier James Hill, Commander 3rd Parachute Brigade, watch a training jump.
(Courtesy: Brig Hill)

U.S. airborne men band together before advancing through barbed wire defences. A parachute hangs in the tree at left.
(Courtesy: USAMHI)

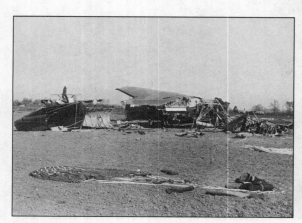

A wrecked glider. (IWM #BV2546)

Lieutenant-Colonel Jeff Nicklin, Co 1st Canadian Parachute Battalion. (Courtesy: Lt-Col Fraser Eadie)

battalion. They had seen half their number killed or wounded in the D-Day invasion and the subsequent three-month offensives in Normandy and the Ardennes. Now they were back to strength, well trained and fit. Morale had never been higher.

Prospects were certainly less reassuring for parachutists of Major-General Miley's 17th U.S. Airborne Division. Operation Varsity would be the division's first airborne assault. After fighting in an infantry role during the German counter-attack in the Ardennes, "Bud" Miley's "Golden Talons" had been seriously depleted by heavy casualties.

"The stupendousness of the task ahead in preparing for an airborne operation on such short notice was apparent," Miley noted. "The division had just completed the most rigorous campaign the American army had ever fought. Casualties had been so heavy that some rifle companies had less than 40 men of their original strength and some were without officers. The division was about 4,000 officers and men under strength."

Moving to their divisional headquarters at Chalons-sur-Marne in France during the second week of February, they found that not only were their quarters not completed, but they were engulfed in mud from the spring thaws. Miley gave the division four days to set up new housekeeping facilities, pitch tents, repair roads, and build kitchen and latrine facilities.

Troop carrier units from 9th U.S. Troop Carrier Command similarly discovered that only a dozen battered, shell-cratered airfields were available from which to launch their part of the operation. Frantic efforts were made by over 3,000 Allied engineers and 750 French construction workers to restore the airstrips to usable condition.

The 17th Airborne faced the urgent task of training fresh reinforcements, some of whom were unfamiliar with gliders and combat jumping. Of the division's three regimental combat teams in Operation Varsity (the 513th and 507th Parachute Infantry Regiments and the 194th Glider Infantry Regiment), only the 507th — "Raff's Ruffians," under command of Colonel Edson Raff — had had combat experience prior to the Ardennes battle. Raff had led his men on combat missions in North Africa and later in Normandy.

But many of the parachutists of the 513th U.S. Parachute Infantry Battalion were — until Varsity — callow youngsters. "I guess you'd call us a rowdy bunch," Captain Albert Wing, company commander in the 513th, remembers. "We had one boy who was only 15 when he came (I found out later), about a dozen that were 16, and a couple of dozen were 17. The 15s and 16s were illegal; the 17s with parental permission were OK.

"Another thing, most of them were shorter than I was (I was only five-foot-ten) and weighed about 145 to 150 pounds. We used to handle heavy loads and I remember we were concerned about the little fellows being able to carry that much weight." (Each soldier carried his own rifle valise containing rifles, ammunition, radio batteries, explosives, and other battle essentials. The weight of the bag — 200 pounds or more — made it necessary to lower it on a 12-foot length of rope at the critical moment to slow the descent of the jumper just before he landed.)

In fact, the CO of 2nd Battalion of the 513th, Lieutenant-Colonel Allen C. Miller, was only five-foot-four. His helmet came down over his eyebrows and his jump boots reached almost to his knees; to the GIs who had followed him through the Battle of the Bulge he was "Boots and Helmet."

Besides breaking in young and green troops for Operation Varsity, the American division would be using two new weapons for the first time: the 57mm and 75mm recoilless rifles — both capable of knocking out a German tank. Moreover, Miley was told that one of his regiments — Colonel James Coutts's 513th Parachute Infantry — would jump from the new C-46s, a plane never before flown in combat. Larger and faster than their C-47 counterparts, and with doors on two sides instead of one to facilitate paratroop drops, these new aircraft would require considerable experimental work in jumping.

The pilots of the glider regiment would fly the Waco CG-4A compact steel-and-fabric gliders, which could hold 15 men or one jeep. While the primary pilots were seasoned veterans of three combat operations, many of the co-pilots were "virgins" — men with only minimal training who had never flown gliders in combat.

In the midst of all this strenuous preparation it was decided to completely reorganize the 17th Airborne. "The division reverted from having one parachute and two glider regiments to having two parachute and one glider regiment," explains Colonel Carl A. Peterson, then a major and operations staff officer with 194th Glider Infantry Regiment. "The glider regiment — the 194th absorbed the 193rd — became almost twice as strong as it had been. The idea was to give the division more staying power and more firepower to make it a stronger unit."

New troops . . . new weapons . . . new aircraft . . . new crew . . . new organization: the inclusion of so many untested elements with little time to assess and assimilate them added extra burdens to an already weighty operation.

"Virgins" were at the controls of gliders in Britain, too. When the Glider Pilot Regiment was halved by casualties at Arnhem, its dynamic commander, Brigadier George Chatterton, was called upon to pull off what he considered an impossible feat. "My instructions were to prepare a glider force large enough to fly, if required, 2,000 gliders. But with what? I had a casualty list of well over 500 men and no reinforcements. Clearly rapid improvisation would be needed."

Obviously, men could not be trained in just a few months, first to fly, then to fly gliders, and then to fight as combat soldiers. Chatterton turned to a source of already trained pilots: the RAF, with its surplus pool of 46,000 flying personnel.

Flying Officer John Love was one of a handful of RAF pilots who initially responded. When he arrived for glider training, he was amused to see that many of his RAF buddies who had kidded him for making the sucker move of volunteering for glider service had themselves been press-ganged into transferring to fly the "boxes with wings" (or "flying coffins," as they were irreverently known).

Military training was rudimentary: two weeks on small arms, an even shorter assault course, and a few hours' flight training in gliders. Twenty-one-year-old Sergeant-Pilot Bill McFayden was disgruntled enough by this shallow indoctrination to comment, "If I met a six-foot German with a bayonet when I landed, the odds were on the German. I'd never expected to fight on the ground when I joined the RAF, and a bit of hasty training hasn't helped me much."

Still, the meld of air force to army was to prove surprisingly successful — so much so that the RAF reinforcements, catching the spirit of the glider boys, took to wearing (illegally) the elite maroon berets with their blue uniforms when they went on exercises.

Love was assigned to C Squadron. "We felt that we had got the plum posting, and could be pardoned for being a bit big-headed for flying Hamilcars and not the Mark II Horsas."

Small wonder. The Horsa was an ugly, ungainly craft, constructed all of wood, 68 feet long and 20 feet high; its interior has been likened to a section of the London Underground. It weighed seven tons and could haul two 5-cwt vehicles or 28 fully equipped troops. The newer and more sophisticated 16-ton Hamilcar, with a wingspan of 110 feet, was the king of gliders. Dubbed a "whale with wings," its bulbous brow (whence its vehicle cargos exited) and barge-like belly could accommodate one Tetrarch, a light but fast tank designed for this purpose. Both craft had hinged noses so vehicles and cargo could be unloaded quickly, even in battle conditions. A total of 392 Horsas and 48 Hamilcars were allotted to the operation under command of Lieutenant-Colonel Iain Murray, formerly of the Grenadier Guards.

Flying these aircraft required skill and boldness, and, as one Commando member watching the drop was to comment, a decided lack of interest in remaining alive: "It was suicidal," Lieutenant-Colonel David Ward declares. "You got in a plywood box. And you were wobbling on behind this aircraft — a Dakota — tugged by a piece of string. When you arrived where you were going, you pulled the release, and your plywood box was left to fly down to the ground. But if there should be anyone down there shooting at you, you couldn't do anything whatsoever about it. You couldn't duck . . . you couldn't go sideways . . . you just had to go straight on.

"A lot of them crashed. It's surprising how well you could crash a glider and get out . . . as long as you didn't have a jeep and gun inside. But if you stopped, certainly the jeep and gun would just keep going, straight out the craft, trundling happily down into the battlefield.

"It was worse in the Hamilcar, which carried a light tank, weighing about four tons. The tanks were worth their weight in gold once they got down. The problem was in landing them. The pilot and aircrew sat in the upper level; the tanks or carriers — and whoever was driving them — sat below. The idea was you'd start your engine when the pilot released the tow line, keep it running, and theoretically steam out (or be shot out) through the Hamilcar's hinged nose the moment it touched ground. You had to be a very unusual sort of guy to sit in one of those tanks while the glider was coming down."

Colonel Todd Sweeney, then a company commander with 2nd Battalion Oxfordshire & Buckinghamshire Light Infantry, notes that although the glider frequently crashed, the men usually escaped without serious injury. "You had a very rigid body inside that paper and wood. Gliders could hit the ground and break up; nearly always, the wheels would come off and then it would land on its skids. If you were strapped in, you'd probably get away with it."

If a glider carrying a cargo of mortar bombs and fuel caught fire, however, the crew and passengers would have little chance of survival.

Glider personnel did not wear parachutes. "We reckoned we had just as much chance of getting down in a glider as in a parachute," Major Peterson explains. "There was no real gain as far as safety was concerned; in an emergency a glider can cut loose and get down fairly quickly."

Glider men tended to think they could be more effective initially in battle than paratroopers. A glider could deliver 15 men to the target area, with all their equipment ready, 10 seconds after it landed. "Parachutists lost a lot of time scrambling for their gear," Peterson emphasizes. In truth, floating down under a silk canopy with bullets peppering the air around you — and then trying to land on a rough field, rid yourself of the harness, assemble your weapons, and regroup with your unit — did make the parachutist ineffective at first, and terribly vulnerable.

In those first confused moments on the ground, even their senior field officers had command only of those men who happened to be nearby. They trained as strictly as their men trained, jumped when their men jumped, landed in the same perilous conditions. Until they had assembled their headquarters, parachute commanders — in ranks up to general — were just soldiers, fighting it out alone.

Each man had to depend entirely on his own resources. Paratroopers endured intensive parachute training that reflected this need for skill and initiative. There were only two standards of competence: superior or failure. Before he was finally handpicked to join the parachute battalion, the trainee was subjected to all situations encountered in combat jumping. Then he was drilled to perfect these skills. Besides mastering the technique — and conquering the paralyzing fear — of jumping into 1,200 feet of space from a fast-moving aircraft, he was expected to excel in infantry skills when he landed. He was trained in commando tactics and was a superb marksman. With considerable justification, the parachutist considered himself the elite of the armed forces.

He also realized that he was expendable. Unlike other wartime infantry units whose ranks had been depleted by casualties, the parachutists had a large corps of trainees in holding units, all anxious to transfer up into active ranks. Major disciplinary offences were dealt with summarily: the offender would be RTU — returned to (his former) unit.

The ground training for glider troops was equally tough. The danger factor was recognized by additional pay. ''We got an extra shilling a day for being prepared to fly in them,'' Colonel Sweeney remembers.

In a crowded movie theatre in the small French town of Châteaudun, military police stood guard at the doors as the men responsible for transporting many of the attacking force to the battle zone crowded restlessly into the hall to learn their mission.

The 9th U.S. Troop Carrier Command, under the command of Major-General Paul Williams, would fly the paratroops from both the American and British divisions to the drop in 1,397 C-46s and C-47s. They would also fly the tugs that towed the 906 American glider craft into combat.

''They were the scruffiest-looking guys, with baseball hats and cigars, but they were awfully good,'' Major Richard Hilborn recalls. ''It was quite an international force. Here we were, a Canadian battalion in a British division that was in an American corps — being flown by U.S. pilots.''

Piloting the tug airplanes that towed the gliders was especially hazardous in Operation Varsity. There were many more gliders than there were craft to tow them, necessitating a number of perilous double-tows. The extra drag exerted by each lumbering monster slowed its tug plane almost to a standstill before it could take off. Aloft, the heavily laden gliders, buffetted by crosswinds, would sway crazily on the ends of their tow lines. Sometimes they fouled each other's ropes or — and this did not bear thinking about — collided in mid-air and crashed to earth, taking all their passengers with them.

Each of the American carrier pilots who would fly the tugs and ferry the paratroopers intently studied the marker panels and landmarks that would identify the LZs and DZs of the men he was carrying. For a few brief hours, the lives of 20 or 30 strangers, American or British, would be entirely dependent on one man's skill to get them safely to their destination.

Each pilot was uncomfortably aware that in the course of this flight he would almost certainly come under heavy enemy fire. His own survival had to be of lowest priority. Despite the risks, his job was to hold an unerring course and provide a firm take-off base for his gliders to begin their descent or his jumpers to initiate their drop. It was at this point — on a slow, steady approach at 700 to 1,000 feet — that the plane was most vulnerable to flak.

After the training came the briefing. "We were all kept behind barbed wire," recalls Captain Albert Wing. "They set up actual models of the terrain on sand-tables six by ten feet that took up most of a tent. Aerial photographs were lined up on boards outside.

"We had lots of time. We'd bring in small units and brief each one right on the ground. There were quite a few southerners there, so we named some of the woods 'Lee' and 'Jackson' and such. Then we'd ask questions: 'What's the name of this, what's the name of that.' We went over these things so many times that when we got to our assigned area it was almost as if we'd been there before. It got pretty repetitive and tiresome, over and over again, but it paid dividends."

Security was so tight that not even the men knew where the assault would be. "Everybody was guessing," Wing smiles. "We had one practice river jump before we went into the sealed camp — but we all figured it would be the Rhine."

For four days prior to the launch, the operation's 26 airfields in England and France were sealed. Soldiers were moved, some under cover of darkness, into barbed-wire-enclosed transit camps. Armed military police patrolled the barracks, and guards were posted at all briefing areas. Officers leaving camp on official business were required to remove all regimental insignia from their uniforms.

All outgoing mail and telephone calls were curtailed. Incoming communication was restricted to sometimes unsettling newspaper reports. David Hunter, a young Scottish lieutenant, remembers certain disquieting reactions among some of the men of the 5th British Parachute Brigade:

We had no contact with the outside world, but we did get the newspapers and read a headline in a paper saying that the Germans were expecting airborne landings near Wesel — which is where we were going! We could only console ourselves that since this was not an orthodox type of parachute attack, the enemy might have forgotten about us when they saw the infantry river crossing. We hoped we might have an element of surprise.

Hunter and his unit weren't the only ones to hear directly from the enemy that the air drop was expected. Radio Berlin, Goebbels's slick propaganda machine, informed the American airborne troops in France that the Germans were expecting a full-scale airborne strike at Wesel: "We are prepared," announcer Guenther Weber stated grimly.

An even more disconcerting message was heard on Britain's own BBC when Eisenhower protested an intercepted order from the German High Command. The order: Allied airborne soldiers who were captured on enemy territory were to be executed.

The 6th Airborne Division, the British arm of the operation, would meet over Belgium with the American 17th Airborne Division to form the invasion fleet.

Like the American division, the 6th British division comprised three brigades (known as regiments in the U.S.). The 3rd and 5th Parachute Brigades were led by veteran parachutist commanders, Brigadiers James Hill and Nigel Poett. The 6th Airlanding Brigade — the counterpart of the American Glider Infantry Regiment — had a new commander, Brigadier Hugh Bellamy.

Hill's 3rd Parachute Brigade would be the first to land. It was assigned a DZ on the northwest side of the Diersfordter Wood. Its objectives were to clear out the enemy artillery positions entrenched in the woods and nearby farms and villages, capturing the Schneppenberg Rise.

Brigadier Poett would land his 5th Brigade northeast of Hamminkeln, securing a critical stretch of road to prevent the enemy from bringing up reserves through the area. Bellamy would follow with his three airlanding battalions — 2nd Battalion Oxfordshire & Buckinghamshire Light Infantry, 1st Battalion Royal Ulster Rifles, and 12th Battalion Devonshire Regiment — to seize Hamminkeln and the Issel bridges.

"We expected that the Germans would come in and try to dislodge us and destroy us, and thereby cut off the exploitation and the posse itself," Poett noted. "They had every advantage on us when we first landed. They were hidden; we were running about on top looking for our rendezvous.

"We planned the operation so that it wouldn't be jeopardized by casualties. Every single person, whether he was a brigade commander or a company cook, had a back-up; there was immediately someone to take his place."

When Hill examined the original proposal for the assault he was disturbed. The DZ for his men was some distance to the north of the target area. But Hill believed in a technique they had devised for a massed drop that put the men right on their objectives. Attacking the enemy head-on, before defences could be organized, offered the advantages of placing the men where they could come out fighting. The objective could be seized more rapidly and with fewer ground casualties. But there were two great risks: that the men would be more vulnerable to being shot in the air as they descended over an enemy strongpoint; and that the pilot, under fire from ack-ack artillery, could miss the pinpoint target, dropping them off their DZs.

James Hill boldly created a very fine line between success and catastrophe, staking everything on his confidence in the skill and experience of the American pilots. He still reflects on the gamble: "Twenty-two hundred fighting men dropped in a comparatively restricted area in a matter of six minutes. . . . A slight error in judgment on the part of the American colonel leading the massed formation in which our brigade rode into battle could have been disastrous.

"My confidence in the effect of this method of dropping, and in the skill of the American pilots who were carrying us, persuaded me to ask for a change in the DZ."

"The brigadier selected an area on the map, about 800 by 1,000 yards, and asked the troop carrier wing if they could put a full brigade in there," Lieutenant-Colonel Fraser Eadie, then a major and second-in-command of 1st Canadian Parachute Battalion, notes. "They agreed and he got the DZ moved so that we could come in very tight, right on our objectives. A fellow's awfully naked trying to get someplace to even start his fight."

Even if the gamble worked, Hill knew there would be casualties. "You can't land bang in the middle of a German parachute formation without getting a few men shot in the air."

Hill next studied the operation in the context of the diverse abilities of his three battalions and their commanders to achieve their objectives.

"Battalions," the brigade commander reflects, "were rather like children, very human and very different. . . . It soon became apparent which was the right role for each."

Lieutenant-Colonel George Hewetson, tough, barrel-chested North Country wrestler and schoolmaster who commanded 8th Battalion, had brought his men to the same degree of single-minded boldness and determination that he himself displayed. "He would go straight up the gut, get pinned down, and then fight his way out of it," one officer remembers. Hewetson, Hill decided, would lead off the 3rd Parachute Brigade drop on the northwest edge of the Diersfordter Wood. His task was to clear the enemy off the drop zone — including the densely treed strongpoint known as Axe-Handle Wood — before the other battalions landed there.

The 9th Parachute Battalion, under Lieutenant-Colonel Napier Crookenden's discerning command, were the "artists." Their skills lay in executing precise and meticulously coordinated actions. Hill assigned them the critical job of securing the Schneppenberg Rise, which dominated the British and American positions. Crookenden would then link up with the 17th Airborne.

The third battalion in Hill's brigade was composed solely of Canadians. Its task was to clear and hold the southwest corner of the wood between the 8th Battalion and 9th Battalion positions.

"My immediate and urgent task was to clear the Germans from the northern end of the DZ because the road ran through there," Hill recently remarked. "We knew for a certainty there were houses there with Germans in them; it was the strongest occupied point on the DZ. Unless they were silenced, the DZ would be untenable. I had no hesitation in giving this task to my Canadian battalion, whose makeup and spirit made them ideal for the job."

Through a political configuration, the 1st Canadian Parachute Battalion had become the orphan child of the Canadian forces, conceived out of political wedlock. In 1942 the Canadian cabinet's War Committee gave General A.G.L. McNaughton, commander of the Canadian forces overseas, the authority to commit Canadian troops to large-scale operations "in combination" with British troops. Supposedly, this mandate restricted their employment to raids rather than to expeditionary operations such as invasions and occupations. It was a sensitive issue to a country determined to protect its fragile independence.

Nevertheless, the British had been permitted to have continuous command of 1st Canadian Parachute Battalion, and it participated in three campaigns — none of them "raids." It is understandable that, with the indifference shown these volunteers by their native country, the Canadians felt orphaned.

"We called ourselves the forgotten battalion," Eadie divulges, "and nobody was very happy about it. Very few Canadians were aware that we even had a parachute battalion. The Canadian army really had nothing to do with us, ever. We were put 'in combination' with the 6th British Airborne Division, the word 'combination' being key because that allowed Canadian control over major disciplinary actions — courts-martial and such — while we were in every other sense under British command. The only Canadian thing we did was draw pay and battle dress. We even had to draw our other clothing from the Brits — underwear, socks, etc. They treated us just as if we were part of the family."

Curiously, although the fact that these Canadians were ignored by their own country reflected badly on their government, it stamped the volunteers with that special quality of élan in battle that Hill recognized. Trying to understand these "Canucks," as he called them, had produced a delicate and somewhat frustrating period of transition for the brigade commander.

"Brigadier Hill loved the Canadians," Eadie reminisces. "But he said to me one day during the fighting in Normandy, 'I can't understand why you Canucks have to go into battle wearing hard hats' — the guys were wearing bowlers — 'and smoking cigars. And there is one chap there in a multicoloured jersey!' This kid had a hockey sweater on that said 'Flin Flon' with the number 5 on the back. I said, 'If they fight comfortable, sir, let 'em be.' "

The CO of the battalion was Lieutenant-Colonel Jeff Nicklin. Six-foot-three, smartly turned out, and every inch the powerful athlete that he had been in pre-war years playing All-Canadian end with the Winnipeg Blue Bombers from 1935 to 1940, Nicklin was "a real John Wayne type," as one British parachutist recalls.

Shortly after war broke out, Nicklin joined the Royal Winnipeg Rifles, later volunteering for the paratroopers. Like so many other "civilian soldiers," he made the essential transition to being an effective wartime commander only by exerting enormous effort and self-discipline. Now 32, Jeff Nicklin had already earned a reputation as a tough and unyielding CO who got results.

As a consequence he sometimes seemed aloof to fellow officers of the unit. "He was a completely clean-living chap," James Hill recalls, "tremendously proud of Canada and tremendously proud of his parachutists. I would say he was a great disciplinarian, but strait-laced, and he hadn't much sympathy for those who weren't."

"He was a very good commander and he had bags of guts," Nicklin's second-in-command, Eadie, remembers. "He didn't change from lugging a football to lugging a tommy-gun." "He built a pretty darn good regiment," adds Corporal Dennis Flynn. "He puts us back together."

Putting the Canucks back together had been a traumatic task — for all ranks, as Hill painfully recalls. On September 8, 1944, Nicklin, recently promoted to command the regiment, arrived on the Southampton docks to meet the battalion as it returned from the Normandy campaign. He had fully recovered from wounds incurred in July when he stepped on a booby trap in Normandy.

What he saw that day on the Southampton docks shocked him. The parachutists had been through a grim campaign. Over two-thirds of their number, including 24 of their 27 officers, had become casualties — half on the D-Day drop. The survivors had been fighting for three months without reinforcements. And they had been restive and unhappy under the command of their former CO, Lieutenant-Colonel Bradbrooke. It showed: the battalion had become a battered remnant, unkempt and disorderly. Turning to the acting CO of the unit, Major Eadie, Nicklin snapped: ''What have you done to these men? We are going to have to put the boots to these guys to get them back into shape again. Give them leave — then we'll get started.''

The next weeks were tough ones for the officers and men of 1st Canadian Parachute. Determined to make his regiment battle-ready, Nicklin cracked down fiercely. Strenuous training exercises in street fighting, weapons handling, and other combat tactics were coupled with daily long-distance runs and extended route marches. Standards of dress and conduct were strictly enforced.

The camp smouldered. ''We had the old sweats who had just come out of France,'' Eadie recalls. ''Then we also had another whole half-battalion — many of them just kids, not even 21 — coming in to reinforce the men we had lost. Nobody quite understood why Nick was being that tough. He found it a little hard to be compassionate to some of the soldiers because he didn't hold with a lot of things the guys would do — like going out and getting hammered and then ending up in the slammer. Nick didn't like that; he didn't understand that that was a soldier's life.''

''I guess there were two factors involved,'' reflects Sergeant Ron Anderson. ''We really did feel we were a lost battalion — attached to a British division and a British brigade, living on British rations and so on — and the troops just seemed to get frustrated. The other thing of course was that — and I don't mean to be critical of Jeff Nicklin — but he was an absolute fanatic about physical conditioning. It was not uncommon to have reveille at 5 o'clock. He made a lot of the junior officers bloody mad, too, because he personally hauled them out of their bunks to make them go for a run. He was a bugger on 10-mile runs with packs in two hours. He would take names coming back in the gate, and anybody that didn't make it was RTUed. The men were getting pretty mutinous.''

On October 20, 1944, the crisis erupted. The men staged a hunger strike. ''Nick said to me, 'You had better go and see what the troops had for lunch.' I discovered they hadn't eaten anything,'' Eadie recalls. ''It was just corporals and privates involved, and they still worked and would do whatever they had to do. Brigadier Hill was very upset about it. He said to Nick, 'I will come down and talk to them and I don't want any officers or NCOs in that drill hall.' "

"I told them exactly what I thought of the hunger strike," Hill recently explained. "I said that I expected them to get in shape to come and do this operation [Varsity] with me. 'If you think you can achieve that by doing what you have been doing here you are mistaken,' I informed them, 'and it will take very little to replace you. So make up your minds.' And I walked out.

"That night, the men filed through for dinner. It was all over. They realized that they had to start measuring up again and they did. On the Monday following this incident, six ORs [other ranks] from the battalion came to Brigade HQ to apologize in person to me. It was a gesture that I greatly appreciated, and it did much to maintain my very close relationship with the Canadians."

It also marked the turning point for 1st Canadian Parachute Battalion. Under Nicklin's tough discipline and Hill's paternalistic compassion, the battalion shaped into one of Operation Varsity's sharpest units.

"It was drilled into these fellows that when they were thrown into the middle of an operation like Varsity, they were on their own hook. It would be all confusion. To cope with the things that could happen to them — like dropping in the middle of a woods alone, perhaps being wounded — and then find their positions as fast as possible, physical fitness and discipline were the two things that were going to get them there," Eadie explains.

On March 23, the eve of Operation Varsity, the brigadier met separately with each of his three battalions, offering the usual encouragement and optimism of a coach's pre-game pep talk. But when he came to the Canadian barracks, Hill caught the reckless glint in the eyes of some of his Canuck orphans. Hill knew his derring-do Canadians. He realized that they felt curiously compelled to prove themselves. And he knew they were spoiling for a fight.

"I want you Canadians to understand that I don't want any foolishness on that drop zone," Hill told them. "You all know by now that the areas on which you will land will be ringed with enemy small arms, anti-aircraft weapons, and 88mm guns. These enemy positions have been allocated to Lieutenant-Colonel Hewetson's battalion. I want to make it clear that the objectives assigned you are your primary targets. I don't want you engaged in unauthorized targets. Leave the other man's fight to him!"

In those final hours of March 23, the weight of thousands of tons of explosives from Ninth U.S. Army and Second British Army guns fell remorselessly on German paratroops dug deep in their trenches along the Rhine.

Hundreds of miles away, the glider men and parachute troops who would soon be catapulted into the conflict strolled under star-streaked skies in France and England. Some crawled into rough-blanketed cots, heeding the early curfew. Many preferred the stillness of the night to the restless company of their barrack buddies. Others read fitfully or sat quietly chatting, perhaps sharing a thoughtful drink in the mess.

The glider pilots headed for the airfield. Hundreds of craft lined the strip; the tug aircraft were nose-to-tail down the runway. Behind waited the gliders, tow ropes already in place, wing tips overlapping in geometric precision as they jammed the field. Almost compulsively, each glider pilot made yet one more check on the loading of his craft. A sudden shift of cargo and he would be smashed to the ground.

It was the moment when the traditional farewell letter was written to wives, girlfriends, and family, to be posted (censored) after their jump the next day. At least one corporal in the British contingent became so carried away with his destiny that he wrote no fewer than 11 farewell love letters — all swearing devotion to 11 different girls.

In his office in a disused mushroom farm, Jeff Nicklin straightened the papers on his desk, thinking with satisfaction that after the long grind, the work had paid off. The men were ready. Before turning out the light, he penned a cheerful birthday note to the son he had never seen; Jeff, Jr., would be one year old in 12 days' time.

Omnipresent in each man, but shoved brusquely aside, was the issue of his odds for survival. Parachutists, by tradition, tended more to brackish humour than to the macabre. "Hey, Padre!" one would say on his way out the plane, "Let's have your watch — where you're going, you won't be needing it!" Or, holding aloft an unfastened parachute-release hook in front of a man poised to jump: "Wow! You're unhooked!"

If you kidded enough about being killed, it just might not happen . . . not this time, anyway.

22

Now Is When You Pray

THEY MET OVER BELGIUM. Two entire divisions of more than 14,000 Americans and British from 26 airfields in two countries, married up in perfect precision.

Head to tail, the column would have stretched two hours and eighteen minutes long. There were 1,795 troop-carrying transport planes and 1,050 tugs towing 1,305 gliders, all flying at several variations of height and speed, cramming the airspace. Colonel Todd Sweeney, then a company commander with 2nd Battalion Oxfordshire & Buckinghamshire Light Infantry, observed the awesome procession from his glider. "It was a beautiful clear, crisp spring day. Everywhere you looked across the sky there was nothing but gliders, gliders, gliders. Then, another 3,000 or 4,000 feet above, were the fighters, twinkling in the sky and zooming down. Below us, as we neared the Rhine, the parachute planes (faster than we were), with their khaki camouflage on top, passed us. We could see the line of the river and the tiny wake of the boats from the Scottish divisions going across.

"There was a great pall of smoke on the far side of the Rhine created by the dust screen from the bombing of Wesel and the smokescreen. It looked like a great big field kitchen in which they were burning old rubber tires. And because it was a still day, this pall of smoke and cloud was hanging about a thousand feet above the ground. Everything below it and above it was beautifully clear.

"Then we saw the flak coming up — flak from the guns we had been assured that the RAF and artillery would knock out."

See Map 12 (Appendix B).

Shortly before 1000 hours on March 24, an audience of over a million ground troops were waiting to view the armada. Some were lolling on sunny slopes on the west bank, others crouched with blackened faces in the rubble of Wesel or in slit-trenches on the precarious east-bank bridgehead. It seemed unnaturally quiet. After 12 hours of incessant thundering, the 5,000 Allied guns had been abruptly shut down in anticipation of the air drop. The silence stretched ominously; then the restless viewers heard the welcome roar of the approaching planes.

One celebrated group watched from a hilltop vantage point behind Xanten.

"They're here!" Prime Minister Winston Churchill shouted excitedly. Next to him, Field-Marshal Sir Alan Brooke, Supreme Commander General Eisenhower, General William Simpson, and Field-Marshal Sir Bernard Montgomery turned to congratulate the producers of the spectacle: Generals Lewis Brereton and Matthew Ridgway.

As cheers went up, the first American and British parachute carriers crossed the Rhine in tight formation and were swallowed up in the dense smog created by Allied bombing, mortaring, and smoke. In the next 10 minutes, over 8,000 British and American parachutists were dropped. Then, minutes later, the spectators saw the 2,355 gliders and tow craft of the 6th British Airlanding Brigade and the 194th U.S. Glider Infantry Regiment heading over the Rhine towards their designated landing zones.

It was a historic moment: this was the longest combat glider tow in history. It was the first combat double-tow, and the first glider combat landing on fields not previously secured by paratroops. When the terrible tally of lives lost was calculated, it was to be the last glider combat ever attempted.

There were perhaps other 30-minute periods during the war when so dramatic an attack was successfully achieved — or when so large a force of combat troops was destroyed. None, however, was so clearly grandstanded before a million sun-basking witnesses.

As the aircraft reappeared on a homeward course, Churchill's boyish enthusiasm turned to alarm. He saw "with a sense of tragedy aircraft in twos and threes coming back askew, asmoke or even in flames." Sharing his horror, the awed spectators watched as 16 planes crashed, flames belching from them.

Brigadier James Hill, commanding 3rd British Parachute Brigade, capsulized the grim results: "Amidst the sunshine and great clouds of dust from the preliminary bombardment on the banks of the river, some 50 aircraft and 10 gliders were shot out of the sky and about 115 aircraft and 300 gliders were raked by ground fire.''

In those moments, the terrible risks in committing the force to a daylight operation over enemy artillery strongpoints were alarmingly evident: the 4,150 Allied aircraft were in the gun sights of a well-entrenched and waiting enemy force. It was now evident that — despite the RAF's anti-flak program — the German anti-aircraft guns were very much intact and alert to the invasion.

For the next 30 minutes, the troops were confronted by hazards far worse than anyone could have imagined: the flak, the smoke-obscured ground, the confusion, and the unexpectedly flammable aircraft.

Those that survived that half-hour of mayhem fought with brilliance and intensity to overcome those obstacles. Before the day was ended, the Germans had been driven from their strongholds. But what a day it was.

The very measures that had been taken to protect the invading troops were working against them. The planners had insisted on stopping the barrage 10 minutes before the arrival of the air armada; intended as a safety margin, the delay backfired. The silence that the onlookers had been uneasily experiencing, and the sudden counter-attacks that the Commandos fighting in Wesel were experiencing, were the clues to the disaster.

The air column arrived nine minutes early. Thus the scheduled 30-minute counter-battery artillery bombardment, the effort to silence the deadly ack-ack guns, was forced by the parachutists' premature arrival to abort after only 21 minutes. This period so reduced the fire plan's striking power that its neutralizing effect had worn off by the time the airborne troops landed, except for the positions that had actually been destroyed by direct hits or near misses.

The thick layer of smog created by the smokescreen, the barrage, and the bombings also backfired. It proved to be more of a hindrance than help. While it served its purpose of shielding the troops on the west bank from direct observation, many of the glider pilots became blinded by the smoke and disoriented, preventing them from landing on their objectives. It also obscured enemy positions from attacking fighter planes.

''The gliders were released as they got over the Rhine at about five, six, or seven thousand feet,'' Sweeney recounts. ''When they came below the pall of smoke, still looking for a place to land, those anti-aircraft gunners of the German army had the best and finest day of their lives. And we at the brigade had something like 40 to 50 per cent casualties in the air."

The onslaught of enemy fire was unexpectedly savage. The men had been assured in briefings that it would have been quelled. The enemy ack-ack was "much greater than we had been led to expect," affirms Lieutenant-Colonel Crookenden, CO of the British 3rd Parachute Brigade's anchor battalion, the 9th.

Luckiest were the Allied paratroopers dropping in the first sticks (groups of nine men jumping from a single plane). The enemy had not yet entirely recovered from the effects of the bombardment, and flak was considerably lighter than subsequent battalions would experience. When the final sticks jumped some 10 minutes later, the flak had become "so heavy one could walk on it," as one American glider man graphically describes it. "Its effect was to drive the planes higher."

Lieutenant-Colonel Hewetson, CO of the 8th Battalion, was one of the "lucky ones." His unit was the first of Brigadier Hill's 3rd Brigade to jump. Passing over the ruins of Goch, Hewetson heard the "Five minutes to go" signal. He glanced at his watch: 0946 hours. But the 3rd Brigade drop had been timed for 1000 hours. What had gone wrong? Would they land off target? Drop on the wrong side of the Rhine? He looked out, relieved to see at last the silver ribbon of the river. "At 0951 we crossed the Rhine," he noted.

Hewetson recalls the "usual sinking feeling" that precedes any jump. The air turbulence that had caused queasiness in many of the paratroopers was exacerbating the pre-jump nerves. Then suddenly, "Red light . . . green light . . . out . . . parachute open . . . ground fairly hard . . . sigh of relief!" Hewetson was safely down — but unaccountably ahead of schedule.

As he scrambled out of his parachute at the drop zone, the burly North Countryman paused momentarily to gaze at the incredible vista: "Thousands of parachutes drifting slowly to the ground and on the ground. . . . Men getting out of their harness and opening kit bags with feverish haste, talking to anyone within call about the jump. . . . Reassuring puffs of blue and yellow smoke that marked nearby RVs [rendezvous].

"It was a scene of indescribable chaos, yet rapidly men were moving off to the RV, and within 35 minutes 85 per cent of the brigade had reported in."

For the parachutists who had planted two feet firmly on the ground, Captain Nick Archdale recalls "an aura, an intense buildup of morale if you landed safely . . . and that is what made paratroopers such effective soldiers.''

For the glider men who at that moment were plunging through the shrouded mist looking for their LZs, there was quite a different feeling. An AP reporter braced himself nervously as his glider pilot released the tow and dived through the dense smog towards the ground. Flak was exploding everywhere. The sergeant beside him turned pale. ''Now,'' he said, ''is when you pray.''

The two British parachute brigades (3rd and 5th) were dropped with near-pinpoint accuracy on their DZs. However, the two American parachute regiments — Colonel Raff's 507th and Colonel Coutts's 513th — were not as fortunate. Their transport, the new C-46 Commando aircraft, never before used in a parachute operation, constituted another failed element in the complex operation.

These craft were carrying three-quarters of the U.S. parachute assault force: the 2,071 men of Coutts's 513rd combat unit and half the troops of the 507th as well. The C-46s were larger and faster than the C-47s and had the advantage of being able to carry 33 men into battle (as opposed to 18 men in the C-47), with two exit doors to facilitate a fast bail-out. But the drastic flaw in the craft revealed itself in mid-air over the Rhine: punctured, they became chariots of fire. ''You could hit that airplane most anywhere and get something on fire,'' one pilot asserted. ''It was a tender airplane, very flammable.''

Unlike the C-47s, the C-46's fuel tanks were not self-sealing. When the wide-bellied craft were punctured, the fuel leaked out into the fuselage. Peppered with shot as they flew over the intense flak to their 500-foot drop level, the planes erupted in flames. Over three-quarters of the 71 C-46 planes were severely damaged in this way. Nineteen of these did not make it home, crashing in flames with crew and many of the parachutists still aboard. Some of the parachutists escaped through the dual jump doors. The aircrew hung on doggedly at the controls to keep the planes steady for the drop. Many went down with their planes.

Jumping from a flaming aircraft was a harrowing experience. ''When we were hit,'' Captain Albert Wing, a company commander with the 513th, recalls, ''I had this wild thought: Who in the hell is throwing gravel at the plane? That's what it sounded like. One boy, he got his little finger nearly severed completely. We had a bit of a flap what to do, then finally we cut his finger off, wrapped a handkerchief around it, and put it in his pocket, and he went out with us. He figured — we all did — that it was safer to be on the ground.''

More problems awaited the troopers of the 513th. The superbly powered C-46s reached the Rhine earlier than scheduled. This factor, plus the confusion of smoke and the inexperience of the pilots, caused the regiment to overfly its DZ and come down in the British zone, two to three miles north of the planned target.

Colonel Coutts had crossed the Rhine when his port engine broke out in flames. ''I glanced at my wristwatch,'' he remembers, ''wondering if the ship would get us there. Our pilot kept us steadily in formation in spite of flak and flames for a little more than three minutes. Over the roar of the many motors I now discerned the sharp reports of gunfire. I knew we were close. In a moment the light changed to green and we were out of the burning plane.''

Once down, Coutts looked around for landmarks: ''I started looking for orienting terrain features that I had memorized, but couldn't find them. I noticed more and more British paratroopers, their cherry berets. I saw British Horsa gliders landing. Either the British or we were in the wrong place. Through an interpreter we learned from a very scared German family that we were northwest of Hamminkeln rather than southwest. The British were in the right area, we were wrong.''

The 513th's drop on the 6th British Airlanding Brigade's zone was just in time, as it turned out, to assist their allies in knocking out German batteries waiting to decimate the incoming British gliders. ''If it had not been for the fact that the 513th dropped wrong, our casualties would have been considerably higher,'' a senior officer of 6th Airborne Division states gratefully.

The plane of Lieutenant-Colonel Allen Miller, CO of 2nd Battalion, the lead assault battalion of the 513th, was one of the first to be ignited. He relates: ''My plane, flying at 400 feet, was hit by small-arms fire. The left wing was consumed and as it lost its ability to support the fuselage, the plane veered to the left. I yelled, 'Let's go' and jumped — but too late for some of my staff and for the plane crew.''

Miller landed in a pigpen. There was total confusion on the ground, with fighting at close quarters. ''The Germans were well dug in and we were very much exposed. As this sharp action progressed, 6th Airborne Division gliders began landing all about us. It was then that I realized we had swung to the left into the

6th's landing zone. As I watched, a big British Horsa glider landed in the field immediately to our front and out rolled an armoured car with a 6th AB soldier standing in the machine-gun turret. He was immediately engaged by the enemy and returned the fire. The armoured car burst into flames. My last impression was of the gunner enveloped in flames but bravely firing his machine gun."

Twenty-seven per cent of Miller's transport planes had been shot down. His casualties were severe and his unit was dispersed and separated from both its assembly point and the 513th Combat Team Artillery (which had landed in its correct DZ). Nevertheless, in small groups the men worked their way back, attacking and destroying pocket after pocket of enemy as they went. By nightfall, the unit had reduced six enemy 88mm guns and captured 1,252 POWs. The 2nd Battalion was awarded a Unit Citation for its outstanding effort.

Meanwhile, the CO and operations officer of the regiment's 1st Battalion — also searching for the rendezvous — were taken prisoner. They were held three hours before talking their captors into surrendering.

Colonel Raff and nearly 700 of his "Raff's Ruffians" of the 507th U.S. Parachute Infantry had also landed some two miles off the table, and were attacking their way back to their objectives. One stick of Raff's paratroopers came under intense fire from a machine-gun position until it was charged single-handedly and destroyed by Private George Peters, a signaller. Peters was cut down by fire twice as he ran 75 yards head-on against the gun. Twice he struggled forward, until he was close enough to throw his grenades on the German position. He died of his wounds as the battery exploded. Peters was awarded the Congressional Medal of Honor posthumously — one of four awarded to young Americans that day.

Raff collected the battalion and headed south towards their RV. On his way, he intercepted his remaining battalions, which had landed correctly, and laid on an attack at noon on their objectives: the village of Diersfordt and its castle. Two German tanks heading in the direction of the parachute drop zones emerged from Schloss Diersfordt just as he arrived. The American tank hunter team persuaded the first tank to surrender by force of a Gammon bomb; the second was set afire with the new 57mm recoilless rifle.

"3rd Battalion systematically reduced the castle room-by-room," the 507th Combat Team reported. "Within an hour the largest part of the castle was ours and the last bit of resistance, consisting of a large group of officers holding out in an isolated turret, was overcome that evening. The strongpoint yielded 500 prisoners . . . including two colonels, two Mark V tanks destroyed and two captured.''

At 1300 hours, their objectives achieved, the 507th made contact with advance patrols of the 15th Scottish. Six hours later, as their final mission, the American paratroopers linked up with the British airborne.

While the Americans were fighting their way back to their DZs, the British and Canadian parachutists had landed squarely on top of stiff opposition. Brigadier Hill's confidence in the American pilots had not been misplaced; his 2,200 fighting men of 3rd Parachute Brigade had been dropped on ''that nice piece of ground, 800 by 1,000 yards'' — right on the enemy, as requested.

But no one had expected that this enemy would be capable of such depth of fire. As Sergeant Ron Anderson reported, the DZ was being raked heavily: it ''had not been neutralized at all.''

The field was a lethal no-man's-land, with the Canadians and British holding one side of it, German machine-gunners and snipers peppering fire across from the other side, and parachutists and then gliders careening into its centre. Wounded and dead littered the green meadow.

The brigade was in trouble. Hewetson's 8th Battalion had not been able to clear the DZ before the Canadians (and immediately after them, the British 9th Battalion and the gliders carrying brigade equipment) landed. Forty Germans, well dug into Axe-Handle Wood, began lacerating them with fire.

Lieutenant Bob Firlotte commanded 3rd Brigade's Defence Platoon in the drop. ''We were fighting right on the dropping zone immediately we landed. Seven of my platoon of 30 were casualties, one killed. It was pretty bad.''

''The Germans were still in control,'' Hill recounts. ''I realized that the whole thing might be kiboshed. I got hold of Major James Kippen, 8th Para, and said, 'You've got to collect some of your chaps and go in and get the Germans out of that wood.' ''

Kippen and one of his platoon commanders raised an attack. The enemy beat them off and both men were shot dead. Another platoon attacked with grenades from a different direction and succeeded in infiltrating the enemy-held wood. Finally, with fierce hand-to-hand fighting, the British captured the strongpoint. They found trenches choked with German dead and wounded. In the trees hung several British parachutists who had been picked off in the air, or shot while snagged on a tree limb.

Then Hewetson himself was in trouble: "I was standing at the entrance to the wood. . . . Suddenly, with a terrific crash, a glider came through the trees and I found myself lying under the wheel of a jeep. I managed to crawl out from the wreckage to find the glider, one of the medical Horsas of 9th Parachute Battalion, completely written off. The crew had been killed and my IO and two sergeants were also dead."

"At this point," Lieutenant-Colonel Eadie relates, "Hewetson came out from under the wreckage madder than hell and stiff as a poker, every bone aching, yelling his famous 'How now you whorin' bastard shite!' all over the forest so everyone knew he was *really* mad."

The German paratroops "fought like tigers." Despite Brigadier Hill's warning, a number of Canadians stopped by the lethal woods to help their comrades. Lieutenant Jack Brunnette of B Company was killed "fighting someone else's battle." Many of his platoon were shot up. The company commander, Captain Sam McGowan, was hit by a round that entered through the front of his helmet and came out the back.

But Lieutenant-Colonel Jeff Nicklin had not turned up. Jumping four minutes after 8th Battalion, Nicklin and his friend and second-in-command Eadie, each leading his stick from adjacent planes, had planned to jump simultaneously.

"He and I doped it out the night before," Eadie said. "We agreed what we'd do was, when we saw the Emmerich road, we'd give it a quick one, two . . .,and out! Our objective was to land 50 yards in front of the small wood near Axe-Handle Wood. I landed about 30 yards from it. On the way down there were three rounds that came awfully close; there were about five Germans dug into that little wood shooting at me."

Eadie quickly rolled into a furrow in the field and cut himself out of his harness. "Then I laid on a couple of blasts with my tommy-gun and ran to beat hell for my objective."

When Nicklin failed to show up, Eadie, deeply disturbed, swiftly took charge. And word swept worriedly through Canadian ranks: "The Colonel's missing."

Meanwhile, Sergeant Anderson of B Company dropped with his platoon in a tight landing on the edge of the woods. The Canadians noted with relief that their landmarks truly were materializing: "Everything was familiar from the sand-tables and photographs: there's the tree, there's the outhouse, there's the farm building, it's got three doors on it and the windows are exactly where I expected them."

When Brigadier Nigel Poett's 5th Parachute Brigade arrived at its DZ — eight minutes after Hill and some two miles inland from 3rd Brigade positions — the surprise element was gone.

"Everybody was waiting for us," Poett recalls. "There was a lot of flak up there. The American pilots kept completely steady. When an aircraft was hit, the pilot would fly on and get rid of his parachutists and only then would he abandon ship or turn and try to get back."

Captain Nick Archdale, platoon commander in 7th Battalion, saw explosives hit his plane as they came in for the drop. "The pilot was brilliant. The aircraft was on fire and semi out of control as he was struggling to get us to the right place. But I landed within yards of my DZ with the rest of the company nearby."

For Lieutenant David Hunter, the heavy enemy small-arms fire and shelling he and his platoon witnessed as their Dakota came in confirmed the suspicions they had felt in transit camp that the Germans had been expecting them. Hunter jumped, grateful to be free of the lurching craft that had been giving him queasy feelings. He realized that he had been dropped far too high, about 1,000 feet instead of the planned 500 — a long drop, making, he thought uneasily, an easy target for a German machine gun.

Poett hadn't reckoned — nor had any of the planners — that the dense smog that so completely obscured the target area would slow up the rallying of the men. In the confusion of trying to reassemble and reach designated RVs, many companies were delayed for an hour.

"The vast bulk of our casualties occurred after we'd touched down," Poett observed, "until we'd been able to winkle out the enemy dispositions and mop them up." Three hundred men of 5th Brigade became casualties in the drop, almost all incurred in that first period.

At 1030 hours, while the parachute troops were still battling to clear the glider landing zones, the first American Waco CG-4A gliders of Colonel James Pierce's 194th Glider Infantry appeared. The forerunners of the 1,300-craft glider armada, they immediately plunged into a black hell-hole of enemy fire.

The gliders felt the full fury of the now-alert enemy anti-airborne artillery forces. "Get the gliders first," Major Krafft had urged his German anti-aircraft crews. "Nearly every shot gets home." The advice was heeded.

To land, the glider plane would dive sharply to keep up its speed, then flatten out towards the end and finally lose height and drop to the ground. The British glider pilots had been trained to release their tow ropes at 2,500 or even 3,500 feet, well above the dense ribbon of smog suspended 1,000 feet above the ground. With their long descent, they were more vulnerable to flak than their American counterparts, who released at 500 feet. However, the planes that towed the American gliders, flying in at that low level, were more subject to flak than the British tugs. These tug pilots could not take evasive action. Their job was to hold the controls steady, ignoring the buffetting shells, the searing flames, the gunfire squirting up through the floorboards. Almost half of the tug craft were hit. Enemy flak smashed 12 out of the air; 140 more were damaged but managed to stay aloft.

"The troop-carrier pilots did a splendid job," reported Major-General James Gavin, whose observer plane hovered above the assaulting force. "After delivering their troops, a surprising number of troop-carrier pilots we saw on their way back were flying planes that were afire. The crew I was with counted twenty-three ships burning in sight at one time. But the incoming pilots continued on their courses undeterred by the awesome spectacle ahead of them."

The British glider pilots dived for the ground, peering down anxiously, trying to pick up familiar landmarks of LZs screened by smoke as they weaved and swerved to avoid the low-aiming German defense artillery. Silhouetted against the haze, they were easy targets for enemy flak. Their underbellies were mercilessly lacerated. Some collided as they attempted to land. The air was filled with the sounds of whining bullets cracking upwards, and the screams of gliders crashing down. The fragile plywood Horsas and Hamilcars splintered like matchsticks.

Then yet another element of the operation went awry. "The mistake we made at Varsity was, we not only flew in the rifle platoons right slap on the objective, but we also flew in the support platoons and vehicles," Colonel Sweeney reported.

"We had three platoons of mortars, two platoons of anti-tank guns, and one or two platoons of machine guns. When they were hit, the fire set off the mortar bombs and they blew up."

In 10 minutes, half of the total strength of Sweeney's unit, 2nd

Oxfordshire & Buckinghamshire, was lost. "We had 110 people killed and quite a lot wounded in that landing, and that was due to anti-aircraft fire," Sweeney said. "Of 600 hard scale [troops making the attack], 300 were not effective at the end of the day. But the worst feature perhaps was that the proportion of killed to wounded was very high." Delaying this fly-in until a second wave when the opposition had been subdued would have prevented the carnage.

Of the 416 British glider planes making the attack, 300 were damaged, many severely. Thirty-two were destroyed with all on board lost. Thirty-eight per cent of the British RAF glider pilots — 100 men — became casualties in those frantic few minutes.

Diving at a whistling 120 miles per hour, the fabric-covered American Wacos of the 194th Glider Infantry Regiment also suffered grievous casualties. Their flimsy framework buckled and snapped, sounding like "a paper sack full of popcorn kernels." The pilots wore flak suits, but the passengers had no such protection from the lethal ack-ack and machine-gun fire being pumped in from below — or from the suddenly erupting fire within the craft as fuel jerry-cans exploded.

Second Lieutenant F. Tipton Randolph, a glider pilot with 80th Squadron, 436th U.S. Troop Carrier Group, ran into yet another unexpected situation: "Along with regular flak type stuff, the Germans were using a phosphorus-type shell. This phosphorus shell was responsible for catching quite a few gliders on fire, because if it hit in the wing it would just stay there and start smouldering in the wood.

"In building the main spars on some of the gliders, they had not done much of a job of cleaning the sawdust out. That sawdust came out of there like little fireflies as the phosphorus was burning. There were four gliders in our squadron that burnt the fabric clear off, all except a little bit around the nose."

Although 90 per cent of the 345 Wacos of the 194th landed on their designated LZs, 293 were damaged to some extent. Most crash-landed, barrelling across fields and smashing fences, trees, and telephone poles. Seven were destroyed by four 88mms on the field where they landed.

The instant they touched down, the three glider infantry battalions plunged into fierce combat, knocking out the lethal gun positions. This aggressive action prevented more gliders and glider men from being knocked out.

Over 300 glider men were casualties that day, 105 killed. The majority of these casualties occurred in the first moments of landing.

"The enemy's most effective weapon was to mow down the load as it debouched from the glider," recalls Colonel Carl Peterson. "I saw two glider loads wiped out in this way."

The glider man's most effective weapon proved to be the glider itself. The very fact that these craft kept landing helter-skelter throughout the area instead of in a planned pattern actually disrupted the enemy. As they took aim on one craft, another would come in behind. "Our gliders were coming from all directions," Peterson remembers. "Just their presence tended to be an offensive weapon."

To cap off the confusion, the CO and the entire staff of the German 1052nd Infantry Regiment were captured 10 minutes after landing. "The consequent disorganization among the Germans was tremendous," Peterson noted.

"One hundred and fifty small battles were fought simultaneously on the landing zone in the first half hour," the 194th Glider Infantry Regiment noted. "Despite the organized resistance and persistent sniper fire . . . all initial objectives, including seizure of crossings of the Issel River and Canal, were taken within two hours of the landing." Forty-two German guns, five self-propelled guns, and ten tanks were destroyed or captured, and 1,150 German prisoners were taken.

The troops of 6th British Airlanding Brigade had two objectives: the first was the village of Hamminkeln, to be taken by 12th Battalion, the Devonshire Regiment. The second objective was the bridges over the Issel River and Canal. This assignment was shared by the American glider men and by coup-de-main bridge-raiders of the 2nd Battalion Oxfordshire & Buckinghamshire Light Infantry and the Royal Ulster Rifles.

After sharp fighting with elements of Battle Group Karst — the special German anti-air landing formation made up of paratroops, SS, or Waffen-SS — 12th Devons captured Hamminkeln in less than three hours, taking some 500 prisoners.

The coup-de-main parties were seasoned volunteers with special training and special orders. Their glider pilots landed eight gliders at pinpoint targets on two strategically important bridges over the Issel, three Horsas on the east or far side, and five on the west.

This was the first time that an airborne division had attempted a tactical landing on an objective by a glider. The craft landed (or crash-landed) just yards from their LZs — a brilliant feat in view of the heavy opposition and obliterated targets.

The bridge-raiders swung into action to seize the bridges. Despite their heavy casualties, they fought a brisk action and were consolidating on their objectives by midday.

The 2nd Oxf & Bucks were strongly counter-attacked later in the night by German infiltrators who set fire to unoccupied houses and caused a number of casualties. The British forced the enemy back across the river and blew up one of the bridges to prevent further encroachment.

By 1230 hours — two and a half hours after the attack was launched — all the airborne troops were on the ground and most were on their objectives. As well, 109 tons of ammunition, 695 vehicles, and 113 artillery pieces had been successfully landed in the gliders. But the enemy ack-ack had still not been subdued.

At 0100 hours, a giant shadow was cast over the battling troops, and the skies exploded with the ear-pounding roar of a thousand engines. It was the promised low-level resupply. A fleet of 240 four-engine Liberator bombers of the Eighth U.S. Air Force, flying at 300 feet, dropped 582 tons of ammunition, fuel, and food. Even these mammoth aircraft were not immune to the flak. Fifteen were shot down as they turned for home; 104 more were damaged. One man plunged to the ground as he was kicking supply boxes out of the hold.

During the rest of the day, violent and confused fighting erupted spasmodically in every sector. Holding the northernmost sector of the airborne assault zone, Brigadier Poett had expected enemy counter-attacks, and he got them. Lieutenant William (Pat) Patterson, a Canadian officer commanding a platoon of 7th Battalion, hung on for 22 hours, beating back countless enemy attacks.

The Allied air forces flew 7,700 sorties, with the loss of 56 aircraft. Bombers and fighters from the Eighth U.S. Air Force, the 9th Tactical Air Command (USAAF), and the RAF attacked airfields and marshalling yards and swept the skies for enemy aircraft (53 were destroyed, including a handful of jets).

The tactical air forces were invaluable flying in direct support of ground troops. Four squadrons of Typhoons from 123 Wing RAF carried out 97 sorties. They succeeded in demolishing many enemy gun batteries without casualties to their pilots or their own land troops. "It was noted," Wing Commander J.R. Baldwin reported drily, "that as soon as a dive was made, [enemy] fire almost always stopped immediately."

With the troops was another supporting arm — one that carried bottles of plasma into battle instead of bandoliers of bullets.

It was Corporal George Topham's assignment to help clear the casualties from the 1st Canadian Parachute Battalion DZ. A blond giant of a man, Topham had earned a reputation for being a reserved and mild-mannered fellow.

His superb physical conditioning, a legacy from working in the rugged mines of northern Canada before the war, had made him a prime candidate for Major Pat Costigan's tough new training program for his medical orderlies. At about the time that Jeff Nicklin was force-feeding discipline to his troops, Costigan, the medical officer of the battalion, was hand-picking the biggest, strongest men he could find for special infantry-cum-paramedical training. Men on the course were taught the essentials of dealing with casualties on the field: making simple incisions, stitching wounds, giving hypodermic needles. Topham jumped with C Company and immediately started evacuating the wounded.

Two men from 224th Parachute Field Ambulance Battalion went into the field to rescue a casualty. As Topham watched, a burst of enemy fire cut them down. He ran past the mortally wounded orderlies to the man still lying in the exposed area. Shots rained about him as he tended the wounded soldier; one bullet ripped across his cheek and another through his nose.

"Toppy refused to be evacuated," remembers Lieutenant-Colonel Eadie. "He went back out there again and again and continued evacuating the drop zone until he had cleared it. It wasn't until then that he finally agreed to sit down and listen to reason and let the doctors work on him. Even then he refused to be evacuated."

It was on his way back from the aid station that Topham came across a Bren-gun carrier that had received a direct hit. Corporal Dawson Einarson, Vickers Machine-Gun Platoon, was returning from Battalion HQ with fresh belts of ammunition at that moment: "I saw a man jump up on top of the carrier and literally lift the occupants out — the driver, the co-driver, and the people behind and hand them down. I thought the person was absolutely out of his mind, being up on top of the carrier when the thing was literally exploding and burning and popping underneath him. As I moved down the road, I looked back and saw him jump off. Then the carrier exploded. The man was George Topham.''

Topham's acts of valour that Friday morning were to win him the Victoria Cross — the first VC won by the 6th British Airborne Division, and the third VC awarded to a Canadian in the Rhineland campaign.

On the American sector, one of the last serials of gliders in the fly-in was a group of 50 craft carrying medical personnel and supplies. Sixteen of the medics were killed by enemy fire on the LZ. Within an hour, the field surgical team was treating the wounded at a casualty clearing station at the end of the zone. Most were evacuated later in the day by boat.

Medical units attached to the glider battalions dealt with hundreds of severely wounded casualties on the field. ''The wounded were remarkably patient and cheerful,'' the regiment history reported. ''They well knew that there was no chance for them to be evacuated until the ground forces linked up with us, but they hung on.''

Some, like Corporal Dennis Flynn, got their initial help from the enemy. In the early afternoon of D-Day, Flynn led one of the patrols sent out to intercept German infiltrators. Suddenly, a bullet ripped into his thigh, tearing a jagged, three-inch splinter of bone from his femur.

Flynn recalls: ''I called for a stretcher-bearer and a German POW, a medic, came over to take care of me. He dressed my wound, gave me my morphine that I supplied to him, and then he got the guys to come and make a very quick litter to carry me back. We were going down the road when we were shelled by mortars. This German fellow threw his body right on top of me to protect me. He took me to 224th Field Ambulance and that was the last I saw of him; I guess he saved my life.''

The Varsity planners had anticipated that in a drop on a defended area it could take as much as 36 to 48 hours before they were relieved by ground troops. The personnel of the British 224th Parachute Field Ambulance, attached to 3rd Parachute Brigade, carried sufficient emergency equipment when they were parachuted in to handle casualties for that period. With pre-sterilized instruments, anaesthesia, and antibiotic drugs, unit surgeons could set up in a woods if necessary.

A church and an adjoining priest's parish home were expropriated for a dressing station, as the unit history describes:

Everything that cumbered the rooms was pushed out of the windows: coal-skuttles and crockery, and dishes with the remains of meals on them, all went to join the piles of rubble and broken glass outside. The owner, in his black clerical hat, moved gloomily about the house. . . . At half-past two the first patient was on the operating table.

In the next 45 hours the two surgeons, Major H. Daintree-Johnson and Major N.A. Miller, each did 14 major operations in the priest's house, all on men in too desperate a condition to survive evacuation across the Rhine. "Of the 28 theatre cases [the history states], 15 had multiple wounds, about two-thirds resulting from gunshot and the remainder from shells and mortar bombs."

Four chaplains jumped with the troops of 3rd Parachute Brigade. Two were killed in the drop: one, Honorary Captain Kenny, a Roman Catholic padre, was shot in the trees. The priest's reserve sacrament, which he had carried in the jump, was rescued by the Canadian chaplain, Honorary Captain Douglas Candy, and turned over to an RC chaplain in another brigade. (Throughout the Northwest Europe Campaign, Captain Candy was the only airborne padre to escape the casualty list.)

Top Secret. Personal and Eyes Only for CIGS from Field-Marshal Montgomery, 24 Mar 45:
I can now say that the first day's operations in Plunder have been most successful. We have got 6 divs over the Rhine, including the 2 airborne. We have captured 5500 prisoners. Our total casualties are about 1200. The bridging is proceeding very satisfactorily except on the left about Rees.
16 corps of 9th Army have got 79 div and 30 div over the river and one class 40 bridge is already in position. In 30 Corps sector, 51 div have had very tough fighting against a parachute division. A good bridgehead has been gained about 4000 yds deep but the town of Rees itself has not been completely captured and this has hampered ferrying and rafting and bridging preparations generally. . . . The town of Rees is being assulted tonight by 2 battalions and I have every hope that it will be clear of the enemy before daylight.

In six hours, it was all over. Most of the objectives had been secured and the ground troops had fought their way inland to form a firm link with the airborne. The 507th Parachute Infantry Regiment joined up with the British Commandos; 17th U.S. Airborne troops touched base with the 15th Scottish Division.

Bone-weary and elated, British and American airborne troops mingled, swapping K-rations for Compo-pacs and passing flasks of whiskey as they mulled over the day's events.

Later that night and all through the next day, casualties were ferried across the Rhine. Glider pilots joined the westward trek over the river, shepherding dispirited Germans to POW cages. A large, hand-printed sign awaited them: "The Rhine Hotel — Glider Pilots a Speciality."

The tug aircraft — their jobs done — had run for home, fast. Flight Sergeant Malcolm Guthrie recalls "the most fantastic piece of low flap flying I think I've ever done.

"It was every man for himself. We left the throttle wide open and put the nose down and weaved. . . . One thing I clearly remember, we were crossing Denmark with the coast in sight and we pulled out to clear one line of trees. The skipper put the nose right down the other side. I suppose we were probably no more than 20 or 30 feet up and there was a herd of cows with a farmer sitting on a stool milking them. I can remember seeing the cow giving a tremendous kick and sending the farmer flying."

A Canadian signals officer, Captain Dean Steadman, serving with the Irish glider troops of the Royal Ulster Rifles, was tickled by an impromptu entertainment that erupted on the still-warm battlefield: "Our crazy American cousins were hopping around on these farm horses — in their wild and wonderful way, they'd improvised a game of polo."

In their wild and wonderful way, the troops of 6th British and 17th U.S. Airborne Divisions had sliced through the enemy guns, silencing them forever. The casualties had been disastrous; the day was pandemonium — but the way was now clear for the ground troops to break out over the Rhine's defences and penetrate the last inner core of Germany.

On a balmy Palm Sunday, 48 hours after the landing, Todd Sweeney stood at the side of the road and watched, transfixed, as the tanks rolled by: "Hour after hour after hour they went by, on their way into Germany.

"The operation was very heavy on our battalions," Sweeney notes, "but it probably saved as many if not more lives in the armour and the infantry who'd have had to fight their way through if we hadn't seized these points."

Lieutenant-General Sir Napier Crookenden recently wrote: "Perhaps the most important gain was the destruction of 90 German artillery pieces, ranging from 155mm down to 76mm, a large number of 20mm guns in multiple mountings and hundreds of machine guns."

Yet the official U.S. military historian, Colonel Charles Mac-Donald, questions whether Operation Varsity was "necessary or even justified." He suggests that while the operation aided British ground troops, the cost in American losses was out of proportion. General Bradley was also to denigrate the usefulness of the operation, dismissing the enemy defences on the east bank of the Rhine as "disorganized and unimaginative."

"It gave us a running start," disagrees U.S. glider veteran Carl Peterson. "Taking that position by ground troops would have resulted in considerably more casualties and would have taken longer."

Even in the face of defeat, the Germans had managed to withdraw their artillery pieces from the Ardennes battle, employing them again against the advancing Allies in the Rhineland. They withdrew them once again over the Rhine River and repositioned them on the east bank to stave off invaders.

The airborne assault assured one thing: those guns would never again be fired.

Thirty-six hours after the parachute drop, a patrol from 1st Canadian Parachute Battalion found Jeff Nicklin. His boots still gleamed; the crease in his pants was still immaculate. They cut him down from the tree where his riddled body had lodged, and they buried him in the winter-torn Westphalian scrubland. Nicklin had restored the spirit of his battalion, but he had not lived to see it soar.

Eleven hundred other parachutists, glider men, and aircrew died — most as nobly and as miserably as Nicklin. Another 1,800 were wounded, some severely, on that tiny tract of land, six miles long and five miles wide — punishment meted out by an "uninspired" enemy.

It had taken six agonizing weeks for the million men from Second British Army, Ninth U.S. Army, and First Canadian Army to inch forward 25 miles from their start line just to reach the Rhine. It took 12 hours for the land and airborne troops to achieve a successful crossing.

Grenade, Veritable, and Blockbuster had got them to the river. Plunder propelled them over. Varsity ensured their bridgehead and ensuing breakout.

Epilogue

The soldiers' war was drawing to an end. But the war of the generals was not.

One hundred and fifty miles south of Wesel, the small Rhine town of Oppenheim had long been noted for the fine Niersteiner wines produced on its sunny slopes. On the night of March 22, twenty-four hours before Operation Varsity was due to be launched, Lieutenant-General George Patton "sneaked" a regiment of 5th U.S. Infantry Division across the Rhine at Oppenheim, giving the hamlet a new prominence and giving the U.S. Army a new bridgehead. Patton achieved this feat in a silent attack without artillery or air bombardment, and with only 20 casualties. As with the Remagen coup, the location was so unlikely and unpromising that the Germans were surprised. By the next day, the whole division was across and an armoured division was preparing to follow.

Here was Patton's longed-for breakout. Now he could get such a major force committed in so far-reaching a campaign that "Americans rather than British could carry the ball."

"Wait until tomorrow to announce it," his deputy suggested. And just as Montgomery's troops were launching their attack across the Rhine, Patton called his chief.

"Brad," he shrilled excitedly to his senior commander, "for God's sake tell the world we're across! I want the world to know Third Army made it before Monty starts across."

"[Patton] wanted a quick, spectacular crossing . . . to produce newspaper headlines like those generated by the First Army's seizure of a bridge at Remagen," American military historian Charles MacDonald speculates. "Most of all he wanted it in order to beat a certain British field-marshal across the river."

The Allies now had three bridgeheads across the Rhine. Although Remagen and Oppenheim were valuable pressure points on a faltering enemy, Eisenhower himself maintained that it was the bridgehead at Wesel that opened the way for the Allies to capture the Ruhr. ''The March 24 operation sealed the fate of Germany,'' he concluded.

The American ''torpor'' of the fall and early winter had given way to a dynamic resurgence of optimism and energy. Seven allied armies fanned out in a spectacular six-week 200-mile armoured drive across Germany that culminated in the German surrender on May 8.

On the left flank, 21st Army Group — Dempsey's Second British Army and Crerar's First Canadian Army, finally on an all-out armoured blitz — shot forward towards the northern sectors of Holland and Germany. Second British Army reached Hamburg on the Elbe River on April 19. The Canadian 1 Corps liberated Amsterdam, and 2 Corps drove north to Groningen, Emden, and Oldenburg.

Temporarily attached to Montgomery's force, the British and American divisions of Ridgway's 18 Airborne Corps — those multiskilled winged soldiers — stayed on to fight as land troops, gratefully hitching rides on the tanks of armoured divisions as they spearheaded the drive to the Baltic Sea. They met the Russian armies at Wismar.

''It went like clockwork,'' Colonel Carl Peterson recalls. ''It was almost like moving pieces on a chessboard. We leapfrogged regiments, leapfrogged battalions within regiments, and just kept going.''

Simpson's Ninth Army reverted back to the command of General Bradley's 12th U.S. Army Group, completing the encirclement of the Ruhr in conjunction with Hodges's First Army. By April 19, 325,000 Germans trapped in the Ruhr had been taken prisoner. The two armies then pushed eastwards on parallel courses into central Germany, making contact with the Russians on April 25 on the Elbe.

On the right, Patton's Third Army cut southeast to Pilsen in Czechoslovakia and Linz in Austria. Patton, irrepressible to the end, made a cavalier and costly 60-mile detour to rescue his son-in-law from POW camp. Of his strike force of 307 men, only 15 returned.

The 6th U.S. Army Group (Seventh U.S. Army and First Free French Army), under General Jacob Devers, advanced through southern Germany, capturing Nuremberg and Stuttgart.

During April, the Allies took more than 1,650,000 prisoners. On May 8, the German forces in Northwest Europe formally surrendered.

It took as long to conquer the 20 miles to the Rhine as it did to cross those next 200 miles into the heart of Nazi Germany, and the cost was much higher. In the Rhineland campaign, a total of 9,284 Americans and 17,685 British and Canadians were casualties. The strategists of the three nations must share the responsibility for many of these losses.

That the British and Canadian casualties were double those of the Americans can be attributed to the ill-planned and ill-commanded Huertgen campaign and, subsequently, to Bradley's failure to capture the Roer dams. This gave the German defenders a 15-day reprieve during which they could concentrate all their resources against the First Canadian Army assault without concern for their southern flank.

Eisenhower's vacillation delayed the launching of Operation Veritable by the critical few weeks that meant the difference between winter and spring — between hard ground and mud. Montgomery compounded the folly by insisting on going ahead with a flawed battle plan. The resulting grind across the Rhineland exacted a high price. The cost was inflated even more by senior commanders who had lost touch with the realities of the battlefield. In the Huertgen Forest and in the Hochwald Gap, the fog of war took a terrible toll.

The Allied air forces were stubbornly short-sighted in refusing to concentrate their air power on knocking out the Roer dams and the Rhine bridges. This allowed General Schlemm to evacuate almost all of his artillery. It was these guns that inflicted so much damage on the airborne troops.

The Rhine was won despite the weather, despite enemy resistance, and — especially — despite the high-level inter-Allied bickering and jealousy. The Rhine was won because the officers and men fighting for it carried through ill-conceived plans with dogged courage and brilliance.

The troops at the sharp end had learned to fight together. The integrated assault that saw Americans, British, and Canadians commingling in battle was historically unique and militarily successful. It gave justification to the often-abused word "Allied."

The Welsh and Irish linked up cheerfully with the English, Americans, and Canadians. Armour and infantry finally sealed a workable partnership.

The 117,000 men from both sides of the hill who lost their lives, their limbs, and, sometimes, their freedom in that slog to the banks of the Rhine left a permanent imprint — not just in yards gained and battles won, but in the sense of decency to which they stubbornly clung throughout the ugly campaign.

Fighting men found a common denominator: humanity. On the battle-torn slopes of Moyland Wood, German troops crossed the field to take fresh milk to Canadian casualties; at the Goch-Calcar road, two wounded enemies touched hands and became friends; a German woman, Wilma Kuhler, wrote a young Welsh private to thank him for burying her husband.

"Wars settle nothing," she said.

Appendix A

ORDER OF BATTLE

21ST ARMY GROUP

FIRST CANADIAN ARMY (FOR OPERATION VERITABLE)

30 British Corps
GUARDS ARMOURED DIVISION
  5th Guards Armoured Brigade
    2 Grenadier Guards
    1 Coldstream Guards
    2 Irish Guards
    1 Grenadier Guards (Motor)
  32nd Guards Infantry Brigade
    3 Irish Guards
    5 Coldstream Guards
    2 Scots Guards
    4 Grenadier Guards
11TH ARMOURED DIVISION
  29th Armoured Brigade
    8 Bn The Rifle Brigade
    23 Hussars
    2 FS Yeomanry
    3 Royal Tanks
  159th Infantry Brigade
    4 King's Own Shropshire Light Infantry
    1 Herefordshire Regiment
    1 Cheshire Regiment
INDEPENDENT ARMOURED BRIGADES
  6th Guards Tank Brigade
    4 Tank Grenadier Guards
    4 Tank Coldstream Guards
    3 Tank Scots Guards

13/18 Royal Hussars
Nottinghamshire Yeomanry Regiment
12 King's Royal Rifle Corps (Motor)
34th Armoured Brigade
  107 Royal Armoured Regiment
  147 Royal Armoured Regiment

3RD BRITISH INFANTRY DIVISION
8th Infantry Brigade
  1 Suffolk Regiment
  2 East Yorkshire Regiment
  1 South Lancashire Regiment
9th Infantry Brigade
  2 Lincolnshire Regiment
  1 King's Own Scottish Borderers
  2 Royal Ulster Rifles
185th Infantry Brigade
  2 Royal Warwickshire Regiment
  1 Royal Norfolk Regiment
  2 King's Own Shropshire Light Infantry

15TH SCOTTISH DIVISION
44th (Lowland) Brigade
  8 Royal Scots
  6 Royal Scots Fusiliers
  6 King's Own Scottish Borderers
46th (Highland) Brigade
  9 Cameronians
  2 Glasgow Highlanders
  7 Seaforth Highlanders
227th (Highland) Brigade
  10 Highland Light Infantry
  2 Gordon Highlanders
  2 Argyll & Sutherland Highlanders

43RD WESSEX DIVISION
129th Infantry Brigade
  4 Somerset Light Infantry
  4 Wiltshire Regiment
  5 Wiltshire Regiment
130th Infantry Brigade
  7 Hampshire Regiment
  4 Dorsetshire Regiment
  5 Dorsetshire Regiment
214th Infantry Brigade

7 Somerset Light Infantry
1 Worcestershire Regiment
5 Duke of Cornwall's Light Infantry

51ST HIGHLAND DIVISION

152nd Highland Brigade
2 Seaforth Highlanders
5 Seaforth Highlanders
5 Queen's Own Cameron Highlanders
153rd Highland Brigade
5 Black Watch (RHR)
1 Gordon Highlanders
5/7 Gordon Highlanders
154th Highland Brigade
1 Black Watch (RHR)
7 Black Watch (RHR)
7 Argyll & Sutherland Highlanders

52ND LOWLAND DIVISION

156th Infantry Brigade
4/5 Royal Scots Fusiliers
6 Cameronians
7 Cameronians
155th Infantry Brigade
7/9 Royal Scots
4 King's Own Scottish Borderers
5 King's Own Scottish Borderers
157th Infantry Brigade
5 Highland Light Infantry
6 Highland Light Infantry
1 Glasgow Highlanders

53RD WELSH DIVISION

71st Infantry Brigade
4 Royal Welch Fusiliers
1 Oxfordshire & Buckinghamshire Light Infantry
1 Highland Light Infantry
158th Infantry Brigade
7 Royal Welch Fusiliers
1 East Lancashire Regiment
1/5 Welch Regiment
160th Infantry Brigade
2 Monmouthshire Regiment
4 Welch Regiment
6 Royal Welch Fusiliers

1ST COMMANDO BRIGADE
  45 Royal Marine Commando
  46 Royal Marine Commando
  3 Army Commando
  6 Army Commando

2 Canadian Corps
4TH CANADIAN ARMOURED DIVISION
  4th Canadian Armoured Brigade
    Lake Superior Regiment (Motor)
    British Columbia Regiment
    Governor General's Foot Guards
    Canadian Grenadier Guards
    South Alberta Regiment (Recce)
  10th Canadian Infantry Brigade
    Algonquin Regiment
    Lincoln & Welland Regiment
    Argyll & Sutherland Highlanders of Canada
2ND CANADIAN ARMOURED BRIGADE
  Fort Garry Horse
  The Sherbrooke Fusiliers Regiment
  1st Hussars
  18th Manitoba Car Regiment (12th Manitoba Dragoons)
2ND CANADIAN INFANTRY DIVISION
    Toronto Scottish Regiment (M.G.)
    8th Reconnaissance Regiment
  4th Canadian Infantry Brigade
    Royal Regiment of Canada
    Royal Hamilton Light Infantry (Wentworth Regiment)
    The Essex Scottish Regiment
  5th Canadian Infantry Brigade
    Black Watch (RHR of C)
    Calgary Highlanders
    Le Régiment de Maisonneuve
  6th Canadian Infantry Brigade
    Les Fusiliers Mont-Royal
    Queen's Own Cameron Highlanders of Canada
    South Saskatchewan Regiment
3RD CANADIAN INFANTRY DIVISION
    7 Reconnaissance Regiment
    The Cameron Highlanders of Ottawa (M.G.)

7th Canadian Infantry Brigade
   Regina Rifle Regiment
   Royal Winnipeg Rifles
   1 Canadian Scottish Regiment
8th Canadian Infantry Brigade
   Queen's Own Rifles of Canada
   Le Régiment de la Chaudière
   North Shore Regiment
9th Canadian Infantry Brigade
   Highland Light Infantry of Canada
   Stormont, Dundas & Glengarry Highlanders
   North Nova Scotia Highlanders

NINTH U.S. ARMY (FOR OPERATION GRENADE)

13 Corps
5TH ARMORED DIVISION
   10 Tank Battalion
   34 Tank Battalion
   81 Tank Battalion
   15 Armored Infantry Battalion
   46 Armored Infantry Battalion
   47 Armored Infantry Battalion
   620 Tank Destroyer Battalion
84TH INFANTRY DIVISION
   333 Infantry Regiment
   334 Infantry Regiment
   335 Infantry Regiment
102ND INFANTRY DIVISION
   405 Infantry Regiment
   406 Infantry Regiment
   407 Infantry Regiment
   771 Tank Battalion
16 Corps
8TH ARMORED DIVISION
   18 Tank Battalion
   36 Tank Battalion
   80 Tank Battalion
   7 Armored Infantry Battalion
   49 Armored Infantry Battalion

58 Armored Infantry Battalion
809 Tank Destroyer Battalion
35TH INFANTRY DIVISION
134 Infantry Regiment
137 Infantry Regiment
320 Infantry Regiment
784 Tank Battalion
79TH INFANTRY DIVISION
313 Infantry Regiment
314 Infantry Regiment
315 Infantry Regiment

19 Corps
2ND ARMORED DIVISION
66 Armored Regiment
67 Armored Regiment
41 Armored Regiment
702 Tank Destroyer Battalion
29TH INFANTRY DIVISION
115 Infantry Regiment
116 Infantry Regiment
175 Infantry Regiment
30TH INFANTRY DIVISION
117 Infantry Regiment
119 Infantry Regiment
120 Infantry Regiment
83RD INFANTRY DIVISION
330 Infantry Regiment
331 Infantry Regiment
332 Infantry Regiment

7 Corps
3RD ARMORED DIVISION
104TH INFANTRY DIVISION
413 Infantry Regiment
414 Infantry Regiment
415 Infantry Regiment
8TH INFANTRY DIVISION
13 Infantry Regiment
28 Infantry Regiment
34 Infantry Regiment

18 AIRBORNE CORPS (FOR OPERATION VARSITY)

17TH U.S. AIRBORNE DIVISION
194 Glider Infantry Regiment
507 Parachute Infantry Regiment
513 Parachute Infantry Regiment
6TH BRITISH AIRBORNE DIVISION
3rd Parachute Brigade
9 Parachute Battalion
8 Parachute Battalion
1 Canadian Parachute Battalion
5th Parachute Brigade
7 Parachute Battalion
12 Parchute Battalion
13 Parachute Battalion
6th Airlanding Brigade
2nd Oxfordshire & Buckinghamshire Light Infantry
12 Devonshire Regiment
1 Royal Ulster Rifles

NINTH U.S. ARMY (FOR OPERATION PLUNDER)

30TH INFANTRY DIVISION
79TH INFANTRY DIVISION

SECOND BRITISH ARMY (FOR OPERATION PLUNDER)
Formations in Operation Veritable

Appendix B

MAPS

MAP 1

THE WESTERN FRONT 8 FEB 45

MAP 2

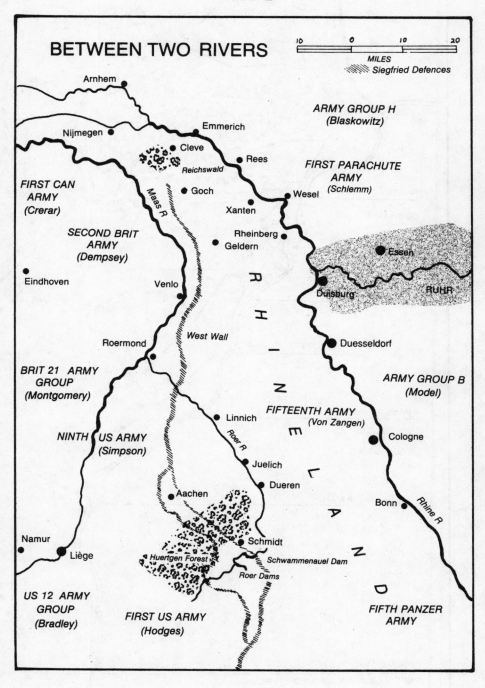

BETWEEN TWO RIVERS

10   0   10   20

MILES

Siegfried Defences

Arnhem

ARMY GROUP H
(Blaskowitz)

Nijmegen

Emmerich

Cleve

Reichswald

Rees

FIRST PARACHUTE
ARMY
(Schlemm)

FIRST CAN
ARMY
(Crerar)

Goch

Wesel

SECOND BRIT
ARMY
(Dempsey)

Maas R

Xanten

Rheinberg

Geldern

Essen

Eindhoven

Venlo

RHINE

Duisburg

RUHR

Roermond

West Wall

Duesseldorf

BRIT 21 ARMY
GROUP
(Montgomery)

ARMY GROUP B
(Model)

NINTH US ARMY
(Simpson)

Linnich

Roer R

FIFTEENTH ARMY
(Von Zangen)

Cologne

Juelich

Aachen

Dueren

Bonn

Rhine R

Namur

Liège

Schmidt

Schwammenauel Dam

Huertgen Forest

Roer Dams

US 12 ARMY
GROUP
(Bradley)

FIRST US ARMY
(Hodges)

FIFTH PANZER
ARMY

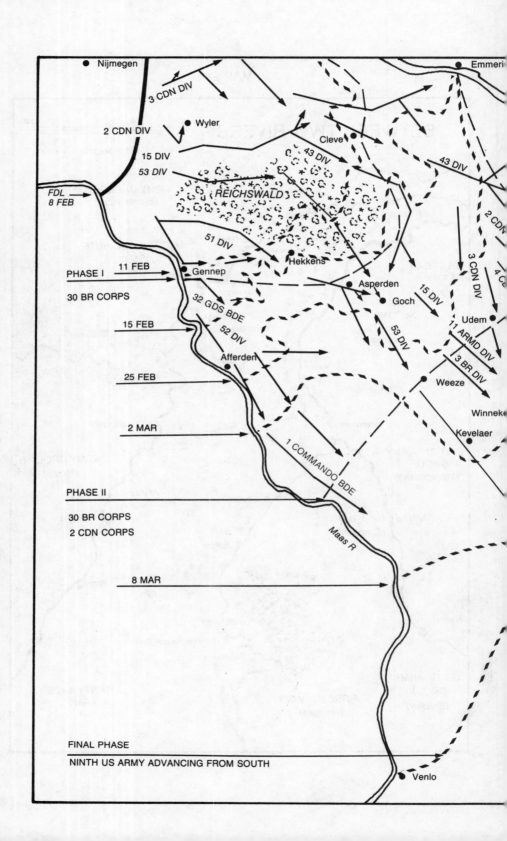

Nijmegen

3 CDN DIV

2 CDN DIV

Wyler

Emmeri

Cleve

15 DIV

43 DIV

43 DIV

53 DIV

2 CDN

FDL
8 FEB

REICHSWALD

3 CDN DIV

51 DIV

4 C

Hekkens

PHASE I   11 FEB

Gennep

Asperden

15 DIV

Udem

30 BR CORPS

32 GDS BDE

Goch

11 ARMD DIV

15 FEB

52 DIV

53 DIV

3 BR DIV

Afferden

25 FEB

Weeze

Winneke

2 MAR

Kevelaer

1 COMMANDO BDE

PHASE II

30 BR CORPS
2 CDN CORPS

Maas R

8 MAR

FINAL PHASE

NINTH US ARMY ADVANCING FROM SOUTH

Venlo

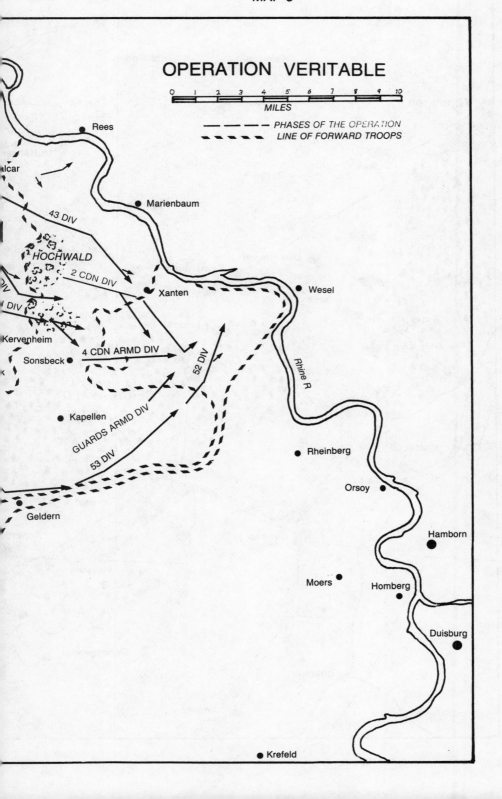

MAP 3

OPERATION VERITABLE

0 1 2 3 4 5 6 7 8 9 10
MILES

– – – – – *PHASES OF THE OPERATION*
▄ ▄ ▄ ▄ ▄ *LINE OF FORWARD TROOPS*

Rees

lcar

Marienbaum

43 DIV

HOCHWALD

2 CDN DIV

Xanten

Wesel

DIV

Kervenheim

4 CDN ARMD DIV

Sonsbeck

52 DIV

Rhine R

Kapellen

GUARDS ARMD DIV

53 DIV

Rheinberg

Orsoy

Geldern

Hamborn

Moers

Homberg

Duisburg

Krefeld

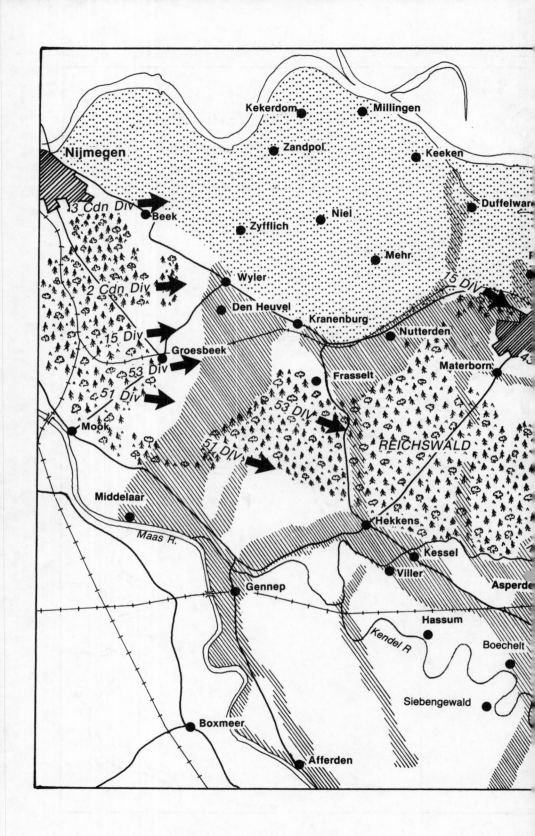

MAP 4

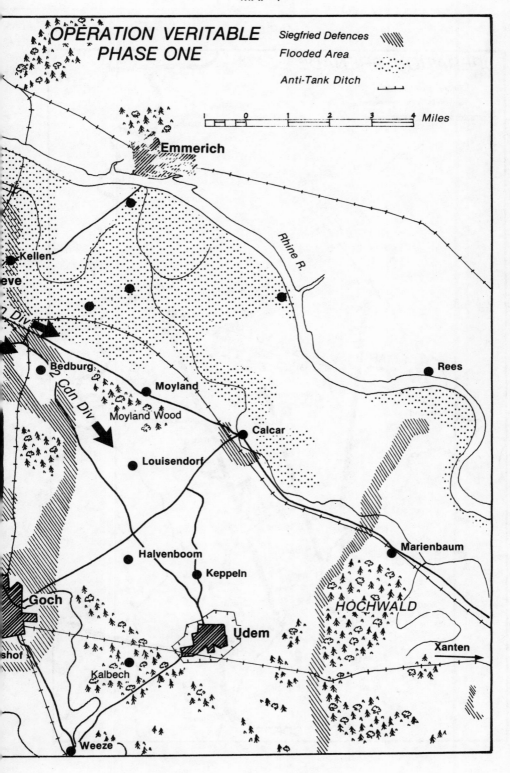

OPERATION VERITABLE
PHASE ONE

Siegfried Defences
Flooded Area
Anti-Tank Ditch

0 1 2 3 4 Miles

Emmerich

Rhine R.

Kellen

eve

7 Div

Bedburg

2 Cdn Div

Moyland

Moyland Wood

Rees

Calcar

Louisendorf

Halvenboom

Keppeln

Marienbaum

HOCHWALD

Goch

Udem

Xanten

shof

Kalbech

Weeze

MAP 5

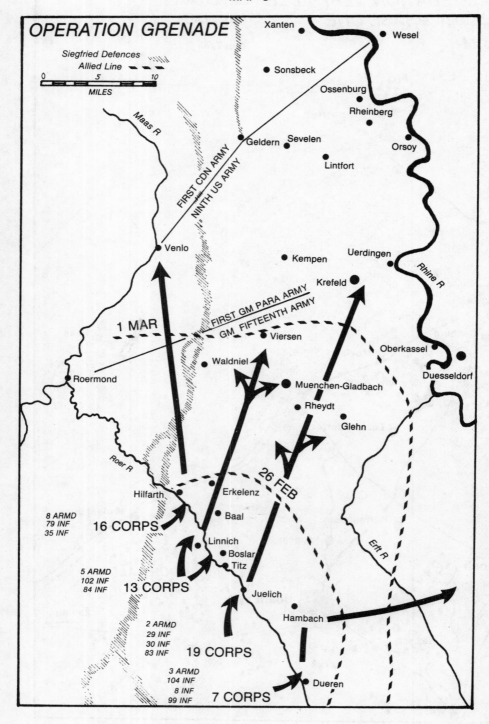

OPERATION GRENADE

Siegfried Defences ///////////
Allied Line ━ ━ ━

0   5   10
MILES

Xanten
Wesel
Sonsbeck
Ossenburg
Rheinberg
Maas R
Geldern   Sevelen
Orsoy
Lintfort
FIRST CDN ARMY
NINTH US ARMY
Venlo
Kempen   Uerdingen
Krefeld
Rhine R
FIRST GM PARA ARMY
1 MAR
GM FIFTEENTH ARMY
Viersen
Oberkassel
Waldniel
Duesseldorf
Roermond
Muenchen-Gladbach
Rheydt
Glehn
Roer R
26 FEB
Hilfarth   Erkelenz
8 ARMD
79 INF
35 INF
Baal
16 CORPS
Erft R
Linnich
5 ARMD
102 INF
84 INF
Boslar
Titz
13 CORPS
Juelich
2 ARMD
29 INF
30 INF
83 INF
Hambach
19 CORPS
3 ARMD
104 INF
8 INF
99 INF
Dueren
7 CORPS

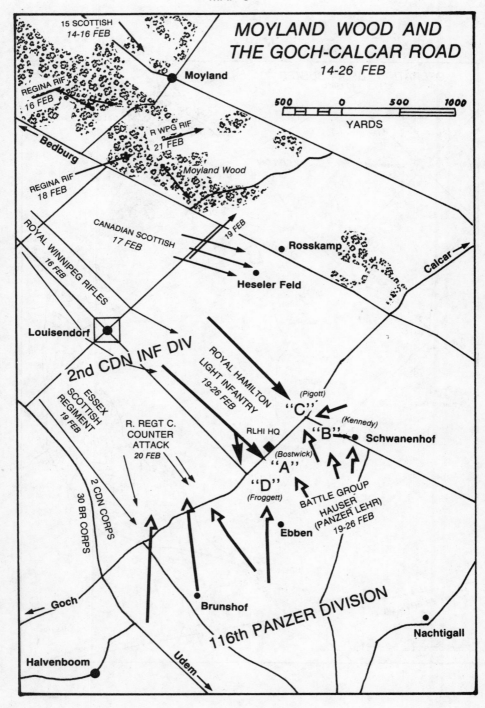

MAP 6

MOYLAND WOOD AND THE GOCH-CALCAR ROAD
14-26 FEB

500   0   500   1000
YARDS

15 SCOTTISH
14-16 FEB

Moyland

REGINA RIF
16 FEB

Bedburg

R WPG RIF
21 FEB

REGINA RIF
18 FEB

Moyland Wood

CANADIAN SCOTTISH
17 FEB

19 FEB

Rosskamp

Calcar

ROYAL WINNIPEG RIFLES
16 FEB

Heseler Feld

Louisendorf

2nd CDN INF DIV

ROYAL HAMILTON
LIGHT INFANTRY
19-26 FEB

(Pigott)
"C"

(Kennedy)
"B"   Schwanenhof

ESSEX SCOTTISH REGIMENT
19 FEB

R. REGT C.
COUNTER
ATTACK
20 FEB

RLHI HQ

(Bostwick)
"A"

2 CDN CORPS

"D"
(Froggett)

BATTLE GROUP
HAUSER
(PANZER LEHR)
19-26 FEB

30 BR CORPS

Ebben

Goch

Brunshof

116th PANZER DIVISION

Nachtigall

Halvenboom

Udem

MAP 7

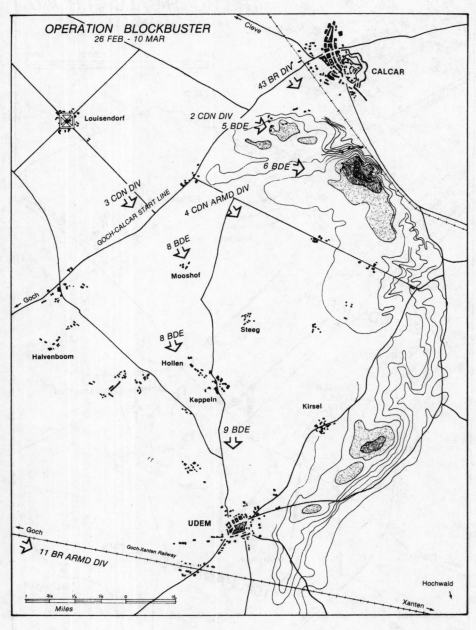

OPERATION BLOCKBUSTER
26 FEB - 10 MAR

Cleve

43 BR DIV

CALCAR

Louisendorf

2 CDN DIV
5 BDE

6 BDE

3 CDN DIV

GOCH-CALCAR START LINE

4 CDN ARMD DIV

8 BDE

Mooshof

Goch

Steeg

8 BDE

Halvenboom

Hollen

Keppeln

Kirsel

9 BDE

UDEM

Goch

11 BR ARMD DIV

Goch-Xanten Railway

Hochwald

Xanten

Miles

MAP 8

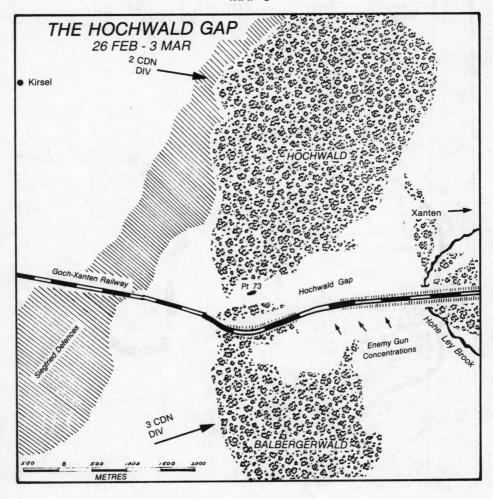

THE HOCHWALD GAP
26 FEB - 3 MAR
2 CDN DIV

Kirsel

HOCHWALD

Xanten

Goch-Xanten Railway

Pt 73

Hochwald Gap

Hohe Ley Brook

Siegfried Defences

Enemy Gun Concentrations

3 CDN DIV

BALBERGERWALD

500   0   500   1000   1500   2000
METRES

MAP 9

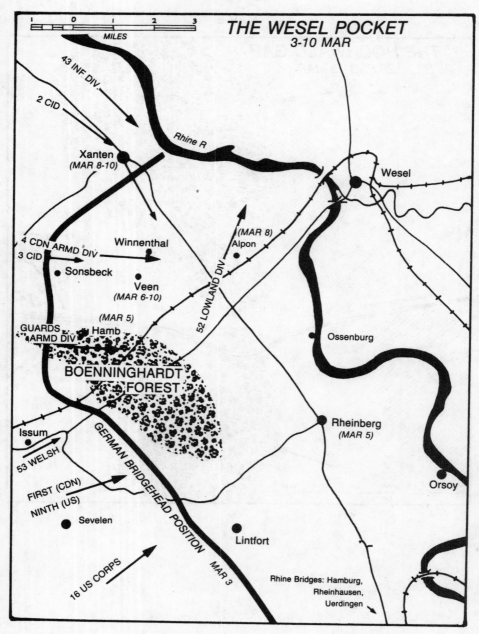

THE WESEL POCKET
3-10 MAR

MILES

43 INF DIV

2 CID

Rhine R

Xanten
(MAR 8-10)

Wesel

Winnenthal

(MAR 8)
Alpon

4 CDN ARMD DIV

3 CID

Sonsbeck

Veen
(MAR 6-10)

52 LOWLAND DIV

(MAR 5)

GUARDS
ARMD DIV

Hamb

Ossenburg

BOENNINGHARDT
FOREST

Issum

GERMAN BRIDGEHEAD POSITION

53 WELSH

FIRST (CDN)

NINTH (US)

Sevelen

Rheinberg
(MAR 5)

Orsoy

Lintfort

16 US CORPS

MAR 3

Rhine Bridges: Hamburg,
Rheinhausen,
Uerdingen

MAP 10

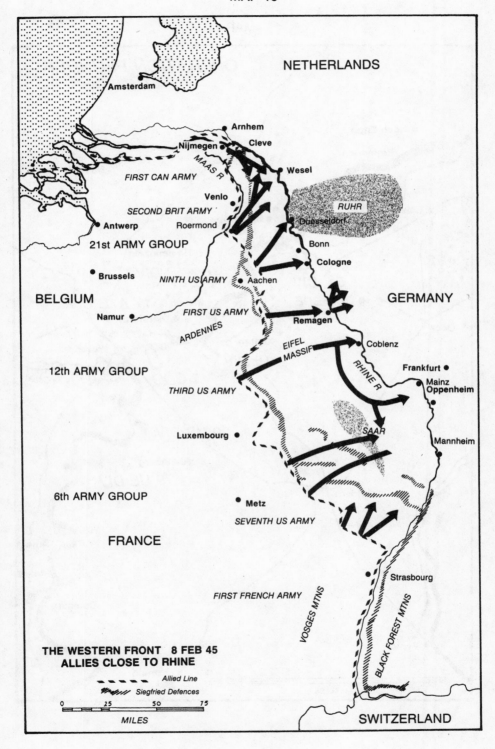

NETHERLANDS

Amsterdam

Arnhem
Nijmegen
Cleve

Wesel

FIRST CAN ARMY

MAAS R

Venlo

RUHR

SECOND BRIT ARMY

Roermond
Duesseldorf

Antwerp

Bonn

21st ARMY GROUP

Cologne

Brussels

NINTH US ARMY
Aachen

BELGIUM

FIRST US ARMY

GERMANY

Namur

Remagen

ARDENNES

Coblenz

EIFEL
MASSIF

RHINE R

12th ARMY GROUP

Frankfurt

THIRD US ARMY

Mainz
Oppenheim

SAAR

Luxembourg

Mannheim

6th ARMY GROUP

Metz

SEVENTH US ARMY

FRANCE

Strasbourg

FIRST FRENCH ARMY

VOSGES MTNS

BLACK FOREST MTNS

**THE WESTERN FRONT   8 FEB 45
ALLIES CLOSE TO RHINE**

- - - - -   Allied Line

〰〰〰   Siegfried Defences

0   25   50   75

MILES

SWITZERLAND

MAP 11

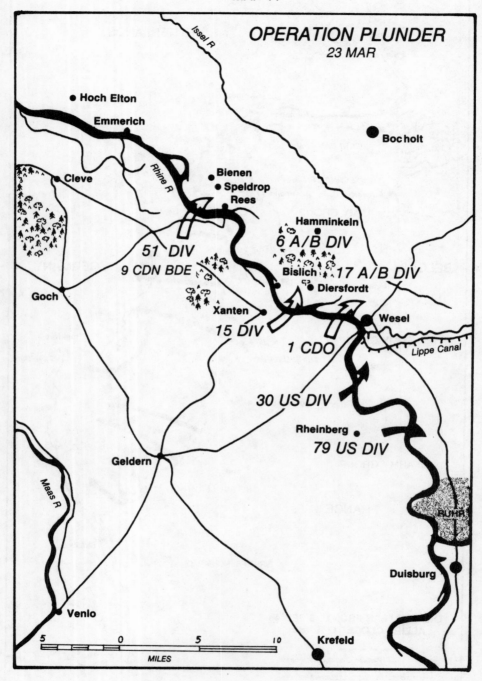

MAP 12

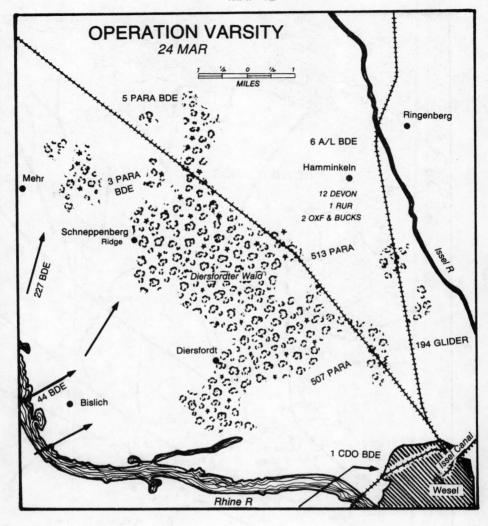

OPERATION VARSITY
24 MAR

MILES

5 PARA BDE

Ringenberg

6 A/L BDE

Mehr

3 PARA BDE

Hamminkeln

12 DEVON
1 RUR
2 OXF & BUCKS

Schneppenberg Ridge

227 BDE

513 PARA

Issel R

Diersfordter Wald

194 GLIDER

Diersfordt

44 BDE

507 PARA

Bislich

1 CDO BDE

Issel Canal

Wesel

Rhine R

MAP 13

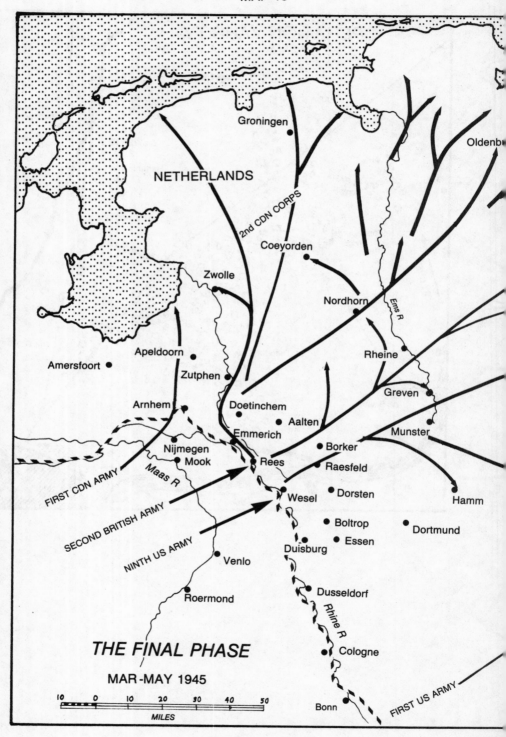

THE FINAL PHASE

MAR-MAY 1945

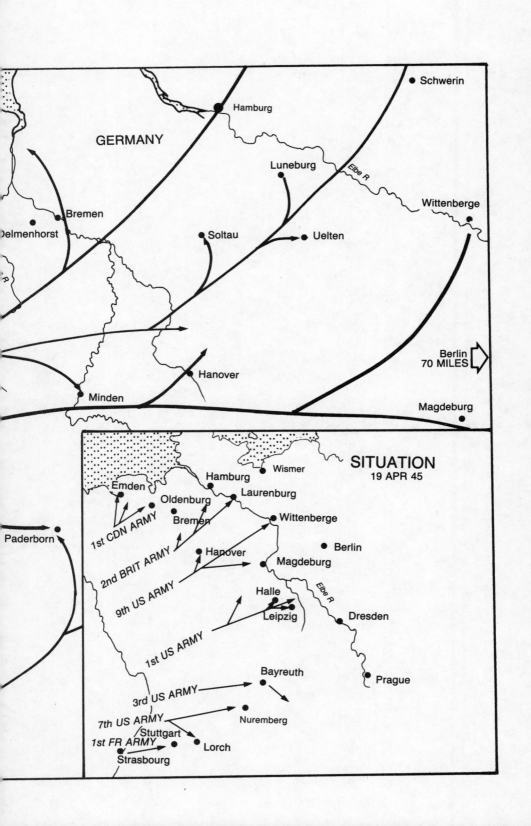

GERMANY

Schwerin

Hamburg

Luneburg

Elbe R

Wittenberge

Bremen

Delmenhorst

Soltau

Uelten

Berlin
70 MILES

Hanover

Minden

Magdeburg

SITUATION
19 APR 45

Wismer

Emden

Hamburg

Oldenburg

Laurenburg

1st CDN ARMY

Bremen

Wittenberge

2nd BRIT ARMY

Hanover

Berlin

9th US ARMY

Magdeburg

Paderborn

Elbe R

Halle

Leipzig

Dresden

1st US ARMY

Bayreuth

Prague

3rd US ARMY

7th US ARMY

Nuremberg

Stuttgart

1st FR ARMY

Lorch

Strasbourg

Glossary

AA Anti-aircraft
ADC Aide-de-camp
AGRA Army Group Royal Artillery
AP Armoured-piercing
APC Armoured personnel carrier
Artillery targets MIKE (regimental), UNCLE (divisional)
AVRE Armoured Vehicle Royal Engineers
Bailey bridge Portable steel bridge
BAR Browning automatic rifle
Bazooka Anti-tank rocket launcher
Bde Brigade
Bn Battalion
Bofors 40mm AA gun used by British and Canadian troops
BS Bronze Star
Buffalo (LVT) An amphibious troop carrier
Canloan Canadian officers loaned to the British army in 1944
CCA Combat Command A — Strike force (United States)
CCB Combat Command B — Strike force
CCR Combat Command Reserve — Strike force
CIB Canadian Infantry Brigade
CID Canadian Infantry Division
C-in-C Commander-in-Chief
CIGS Chief of the Imperial General Staff
CO Commanding officer
CP Command post
CRA Commander Royal Artillery
CRE Commander Royal Engineers
DAQMG Administrative officer: deputy assistant quartermaster general
DCM Distinguished Conduct Medal
DD Tank Duplex drive tank: Sherman tanks made waterproof and amphibious with inflatable air tubes
D-Day Day on which an operation commences or is to commence
DIS Disabled
DSO Distinguished Service Order
DUKW 2.5-ton amphibious troop or supply carrier

DZ Drop zone

FDLs Forward defence lines

FOO Forward observation officer

FS Fallschirmtruppen (German parachute troops)

Funnies Tanks of the 79th Armoured Division designed to overcome specific obstacles: Flail (mine-destroyer), Crocodile (flamethrower), AVREs (petards, ditch-spanning equipment)

FUP Forming up place (where troops assemble before going into battle)

GC Group Captain

GOC General Officer Commanding

GSO General staff officer

GPO Gun position officer

Grenades 36 grenade (fragmenting); 77 grenade (smoke), stick grenade (German model with stick to aid throwing)

H-Hour Exact time on D-day at which a specific operation commences

HE High explosive

HQ headquarters

Inf Infantry

IO Intelligence officer

Kangaroo A type of APC (Priest)

KIA Killed in action

Lagger Tank circular defensive position assumed at night

LMG Light machine gun

LO Liaison officer

LOB Left out of battle

LVT Landing vehicle tracked

LZ Landing zone

MC Military Cross

Me-262 Jet aircraft (introduced by Germans in 1945)

Magen/Ohren Battalions German units whose personnel had physical weaknesses (intestinal or ear)

MM Military Medal

MMG Medium machine gun (Vickers)

Monty's Moonlight Beams bounced off clouds to create artificial light for night fighting

Nebelwerfer 150mm German mortar ("Moaning Minnie")

NRMA National Resources Mobilization Act

O Group Briefing by a commander for oncoming tactical activity

Oberleutnant Lieutenant-colonel

OC Officer Commanding (usually a company)
OKW Oberkommando der Wehrmacht
OP Observation post
Panzer (Pz) Tank
Panzerfaust German anti-tank weapon
PIAT British/Canadian anti-tank weapon
POW Prisoner of war
RAP Regimental aid post
RCAMC Royal Canadian Army Medical Corps
RCASC Royal Canadian Army Service Corps
RCCS Royal Canadian Corps of Signals
Recce Reconnaissance
RE (RCE) Royal (Canadian) Engineers
RTU Return to unit
Sapper British engineer
Schmeisser German short hand-held rapid-firing light machine gun
Schu-mine German anti-personnel mine
Set-piece attack Attack carefully planned in detail
SHAEF Supreme Headquarters Allied Expeditionary Force
Sitrep Situation report
SP Self-propelled
Spandau 34 or 42 model light machine gun
SS Silver Star
Tac HQ Tactical headquarters
Trenching tool Short spade carried by infantry for digging slit trenches
Typhoon Rocket-carrying fighter aircraft
U.S. staff S-1 (Personnel), S-2 (Intelligence), S-3 (Operations), S-4 (Supply), S-5 (Military government). G-1, G-2, and so on are used for General Officer's Staff
Volkssturm People's militia formed as last resort by Germans
Weasel Broad tracked semi-amphibious vehicle
WIA Wounded in action

Notes on Sources

The main sources of primary material for our book were found in archival collections in four countries: Great Britain, Canada, the United States, and West Germany.

GREAT BRITAIN

Imperial War Museum (IWM), London

Under the direction of Mr. Roderick Suddaby, Keeper of the Department of Documents, the papers of Field-Marshal Viscount Montgomery of Alamein have been catalogued by Mr. Stephen Brooks of the IWM research department and stored on microfilm. Sixteen boxes are currently available (material dated from 1948 onwards has not been released to the public), catalogued as The Papers of FM Viscount Montgomery of Alamein, KG, GCB, DSO, DL 1887–1976. Section E, Reels 7 to 14, includes Montgomery's Papers 1944–1946, and personal and private signals to CIGS (BLM 72 – BLM 174). Of special interest is Reel 7, comprising "Notes on the Campaign in North-West Europe." This personal diary, written almost daily in longhand in pencil on foolscap paper by the Field-Marshal and transcribed by his MA, Lt-Col C.P. "Kit" Dawnay, was classified until its release to researchers in 1986.

Other IWM material: De Guingand Papers. Papers of Lt-Col T.S. Bigland. The IWM has the BBC Sound Library and a vast collection of documents, diaries, letters, and combat narratives that have passed into the Department of Documents from veterans and their families over many years. The Department of Printed Books contains a comprehensive collection of military histories.

Public Record Office (PRO), Kew, Richmond, Surrey

Battlefield Tours BAOR (British Army on the Rhine): Operations Veritable, Plunder, Varsity (WO 222). Combat Narratives: Cabinet Records (CAB 106). CMHQ (Canadian Military Headquarters) Historical Narratives (CAB 44). Operations Reports, War Diaries, and Combat Reports for all British divisions and battalions involved in the Rhineland campaign: War Office Records (WO 171). Weekly Intelligence Summaries (WO 208). Interrogation of German Generals (WO 106).

Liddell Hart Centre for Military Archives (LHCMA), King's College, London (Curator: Dr Patricia Methuen)
Liddell-Hart Papers. Chester Wilmot Papers (15/15/3). Alanbrooke Diary (Alanbrooke 3/B/XV LHCMA). Alanbrooke Papers (14/7). Special Interrogation Report: Gen Alfred Schlemm, Commander First Parachute Army (LH 9/24/135 LHCMA). Special Interrogation Report: Gen Heinrich Freiherr von Luettwitz, Commander 2 Panzer Division and 47 Panzer Corps (LH 9/24/123: LHCMA). Special Interrogation Report: Gen Eugen Meindl (LH 9/24/126): LHCMA). Special Interrogation Report: FM Gerd von Rundstedt (LH 9/24/132 LHCMA). Special Interrogation Report: Maj-Gen Heinz Fiebig, Commander 84 Infantry Division (LH 9/24/104: LHCMA). "The Forces in the Reichswald" (LH 9/24/142 LHCMA). "44 R.T.R. at the Rhine Crossing" (LH 15/15/30). Chester Wilmot Papers, "Notes of Gen Ismay and Gen Jacob," 26 May 1949 (LH 15/15/3 LHCMA). "Letter written 14 May 1946 by Maj A.D. Parsons, 4th Battalion the Wiltshire Regiment, to Chester Wilmot" (LH 15/15/54 LHCMA).

National Army Museum, London

Royal Staff College, Tactical Doctrine Retrieval Cell, Camberley, Surrey (Staff Officer: Lt-Col George Truell)
BAOR Battlefield Tours: These comprise on-site studies of specific battles several years after they occurred. Veterans who were involved in each battle return to the battleground and for several days walk through the various stages of the conflict, examining it from many aspects: infantry, armour, artillery, supply, engineers, and so on, and from many levels from army and division down to battalion and company. Military students follow the action, and notes are recorded as each veteran describes his role. Such studies are repeated after intervals of several years and offer fresh information as the personnel changes. These studies are made available to military students, and copies are to be found at a number of military archives in the U.K. and Canada.

Airborne Forces Museum, Browning Barracks, Aldershot (Director: Maj Geoffrey Norton)

Wiltshire Regimental Museum, Salisbury, Wiltshire (Col D. I. M. Robbins)

Royal Scots Regimental Museum, The Castle, Edinburgh

King's Own Scottish Borderers Regimental Museum, The Barracks, Berwick on Tweed (Director: Lt-Col David Ward)

Royal Welch Fusiliers Comrades Association, Wrexham, Clwyd (Secretary: Capt P.H. Shinn)

Queen's Own Highlanders Headquarters (Seaforth and Camerons), Cameron Barracks, Inverness

Regimental Headquarters, Grenadier Guards, London (Director: Col A. T. W. Duncan).

Commando Association of Great Britain, London (Secretary: Henry Brown)

Private Collections
The following unpublished accounts were kindly lent to the authors.
"2nd Bn The Seaforth Highlanders: Account of the Battle of the Rhine." A personal unpublished account by Col GW Dunn, CBE, DSO, MC, TD, DL.
"The Reichswald Battles." A personal unpublished account by Col A.I.R. Murray, OBE, 2nd Bn Seaforth Highlanders.
"Battle of the Reichswald." A personal unpublished account by Lt-Col C.P. Dryland, Royal Welch Fusiliers.
"Reichswald Revisited." A personal unpublished account by Donald F. Callander.
"Operation Veritable." A personal unpublished account by Maj K.J. Irvine, Adjutant, 2 Bn Gordon Highlanders.
Diary of Lt-Col Ivor Reeves, DSO & Bar, MC, and "Letters written by I.L.R. to his wife and father, 1943–1944" (IWM).

CANADA

Public Archives of Canada (PAC), Ottawa (Military Archivist: Barbara M. Wilson)
During World War II, the Official Canadian Military Historian, Col Charles P. Stacey was stationed with CMHQ in London. He coordinated the efforts of a team of trained historians who visited battlefields after an engagement and interviewed personnel involved. These are found as Battle Narratives, CMHQ Historical Officer's Reports, Record Group (RG) 24, G3. In addition, every Canadian

field unit was required to keep a War Diary. Besides offering an accurate chronicle of events, these also contain combat reports (RG 24, Vol. 14,000 – 16,000). Also at PAC: Crerar Papers (MG 30, E 157); Special Interrogation Report: Gen Erich Straube, Commander 86 Infantry Corps (RG24 Vol. 20437)

Department of National Defence (DND), Historical Branch, Ottawa (Dr. W.A.B. Douglas, Director, Directorate of History) The department contains many of the documents stored at the Public Archives of Canada, including the CMHQ Historical Officers' and Combat Reports. The DND collection also includes: Maj-Gen C.C. Mann, CBE, DSO, *The Campaign in North-west Europe, Vol. 3, No. 4., July 1949*, published by the Directorate of Military Training under authority of the Chief of the General Staff; and Lt-Col W.R. Sawyer, *Report on Smoke Screens carried out by First Canadian Army*, printed in the field by 1 Canadian Mobile Printing Section, RCASC, 15 July 1945.

Royal Canadian Military Institute (RCMI), Toronto (Chairman Library Committee: Fl-Lt W.B. Richardson; Librarian: Ms Ann Melvin) RCMI has Canadian and British regimental histories. Also, "An Account of the Operations of Second Army in Europe 1944-1945, Vol. II," compiled by Headquarters Second Army, Secret Copy no. 13, Lt-General Sir N.M. Ritchie, presented to the RCMI in 1979.

Personal papers and diaries were generously lent to the authors. The personal diary of Brig N.E. Rodger, Chief of Staff, 2 Canadian Corps, was lent to us by courtesy of Lt-Gen Rodger. Papers of Lt-Gen G.G. Simonds were lent by his son, Col Charles Simonds. Lt-Gen Daniel Spry and Maj Lawrence Dampier lent us 3 CID GOC Operations Reports.

Theses
Geoffrey William Hayes, "The Friction of War: A Study of the Lincoln and Welland Regiment 1940-1945," master's thesis, Wilfrid Laurier University, Waterloo, 1985.
Martha Ann Hooker, "In Defence of Unity: Canada's Military Policies, 1935-1944," master's thesis, Carleton University, Ottawa, 1985.

UNITED STATES

National Archives (NA), Washington, D.C. (Mr Richard L. Boylan, Assistant Chief, Military Field Branch, Military Archives Division, Suitland, Maryland)

NA has amassed a comprehensive chronicle of the events of World War II. In the wake of each attack, trained historians — many of them still noted figures in their field today — interrogated front-line troops and their commanders intensively. These combat interviews and After Action Reports were usually conducted within 48 hours of each action. The result is some 8,000 cubic feet of data catalogued in 25,000 boxes. More than a third of it is directed to the European war. The interviews are catalogued in Record Group (RG) 407, Adjutant General's Office (AGO), Records of United States Army Command, European Theatre of Operations, Com bat Interviews 1944-45 (edited by James G. Bradsner, compiled by King Merendine and John B. Meyer, General Archives Division).

Also at NA: Mission Reports (RG 18) for all American units in the Rhineland Campaign. Interrogation Reports of German Generals (RG 319): Meindl, Eugen F.S., General and Command- ing General of 2 FS Corps (MS no. B-093, RG 338). "The 84th Infan- try Div during the fight from the Reichswald to Wesel" by Heinz Fiebig, Major-Gen, retired cmdr 84th Infantry Div, written April 1948. "116th Panzer Division: 4 to 10 March 1945: Operations in the Wesel Pocket" by Generalleutnant Gustav Hoehne (MS #B-224). "History of Panzer Lehr Div 15/25 Feb 45" by Maj A.D. Helmut Hudel. "First FS Army: Report of the Commander," prepared by Gen FS Alfred Schlemm at #11 POW Camp, Wales (MS #B-084). "84th Inf Div from the Roer to the Rhine." "The 84 Inf Div in the Battle for Germany." "104th Infantry Div: Report by Maj Hugh L. Carrie, S-3, 415 Infantry Rgt 104 Div."

U.S. Army Military History Institute (USAMHI), Carlisle Barracks, Pa. (Deputy Director: Lt-Col Martin W. Andresen; Archivist Manuscripts: Dr John Sommers; Chief Historian Reference Branch: John J. Slonaker; Historian Reference Branch: David Keough).

Office of the Chief of Military History (OCMH) Collection, Supreme Command Box: Interviews by Dr Forrest Pogue with Brig Sir Edgar T. Williams, Lt-Gen Walter Bedell Smith, Maj-Gen A.W. Kenner, and Lt-Gen Sir Frederick E. Morgan. Papers of Gen Omar Brad- ley, Wm. G. Sylvan, Gen Wm Simpson, Gen Floyd Lavinius Parks. Chester B. Hansen Papers and Diary. Senior Officers Oral History

Program (1975–   ): Lt-Gen Elwood R. Quesada, Gen James E. Moore, Col Charles G. Patterson (''Reflections on Gen Courtney Hodges''). Excerpts from the private correspondence of John S. Wade Jr. Reference material includes regimental and battalion histories (many of them now out of print), manuscripts, and private collections.

The works of two historians — Col C.P. Stacey, the official Canadian military historian, and his counterpart in the United States, Col Charles B. MacDonald, Deputy Chief Historian of the U.S. Army, who served as an infantry company commander in four European campaigns in World War II — were used widely in every chapter in this book and will not be referenced in every instance. Their works, which are listed in the bibliography, present an excellent overview of the Northwest Europe campaign as well as focussing on actions involving Canadian and American units. These men were also unfailingly encouraging and helpful to us during our research.

WEST GERMANY

Bundesarchiv-Militaer Archiv, Freiburg

Militaergeschichtliches Forschungsamt, Freiburg (Oberstleutnant Kindler)
Biographical information on Generals von Waldenburg, Fiebig, Schlemm, Guderian, von Luettwitz, supplied by Dr Friedhelm Kruger-Sprengel, Minister of Defence, and the Military Historical Research Dept. Translation by Elizabeth Carlson, Toronto.

Archiv Landkreis, Kleve

PROLOGUE

Authors' interview with Col Charles MacDonald. On Gen Bradley, in this and the following chapters: Bradley Papers, Chester B. Hansen Papers, OCMH Collection (USAMHI). Bradley and Blair, *A General's Life*. Gavin, *On to Berlin*. MacDonald, *The Mighty Endeavor, The Last Offensive, The Battle of the Huertgen Forest*.

CHAPTERS ONE and TWO
On Germany: Authors' interview with Maj-Gen Heinz Guenther Guderian. General Straube Interrogation Report (PAC). ''Trans-

lation of Captured Document,'' Intelligence Summary #144 (PRO). Chester Wilmot Papers, ''Notes of Gen Ismay and Gen Jacob,'' 26 May 1949 (LHCMA). Correspondence of John S. Wade Jr. (USAMHI). Cooper, *The German Army*. Trevor-Roper, *Hitler's War Directives*. Speer, *Inside the Third Reich*. Kee, *The World We Fought For*. Armstrong, *Unconditional Surrender*. Shulman, *Defeat in the West*.

On Eisenhower, Bradley, and Hodges: as above. William G. Sylvan Diary (USAMHI). Weighley, *Eisenhower's Lieutenants*. Ambrose, *The Supreme Commander*. Wilmot, *Struggle for Europe*. Bradley and Blair, *A General's Life*.

On Montgomery, the most definitive biography is Nigel Hamilton's three-volume work based largely on the same papers at the IWM to which we gained access in 1986. Volume III, *Monty: The Field-Marshal*, deals with the period 1944–1976. Montgomery Papers (IWM). Pogue interviews of Lt-Gen Sir Frederick Morgan and Brig Williams (USAMHI). Authors' interview with Cpl Peter Huntley. Patton, *War As I Knew It*.

On LOs: authors' interview with Lt-Col Trumbull Warren. Papers of Lt-Col T.S. Bigland (IWM). Broadcast to the European Service of the BBC, October 8, 1948, by Chester Wilmot: ''First Soldier of Europe'' (LH).

On Lt Nichols: Hutchison, *Canada's Black Watch*. Straube Interrogation. Personal Diary of Brig N.E. Rodger.

CHAPTER THREE

Signals from Montgomery to CIGS throughout the text: Montgomery Papers (IWM).

On preparations and problems before Veritable: authors' interviews with Maj-Gen Roger Rowley, Gen Geoffrey Walsh, Maj-Gen A. Bruce Matthews, Lt-Gen L.G.C. Lilley, Maj Donald Callander, Maj A.W. Gaade, Col Brian A. Fargus. ''Watch on the Maas,'' CMHQ Historical Officer's Report (DND); battalion war diaries and histories (PAC and PRO). Nicholson, *The Gunners of Canada*, Vol. II. Battle Narrative, Operation Veritable (PAC). 43 Div Intelligence Summary (PRO). Regimental histories: Queen's Own Rifles of Canada, Royal Scots Fusiliers, 2 Bn Argyll & Sutherland Highlanders, 1 Cdn Scottish Regt.

On Gen Crerar: authors' interviews with Lt-Gen Wm Anderson, Brig G. E. Beament, Pvt Thomas MacDonald, Capt Finley Morrison, Maj-Gen Dan Spry, Peggy Palmer (Gen Crerar's daughter), and Maj H.Z. Palmer (Gen Crerar's son-in-law). Crerar Papers and GOC War Diary (PAC).

On Gen Horrocks: authors' interviews with Maj David Russell and Maj Thomas Landale Rollo. Horrocks, *Corps Commander*. Obituary by Brig James Oliver, *Soldier Magazine*, April 1985. Warner, *Horrocks: The General Who Led from the Front*.

CHAPTER FOUR

Authors' interviews with Maj-Gen John Graham, Brig P.A.S. Todd, Maj-Gen Roger Rowley, Lt-Col Trumbull Warren, Lt-Gen Wm. Anderson, Lt-Col George Pangman, Gen Geoffrey Walsh, Brig-Gen Frank Lace, Maj H.Z. Palmer, Maj R.K. MacKenzie, Capt C.P. Dryland, Lt Guy de Merlis, Maj-Gen D.C. Spry, Maj J.T. Hugill, Capt Blake Oulton, Maj William Matthews, Lt-Col F. Arthur Sparks, Heinz Bosch (Geldern), Wilhelm Michels (Cleve), Wilhelm and Elizabeth Haas (Cleve), Herbert von Bebber (Xanten).

Interrogation report Maj-Gen Fiebig (NA). Crerar Papers Vol. 1 (PAC). "Capture of Wyler," Memo of Account by Maj. W.D. Heyland given to Historical Officer, 2 CID, 15 Feb 45 (DND). "Account by W.J. Megill of Operations Veritable and Blockbuster" (PAC). Lecture notes given to the authors by GOC 3 CID Daniel Charles Spry. Report on Operation Veritable prepared by RCE 3 CID (PAC). CRE Account 8 Feb-12 Mar (PAC). Horrocks, *Corps Commander*. Woolcombe, *Lion Rampant*. Middleford and Everitt, *The Bomber Command War Diaries*. Martin, *The History of the 15th Scottish Division*. Nicholson, *The Gunners of Canada*. Shulman, *Defeat in the West*. Roy, *Ready for the Fray*.

CHAPTER FIVE

Authors' interviews with Brig Charles Richardson, Lt-Col E. Remington-Hobbs, Lt Robt Jackson, Sgt Alex Kidd, Capt Derek Ford, Brig David McQueen, Maj Harry Morton, Lt-Col R.B. Wilkinson, Sgt James Sinclair, Maj Victor Beckhurst, Sgt Leslie R. Knight, Col Brian A. Fargus, Capt J.L. Meredith, Capt Tom Powell, Capt Gordon Wright. Correspondence with Maj K.J. Irvine. Simpson Papers and William G. Sylvan Diary (USAMHI). Letter from Maj A.D. Parsons to Chester Wilmot, 14 May 46 (LH). Notes of Discussion, Chester Wilmot and Brian Horrocks (LH). Horrocks, *Corps Commander*. Essame, *Battle for Germany* and *43rd Wessex Division at*

War. Draper, *84th Infantry Division*. Hamilton, *Monty: The Field-Marshal*. Division history, regimental histories, and war diaries of all battalions of 15th Scottish Division (PRO and IWM).

CHAPTER SIX

Authors' interviews with Maj-Gen Heinz Guderian, Lt Alexander Uhlig, Cpl Mobel Rexing, Sgt Leslie Knight, Maj Fred Tilston, Lt-Col G.P. Wood, Maj James Gammie. Letter from Maj A.D. Parsons to Chester Wilmot, 14 May/46 (LH).

Interrogation reports, Gens Heinrich von Luettwitz, Alfred Schlemm, Eugen Meindl, and Heinz Fiebig (LHCMA). Biographical information supplied by Dr Friedhelm Kruger-Sprengel, Ministry of Defence, and the Military Historical Research Dept, Freiburg, West Germany (translation by Elizabeth Carlson, Toronto). Battlefield Tour Operation Veritable: A Summary of German Operations. Montgomery, *Normandy to the Baltic*. Ewing, *29 Let's Go!*. Hewitt, *Workhorse of the Western Front*. Bennett, *Ultra in the West*.

CHAPTER SEVEN

Authors' interviews with Lance Cpl and Mrs Peter V. Huntley, Maj A.W. Gaade, Maj John Chaston, Col Christopher Hill, Sgt Raymond Howell, Maj Jack Catley, Pvt David Edwards, Capt C.P. Dryland, Col Brian Fargus, Father G. Thuring (Bredeweg, Netherlands). "7 Days Fighting through the Reichswald: Report on 34 Armoured Brigade" (IWM). "Wonderful Feats of Endurance" by Joe Illingworth, *Yorkshire Post* war correspondent (private collection). Bolland, *Team Spirit*. Division history, regimental histories, and war diaries of all battalions of 53rd Welsh Division (PRO and IWM). Perrett, *Through Mud and Blood*. Lindsay, *So Few Got Through*.

CHAPTER EIGHT

Authors' interviews with Lt-Col Thomas Landale Rollo, Maj David Russell, Maj Donald Fraser Callander, Maj James Ian Gammie, Maj-Gen J.D.C. Graham, Lt Ross LeMesurier, Col Maurice Carter, Col Ian Murray, Brig G.L.W. Andrews, Lt Nevil Wykes, CSM George Morrice, Col Hector Mackenzie, Lt-Col G.P. Wood, Father Hans Hueneborn. Lang, *Return to St. Valéry*. 51st Highland Division history, regimental histories, and war diaries of all battalions of 51st Highland Division (PRO and IWM).

CHAPTER NINE

Correspondence with Lt-Col Ivor Reeves. Authors' interviews with Lt-Col Edward Remington-Hobbs, Capt Robert Hemmingsen, Lt Robt Jackson, Staff Sgt Rufus Wilkes, Maj Victor Beckhurst, Capt Derek Ford, Brig David McQueen, Lt-Gen Wm. Anderson, Brig G.E. Beament, Brig P.A.S. Todd, Maj-Gen Dan Spry, Lt-Gen N.E. Rodger, Brig Frank Lace, Maj-Gen Bruce Matthews, Capt Marshall Stearns, Col Hugh Rose, Maj Donald Callander, Lt-Col G.P. Wood.

Combat Interviews, AGO (NA). After Action Report, "Publicity & Psychological Warfare," 17 Feb 45 (NA). Mick, *With the 102d Infantry Division*. Diary of Lt-Col Ivor Reeves, DSO & Bar, MC, and "Letters written by I.L.R. to his wife and father, 1943–1945" (IWM). Papers of N. Chaston: "Diary of a Ranger" (IWM). Interrogation of Gen Schlemm (NA). Essame, *43rd Wessex Division at War*. "Four Days in the Wood of Hellfire," *The People's Journal*, April 8, 1967 (lent to the authors by Lt-Col Remington-Hobbs). Diary of Capt Peter Dryland (lent to the authors by Capt Dryland, Wrexham, Wales). Lindsay, *So Few Got Through*.

CHAPTER TEN

Authors' interviews with Brig David McQueen, Brig George Andrews, Col Ian Murray, Lt-Col Thomas Landale Rollo, Col Brian A. Fargus, Maj J.H.F. Morton, Lt-Col G.P. Wood, Col John Chaston, Maj Victor Beckhurst, Lt Ross LeMesurier, Capt J.A. Clovis, Pvt David Edwards, Sgt James Sinclair Cornwall, Sgt Alexander Kidd, CSM George Morrice. Letter to the authors from Baron Adrian von Steengracht, Moyland, Germany, January 2, 1988. Interrogation of Gen Schlemm (NA). Rosse, *Story of the 6th Army Tank Brigade*. Lindsay, *So Few Got Through*. Shulman, *Defeat in the West*. Diary of Maj K.J. Irvine, lent by his kind permission. Joe Illingworth, "Wonderful Feats of Endurance," *Yorkshire Post* (private collection). Narrative by A. Fieber. 1 Manchester Regt, "And I Never Fired a Shot" (IWM). "Translation of Ey Document, captured by 17th Abn Div on 26 March 1945" (NA). "Report by Lt-Col J.A. Peterkin, CO 1st Bn Gordon Highlanders, 26 Feb 45"

(PRO). After Action Reports (NA). Address by Dr G. de Ward, curator, during a ceremony (attended by the authors) awarding a medal to the late Maj R.E. Balfour, September 14, 1985, in the Stadhalle, Cleve, West Germany. Horrocks, *A Full Life*. Division and regimental histories and war diaries of the 15th Scottish and 51st Highland Divisions.

CHAPTER ELEVEN

Authors' interviews with Maj-Gen D.C. Spry, Maj-Gen Heinz-Guenther Guderian, Capt Harvey Bailey, Sgt John Campbell, Lt-Col L.R. Fulton, Maj Wm. Matthews. Capt Norman Donahue, "The Clearing of Moyland Wood by 7 Canadian Inf Brigade" (PAC). Essame, *Battle for Germany*. 3rd Canadian Infantry Division, Operations Veritable and Blockbuster. Spry Papers and Dampier Papers (lent by the kind permission of Gen D. Spry and Maj L. Dampier). Regimental histories and war diaries of all battalions of 7th Canadian Infantry Brigade.

CHAPTER TWELVE

Authors' interviews with Maj Joseph Pigott, Maj Louis Froggett, Lt R.W. Wight, Lt Ken Dugall, Col John Williamson, Sgt Peter Bolus, Cpl Eldrid Severin, Capt Lyle Doering, CSM Robert Hibberd, Capt H.P. Kelley, Lt John Simpkins, Lt Ken Wharton, Maj Ken McIntyre, Maj Cy Steele, Maj Paul Cropp, Capt Tom Stewart, Capt Frank Walton, Maj Charles Barrett, Maj Harvey Theobold, Maj-Gen Heinz Guderian. Report by Lt-Col Heinz Guderian, February 28, 1945 (PA). Kelly, *There's a Goddamn Bullet for Everyone*. "The Struggle for the Goch Calcar Road," Account by Brig F.N. Cabeldu, DSO, ED, given to the Historical Officer 2nd Canadian Infantry Division (PA). "History of the Panzer Lehr Div 15/25 Feb" by Maj A.D. Helmut Hudel (NA). "Die Geschichte der Panzer Lehr Division im Westen 1944–1945" (Stuttgart 1978), excerpt translated for the authors by Oberst A.D. Helmut Ritgen.

CHAPTER THIRTEEN

Authors' interviews with Maj-Gen Carrol Dunn, Lt-Col Harold Hassenfelt, Capt Victor Salem, Capt Frank Hallahan, Lt Robert Truitt, Staff Sgt Rufus Wilkes, Sgt Phillip Polozotto, PFC John Emerich, Lt Norvan Nathan, Col John Carbin, Lt-Col Saul Solow, Maj Frank

Towers, T/5 Robert Bacher, Maj Ken Allison, Lt-Col John Gloriod, Lt-Col Warren Robinson, Lt-Gen Lewis Truman, Lt William Ray, Capt Harold Leinbaugh, Maj Wm Johnson, Cpl Wilson Toups, Cpl Dan Callahan, Sgt Howard Bedney. Oral history interview of Gen James E. Moore, Ninth U.S. Army Chief of Staff (1984), and Elwood R. Quesada Papers (1975) (USAMHI). Ninth U.S. Army Report: "Rehearsal for the Rhine" (NA). Combat Interviews and After Action Reports (NA). First FS Army: Report of the Commander Gen FS Alfred Schlemm (NA). "84th Inf Div from the Roer to the Rhine" (NA). "The 84 Inf Div in the Battle for Germany" (NA). "104th Infantry Div: Report" (NA).

CHAPTER FOURTEEN

Authors' interviews with Maj-Gen Roger Rowley, Col H.E. Dalton, Col Blake Oulton, Lt-Col Stephen Lett, Maj Jim Currie, Col D. Atkinson, Lt-Col Ray Hodgins, Capt R.G. Elliot, Lt Guy de Merlis, Rfn Norman Selby, Rfn Don Chittenden, Maj M. Clevett, Capt Peter Rea, Sgt Charles Lynch, Capt Don Pearce, Maj Ross Martin, CSM Wm. Bailey, H/Capt Jock Anderson, Lt George Pollard.

Jacques Govin, *Bon Coeur et Bon Bras*. Nicholson, *The Gunners of Canada*, Vol. II. Essame, *Battle for Germany*. Dunkelman, *Dual Allegiance*. Eyewitness testimony by Sgt C.R. Anderson, submitted in recommendation of the awarding of the VC to Sgt Aubrey Cosens (courtesy of Col Brandron Conron). Lindsay, *So Few Got Through*. Horrocks, *Corps Commander*. Regimental histories and war diaries of 8th and 9th Canadian Infantry Brigades (PAC). CMHQ: Operation Blockbuster (PAC).

CHAPTERS FIFTEEN and SIXTEEN

Authors' interviews with Maj-Gen Heinz Guderian, Brig-Gen G.D.S. Wotherspoon, Brig-Gen Sidney Radley-Walters, Brig-Gen E.A.C. Amy, Brig-Gen R.W. Moncel, Brig M.J.P. O'Cock, Lt-Col E.R. Hill, Lt-Col G.P. Wood, Maj George Hale, Maj Ivor J. Crosthwaite, Maj John Munro, Maj Donald Callander, Maj Curtis Greenleaf, Col John Chaston, Lt-Col George L. Cassidy, Maj R.D. MacKenzie, Maj John Martin, Maj James Swazey, Capt Donald Muir, Maj Wm. Whiteside, Capt P.C. Neil, Capt Robert Hemmingson, Tpr Alex Graham, Tpr Arnold Boyd, Tpr James Love, Tpr Al LaRose, Lt Stan L. Dunn.

Cassidy, *Warpath*. Ellis, *Sharp End of War*. "A Jaundiced View of Tanks" by Master-Sgt (Retired) R.E. Rogge, *Armour Magazine*, Sept-Oct, 1982. "Operation Blockbuster," including a report by A/Maj D.H. Bradley, Sherbrooke Fusiliers Regt, CMHQ (PAC). Forbes, *The Grenadier Guards*. Essame, *Battle for Germany*. Geoffrey William Hayes, "The Friction of War: A Study of the Lincoln and Welland Regiment." Wilfred Laurier University, 1985. "Operation Churchill," a report by the Lake Superior Regiment 28 Feb/44 (DND). Regimental histories and war diaries of all regiments of the 4th Canadian Armoured Division.

CHAPTER SEVENTEEN

Authors' interviews with Col Fred Tilston, Dr Clifford Richardson, Maj Paul Cropp, Maj Alf Hodges, Maj K.W. McIntyre, Capt Tom Stewart. Smyth, *Great Stories of the Victoria Cross*. *The Legionary*, March 1955. Swettenham, *Valiant Men*. Stacey, *Arms, Men and Governments*.

CHAPTER EIGHTEEN

Authors' interviews with Lt-Gen Lewis W. Truman, 1st Lt Robert Truitt, Cpl Dan Callahan, Lt Norvan Nathan, Col John Carbin, Lt-Col Saul Solow, Maj Frank Towers, T/5 Robert Bacher, Maj Ken Allison, Lt-Col John Gloriod, Lt-Col Warren Robinson, Lt William Ray, Capt Harold Leinbaugh, Maj Wm Johnson, Cpl Wilson Toups, Sgt Howard Bedney.

Ninth U.S. Army Report: "Rehearsal for the Rhine" (NA). After Action Reports (NA). First FS Army: Report of the Commander Gen FS Alfred Schlemm (NA). Regimental histories of all Ninth Army regiments (USAMHI). Combat interviews Operation Grenade (NA). Leinbaugh, *The Men of Company K*.

CHAPTER NINETEEN

Authors' interviews with Maj-Gen Heinz-Guenther Guderian, Maj R.H.S. O'Grady, Col Hugh Rose, Col A.M.H. Gregory-Hood, Lt-Col Morgan G. Roseborough, Lt-Col Tracey Harrington, Maj Henry Rothenberg, Maj J.S. Holland, Pvt Gideon Lumsden, Maj Harry Bannatyne.

Special Interrogation Reports: Gen Schlemm, Field-Marshal von Rundstedt, Maj-Gen Fiebig, Gen von Luettwitz, Gen Eugen Meindl. "The 84th Infantry Div during the fight from the Reichswald to Wesel" by Heinz Fiebig (NA). "116th Panzer Division: 4 to 10 March 1945" (NA). Combat Interviews Ninth U.S. Army and 5th Armoured Div, 17th Armoured Engineer Battalion, 134 Infantry Regiment (NA). William H. Simpson Papers, Diary of March 1945 (USAMHI). Operation Blockbuster (DND). Citation for Distinguished Service Cross for Capt Kemble Tucker (NA). Bolland, *Team Spirit*. Verney, *Story of the Guards Armoured Division*. Fitzgerald, *History of the Irish Guards*. De Guingand, *Operation Victory*. Toland, *Last 100 Days*. Wilmot, *Struggle for Europe*. Leach, *In Tornado's Wake*. Kesselring, *Memoirs*. Blake, *Mountain and Flood*. Kemp, *History of the Royal Scots Fusiliers*.

CHAPTER TWENTY

Authors' interviews with Maj-Gen John C. Graham, Lt-Col R.B. Wilkinson, Col Hugh Rose, Col Brian A. Fargus, Lt Hubert A. Campbell, Lt-Col Thomas Landale Rollo, Lt-Col G.P. Wood, Maj Wm. Whiteside, Capt John McVie, Capt J.A. Clovis, Col A.D. Lewis, Lt-Col David Ward, Lt-Col Harold Hassenfelt, Capt Derek Ford, Brig Charles Richardson.

Combat interviews with 117th Inf Regt, 30 Inf Div, and 315 Regt, 79 Inf Div. Battlefield Tours: The Battle of the Rhine (DND). Personal Account by Lt-Col C.G. Hopkinson, CO 44 R Tks (Royal Staff College, Camberley). HQ European Theatre of Operations US Army Immediate Report #99: Deceptive Measures, CAB 106/964 73037 (PRO). Horrocks, *A Full Life*. Borthwick, *Sans Peur*. "30th Division Crosses the Rhine" (NA). William H. Simpson Papers, Diary of March 1945 (USMHI). "29 ID Roer to Rhine" (NA). The Battle of the Rhine (DND). Pogue (interview of Brig Williams (USAMHI)). Chaston narrative: "The Diary of a Ranger" (IWM). Summary First FS Army (NA).

Bradley and Blair, *A General's Life*. Speer, *Inside the Third Reich*. Hart, *History of the Second World War*. Chatterton, *Wings of Pegasus*. Shulman, *Defeat in the West*. Kesselring, *Memoirs*. Bird, *North Shore (New Brunswick) Regiment*. McElwee, *History of the Argyll and Sutherlanders 2nd Battalion*. Tullett, *From Flushing to Bremen*. Mills-Roberts, *Clash by Night*. Martin, *History of the 15th Scottish Division*.

CHAPTERS TWENTY-ONE and TWENTY-TWO

Authors' interviews with Group Capt Paul Davoud, Sgt R.F. Anderson, Col Albert Wing, Col Carl A. Peterson, Lt-Col David Ward, Col H.J. Sweeney, Gen Sir Nigel Poett, Lt-Gen Sir Napier Crookenden, Brig James Hill, Lt-Col Fraser Eadie, Maj Richard Hilborn, Lt David Hunter, Capt Nick Archdale, Dr Dawson Einerson, Lt Robert Firlotte, Cpl Dennis Flynn, 2nd Lieut F. Tipton Randolph, Capt Dean Steadman, A/Capt Douglas Candy, Maj Peter Griffin, Cpl Ron Knowles, Lt John Marr.

Authors' correspondence with Lt-Col Allen C. Miller II. Battlefield Tours, Operation Varsity and "Ex Varsity Ghost, 28 Feb/63" (PRO). Special Interrogation Reports, Gen. Schlemm, Gen von Luettwitz, Gen Eugen Meindl (NA). War Diary, 1 Canadian Para Bn. Martha Ann Hooker, "In Defence of Unity: Canada's Military Policies, 1935–1944," master's thesis, Carleton University, 1985. Lt R.W. Allanson, ed., "The Papers of Col C.J.L. Allanson" (IWM). After Action Report, 17th Airborne Division (NA). Unit Citation Report, 513th Parachute Infantry (NA). "Airborne Invasion-Glider Story" by Frank Langston, 1st Lt 194th Glider Inf (NA). Letter from George L. Streukens to Richard J. Sommers Aug 3, 1983 (USMHI). *Pegasus, Journal of the Parachute Regiment and Airborne Forces:* Vol. XL, No. 2, August 1985. Crookenden, *Airborne at War.* Lloyd, *The Gliders.* Chatterton, *Wings of Pegasus.* Blair, *Ridgway's Paratroopers.* Mrazek, *Glider War.* Churchill, *Triumph and Tragedy.* After Action Reports: 1 Battalion 513 Para Regt and 3 Battalion 507 Para Regt. Dank, *Glider War.* "The Bridge," by Major A.J. Dyball, Coy Commander of the 1st Royal Ulster Rifles, 6 Airlanding Brigade (PRO). History of the 52nd Light Infantry. *Over the Rhine: A Parachute Field Ambulance in Germany,* by members of 224 Parachute Field Ambulance (Canopy Press, 1946), lent to the authors by the courtesy of Brig Hill.

References

Allen, Ralph. *Ordeal by Fire*. Vol. 5. Toronto: Doubleday, 1961.

Ambrose, Stephen E. *The Supreme Commander*. Garden City, N.Y.: Doubleday, 1970.

Armstrong, Ann. *Unconditional Surrender: The Impact of the Casablanca Policy upon World War II*. New Brunswick, N.J.: Rutgers University Press, 1961.

Blair, Clay. *Ridgway's Paratroopers*. Garden City, N.Y.: Dial Press, 1985.

Blumenson, Martin. *The Patton Papers 1940–1945*. Boston: Houghton Mifflin, 1974.

Bradley, Omar N. *A Soldier's Story*. New York: Henry Holt & Co., 1951.

Bradley, Omar N., and Blair, Clay. *A General's Life: An Autobiography by General of the Army Omar N. Bradley*. New York: Simon & Schuster, 1983.

Brett-Smith, Richard. *Hitler's Generals*. London: Osprey, 1976.

British Broadcasting Corporation. *War Report: A Record of Dispatches Broadcast by the BBC's War Correspondents with the Allied Expeditionary Force, 6 June, 1944 – 5 May, 1945*. London: Oxford University Press, 1946.

Bryant, Sir A. *Triumph in the West*. London: Collins, 1959.

Burns, Maj-Gen E.L.M., DSO, OBE, MC. *Manpower in the Canadian Army 1939–45*. Toronto: Clarke, Irwin, 1956.

Chatterton, Brig George, DSO (Retd). *The Wings of Pegasus: The Story of the Glider Pilot Regiment*. London: MacDonald, 1962.

Cooper, Matthew. *The German Army 1933–1945*. London: MacDonald & Jane's, 1978.

Crookenden, Napier. *Airborne at War*. London: Ian Allan, 1978.

———*Drop Zone Normandy: The Story of the American and British Airborne Assault on D-Day 1944*. London: Ian Allan, 1976.

Dank, Milton. *The Glider Gang: An Eyewitness History of World War II Glider Combat*. New York: Lippincott, 1977.

De Guingand, Maj-Gen Sir Francis, KBE, CB, DSO. *Operation Victory*. London: Hodder & Stoughton, 1947.

Devlin, Gerard M. *Paratrooper: The Saga of U.S. Army and Marine Parachute and Glider Combat Troops During World War II*. New York: St. Martin's Press, 1979.

Douglas, W.A.B., and Greenhous, B. *Out of the Shadows: Canada in the Second World War*. Toronto: Oxford University Press, 1977.

Dunkelman, Ben. *Dual Allegiance*. Toronto: Macmillan, 1976.

Eis, Egon. *The Forts of Folly: The History of an Illusion*. London: O. Wolff, 1959.

REFERENCES

Eisenhower, Gen Dwight D. *Crusade in Europe*. New York: Doubleday, 1948.

Eisenhower, John. *The Bitter Woods*. Toronto: Longmans, 1969.

Ellis, John. *Sharp End of War: The Fighting Man in World War II*. Newton Abbot, Devon: David & Charles, 1980.

Ellis, Maj L.F., CVO, CBE, DSO, MC. *History of the Second World War. Vol. 2: Victory in the West*. London: Her Majesty's Stationer, 1962.

Essame, Maj-Gen Hubert. *Battle for Germany*. New York: Scribners, 1969.

———*The 43rd Wessex Division at War 1944–1945*. London: Clowes, 1952.

Farago, Ladislas. *Patton: Ordeal and Triumph*. New York: Astor-Honour, 1964.

Feis, Herbert. *Churchill, Roosevelt, Stalin: The War They Waged and the Peace They Sought*. London: Oxford University Press, 1957.

Garlinski, Joseph. *Hitler's Last Weapons*. Toronto: Fitzhenry & Whiteside, 1978.

Gavin, James M. *On to Berlin: Battles of an Airborne Commander 1943–1946*. New York: Viking Press, 1978.

Gilbert, Felix G. *Hitler Directs His War*. London: Oxford University Press, 1950.

Granatstein, J.L. *Canada's War: The Politics of the Mackenzie King Government, 1939–1945*. Toronto: Oxford University Press, 1975.

Hamilton, Nigel. *Monty: The Field Marshal, 1944–1976*. London: Hamish Hamilton, 1986.

———*Monty: The Making of a General*. New York: McGraw-Hill, 1981.

Hart, Liddell. *History of the Second World War*. London: Cassell, 1970.

———*The Other Side of the Hill*. London: Cassell, 1948.

Horrocks, Sir Brian. *A Full Life*. London: Collins, 1960.

Horrocks, Sir Brian, with Belfield, Eversley, and Essame, Maj-Gen H. *Corps Commander*. Toronto: Griffin House, [1977].

How, Douglas, ed. *The Canadians at War*. Montreal: Readers Digest Association, 1969.

Hutchison, Bruce. *The Incredible Canadian*. Toronto: Longmans, Green, 1952.

Irving, David. *Hitler's War*. New York: Viking, 1977.

———*The War Between the Generals*. New York: Congdon & Lattes, 1981.

Jacobsen, Hans A., ed. *Decisive Battles of World War II*. London: A. Deutsch, 1965.

Jewell, Brian. *Over the Rhine: The Last Days of War in Europe*. Tunbridge Wells: Spellmount, 1985.

Kee, Robert. *The World We Fought For*. London: Hamish Hamilton, 1985.

Kelly, Arthur. *There's a Goddamn Bullet for Everyone*. Paris, Ont.: Arts and Publishing, 1979.

Kesselring, Field-Marshal Albrecht. *Memoirs of Field-Marshal Kesselring*. London: Wm. Kimber, 1953.

Kirkconnell, Watson. *Canada, Europe and Hitler*. London: Oxford University Press, 1939.

Lang, Derek. *Return to St Valéry*. London: Leo Cooper, 1974.

Leasor, Sir James. *War at the Top*. London: Michael Joseph, 1959.

Leinbaugh, Harold P., and Campbell, John D. *The Men of Company K*. New York: Morrow, 1985.

Lewin, Ronald. *Ultra Goes to War*. London: Hutchinson, 1978.

Lewin, Ronald, ed. *The War on Land: The British Army in World War II*. New York: Morrow, 1970.

Lindsay, Lt-Col Martin. *So Few Got Through: The Personal Diary of Lt-Col Martin Lindsay.* London: Collins, 1946.

Lloyd, Alan. *The Gliders.* London: Leo Cooper, with Secker & Warburg, 1982.

Lyon, Peter. *Eisenhower: Portrait of a Hero.* Toronto: Little, Brown, 1974.

MacDonald, Charles B. *The Battle of the Huertgen Forest.* New York: Jove Publications, 1984.

———*The Last Offensive: The History of the U.S. Army in World War II,* Vol. 3. Washington: Office of the Chief of Military History, United States Army, 1973.

———*The Mighty Endeavor: The American War in Europe.* New York: Morrow, 1986.

———*The Siegfried Line Campaign.* Washington: Office of the Chief of Military History, United States Army, 1963.

———*A Time for Trumpets: The Untold Story of the Battle of the Bulge.* New York: Morrow, 1985.

Malone, Col Richard, OBE. *Missing from the Record.* Toronto: Collins, 1946.

McKee, Alexander. *The Race for the Rhine Bridges.* London: Souvenir Press, 1971.

Mellenthin, Friedrich Wilhelm von. *German Generals of World War II: As I Saw Them.* Norman: University of Oklahoma Press, 1977.

Montgomery, Field-Marshal Bernard. *The Memoirs of Field-Marshal Montgomery.* London: Collins, 1958.

———*Normandy to the Baltic: A Personal Account of the Conquest of Germany.* London: Hutchinson, 1947.

Moorhead, Alan. *Eclipse.* London: Hamish Hamilton, 1967.

Mrazek, James. *The Glider War.* London: Hale, 1975.

Munro, Ross. *Gauntlet to Overlord: The Story of the Canadian Army.* Toronto: Macmillan, 1945.

Nicholson, Col G.W.L. *The Gunners of Canada: The History of the Royal Canadian Artillery.* Vol. II. Toronto: McClelland & Stewart, 1967–72.

———*Seventy Years of Service: A History of a Royal Canadian Army Medical Corps.* Ottawa: Borealis Press, 1977.

North, John. *Northwest Europe 1944–1945: The Achievement of 21st Army Group.* London: Her Majesty's Stationer, 1953.

Patton, George. *War As I Knew It.* Boston: Houghton, 1947.

Pearce, Donald. *Journal of a War.* Toronto: Macmillan, 1965.

Perrett, Peter. *Through Mud and Blood: Infantry/Tank Operations in World War II.* London: Hale, 1975.

Powley, A.E. *Broadcast from the Front: Canadian Radio Overseas in the Second World War.* Toronto: Hakkert, 1975.

Shulman, Milton. *Defeat in the West.* London: Secker & Warburg, 1947.

Sixsmith, E.K.G. *Eisenhower as a Military Commander.* London: B.T. Batsford, 1973.

Smyth, Brig the Rt Hon Sir John, Bt, VC, MC. *Great Stories of the Victoria Cross.* London: Arthur Barber, 1977.

Snyder, Louis. *The Great Moments of World War II.* New York: Julian Messner, 1962.

Speer, Albert. *Inside the Third Reich.* New York: Macmillan, 1962.

Stacey, Col C.P., OC, OBE, CD, AM, PhD, DLitt, LLD, FRSC. *Arms, Men and Governments: The War Policies of Canada, 1939–1945.* Ottawa: Queen's Printer, 1970.

————*The Canadian Army 1939–1945: An Official Historical Summary.* Ottawa: King's Printer, 1948.

————*A Date With History: Memoirs of a Canadian Historian.* Toronto: Deneau, 1983.

————*The Victory Campaign: The Operations in Northwest Europe, 1944–45.* Vol. III, Official History of the Canadian Army in the Second World War. Ottawa: Queen's Printer, 1960.

Strong, Maj-Gen Sir Kenneth. *Intelligence at the Top.* New York: Doubleday, 1968.

Swettenham, John, ed. *Valiant Men: Canada's Victoria Cross and George Cross Winners.* Toronto: Hakkert, 1973.

Thompson, R.W. *Battle for the Rhineland.* London: Hutchinson, 1958.

Toland, John. *The Last 100 Days.* New York: Random House, 1965.

Trevor-Roper, H.R. *Hitler's War Directives, 1939–1945.* London: Sidgwick & Jackson, 1964.

Urquhart, R.E. *Arnhem.* London: Cassell, 1958.

Warlymont, Walter. *Inside Hitler's Headquarters 1939–1945.* Bristol, England: Western Printing Services, 1963.

Warner, Philip. *Horrocks: The General Who Led from the Front.* London: Hamish Hamilton, 1984.

Weighley, Russell. *Eisenhower's Lieutenants.* London: Sidgwick & Jackson, 1981.

Wilmot, Chester. *The Struggle for Europe.* London: Collins, 1952.

Winterbotham, F.W., CBE. *The Ultra Secret.* New York: Harper & Row, 1974.

REGIMENTAL HISTORIES

Baggaley, Capt. J.R.P., MC. *The 6th (Border) Battalion the King's Own Scottish Borderers 1939–1945.* 1945.

Barclay, Brig C.N., CBE, DSO. *The History of the Cameronians (Scottish Rifles). Vol. III: 1933–1946.* London: Sifton Praed, 1946.

————*The History of the 53rd (Welsh) Division in the Second World War.* London: Clowes, 1955.

Barker, A.J. Edited by Lt-Gen Sir Brian Horrocks. *The East Yorkshire Regiment (the 15th Regiment of Foot).* London: Leo Cooper, 1971.

Barnard, Lt-Col W.T., ED, CD. *Queen's Own Rifles of Canada 1860-1960.* Don Mills, Ont.: Ontario Publishing, 1960.

Barrett, L.W.W. *The History of 13 Canadian Field Regiment, Royal Canadian Artillery, 1940-1945.* n.p., n.d.

Bartlett, Jack Fortune. *The Highland Light Infantry of Canada (1st Battalion) 1940-1945.* Galt, Ont.: Highland Light Infantry of Canada Association, [1951].

Baylay, George Taylor, ed. *The Regimental History of the Governor General's Foot Guards.* Ottawa: privately printed, 1948.

Binkoski, J., and Plaut, A. *The 115th Infantry Regiment in World War II.* Washington: Infantry Journal Press, 1948.

Bird, Will R. *No Retreating Footsteps: The Story of the North Nova Scotia Highlanders.* Kentville, N.S.: Kentville Publishing, 1954.

————*North Shore (New Brunswick) Regiment.* Fredericton, N.B.: Brunswick Press, 1963.

Birdwood, Lt-Col Lord, MVO. *The Worcester Regiment 1922–1950*. Aldershot: Gale and Polden, 1952.

Blake, George. *Mountain and Flood: The History of the 52nd (Lowland) Division 1939–1946*. Glasgow: Jackson, Son & Co., 1950.

Bolland, Maj A.D. *Team Spirit: The Administration of the 53rd Welsh Division During Operation Overlord, June 1944 to May 1945*. Aldershot: Gale & Polden, 1948.

Borthwick, Alastair. *Sans Peur: History of the 5th (Caithness & Sutherland) Battalion the Seaforth Highlanders 1942–1945*. Stirling, Scotland: Eneas Mackay, 1946.

Boss, Lt-Col W., CD. *The Stormont, Dundas and Glengarry Highlanders (1783–1951)*. Ottawa: Runge Press, 1952.

Brett, Lt-Col G.A., DSO, OBE, MC. *History of the South Wales Borderers and the Monmouth Regiment. Part II: The 2nd Battalion the Monmouth Regiment*. Pontypool, U.K.: Griffin Press, 1953.

–––––*A brief History of the 4th Canadian Armoured Brigade in Action, July 1944 – May 1945*.

Buchanan, Lt-Col G.B., MBE, *The March of the Prairie Men: A Story of the South Saskatchewan Regiment*. Weyburn, Sask.: privately printed, [1957].

Cameron, Capt. Ian C. *History of the Argyll and Sutherlanders 7th Battalion: From El Alamein to Germany*. London: Nelson, 1946.

Cassidy, Maj. George L., DSO. *Warpath: The Story of the Algonquin Regiment 1939-1945*. Toronto: Ryerson Press, 1948.

Castagna, Capt E. *The History of the 771st Tank Battalion*. Berkeley, Cal., 1946.

Cent ans d'histoire d'un régiment canadien-français: les Fusiliers Mont-Royal, 1869–1969. Montreal: Éditions du Jour, 1971.

Combat History of the 8th Infantry Division. 1945.

Conquer: The Story of the Ninth Army. Washington: Infantry Journal Press, 1947.

Conron, A. Brandron, ed. *A History of the First Hussars Regiment, 1856–1980*, London, Ont., 1981.

The Cross of Lorraine: A Combat History of the 79th Infantry Division, June 1942–December 1945. [Baton Rouge, Army & Navy Publ. Co., 1946].

Darby, Hugh, and Cunliffe, Marcus. *A Short Story of 21 Army Group*. Aldershot: Gale and Polden, 1949.

Draper, Lt Theodore. *The 84th Infantry Division in the Battle of Germany, November 1944–May 1945*. New York: Viking, 1946.

Duguid, Col Archer Fortescue. *History of the Canadian Grenadier Guards, 1760–1964*. Montreal: Gazette Printing Co., 1965.

Elliot, Maj S.R. *Scarlet to Green: A History of Intelligence in the Canadian Army 1903–1963*. Toronto: Canadian Intelligence and Security Association, 1981.

Ewing, Joseph H. *29 Let's Go! A History of the 29th Infantry Division in World War II*. Washington: Infantry Journal Press, 1948.

Farran, Maj Roy, DSO, MC. *The History of the Calgary Highlanders, 1921–1954*. Calgary: Bryant Press, 1954.

Feasby, W.R. *Official History of the Canadian Medical Services 1939–1945*. Vols. 1-2. Ottawa: Queen's Printer, 1956.

Fergusson, Bernard. *The Black Watch and the King's Enemies*. London: Collins, 1950.

–––––*The Watery Maze: The Story of Combined Operations*. London: Collins, 1961.

1 Battalion, The Essex Scottish Regiment (Allied with the Essex Regiment) 1939–1945. Welland, Ont.: The Wellington Press, 1946.

REFERENCES

1st Battalion, The Regina Rifle Regiment, 1939–1946. Regina, Sask.: The Regiment, [1946].

Fitzgerald, Maj Desmond J.L., MC. *History of the Irish Guards in the Second World War.* Aldershot: Gale and Polden, 1952.

Forbes, Patrick. *The Grenadier Guards 1939–1945. Vol. One.* Aldershot: Gale and Polden, 1949.

From Normandy to the Baltic: The Story of the 44th Lowland Brigade of the 15th Scottish Division. Germany, 1945.

Goodspeed, Maj. D.J. *Battle Royal: A History of the Royal Regiment of Canada: 1862–1962.* Toronto: Royal Regiment of Canada, 1962.

Govin, Jacques, ed. *Bon Coeur et Bon Bras: Regimental History of the Régiment de Maisonneuve 1880–1980.* Montreal: Régiment de Maisonneuve, 1980.

Grant, Maj D.W. *"Carry On": The History of the Toronto Scottish Regiment (M.G.) 1939–1945.* Toronto: privately printed, 1949.

Greenhous, Brereton. *Semper Paratus.* Hamilton, Ont.: The Royal Hamilton Light Infantry Historical Association, 1977.

Haas, Wilhelm. *Niederrheinisches Land im Krieg.* Kleve. Boss-Druck und Verlag, 1964.

Harker, Douglas E. *The Dukes: The Story of the Men Who Served in Peace and War with the British Columbia Regiment (D.C.O.), 1883–1973.* Privately printed, 1974.

Hart, Capt Liddell B.H. *The Tanks: The History of the Royal Tank Regiment. Vol. Two: 1939–1949.* London: Cassell, 1959.

Hayes, Geoffrey William. "The Friction of War: A Study of the Lincoln and Welland Regiment 1940–1945." Master's thesis, Wilfrid Laurier University, 1985.

Henry, C.E. *Regimental History of the 18th Armoured Car Regiment (XII Manitoba Dragoons).* Deventer, Neth.: privately printed, n.d.

Hewitt, R.L. *Workhorse of the Western Front: The Story of the 30th Infantry Division.* Washington: Infantry Journal Press, 1946.

The History of 6th (Lanarkshire) Battalion, the Cameronians (S.R.) World War II. Glasgow: John Cossar Publishing.

Hoegh, L.A., and Doyle, H.J. *Timberwolf Tracks: The History of the 104th Infantry Division 1942-1945.* Washington: Infantry Journal Press, 1946.

Huston, J.A. *Biography of a Battalion.* Gering, Nebraska: Courier Press, 1950.

Hutchison, Col. Paul P., ED. *Canada's Black Watch: The First 100 Years (1862-1962).* Don Mills, Ont.: The Black Watch (RHR) of Canada, 1962.

Jackson, Lt-Col H.M., MBE, ED, ed., et al. *The Argyll and Sutherland Highlanders of Canada (Princess Louise's) 1928–1953.* Montreal: privately printed, 1953.

Jackson, Lt-Col H.M., MBE, ED. *The Sherbrooke Regiment (12th Armoured Regiment),* 1958.

Kemp, Col J.C., MC. *The History of the Royal Scots Fusiliers 1919–1959.* Glasgow, 1963.

Kemp, Lt-Cmdr P.K. *The History of the 4th Battalion King's Shropshire Light Infantry (T.A.) 1745–1945.* Shrewsbury: Wilding & Son, 1955.

———and John Graves. *The Story of the Royal Welch Fusiliers 1919–1945.* Aldershot: Gale and Polden, 1960.

Kemsley, Capt. W., and Riesco, Capt M.R. *The Scottish Lion on Patrol: the 15th Scottish Reconnaissance Regiment 1943–1946.* Bristol: White Swan Press, 1950.

REFERENCES

Kenrick, Col N.C.E., DSO. *The Story of the Wiltshire Regiment (Duke of Edinburgh's): The 62nd and 99th Foot (1756–1959).* Aldershot: Gale and Polden, 1963.

Ladd, James. *Commandos and Rangers of World War II.* London: MacDonald & Jane's, 1978.

Leach, Capt C.R. *In Tornado's Wake: A History of the 8th Armoured Division.* Published by the 8th Armoured Division, 1956.

Martin, Lt-Gen H.G., CB, DSO, OBE. *The History of the 15th Scottish Division 1939–1945.* Edinburgh and London: Blackwood, 1948.

McElwee, Maj W.L., MC. *History of the Argyll and Sutherlanders 2nd Battalion (Reconstituted): European Campaign 1944–1945.* London: Nelson, 1949.

McMath, Capt J.S. *The 5th Battalion the Wiltshire Regiment in North West Europe, June 1944–May 1945.* London: Whitefriars Press, 1946.

Meredith, Capt J.L.J., *From Normandy to Hanover: The Story of the Seventh Battalion the Somerset Light Infantry (Prince Albert's).* Hanover, W. Germany: The Regiment, 1945.

Mick, Maj A.H., ed. *With the 102d Infantry Division Through Germany.* Washington: Infantry Journal Press, 1947.

Middleford, Martin and Everitt, Chris. *The Bomber Command War Diaries.* London: Viking, 1985.

Miles, Wilfrid. *The Life of a Regiment. Vol 5: The Gordon Highlanders 1919–1945.* Aberdeen: The University Press, 1961.

Mills-Roberts, Derek. *Clash by Night — A Commando Chronicle.* London: Kimber, 1956.

Muir, Augustus. *The First of Foot: the History of the Royal Scots (The Royal Regiment).* Edinburgh: Royal Scots History Committee, 1961.

Nicholson, Capt Nigel, and Forbes, Patrick. *The Grenadier Guards in the War of 1939–1945. Vol. 1.* Aldershot: Gale & Polden, 1949.

Parsons, Maj A.D., MC; Robbins, Maj D.I.M., OBE, MC; Gibson, Maj D.C., MC, eds. *The Maroon Square: A History of the 4th Battalion the Wiltshire Regiment (Duke of Edinburgh's) in North West Europe 1939–1946.* London: Franey, [1946].

Paths of Armour: The Fifth Armoured Division in World War II. Tennessee: Battery Press, 1950.

Paterson, Maj R.A. *A History of the 10th Canadian Infantry Brigade.* Privately printed, 1945.

Pavey, Walter G. *An historical account of the 7th Canadian Reconnaissance Regiment (17th Duke of York's Royal Canadian Hussars) in the World War, 1939–1945.* Montreal: 7th Canadian Reconnaissance Regiment, 1948.

Pereira, Capt. J. *A Distant Drum: War Memories of the Intelligence Officer of the 5th Battalion Coldstream Guards 1944–1945.* Aldershot: Gale & Polden, 1948.

Popham, Hugh. *The Somerset Light Infantry. Famous Regiments,* ed. Lt-Gen Sir Brian Horrocks. London: Hamish Hamilton, 1968.

Queen-Hughes, R.W. *Whatever Men Dare: History of the Queen's Own Cameron Highlanders of Canada, 1935–1960.* Winnipeg: The Regiment, 1960.

Rogers, Maj R.L. *History of the Lincoln and Welland Regiment.* St. Catharines, Ont.: The Regiment, 1954.

Ross, Maj Armand, DSO, and Gauvin, Maj Michel, DSO. *Le Geste du Régiment de la Chaudière.* Lévis, Que.: The Regiment, 1968.

REFERENCES

Ross, Lt-Col Richard M. *The History of the 1st Battalion Cameron Highlanders of Ottawa (M.G.)*. Ottawa: The Regiment, 1946.

Rosse, Capt Laurence, 6th Earl of, MBE. *The Story of the 6th Army Tank Brigade*.

Rosse, Capt Laurence, 6th Earl of, and Hill, Col. E.R., DSO. *The Story of the Guards Armoured Division*. London: G. Bles, 1956.

Roy, R.H. *Ready for the Fray: History of the Canadian Scottish Regiment*. Vancouver, B.C.: Evergreen, 1958.

Royal Winnipeg Rifles Pamphlet, 75th Anniversary, 1883–1958.

Salmond, J.B. *The 51st Highland Division*. Edinburgh and London: Blackwood & Sons, 1953.

Saunders, Hilary St George, and Richards, Denis. *Royal Air Force 1939–1945*. London: Her Majesty's Stationer, 1975.

Service, Capt G.T., and Marteinson, Capt J.K., ed. *The Gate: A History of the Fort Garry Horse*. Calgary: privately printed, 1971.

A Short History of the 6th (Caernarvon and Anglesey) Battalion the Royal Welch Fusiliers: North West Europe, June 1944 to May 1945. 1946.

The 6th Battalion Royal Scots Fusiliers 1939–46. Ayr: Printed by T.M. Gemmell, [1946?].

Stanley, George. *In The Face of Danger: The History of the Lake Superior Regiment*. Port Arthur, Ont.: The Regiment, 1960.

Story of the 320 Infantry. Hamelin, Germany; 1945.

Sym, Col John, ed. *Seaforth Highlanders*. London: Gale and Polden, 1962.

Tascona, Bruce, and Wells, Eric. *Little Black Devils: A History of the Royal Winnipeg Rifles*. Winnipeg: Frye Publ., 1983.

Taurus Pursuant: A History of the 11 Armoured Division. BAOR, 1945.

The 35th Infantry Division in World War II. 1946.

Tullett, Capt E.V. *From Flushing to Bremen: A History of the Fifth Battalion the King's Own Scottish Borderers from 19 October 1945 until V.E. Day*. Minden, Germany; 1945.

Vanguard: The Fort Garry Horse in the Second World War. Winnipeg: The Fort Garry Horse Association, 1945.

Verney, Maj-Gen G.L., DSO, MVO. *The Story of the Guards Armoured Division*. London: Hutchinson, 1955.

Wake, Maj-Gen Sir Hereward, Bt, CB, CMG, DSO and Deedes, Maj W.F., MC, eds. *Swift and Bold: The Story of the King's Royal Rifle Corps in the Second World War 1939-1949*. Aldershot: Gale and Polden, 1949.

War History 1939–1945, The Fourth Battalion King's Own Scottish Borderers. Galashiels, Selkirkshire, Scotland: War History Committee, 1945.

Warren, Arnold. *Wait for the Waggon: The Story of the Royal Canadian Army Service Corps*. Toronto: McClelland & Stewart, 1961.

Willes, John A., assisted by Mark H. Lockyer. *Out of the Clouds: The History of the 1st Canadian Parachute Battalion*. Kingston, Ont., 1981.

Wilson, Rev. W.I.G., CF. *A Short History of the First Battalion The King's Own Scottish Borderers in North-west Europe from 6 June 1944–8 May 1945*. 1945.

Woolcombe, Robert. *Lion Rampant: The 15th Scottish Division — Normandy to the Elbe*. London: Leo Cooper, 1955.

Interviews

The following veterans of the Rhineland campaign kindly helped us by granting us interviews about their part in the battle. (Ranks indicated were as of March 1945. Present ranks are in brackets.)

Maj Ken Allison, BS 3, Staff Officer (G-3), 79 Inf. Div, 9 US Army
Lt-Col. Mowbray Alway, DSO, 8 Recce Regt, 2 CID , 1 Cdn Army
Lt-Col. (Brig-Gen), E.A.C. Amy, DSO, MC, Grenadier Guards, 4 CAB (4 CAD), 1 Cdn Army
H/Capt Jock Anderson, MC Bar, Highland Light Infantry, 9 CIB (3 CID), 1 Cdn Army
Lt. John Anderson (Canloan), 5/7 Gordons, 153 Bde (51 H), 2 Brit Army
Sgt Ron Anderson, 1 Cdn Para Bn, 3 Para Bde (6 AB), 18 AB Corps
Lt-Col (Lt-Gen) Wm. Anderson, RCA, Col GS, 1 Cdn Army
Lt-Col (Brig) G.L.W. Andrews, CBE, DSO, 2 Seaforth, 152 Bde (51 H), 2 Brit Army
Capt. Nick Archdale, 7 Para Bn, 5 Para Bde (6 AB), 18 AB Corps
Capt. W.A. Atkinson, MC, Régiment de la Chaudière, 8 CIB (3 CID), 1 Cdn Army

T/5 Robert R Bacher, 320 Inf Regt, 35 Inf Div, 9 US Army
Capt Harvey Bailey, 1 Cdn Scottish, 7 CIB (3 CID), 1 Cdn Army
CSM Wm. Bailey, MM, North Nova Scotia Highlanders, 9 CIB (3 CID), 1 Cdn Army
Maj Harry Bannatyne, 7 Cameronians, 156 Bde (52 L), 2 Brit Army
Maj Charles Barrett, Staff Officer (BM), 4 CIB (2 CID), 1 Cdn Army
Col (Brig) G.E. Beament, OBE, CM, ED, CD, Col GS, 1 Cdn Army
Maj (Col) David S. Beatty, Royal Regt of Canada, 4 CIB (2 CID), 1 Cdn Army
Lt George Beck (Canloan), 7 South Staffordshire, 59 Inf Div, 2 Brit Army

Maj Victor Beckhurst, MC, 4 Somerset Light Infantry, 129 Bde (43 W), 2 Brit Army

Sgt Howard Bedney, 104 Inf Div, 1 US Army

Lt J. D. Bell, Royal Hamilton Light Infantry, 4 CIB (2 CID), 1 Cdn Army

Lt-Col Peter Bennett, DSO, Essex Scottish, 2 CID, 1 Cdn Army

Capt George R.Blackburn, MC, 4 Fd Regt, RCA, 2 CID, 1 Cdn Army

CSM Charles Bolton, Black Watch (RHR of C), 5 CIB (2 CID), 1 Cdn Army

Sgt Peter Bolus, Royal Hamilton Light Infantry, 4 CIB (2 CID), 1 Cdn Army

Tpr David Bonnell, Sherbrooke Fusiliers, 2 CAB, 1 Cdn Army

Heinz Bosch, civilian, Geldern, Germany

Tpr Arnold Boyd, Sherbrooke Fusiliers, 2 CAB, 1 Cdn Army

Maj E.J. Brady, Lincoln & Welland Regt, 10 CIB (4 CAD), 1 Cdn Army

Brig A.E.C. Bredin, DSO, MC, 5 Dorsets, 130 Bde (43 W), 2 Brit Army

Maj G.B. Buchanan, MBF, South Saskatchewan Regt, 6 CIB (2 CID), 1 Cdn Army

Lt-Col (Brig) Ian Buchanan-Dunlop, CBE, DSO, 6 Cameronians, 156 Bde (52 L), 2 Brit Army

Maj Herb Burton, Royal Hamilton Light Infantry, 4 CIB (2 CID), 1 Cdn Army

Pte Al Butler, Royal Regt of Canada, 4 CIB (2 CID), 1 Cdn Army

Capt Don Bythell, Staff Officer (IO), 4 CIB (2 CID), 1 Cdn Army

Cpl Dan Callahan, 1106 Eng Gp, 104 Inf Div, 1 US Army

Maj Donald F. Callander, OBE, MC Bar, 5 queen's Own Cameron Highlanders, 152 Bde (51 H), 2 Brit Army

Lt (Maj) Hubert A. Campbell CD (Canloan), 5 Black Watch, 153 Bde (51 H), 2 Brit Army

Sgt John Campbell, Regina Rifle Regt, 7 CIB (3 CID), 1 Cdn Army

H/Capt Doug Candy, 1 Cdn Para Bn, 3 Para Bde (6 AB), 18 AB Corps

Col John Carbin, Staff Officer (G-3) 30 Inf Div, 9 US Army

Lt (Col) Maurice Carter, MC (Canloan), 2 Seaforth, 152 Bde (51 H), 2 Brit Army

Maj (Lt-Col) George Cassidy, DSO, Algonquin Regt, 10 CIB (4 CAD), 1 Cdn Army

Maj Jack Catley (Canloan), 1/5 Welch Regt, 158 Bde (53 W), 2 Brit Army

Maj Gilles Charlebois, DSO, CD, Régiment de Maisonneuve, 5 CIB (2 CID), 1 Cdn Army

Maj John Chaston, CBE, MC, 2 Monmouthshire Regt, 160 Bde (53 W), 2 Brit Army

Capt Frederick Chesham (Canloan), 7 Royal Hampshire Regt, 130 Bde (43 W), 2 Brit Army

Rfn Don Chittenden, Queen's Own Rifles, 8 CIB (3 CID), 1 Cdn Army

Lt Arne Christianson, SS, BS, 194 Glider Inf Regt, 17 AB Div, 18 AB Corps

Maj M. Clennett, DSO, North Nova Scotia Highlanders, 9 CIB (3 CID), 1 Cdn Army

Maj M. Clevett, North Shore Regt, 8 CIB (3 CID), 1 Cdn Army

Capt J.A.Clovis, MBE, 6 Army Cdo, 1 Cdo Bde, 2 Brit Army

Lt-Col (Brig) Rowan Coleman, DSO, Lincoln & Welland Regt, 10 CIB (4 CID), 1 Cdn Army

Maj (Col) Brandron Conron, 1 Hussars, 2 CAB, 1 Cdn Army

Sgt James Cornwall, 8 Royal Scots, 44 Bde (15 S), 2 Brit Army

Lt-Col (Lt-Gen) Sir Napier Crookenden, KCB, DSO, OBE, 9 Para Bn, 3 Para Bde (6 AB), 18 AB Corps

Maj Paul Cropp, MC, Essex Scottish, 4 CIB (2 CID), 1 Cdn Army

Maj Ivor J. Crosthwaite, DSO, 4 Grenadier Guards, 6 Guards Tank Bde, 2 Brit Army

Maj James Currie, North Shore Regt, 8 CIB (3 CID), 1 Cdn Army

Maj (Col) H.E. Dalton, DSO, ED, CD, Queen's Own Rifles, 8 CIB (3 CID), 1 Cdn Army

Maj (Lt-Col) Larry Dampier, OBE, Staff Officer (G-2), 3 CID, 1 Cdn Army

1st Lt. Milton Dank, 91 Glider Squadron, 439 Troop Carrier, 18 AB Corps

GC Paul Davoud, DSO, DFC, OBE, 83 Group RAF

Lt Guy de Merlis, Régiment de Maisonneuve, 5 CIB (2 CID), 1 Cdn Army

Capt Donald Diplock (Canloan) 1/5 Welch Regt, 158 Bde (53 W), 2 Brit Army

Capt Lyle Doering, Royal Hamilton Light Infantry, 4 CIB (2 CID), 1 Cdn Army

Capt Norman Donahue, Royal Winnipeg Rifles, 7 CIB (3 CID), 1 Cdn Army

Maj (Lt-Col) Melvin R.Douglas, Regina Rifle Regt, 7 CIB (3 CID), 1 Cdn Army

Col James Drum, SS, DSO, 334 Inf Regt, 84 Inf Div, 9 US Army

Capt (Lt-Col) Peter Dryland, MBE, MC, 7 Royal Welch Fusiliers, 158 Bde (53 W), 2 Brit Army

Lt Ken Dugall, Royal Hamilton Light Infantry, 4 CIB (2 CID), 1 Cdn Army

Lt-Col (Maj-Gen) Carrol Dunn, SS, 105 Eng Bn, 30 Inf Div, 9 US Army

Lt. Stan Dunn, Sherbrooke Fusiliers, 2 CAB, 1 Cdn Army

Lt-Col Fraser Eadie, DSO, 1 Cdn Para Bn, 3 Para Bde (6 AB), 18 AB Corps

Pte David Edwards, 2 Monmouthshire Regt, 160 Bde (53 W), 2 Brit Army

Cpl Dawson Einarson, 1 Cdn Para Bn, 3 Para Bde (6 AB), 18 AB Corps

Capt. R.G. Elliot, Queen's Own Cameron Highlanders, 6 CIB (2 CID), 1 Cdn Army

PFC John Emerich, 407 Inf Regt, 102 Inf Div, 9 US Army

Capt (Col) Brian A. Fargus, OBE, 8 Royal Scots, 44 Bde (15 S), 2 Brit Army

Lt Robert R. Firlotte, 1 Cdn Para Bn, 3 Para Bde (6 AB), 18 AB Corps

Cpl Jack Fleger, 6 Fd Regt RCE, 3 CID, 1 Cdn Army

Cpl Dennis Flynn, 1 Cdn Para Bn, 3 Para Bde (6 AB), 18 AB Corps

Capt John Forbes (Canloan), 6 Royal Welch Fusiliers, 160 Bde (53 W), 18 AB Corps

Lt (Capt) D.N.A. Ford, 7 Somerset Light Infantry, 214 Bde (43 W), 2 Brit Army

Maj Louis Froggett, DSO, ED, Royal Hamilton Light Infantry, 4 CIB (2 CID), 1 Cdn Army

Lt-Col L.R. Fulton, DSO, ED, Royal Winnipeg Rifles, 7 CIB (3 CID), 1 Cdn Army

Maj A. W. Gaade, MC, 4 Royal Welch Fusiliers, 71 Bde (53 W), 2 Brit Army

Maj James Gammie, MC, 5/7 Gordons, 153 Bde (51 H), 2 Brit Army

Capt. M. Gervais, Royal Hamilton Light Infantry, RCAPC, 1 Cdn Army

Fritz Getlinger, parachutist, 1 Para Army, Germany

Capt (Lt-Col) D.C. Gilson, MC, 4 Wiltshire Regt, 129 Bde (43 W), 2 Brit Army

Lt-Col John A. Gloriod, Staff Officer (S-3), 79 Inf Div, 9 US Army

Maj (Brig-Gen) Neil Gordon, DSO, North Shore Regt, 8 CIB (3 CID), 1 Cdn Army

Lt Frank Gosman, Royal Winnipeg Rifles, 7 CIB (3 CID), 1 Cdn Army

Tpr Alex Graham, Sherbrooke Fusiliers, 2 CAB, 1 Cdn Army

Maj (Maj-Gen) J.D.C. Graham, CB, CBE, 2 Argyll & Sutherland Highlanders, 227 Bde (15 S), 2 Brit Army

Maj Kirk Greenleaf, Cdn Grenadier Guards, 4 CAB (4 CAD), 1 Cdn Army

Maj (Col) A.M.H. Gregory-Hood, MC Bar, 2 Grenadier Guards, 5 Guards Armd Bde (Guards Armd Div), 2 Brit Army

Maj Peter Griffin, MC, 1 Cdn Para Bn, 3 Para Bde (6 AB), 18 AB Corps

Lt-Col (Maj-Gen) Heinz Guenther Guderian, 116 Pz Div, 1 Para Army, Germany

Capt Montgomery Gunn, 30th Battery, RCA, 1 Cdn Army

Wilhelm Haas, civilian, Cleve, Germany

Elizabeth Haas, civilian, Cleve, Germany

Maj George Hale, DSO, CD, Cdn Grenadier Guards, 4 CAB (4 CAD), 1 Cdn Army

Capt Frank Hallahan, 413 Inf Regt, 104 Inf Div, 1 US Army

Capt Horst Hanemann, 1st Bn, Pz Lehr Regt, 1 Para Army, Germany

Lt-Col Tracey Harrington, Recce Regt, 8 Armed Div, 9 US Army

Lt-Col Harold Hassenfelt, Staff Officer (G-3), 30 Inf Div, 9 US Army

Tpr Alf Hebbes, Sherbrooke Fusiliers, 2 CAB, 1 Cdn Army

Capt (Maj) Robert Hemmingsen (Canloan), 7 Seaforth, 46 Bde (15 S), 2 Brit Army

Lt-Col Larry Henderson, DSO, 1 Cdn Scottish, 7 CIB (3 CID), 1 Cdn Army

CSM R.M. Hibberd, Royal Hamilton Light Infantry, 4 CIB (2 CID), 1 Cdn Army

Maj Richard Hilborn, 1 Cdn Para Bn, 3 Para Bde (6 AB), 2 Brit Army

Maj (Col) C.E. Hill, DSO, 6 Royal Welch Fusiliers, 160 Bde (53 W), 2 Brit Army

Lt-Col E.R. Hill, DSO, 4 Coldstream Guards, 6 Guards Tank Bde, 2 Brit Army

Brig S.J.L. Hill, DSO Bar, MC Bar, Commander, 3 Para Bde (6 AB), 2 Brit Army

Capt Alf Hodges, MC, Essex Scottish, 4 CIB (2 CID), 1 Cdn Army

Lt-Col Ray Hodgins, Highland Light Infantry of Canada, 9 CIB
(3 CID), 1 Cdn Army

Maj J.S. Holland, 6 Cameronians, 156 Bde (52 L), 2 Brit Army

Sgt Raymond Howell, 6 Royal Welch Fusiliers, 160 Bde (53 W), 2
Brit Army

Maj J.T. Hugill, 2 Chem Warfare, 1 Cdn Army

Lt Hans Hueneborn, 2 Para Regt, 2 Para Div, 1 Para Army,
Germany

Lt David Hunter, MC, 7 Para Bn, 5 Para Bde (6 AB), 18 AB Corps

L/Cpl P.V. Huntley, MM, 7 Royal Welch Fusiliers, 158 Bde (53 W),
2 Brit Army

1st Lt John Hutchins, 313 Inf Regt, 79 Inf Div, 9 US Army

Maj Michael Hutchinson, MC, 4 Somerset Light Infantry, 129 Bde
(43 W), 2 Brit Army

Capt Robert Jackson (Canloan), 10 Highland Light Infantry, 227
Bde (15 S), 2 Brit Army

Maj Wm. R.Johnson, 333 Inf Regt, 84 Inf Div, 9 US Army

Tpr Jim Jones, Sherbrooke Fusiliers, 2 CAB, 1 Cdn Army

S/Sgt Albert Jordan, 142 Armd Squadron, 2 Armd Div, 9 US Army

Capt H.P. Kelley, Royal Hamilton Light Infantry, 4 CIB (2 CID),
1 Cdn Army

Pte Jeffrey Kelly, 1 Cdn Para Bn, 3 Para Bde (6 AB), 18 AB Corps

Sgt Alexander Kidd, 6 King's Own Scottish Borderers, 44 Bde
(15 S), 2 Brit Army

Sgt Leslie R. Knight, 4 Wiltshire Regt, 129 Bde (43 W), 2 Brit Army

Cpl (Sgt) Ron Knowles, 1 Cdn Para Bn, 3 Para Bde (6 AB), 18 AB
Corps

Brig Frank D. Lace, DSO, OBE, CD, CRA, 2 CID, 1 Cdn Army

Tpr Al LaRose, Sherbrooke Fusiliers, 2 CAB, 1 Cdn Army

Maj Harold Leinbaugh, 333 Inf Regt, 84 Inf Div, 9 US Army

Lt Ross LeMesurier, MC (Canloan), 5 Queen's Own Cameron Highlanders,152 Bde (51 H), 2 Brit Army

Lt-Col Stephen Lett, DSO, Queen's Own Rifles, 8 CIB (3 CID), 1
Cdn Army

Lt-Col (Col) A.D. Lewis, DSO, MC, 6 Army Cdo, 1 Cdo Bde, 2
Brit Army

Lt-Col (Lt-Gen) L.G.C. Lilley, DSO, CD, CRE, 2 CID, 1 Cdn Army

2nd Lt Philip Lombardi, 333 Inf Regt, 84 Inf Div, 9 US Army

Tpr James Love, Sherbrooke Fusiliers, 2 CAB, 1 Cdn Army

Pte. Gideon Lumsden, 4 King's Own Scottish Borderers, 155 Bde (52 L), 2 Brit Army

Sgt Charles Lynch, Highland Light Infantry of Canada, 9 CIB (3 CID), 1 Cdn Army

Maj (Col) Charles B. MacDonald, 23 Inf Regt, 2 Inf Div, 1 US Army

Pte Thomas MacDonald, batman to Gen Crerar, 1 Cdn Army

Maj (Col) H.A.C. Mackenzie, OBE, MC, 5 Seaforth, 152 Bde (51 H), 2 Brit Army

Maj (Lt-Col) R.D. Mackenzie, Argyll & Sutherland Highlanders, 10 CIB (4 CID), 1 Cdn Army

Maj. R.K. MacKenzie, 14 Cdn Fd Regt, RCA, 3 CID, 1 Cdn Army

Maj-Gen (Lt-Gen) Sir Gordon MacMillan, KCB, KCVO, CBE, DSO, MC 2 Bars, GOC 51 H Div, 2 Brit Army

Lt John Marr, 507 Para Regt, 17 AB Div, 18 AB Corps

Capt Don Marsh, CCA, 2 Armd Div, 9 US Army

Capt Hilary Marshall, The Royal Scots Greys, 4 Armd Bde, 2 Brit Army

Rfn Jack Martin, Queen's Own Rifles, 8 CIB (3 CID), 1 Cdn Army

Maj John Martin, DSO, Lincoln & Welland Regt, 10 CIB (4 CID), 1 Cdn Army

Maj Ross Martin, Staff Officer (BM), 9 CIB (3 CID), 1 Cdn Army

Maj-Gen A. Bruce Matthews, CBE, DSO, ED, CD, GOC 2 CID, 1 Cdn Army

Maj Wm. Matthews, MC Bar, CD, 1 Cdn Scottish, 7 CIB (3 CID), 1 Cdn Army

Lt (Lt-Col) R.J. McCallum, MC, 3 Scots Guards, 6 Guards Tank Bde, 2 Brit Army

Maj K.W. McIntyre, DSO, Essex Scottish, 4 CIB (2 CID), 1 Cdn Army

Lt Aubrey McIver(Canloan), 2 Monmouthshire Regt, 160 Bde (53 W), 2 Brit Army

Lt Fred McKenna, Toronto Scottish Regt, 2 CID, 1 Cdn Army

Maj (Brig) David McQueen, CBE, DSO, 8 Royal Scots, 44 Bde (15 S), 2 Brit Army

Capt John McVie, 7/9 Royal Scots, 155 Bde (52 L), 2 Brit Army

Capt J.L. Meredith, 7 Somerset Light Infantry, 129 Bde (43 W), 2 Brit Army

Wilhelm Michels, civilian, Cleve, Germany

Lt-Col Allen C. Miller, 513 Para Inf Regt, 17 AB Div, 18 AB Corps

Brig R.W. Moncel, DSO, OBE, Commander, 4 Armd Bde (4 CAD), 1 Cdn Army

CSM George Morrice, MM, 1 Gordons, 153 Bde (51 H), 2 Brit Army

Capt Finley Morrison, Staff Officer (ADC to Gen Crerar), 1 Cdn
Army

Maj J.H.F. Morton, MC Bar, 7 Argyll & Sutherland Highlanders,
154 Bde (51 H), 2 Brit Army

Capt Donald Muir, Lincoln & Welland Regt, 4 CIB (4 CAD), 1 Cdn
Army

Maj John Munro, Cdn Grenadier Guards, 4 CAB (4 CAD), 1 Cdn
Army

Maj (Col) A.I.R. Murray, OBE, 2 Seaforth, 152 Bde (51 H), 2 Brit
Army

1st Lt Norvan Nathan, 116 Inf Regt, 29 Inf Div, 9 US Army

Capt John Neil, MC, Cdn Grenadier Guards, 4 CAB (4 CAD), 1
Cdn Army

Maj (Brig) M.J.P. O'Cock, CBE, MC, 2 Irish Guards, 5 Guards Armd
Bde (Guards Armd Div), 2 Brit Army

Lt (Maj) Robert O'Grady, MC, 3 Irish Guards, 32 Guards Inf Bde
(Guards Armd Div), 2 Brit Army

Capt Blake Oulton, North Shore Regt, 8 CIB (3 CID), 1 Cdn Army

Maj H.Z. Palmer, 30 A-A Battery, RCA, 1 Cdn Army

Mrs. Peggy Crerar Palmer, Canadian civilian

Lt-Col George Pangman, Staff Officer (G-1), 1 Cdn Army

CSM (Lt-Col) C.R. Parrish, 5 Para Bde (6 AB), 18 AB Corps

Capt Don Pearce, MC, Highland Light Infantry of Canada, 9 CIB
(3 CID), 1 Cdn Army

Maj Carl A. Peterson, BS2, 194 Glider Inf Regt, 17 AB Div, 18 AB
Corps

Maj J.M. Pigott, DSO, Royal Hamilton Light Infantry, 4 CIB (2 CID),
1 Cdn Army

Brig (Gen) Sir Nigel Poett, KCB, DSO, Commander, 5 Para Bde
(6 AB), 18 AB Corps

Lt (Capt) George Pollard, Highland Light Infantry of Canada, 9
CIB (3 CID), 1 Cdn Army

Sgt Phillip Polozotto, 314 Inf Regt, 79 Inf Div, 9 US Army

Capt John E. Potts, 313 Regt, 79 Inf Div, 9 US Army

Capt Tom Powell, 4 Wiltshire Regt, 129 Bde (43 W), 2 Brit Army

Maj P.H.B.Pritchard, DSO, 6 Commando, 1 Cdo Bde, 2 Brit Army

Maj (Brig-Gen) Sidney Radley-Walters, DSO Bar, Sherbrooke
Fusiliers, 2 CAB, 1 Cdn Army

Lt F. Tipton Randolph, 80 Squadron, 436 Group, 18 AB Corps

2nd Lt Wm. L.Ray, Jr., 333 Inf Regt, 84 Inf Div, 9 US Army

Capt Peter Rea, Queen's Own Rifles, 8 CIB (3 CID), 1 Cdn Army

Lt-Col Ivor Reeves, DSO Bar, MC, 7 Somerset Light Infantry, 214 Bde (43 W), 2 Brit Army

Lt-Col (Col) Edward Remington-Hobbs, DSO, OBE, KStJ, 9 Cameronians, 46 Bde (15 S), 2 Brit Army

Cpl Mobel Rexing, 116 Pz Div, 1 Para Army, Germany

Lt-Col C.W.P. Richardson, DSO Bar, 6 King's Own Scottish Borderers, 44 Bde (15 S), 2 Brit Army

Maj Cliff Richardson, RCAMC, 4 CIB (2 CID), 1 Cdn Army

Maj D.B. Riddell-Webster, OBE, 6 Cameronians, 156 Bde (52 L), 2 Brit Army

Lt-Col Warren A. Robinson, 314 Inf Regt, 79 Div, 9 US Army

Lt William Robinson(Canloan), Royal Ulster Rifles, 6 AL Bde (6 AB), 18 AB Corps

Brig (Maj-Gen) J.M. Rockingham, CBE, DSO Bar, ED, Commander, 9 CIB (3 CID), 1 Cdn Army

Brig (Lt-Gen) N.E.Rodger, CBE, CD, Staff Officer (C of S), 2 Cdn Corps, 1 Cdn Army

Maj David Rodgers, DSO, Queen's Own Cameron Highlanders, 6 CIB (2 CID), 1 Cdn Army

Maj (Lt-Col) Thomas L. Rollo, MC, 7 Black Watch, 154 Bde (51 H), 2 Brit Army

Col Hugh Rose, CBE, DSO, 7/9 Royal Scots, 155 Bde (52 L), 2 Brit Army

Lt-Col (Maj-Gen) Morgan Roseborough, 49 Armd Inf Regt, 8 Armd Div, 9 US Army

Maj Henry Rothenberg, Recce Bn, 8 Armd Div, 9 US Army

Lt-Col (Maj-Gen) Roger Rowley, DSO Bar, ED, CD, Stormont. Dundas & Glengarry, 9 CIB (3 CID), 1 Cdn Army

Maj David Russell, MC, 7 Black Watch, 154 Bde (51 H), 2 Brit Army

Capt Victor Salem, SS 3, BS, Staff Officer (S-3), 30 Inf Div, 9 US Army

Capt Roy Sampson, Queen's Own Cameron Highlanders, 6 CIB (2 CID), 1 Cdn Army

Maj Victor Schubert, South Saskatchewan Regiment, 6 CIB (2 CID), 1 Cdn Army

Rfn Norman Selby, Queen's Own Rifles, 8 CIB (3 CID), 1 Cdn Army

Lt (Brig) Gordon Sellers, Calgary Highlanders, 5 CIB (2 CID), 1 Cdn Army

Sgt Eldrid Severin, Royal Hamilton Light Infantry, 4 CIB (2 CID), 1 Cdn Army

Lt John Simpkins, Royal Hamilton Light Infantry, 4 CIB (2 CID), 1 Cdn Army

Col Charles Simonds, Staff Officer, Cdn Army

Sgt James Sinclair, 8 Royal Scots, 44 Bde (15 S), 2 Brit Army

S/L William Skelding, 83 Group RAF

Maj K.A. Smith, Queen's Own Cameron Highlanders, 6 CIB (2 CID), 1 Cdn Army

Lt-Col Saul Solow, 120 Inf Regt, 30 Inf Div, 9 US Army

Maj Thomas Somerville, 2 Fd Coy, RCE, 2 CID, 1 Cdn Army

Lt-Col Eric Southward, DSO, 6 Cameronians, 156 Bde (52 L), 2 Brit Army

Lt-Col Arthur Sparkes, DSO, North Nova Scotia Highlanders, 9 CIB (3 CID), 1 Cdn Army

Capt Fred Sparling, 12 Field Dressing Station, RCAMC, 1 Cdn Army

Maj-Gen Daniel Spry, CBE, DSO, CD, GOC 3 CID, 1 Cdn Army

Capt Dean Steadman (Canloan), 1 Royal Ulster Rifles, 6 AL Bde (6 AB), 18 AB Corps

Capt Marshall Stearns, ADC, 2 Cdn Corps, 1 Cdn Army

Maj Cy Steele, Essex Scottish, 4 CIB (2 CID), 1 Cdn Army

Capt Tom Stewart, Essex Scottish, 4 CIB (2 CID), 1 Cdn Army

Lt-Col George Stott, Calgary Highlanders, 5 CIB (2 CID), 1 Cdn Army

Lt-Col Vern Stott, DSO, South Saskatchewan Rifles, 6 CIB (2 CID), 1 Cdn Army

Lt-Col Phillip Strickland, DSO, Highland Light Infantry of Canada, 9 CIB (3 CID), 1 Cdn Army

Maj (Col) James Swazey, DSO, Lincoln & Welland Regt, 10 CIB (4 CID), 1 Cdn Army

Maj (Col) H.J. Sweeney, MC, 2 Oxford & Buckinghamshire, 6 AL Bde (6 AB), 18 AB Corps

Maj Harvey Theobald, MC, Fort Garry Horse, 2 CAB, 1 Cdn Army

Lt Donald Thomson (Canloan), 4 Somerset Light Infantry, 129 Bde (43 W), 2 Brit Army

Father G. Thuring, civilian, Bredeweg, Holland

Capt (Col) Fred Tilston, VC, CD, Essex Scottish, 4 CIB (2 CID), 1 Cdn Army

Brig P.A.S. Todd, CBE, DSO, ED, CD, CCRA, 2 Cdn Corps, 1 Cdn Army

Cpl Wilson Toups, 314 Inf Regt, 79 Inf Div, 9 US Army

Maj Frank Towers, 120 Inf Regt, 30 Inf Div, 9 US Army

1st Lt Robert F. Truitt, BS2, 333 Inf Regt, 84 Inf Div, 9 US Army

Lt-Gen Lewis W. Truman, Staff Officer (C of S), 84 Inf Div, 9 US Army

Lt Alex Uhlig, 3 Iron Crosses, 7 Para Div, 1 Para Army, Germany

Herbert Van Bebber, civilian, Xanten, Germany

Lt Frank Volterman, Royal Hamilton Light Infantry, 4 CIB (2 CID), 1 Cdn Army

Baron Adrian Von Steengracht, civilian, Moyland, Germany

Brig (Gen) Geoffrey Walsh, CBE, DSO, CD, CRE, 1 Cdn Army

Maj (Lt-Col) V.O. Walsh, DSO, Sherbrooke Fusiliers, 2 CAB, 1 Cdn Army

Capt Frank Walton, Essex Scottish, 4 CIB (2 CID), 1 Cdn Army

Lt (Lt-Col) David Ward, 45 RM, 1 Cdo Bde, 2 Brit Army

Lt-Col (Col) Trumbull Warren, OBE, BS, PA to Field-Marshal Montgomery, 21 Army Group

Lt Ken Wharton, Royal Hamilton Light Infantry, 4 CIB (2 CID), 1 Cdn Army

Maj Wm. Whiteside, Argyll & Sutherland Highlanders, 10 CIB (4 CAD),1 Cdn Army

Lt Robert W. Wight, Royal Hamilton Light Infantry, 4 CIB (2 CID), 1 Cdn Army

Maj Thomas Wilcox, Royal Regt of Canada, 4 CIB (2 CID), 1 Cdn Army

S/Sgt Rufus Wilkes, SS, BS, 407 Inf Regt, 102 Inf Div, 9 US Army

Capt Ben Wilkie, Royal Regt of Canada, 4 CIB (2 CID), 1 Cdn Army

CSM (Lt-Col) R.B. Wilkinson, MBE, 2 Gordons, 227 Bde (15 S), 2 Brit Army

Lt (Col) John Williamson, EM, CD, Royal Hamilton Light Infantry, 4 CIB (2 CID), 1 Cdn Army

Sgt Peter Willigen, MM, 6 Fd Coy, RCE, 3 CID, 1 Cdn Army

Capt (Col) Albert Wing, 513 Para Inf Regt, 17 AB Div, 18 AB Corps

Lt (Lt-Col) G.P. Wood, MC, Argyll & Sutherland Highlanders, 154 Bde (51 H), 2 Brit Army

Brig-Gen Gordon S. Wotherspoon, DSO, ED, CD, South Alta Regt, 4 CAB (4 CID), 1 Cdn Army

Capt Gordon Wright, MC Bar (Canloan), 4 Somerset Light Infantry, 129 Bde (43 W), 2 Brit Army

Lt. Nevil Wykes (Canloan), 7 Argyll & Sutherland Highlanders, 154 Bde (51 H), 2 Brit Army

Index

413

BRITISH FORMATIONS

ARMY